Arms reduction

**Note to the reader from the UNU**

The UNU programme on Future Global Change and Modelling is a response to far-reaching transformations in the perception and structure of the world's policies, economics, demography, technology, ecology, and ethics. Under this programme, the UNU seeks to evaluate such changes, their implications, and necessary adjustments.

This volume is based on the proceedings of the 1992 Tokyo Conference on "Arms Reduction and Economic Development in the Post-Cold War Era" – the second in a series of UNU conferences on Future Global Change and Modelling. The objectives of this project are three-fold: (1) to examine global trends and patterns of miliary expenditure; (2) to explore possible arms reduction scenarios and examine their impacts on the world economy with special attention to developing countries; and (3) to stimulate policy dialogue on alternative approaches to achieving arms reduction. By bringing together the views of opinion leaders and experts involved in arms reduction research, this project seeks to create awareness in the world community about coping with this common global issue in an increasingly interdependent and complex world.

# Arms reduction: Economic implications in the post-Cold War era

Edited by Lawrence R. Klein, Fu-chen Lo, and Warwick J. McKibbin

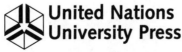

**United Nations University Press**

TOKYO · NEW YORK · PARIS

United Nations University Press
The United Nations University, 53-70, Jingumae 5-chome, Shibuya-ku, Tokyo 150, Japan
Tel: (03) 3499-2811          Fax: (03) 3406-7345
Telex: J25442                Cable: UNATUNIV TOKYO

Typeset by Asco Trade Typesetting Limited, Hong Kong
Printed by Permanent Typesetting and Printing Co., Ltd., Hong Kong
Cover design by David King and Judy Groves

UNUP-881
ISBN 92-808-0881-8
04500 P

# Contents

## Part 4: Political economy of sustainable reductions in military spending

# 1

# An overview

Warwick J. McKibbin

The end of the Cold War presents an unparalleled opportunity for global disarmament. In order to examine the economic, social, and political implications of global reductions in military spending, a conference was organized by the United Nations University in November 1992. To achieve three goals, the conference brought together opinion leaders and experts involved in research on military disarmament from various parts of the world:

1. to examine global trends and patterns of military expenditure;
2. to explore possible arms reduction scenarios and examine their impacts on industrialized and developing countries;
3. to simulate policy dialogue on alternative approaches to achieve a significant and sustainable reduction in the degree of global militarization.

With these three aims in mind, this overview will summarize the major issues raised by conference participants. It is hoped that by stimulating dialogue and bringing together important research and views on the question of military disarmament, this will help clarify the issues facing political leaders who must grasp the unique opportunity for global demilitarization.

The conference was held against the backdrop of the Japanese government's official announcement that Japan's Official Development Assistance (ODA) would be tied to the amount of military expenditures undertaken by recipient countries. This position was outlined in detail at the conference by Mr. Takao Kawakami of the Ministry of Foreign Affairs. The Japanese Official Development Assistance Charter of June 1992 particularly states that, in addition to following the principles of the United Nations Charter, Japan's ODA would also take into account four additional principles:

(1) Environmental conservation and development should be pursued in tandem;
(2) Any use of ODA for military purposes or for aggravation of international conflicts should be avoided;
(3) Full attention should be given to trends in recipient countries' military expenditure, their development and production of weapons of mass destruction, weapons and missiles, their export and import of arms, etc., so as to maintain and strengthen international peace and stability, and from the viewpoint that developing countries should place appropriate priorities in the allocation of their resources for their own economic and social development;
(4) More efforts should be paid to the promotion of democratisation and the introduction of a market-oriented economy, and the situation to secure basic human rights and freedoms in the recipient country.[1]

## Trends in military spending and arms trade

Two of the leading sources of data on military expenditures and arms trade are the Stockholm International Peace Research Institute (SIPRI), which publishes the *SIPRI Yearbook*, and the US Arms Control and Disarmament Agency (ACDA), which publishes the *World Military Expenditures and Arms Transfers*. Leading researchers from these institutions presented papers outlining the recent global trends in military spending and arms trade.

In "Military expenditures and arms trade: Trends and prospects" by Saadet Deger (SIPRI) and "Trends in world arms trade and spending and their implications" by Daniel Gallik (US ACDA), the authors document emerging trends over the recent decade that have been dominated by the decline in the former Soviet Union. The upward trend in world military expenditures during the 1980s began to reverse by 1988 and looks to continue to fall through 1992 and 1993. Although this largely reflects the dominant position of the United States and former Soviet Union, a similar trend occurred in developing countries (adjusting for the Gulf War). In addition, imports of major conventional weapons by developing countries halved from the peak in 1987 to 1990 and continued to fall through 1991. Deger argues that rather than being the result of a concerted effort to reduce arms by international treaties, this reflected tight fiscal constraints facing countries. This was particularly true in the former Soviet Union, where there have been substantial cuts in all categories of defence expenditures. In the United States on the other hand the cuts to date have been focused on procurement with defence R&D expenditures being cut by relatively much less. In Western Europe, military outlays have also fallen but only slowly. As with the United States the largest cuts have been in procurement. In Eastern Europe the cuts have been far more dramatic, reflecting the economic crises in these countries.

An important aspect of the arms trade data is that the arms trade is highly concentrated. Five suppliers (former USSR [42.4 per cent] United States [22.1 per cent], France [8.4 per cent], China [7.2 per cent], and United Kingdom [7.1 per cent]) supplied 87 per cent of the arms exports between 1987 and 1991. Only 15 developing countries imported 80 per cent of total arms imported by the third world over this period.

Deger argues that because the cut-backs in arms trade have been due to severe economic problems in importing countries, any rise in growth in these countries will be likely to lead to a rise in arms imports. However, because the suppliers of arms exports are relatively concentrated, placing limits on arms exports should be only a matter of political will by the five members of the Security Council (who also happen to be the major arms exporters). Despite the possibility of cutting arms trade by focusing on the arms exporters, it is still true that the arms trade is a symptom of regional insecurity. Therefore any attempts to make the current trend decline in military expenditures, a permanent feature of the global economy, will require solutions of the underlying regional problems.

By cutting domestic demand for military equipment an incentive is created for governments or arms exporters within countries to find foreign markets for their excess production. This is particularly severe in countries of Eastern Europe and the former Soviet Union. Selling military equipment is a way for these countries to generate desperately needed foreign exchange. But this is not only a problem in these distressed economies. Gallik points to a recent rising trend in agreements to deliver arms to developing countries by the United

3

States and United Kingdom. This highlights a problem resulting from attempts to scale back defence budgets. It is not only sufficient to scale back government demand for weapons but careful consideration must be given to preventing export of these weapons to other countries. A coordinated effort must be made to limit both military budgets and arms trade. But in addition, the underlying causes of the militarization need to be addressed and these relate to issues of regional security and development.

Monitoring the military expenditures of countries is crucial, especially if proposals to tie development assistance to military spending are implemented. What are the links between development assistance and defence budgets? There are many ways to analyse the data. Paul Armington and Jalaleddin Jalali in "Military spending in developing countries and official development assistance" pool together a comprehensive array of data from a variety of sources including SIPRI and ACDA. The authors then calculate three measures of the degree of militarization: military expenditures relative to GNP; military expenditures as a share of general government expenditures; and military imports as a share of total imports. They compare these three measures of militarization for 114 low and middle-income developing countries, with the receipts of official development assistance (ODA) by these countries.

The authors rank countries by these measures compared to ranking of countries in terms of ODA over the period from 1978 to 1989 and the sub-periods 1978 to 1983 and 1984 to 1989. Countries are classified according to the calculated ratios relative to the median of countries in the sample. The authors find that eight out of the 13 very high military spenders are also in the top half of ODA recipients. The three top ranked receivers of ODA between 1979 and 1989 were India, Syria, and Egypt. The latter two countries were also classified as very high military spenders in the study. Respectively, they spent 67 per cent and 50 per cent of general government expenditures on the military over this period.

Although only a first step, collating and improving data on a variety of measures of military outlays is crucial for monitoring trends and implementing proposals to significantly reduce military budgets.

## Economic and social consequences of demilitarization

The reduction in military budgets in many countries affected by the end of the Cold War is likely to be followed by a difficult period of adjustment. As a number of authors have stressed, it is not a simple and cost-free exercise to reduce military expenditures. Production facilities for military equipment tend to be regionally concentrated. Military bases tend to be economically important to the region in which they are located. The resources that are released by scaling back these facilities may be difficult to absorb immediately into the private economy, either due to the slow process of retooling capital equipment or because it takes time to retrain workers to develop the skills for private sector production. In addition to the micro-economic problems to be faced, there is also the need to understand the national and international macroeconomic consequences of the potentially large adjustments to production, saving, and investment that substantial military cut-backs entail.

Papers at the conference focused on this range of issues from regional impacts in particular countries to global impacts. The many issues involved in conversion from military to civilian production are discussed by Lawrence Klein in "The economics of arms reduction." The extent of possible US cut-backs is documented and a comparison is drawn between the conversion over the next decade and the conversion undertaken at the end of World War II. During the earlier period, conversion was achieved over a five-year period but in conditions that differ from those today. Most significant was probably the extent of suppressed demand built up during the war. In the case of the former Soviet Union, Klein sees the prospects for conversion as less encouraging. In the midst of an economic collapse, the ability of the economy to absorb the resources released from the military sector is very limited. Klein argues that for most countries, the costs of disarmament are substantial and will be incurred in the early years, whereas the gains are also potentially substantial but are realized in future years. This observation is supported by simulation evidence from studies reported below.

In "Defence reductions in the United States in the 1990s," Murray Weidenbaum explores the regional impacts of expected cuts in defence expenditures in the United States. He points out that the regional and economic impacts of reduction in the military budget are uneven within the United States. First, the defence industry is highly concentrated in a small number of firms (in 1988, 25 firms accounted for 50 per cent of defence contracts). Secondly, the major firms supplying defence contracts have a high degree of regional concentration (66 per cent of defence jobs in 10 states in 1988). Thirdly, the cutbacks are not uniform, with weapon systems being cut more than operations and these more than research and development.

Weidenbaum also draws a comparison between conversion problems facing firms after the Cold War versus the ends of previous wars. He notes in particular that in previous wars, manufacturers shifted from civilian production into military production for the duration of the war, and then were able to shift back again to civilian production relatively easily. But in the current situation the major firms have been specializing in defence contracting for a substantial period and have not had to develop skills in marketing, distribution, and large-scale, low-cost production that typifies firms that produce civilian goods. He points to attempts by big military contractors to diversify into civilian production in the last decade that have uniformly met with failure. Although facing a significant conversion problem, Weidenbaum argues that the solution to the conversion problem is not to subsidize the large defence firms and keep them large but to subsidize general research and development, which will enable the scientists and technicians in these corporations to be absorbed elsewhere in the economy.

## Global economic consequences of reductions in military spending

Three papers used multi-country simulation models to focus on the global macroeconomic implications of reductions in military outlays over the next decade. The models include the McKibbin-Sachs Global model (MSG2), maintained at the Brookings Institution in Washington, D.C., the MULTIMOD model maintained at the International Monetary Fund, and the Project LINK model simulated by a team at the United Nations in New York. The advantage of using a modelling framework for analysing this complex issue is the ability to focus on the short-run demand consequences of significant defence cuts and the medium-term supply responses after factors of production are reallocated. A surprising outcome in the three very different models was the degree of consensus that there are costs to conversion in the short run, but the medium-term economic gains to cutting defence spending are significant. Where the models differed most was in the timing of adjustment and the role of announcements of credible future defence cuts in offsetting some of the short-run negative impacts.

In "The impact on the world economy of reductions in military expenditures and military arms exports," Warwick McKibbin and Stephan Thurman use the MSG2 multi-country model to explore the impacts of multilateral expenditure cuts within the OECD. They also focus on the impacts of an embargo on shipments of military weapons to developing countries. The authors simulate a gradual reduction in military expenditures in the OECD with the United States gradually cutting outlays to 3.2 per cent of GDP by 1997 and the other OECD countries cutting outlays to 2 per cent of GDP. The policies are explored with and without any change in monetary policy. The authors find that the impact in the first year of the spending cuts may well be positive because of the fall in long-term interest rates that accompanies the credible reduction in fiscal deficits throughout the OECD. As long-term interest rates fall, private investment rises and there is a strengthening of the global economy before the actual cuts in spending are implemented. The stimulus is quickly offset by the cuts in demand by government in the years from 1994 to 1997. Without any monetary response, industrialized countries lose about 1 per cent of GDP by 1997. With an easing of monetary policy during the period of largest cuts this can be reduced to about 0.5 per cent of GDP. By the turn of the century, the negative effects are dissipated and the world economy grows to reach a higher level of GDP than would have otherwise been experienced.

The authors also consider an embargo on exports of arms from the major arms exporters to developing economies. The global implications of this policy are much smaller and can easily be offset by changes in other macroeconomic policies within the industrial economies.

In "Economic consequences of lower military spending: Some simulation results," Tamim Bayoumi, Daniel Hewitt, and Jerald Schiff use the IMF's MULTIMOD multi-country model to trace the global impacts of a phased-in cut in world military expenditures of 20 per cent from 1993 to 1997. The authors consider a base-case scenario in which the standard MULTIMOD model is used to evaluate the global impacts of the cut-back in military expenditures. They then test the sensitivity of their results to assumptions about the determinants of private investment and the productivity of military expenditures. The authors also consider the implications of a unilateral cut in military expenditures in the United States. Under each assumption, GDP falls on impact but quickly recovers and then rises over time. In the long run there is a clear economic gain from the reduction of military outlays. Private consumption and investment both rise immediately the policy is announced because of the anticipation of higher future output. Present value calculations of future changes in consumption clearly indicate that the policy of reducing

7

military budgets leads to positive benefits. In addition, the authors find that global coordinated cuts in military spending lead to higher welfare for individual countries than achieved by the same cuts made on a unilateral basis.

In "Some macroeconomic aspects of reductions in military expenditure," Simon Cunningham and Kenneth Ruffing focus on the costs and benefits of the peace dividend. The authors argue that the costs of disarmament will be incurred over the next few years, with the benefits being in the longer term. These costs are varied and relate to: the direct regional impacts of closing production and military facilities; cleaning up environmental damage due to defence-related production; the non-trivial costs of weapon destruction with minimal environmental impact; and monitoring arms-reduction agreements. On the problem of short-term conversion, in contrast to the pessimistic assessment of Weidenbaum that conversion was likely to be difficult, the authors point to a number of successful conversions of military bases into industrial and office parks and educational establishments. These conversions resulted in a net increase in employment.

The medium-term effects of disarmament are assessed using the Project LINK global macroeconomic model. Cut-backs in military spending of 1 per cent of GDP in the United States and 2 per cent of GDP in the United Kingdom, France, and Germany phased in from 1993 to 1996 were simulated. Without any other policy offsets, the spending reduction lowers global GDP over the period by up to 0.7 per cent. The authors then attempt to offset the losses with coordinated interest rate reductions in the Group of Seven (G7) economies, increased transfers to developing countries, and a shift of the revenue saved from military production to investment in export sectors of developing countries. Although it is possible to reduce the adjustment costs with policy responses, there are none the less still some short-term losses.

A surprising aspect of these three model-based papers was the overall consensus on the magnitude of effects of similar cut-backs. In the short run the anticipated cut in military outlays may be slightly positive to slightly negative. In the medium term there is likely to be a slow-down of the world economy relative to where it otherwise would have been. However, by the turn of the decade, the returns for shifting resources out of the military sector into the private sector begin to be realized. The adjustment phase requires some other modifications of policy to dampen the negative demand consequences of the shift.

## The political economy of sustainable reductions in military spending

The papers that explored the economic impacts of reductions in military spending and cuts in arms exports to developing countries did not address the many political problems to be encountered in achieving the cuts. A number of other papers presented at the conference raised the global, regional, and national political issues that need to be faced in the next few years. Some authors pointed to the need for international institutions to adapt to a new and evolving international order. Institutional reform should not only focus on the immediate situation at the end of the bipolar world but reform should be planned in the context of the multipolar world that is likely to evolve over the next few decades. With localized conflicts such as the problems in former Yugoslavia, the world is not rid of security problems, but the nature of these problems, and therefore the focus of political actions, has changed dramatically. Regional security issues are now at the forefront. These regional problems need to be tackled while, at the same time, the funds that were previously channelled into the Cold War need to be redirected into solving the development problems still facing many countries.

Robert McNamara in "A new international order and its implications for arms reductions" is a strong proponent of the argument that international institutions should be adapted now to meeting the needs of the next century. McNamara argues that the basis for lasting peace is to ensure collective security. This can be done by creating a mechanism for resolving regional conflicts, setting up a basis for guaranteeing security for each nation state as well as minorities within nation states, by ceasing the flow of military support to conflicts in developing regions, and by increasing the flow of development assistance to raise the living standards within these regions. To facilitate the move to greater global security, McNamara argues for greater leadership in negotiating the complete removal of nuclear weapons, tight limits on the proliferation of other weapons of mass destruction, substantial reductions in military outlays, and substantial reductions in arms transfers between the developed and the developing world. In relation to the last issue, McNamara highlights the social cost in many developing countries of maintaining large military forces at the expense of other social programmes. He strongly argues for the linking of financial assistance by the multilateral institutions to levels of military expenditures in recipient countries. This aspect of the paper was perhaps the most controversial primarily due to the practical problem of who decides what is reasonable for a country to spend on defence. Any evaluation must take into account the perceived threats facing a given country. Traditionally the international aid agencies have resisted tackling the domestic priorities of countries, especially in terms of military outlays.

The policy of using persuasion by international agencies in reducing global military budgets was also a theme in the comprehensive paper on "Enhancing peace and development: Foreign aid and military expenditure in developing countries" by Nicole Ball of the Overseas Development Council. Ball points out that the confluence of events such as the end of the Cold War and the shortage of funds for development purposes means that military imbalances in the budgets of many developing countries need to be rectified. In order to focus on improving both security and development within developing countries, Ball presents a detailed account of the types of leverage available to lenders to accelerate military reform in a variety of different categories of countries.

In reforming the role of the military in many countries, the key aspect that Ball highlights is not only the need to eliminate wasteful expenditures and reduce the size of military outlays but to increase the transparency of military budgets and in the process make governments accountable for their budgetary decisions. Like McNamara, Ball also highlights the need for collective security measures. By tackling the problem of regional security at the same time as assisting governments in managing their military budgets, there is a chance to raise the prospects for increased security and development.

Ball also argues that it is important to distinguish countries where the desire of governments within those countries is to reform their military establishments. It is much easier to instigate a successful programme of military reform if the government is willing to cooperate. In some cases, external pressure can be helpful to governments that would like to undertake reform but due to domestic political considerations cannot commence the process without some external assistance. In particular this can be important for civilian governments that are attempting to restrict the power of an entrenched military élite.

The form of intervention depends on the country considered, but Ball suggests three broad categories of approaches to promote military reform. These differ between unilateral and multilateral aid agencies. The main categories are persuasion, support, and pressure.

By 1989 the IMF and the World Bank began talking of the link between military outlays and development finance. Although these agencies are technically prevented from dictating military budgets, they can and have signalled a change in attitude to military spending that has important implications for the behaviour of unilateral donors. Countries can be persuaded to undertake military conversion if offered financial, technical, and diplomatic support. They can also be subject to specific conditionality in which an economic benefit is tied to meeting specific targets for military outlays. Or they can be rewarded for moving in an appropriate direction. The latter approach has been and is likely to be followed given that donors are usually reluctant to specify exact targets for military spending given the difficulties of evaluating external threat. Again this approach is likely to be effective for countries that already have a commitment to reform.

Ball notes that to date the approach to reducing military budgets has largely been indirect. She makes a number of proposals that directly tackle the reform of military establishments in developing countries. Included in these proposals are: active promotion of military reform by the international community including aid agencies; coordination of efforts by international political and development institutions to promote reform; developing norms for security assessment tied to development assistance; promoting transparency and accountability in military budgeting; that bilateral donors should undertake the same military reforms as those advocated for developing countries; that bilateral donors should support efforts by international financial institutions to promote military reforms.

The issue of how to persuade countries to undertake substantial military reform was a recurring theme in many of the papers presented at the conference. In "Economic incentives for demilitarization," Somnath Sen uses a more formal approach, based on concepts from game theory, to consider the incentives facing countries and how best to change those incentives to achieve the goal of greater global security. He stresses that most recent major military reforms have not resulted from treaties but have been due to large changes in economic circumstances. This is clearly illustrated in the economic collapse of Eastern Europe and the former Soviet Union. In many other cases the cut-backs that have been seen to date have been due to binding budgetary constraints. As these are relaxed it is crucial to have a set of incentives in place to discourage countries from reversing the current trend of demilitarization. The paper focuses on whether economic incentives can be used to promote the goal of greater security as well as enhancing economic development.

Sen constructs a framework in which there are two players, the major powers and the developing countries. He assumes that incentives will be provided by the major powers, while the demilitarization is focused on the developing countries. The trade-off facing countries is between the goals of development and security. The dilemma arises because individual countries are assumed to be concerned only with their own security, where their security is diminished if other countries raise their military spending. With all countries spending more on security, each perceives a greater external threat and therefore spends more on security. The equilibrium is a global overspending on security, which is a similar outcome to that in a classic "prisoner's dilemma." By providing a credible coordinated reduction in military outlays, there can be a global improvement in welfare. Resources are freed for development purposes and overall security is not diminished. The problem is how to structure incentives facing countries that achieve the same overall result. Sen considers a range of possible incentives based on criteria of optimality, efficiency, equity, affordability, and existence.

One economic incentive is via direct foreign aid. In applying this approach of limiting aid to countries that undertake excessive militarization, Sen argues that there is a danger that the general population of that country will suffer without changing the behaviour of the government. From an equity point of view such a policy would be inadvisable. In addition it is important to realize the limitations of using a limited number of targets and instruments, especially when the targets may be difficult to define. Sen argues that concentrating only on military expenditures could be a suboptimal way to proceed. A wider range of policies such as direct payments for good behaviour, trade concessions, in addition to foreign aid should be employed to create the incentives for countries to devote more resources to their own development.

If aid is to be targeted based on some measure of militarization, then Sen proposes that there is a need to create a demilitarization index so that donors can monitor countries. There was a good deal of debate on this issue as well as the use of indicators to tie foreign aid directly to degrees of militarization. It was pointed out that indicators proposed do not take into account the perceived external threat, which is crucial in deciding if some measure is excessive.

The end of the Cold War has shifted focus towards regional conflicts. The Middle East is one area where regional tensions remain high despite recent developments. Amin Hewedy outlined the major issues facing this region in a paper entitled "Arms reduction in the Middle East: Between credibility and illusion." In a pessimistic assessment of the prospect of regional disarmament, Hewedy considers this issue in the context of the regional implication of the old bipolar world versus the new international order. He argues that in a bipolar world it was only possible to change the global balance of power at the margin and therefore regional conflicts were used as proxies of the larger global conflict. The result was massive arms transfers to developing countries. In the new world order it is not possible to cut arms transfers instantly in a discriminatory way to the Middle East because there continue to be arms suppliers such as the former Soviet Union and China. These countries are motivated to transport arms for economic rather than political incentives. Hewedy argues that before a lasting resolution of the problems in the Middle East can be found there must be a cut in all arms transfers to the region rather than selective cuts. In addition there must be enforcement and adherence to UN Security Council resolutions by all countries in the region and a resolution of the underlying political conflicts based on a balancing of interests.

Japan's policy on linking ODA to military expenditures was outlined in a paper by Takao Kawakami entitled "Japan's ODA policies for a peace initiative." A major reason for the new policy is related to the likely scarcity of funds for development assistance in the foreseeable future and the amount of funds that are allocated for military purposes in developing countries (approximately $160 billion in 1991). The Japanese policy is argued to be in the interests of the Japanese taxpayers, the recipient countries, and the region. For Japan, which is the largest provider of ODA, to be able to continue to redirect taxpayers' funds to ODA requires public support. This support is difficult to maintain when the money is perceived to be used for military purposes rather than for enhancing economic development. The recipient countries gain by freeing up some of their own resources for development. In addition reduced military spending contributes to overall regional security.

Kawakami cites a number of issues that he personally argues are crucial in using ODA for encouraging reform of military outlays.

First, there should be monitoring of trends in the size of military expenditures and the allocation between military and non-military domestic spending. The monitoring role could be undertaken by the IMF and the World Bank as part of public expenditure reviews. Secondly, there needs to be greater transparency of military budgets. The United Nations could play a role here in improving data as well as using data from the newly established UN register of Conventional Arms Transfers. Thirdly, policy dialogue is required to encourage diplomatically, as well as through direct means, reductions in military spending. Fourthly, global cooperation between bilateral donors and multilateral institutions is important. The Development Assistance Committee (DAC) of the OECD could play a role in facilitating such cooperation and dialogue. Finally, there needs to be coherence between the behaviour of the donors and the requirements placed on recipient countries. Donors should scale back their own military expenditures, military exports, and military export credits to developing countries.

## Prospects and policies

The conference agenda covered a wide range of issues. Many participants agreed that there is currently a rare opportunity for a global reduction in military budgets and this would indeed be beneficial for all countries. All participants agreed that greater transparency in reporting military budgets and arms transfers and accountability for these budgets was essential to the process of global disarmament. In addition, better data on military expenditures and arms trade are needed for monitoring developments in countries. There was less agreement on how to encourage developing countries to reduce military budgets. On the question of whether multilateral agencies and other donors should follow the Japanese approach of directly tying aid to some indicators of the degree of militarization, there was a good deal of debate. The major point of disagreement arose because no criteria were straightforward and ultimately someone needed to undertake a complete analysis of military budgets in the context of the regional threats facing specific countries. Requiring aid agencies to undertake such an analysis may not be the most appropriate use of resources within those agencies.

In addition, there was some concern that directly restricting arms transfers or imposing military budgets through aid commitments, was only addressing the symptom rather than tackling the more fundamental security problem facing many countries. Direct attempts to impose military cut-backs may not be as effective as devising a system based on institutional arrangements and the use of economic incentives to affect behaviour.

The security problem could be addressed by strengthening regional institutions within a global security framework. Enhancing security through this approach would also require commitment of resources to provide the means to credibly deter military aggression within a region. Secondly, direct economic incentives could be applied to raise the cost to countries of sustaining excessive military budgets. To avoid the problems, repeatedly raised during the conference, of deciding how to define excessive military spending, several options are available. One option raised by Daniel Hewitt could be to levy a tax on countries based on military expenditures that would raise their cost and therefore give countries the incentive to cut them. An alternative that was suggested by Warwick McKibbin is to levy a tax on the exports of military arms to deter countries from exporting weapons to developing countries. The revenue from either tax could be used to strengthen the regional and global security arrangements. The advantages of this approach is that if it encouraged all countries to cut back their military expenditure just a little, then regional security would rise and there would be an incentive to cut expenditures further. Secondly, by actually providing funding for regional security measures that are credible and deter aggression between countries, there can be a further increase in the perceived security and a further cut in military outlays.

Only by focusing on reinforcing regional institutions under a global umbrella and providing incentives in terms of economic resources and greater security will there be a real opportunity to move into the next century with the prospect of greater peace.

## Note

1. From Japan's Official Development Assistance Charter, 30 June 1992, p. 2.

# Part 1
# Recent trends in military spending and arms trade

# 2

# Military expenditure and arms trade: Trends and prospects

Saadet Deger

## I. Introduction

World military expenditure in aggregate rose continuously almost throughout the 1980s. Such a rise was in sharp contrast to the late 1970s, when aggregate world military expenditure saw modest growth and for some groups of countries exhibited a decline. Defence spending began to slow down in the late 1980s and began falling around 1988 at about 5 per cent per annum. In 1990 world military expenditure exceeded $950 billion (US dollars) even after having fallen for two years. The downward trend continued into 1991 in spite of the costly Gulf War. The trend is set to accelerate in 1992 and the rate of decline could approach 10 to 15 per cent during the current year.

The rise and fall of world military expenditure can be principally attributed to the behaviour of the two superpowers (the United States and the former Soviet Union, called FSU hereafter). It was their action–reaction arms race that provoked the rise of aggregate international defence spending in the 1980s. Again, the fall in the

I am indebted to Evamaria Loose-Weintraub, Sten Wicksten, and Miyoko Suzuki for assistance. The views presented here do not necessarily reflect those of the affiliated institution.

aggregate is attributable to the sharp cut-back of military expenditures in the FSU and the newly independent CIS states, as well as to the defence cuts following the attempt to restrain the huge US budget deficits. More fundamental structural and systemic causes are discussed below.

Third world defence spending, which is only a small share of the world total, followed a rather different pattern over the last two decades. During the 1970s the total rose very fast, principally fuelled by the oil price rise. Between 1970 and 1979, military expenditure rose by about 9.7 per cent per annum for all developing countries; 14.9 per cent per annum for OPEC; 6.2 per cent per annum for non-oil developing countries. The rate of growth slowed down but remained positive in the early 1980s. Since 1984/85 military spending of all developing countries, taken as a whole, has fallen consistently. Only in 1991, due to the exceptional military spending of Kuwait, Saudi Arabia, and the United Arab Emirates in financing the Gulf War, did the trend show an increase. Again, by 1992 the downward movement is expected to be firmly established. There are of course substantial regional variations, but the essential trend towards demilitarization is clear across regions with possibly one notable exception (see later).

The volume of arms trade to the developing world followed a similar pattern, although the rise and fall took place on a somewhat different time-scale. The data on the trade in arms should be used cautiously since they reflect a volume index and not actual monies paid or the cost of weapons transactions. Nevertheless, they indicate whether the trade is rising or not. Third world arms importation rose consistently from the early 1970s until 1987. That year saw the end of the long-running Iran–Iraq war and the boom in arms imports by developing countries taken as a whole. Since 1987 the import of *major conventional weapons* by developing countries has collapsed. In 1991 alone the volume of arms imported by the developing world fell by 26 per cent compared to the previous year. From the peak of 1987, imports of major conventional weapons halved between 1987 and 1990. In 1990 the volume of major conventional (non-nuclear) weapons imports of the developing world was almost the same as that in 1971 – 20 years ago. The long cycle was complete.

It is necessary, when analysing military expenditure shares, to note an important characteristic of the data. Both the Stockholm International Peace Research Institute (SIPRI) and the US Arms Control and Disarmament Agency (ACDA), which collect military spending information, rely on domestic budgetary data plus adjustments.

However, international comparisons are facilitated by the use of dollar values. When converting local currencies into dollars, the military expenditure data for the former socialist countries in the former WTO are changed by utilizing Purchasing Power Parities (PPPs). This is particularly important for the former USSR, where the use of official exchange rates would be meaningless in capturing the true resource cost of the military. However, for developing countries, official exchange rates are widely used for conversion (ACDA uses PPPs for China also). Since there may be considerable divergence between exchange rates and PPPs for countries with low per capita income, the aggregation of data is not precise. More specifically, the share of the developing countries in the world total tends to be underestimated.

The central purpose of the paper is to analyse the trends in world military expenditure and arms trade with special reference to the third world. Section 2 discusses defence spending trends of the major powers and the industrial countries. Section 3 analyses the trends in the third world, both for defence expenditure and arms procurement through importation, in terms of various indicators of militarization and shows the evolution during the last decade or so. It also discusses the burden of militarization using some non-traditional indices. Section 4 discusses the causes of the fall in military expenditures in the world generally as well as the reasons for the regional variations. It also briefly tackles a major issue as to whether such declines are sustainable and whether there is a scope for further significant falls. Such a prognosis of future trends is clearly fraught with major uncertainty, particularly at a time of systemic changes. Section 5 concludes briefly.

## II. Military expenditure in the industrial countries

After the rapid rise in industrial countries' military expenditure since the late 1970s, a downward trend has been discernible from the late 1980s. This *steady but slow* decline has been mainly a product of technological and economic factors rather than a product of arms control treaties and negotiations. By the second half of the 1980s, changes in sophisticated technology increased unit costs considerably for weapons systems, unless large procurement orders allowed producers to recoup the gains from increasing returns. Budgetary constraints, in an era of conservative fiscal policies, hindered countries from overspending on the military irrespective of the perceived threats. These two factors produced what may be termed a "scissors

21

crisis" for the proponents of defence spending. Alternatively, one could perceive such a situation as Technological and Structural Disarmament, TESD (see Deger and Sen, 1990). The features of TESD, which were particularly relevant for the major military spenders in NATO and the WTO and in somewhat different fashion for third world countries, is discussed in section 4.

Arms control treaties of the late 1980s did not have a significant additional decelerating effect i.e. over and above what constituted the core impact of TESD. For NATO the ceilings on Treaty Limited Items were high and required little disarmament *per se*, only a slowing down of defence spending. For the former WTO countries the upper limit was more seriously binding. However, at the same time economic constraints had become so adverse that it was impossible to sell the claims of military security to an impoverished nation. Arms control treaties notwithstanding, the structural changes of TESD were sufficient to reduce defence spending and arms acquisition considerably.

It was expected that the profound political transformation since 1989, the so-called end of the Cold War, would have an equally profound impact on defence spending. Spectacular claims of halving military expenditure in a few years were widely made at that time. It was believed that arms industries would face major crises, that defence R&D establishments would be shut down, that personnel would rapidly dwindle, and that military expenditure would collapse. None of these things have happened in NATO and OECD countries by 1992. Among the Central and East European Economies (CEEE), including the CIS countries, rapid demilitarization has actually occurred but this has been a product of systemic change in the whole economic structure. Military spending has been drastically cut but so too have been expenditures on social welfare provisions, including other types of public goods such as education and health. For example, according to the 1992 Gaidar budget for Russia, defence spending could be one-third of total republican budgetary expenditures. The ratio is not fundamentally different from the recent past during the Gorbachev era.

In the OECD countries, military expenditure reductions, and concomitant restructuring, have yet to catch up with political changes taking place in the world. They have also failed to keep pace with the changes in military doctrines that require different forms of capability to match altered threats. The declines that are occurring are slow and steady and motivated by technology and economics rather than systemic political transformation. Rather, new demands for funding alternative defence structures, compensation, and subsidies for industrial restructuring, as well as paying for better quality volunteer armed forces, are potentially expensive and could reduce the slowdown in defence spending.

The hopes of a substantial peace dividend have all but evaporated. Rather, the emphasis is on the costs of demilitarization. It is increasingly stressed that disarmament is like an investment with initial costs (both sunk and fixed costs) and little returns in the short run. However, it is also believed that the returns appear in the longer run when the disarmament dividend could be potentially large. However the crucial question as to "how long is the long run" is as yet unanswerable.

There is little doubt that the decline in defence spending over the last five years or so, in most regions of the world, is irreversible. There are arguments and controversies about how quickly the restructuring will take place and what would be the optimum level of military expenditures (for various major countries and regions) when the stable plateau is reached, possibly at the millennium. But technology, economics, and politics will all contribute to a permanent reduction in global defence spending – although it will take far longer than anticipated at the dawn of the post-Cold War world.

Considering first the United States, currently the largest military spender in the world, during the decade of the 1980s US military expenditure rose rapidly until around 1986–1987 (depending on definition and measurement) and then began a downward fall. Since 1990 the fall has been much more marked and expenditures are expected to fall by 4 to 5 per cent per year until the mid-1990s. However, even in 1990 the value of US defence budgetary outlays was 50 per cent more than in 1980, reflecting the rapidity of rise in the first part of the decade.

The allocation of military expenditures into its constituent parts – personnel, operations and maintenance (O&M), procurement, research and development (R&D) – give an indication of threat perception and how capabilities were built up. During the expansion of aggregate budgets, procurement rose the fastest followed closely by R&D. During the downturn, procurement budgets have been cut most while R&D has been relatively protected. The share of procurement in the total budget authority fell from its peak of 32 per cent in 1986 to 22 per cent in 1991. During the same period R&D expenditures remained stable at around 12 per cent of the aggregate

budget authority. Thus, at a time when expenditures were being reduced, R&D exhibited resilience in the sense that its share was protected even though absolute amounts went down somewhat. Military
personnel shares remained the most stable, while O&M shares fell
during the expansionary phase and rose during the contractionary
phase.

The future reveals large cuts in active and reserve forces and
weapons systems as well as military personnel. In his State of the
Union message to Congress, President Bush announced in January
1992 the termination of: (a) the B-2 bomber – the costliest aeroplane
ever built at $75 million a copy; (b) the Midgetman ICBM; (c) the
W88 nuclear warhead for Trident missiles; (d) the Advance Cruise
missiles after a minimum production run (of 640 missiles to be purchased). SDI has fared relatively better particularly after the Iraqi
war and the spread of tactical missiles in the former Soviet states.
There is also now a modest Tactical Missile Defence Initiative that
could grow in importance given missile proliferation and regional
instability.

It is clear that US military spending is moving firmly downwards.
Its share of GNP, which was around 6.7 per cent in the mid-1980s, is
forecast to fall to 3.4 per cent by 1997 – the lowest share since the end
of World War II. The fall in defence orders has created a small crisis
in the military industrial sectors and the cuts in personnel will affect
unemployment, albeit modestly in terms of total labour force. However, taking a more long-term view, the period from 1980 to 1995
shows the end of a long cycle – not fundamentally unlike the end of
the Vietnam War. The current long cycle has, as usual, been characterized by expansion followed by contraction. For example, even after the recent cuts, military research and development is expected to
be greater by almost 50 per cent in 1995 compared to 1980. By mid-
1990 it is expected that defence spending will have reached a stable
plateau after the completion of the 15-year cycle. Given this relatively
long period of adjustment, industrial restructuring, although painful,
will not be traumatic. Since the markets have been given sufficiently
long time to adjust there is little interest in "conversion" in the
classical sense of the term. Rather the problem is one of industrial
diversification, retraining of skilled workers, and the reorientation of
military R&D towards research in other types of public goods such as
environmental protection (see Deger and Sen, 1990; 1992c). President Clinton will accelerate the cuts already initiated.

We now turn to the FSU (former Soviet Union), where the trans-formation has been truly profound. Defence spending, and the re-source cost of maintaining a large military, depends on perceptions regarding national security. In the Soviet successor states, national security is being defined in terms of a very broad set of parameters. Within this broad framework, national defence itself depends on many factors, not all of which are related to strategic considerations or foreign policy. Internal factors, ethnic unrest and civil disorder, will also affect military related spending. In the FSU, military expen-diture often reflected increases in military capability but also the perceptions of the country towards threat and security. The new states will clearly have a totally different set of priorities. In particu-lar, economic factors will become dominant in determining budgetary trends and the capacity of the state to provide for defence. In addi-tion, economic insecurity will be a far more important factor than threat perceptions of the old type. The level of external debt, or that of foreign aid, could be more critical than new arms procured. In the new group of states the issue will become more complicated than in the past: domestic, foreign, and interrepublican influences create a complex web of relationships that will affect the trends in force and spending levels. Unlike the past, military spending will never be a matter of military security alone.

It is now well known that after a slow-down in the late 1970s Soviet military expenditure rose rapidly in the 1980s, in the process exceed-ing the growth of the national product, which was itself slowing down due to various factors termed "growth retardation." The process was motivated by a variety of factors: the arms race consequent to the Reagan administration's spurt in defence spending; modernization, high R&D, automation and new technologies, a new procurement cycle; as well as military involvement and security assistance in the third world. The military burden rose fast since defence growth ex-ceeded economic growth. The process was halted in 1987, stabilized in 1988, and the decline in spending began earnestly in 1989. The years 1990 and 1991 were characterized by the great "build-down" and substantial reductions in all categories of forces and expenditures were carried out. The particular feature of 1991 was the chaotic nature of the cuts forced by the dissolution of the country and the inability to acquire funding for most projects particularly in defence-related research. The chaos continues in 1992 even though some systematic features are becoming clearer. For example, the investment part of the budget (procurement plus R&D, will be reduced substantially and the consumption part (personnel, construction, pensions share) will go up, albeit with a diminishing total.

The aggregate level of military expenditure in the FSU and the successor states, as well as the proportion of GDP, is still a matter of controversy, although the trends are undeniably downwards. For the first time in 1990 the USSR submitted its official military expenditure budget for 1989 to the United Nations according to the UN matrix information sheet (see Deger, 1991). Although far more comprehensive than in the past many reporting sections are still blank. Given the disintegration of the Union, in the coming years it may not be even possible to get this information at all. What UN and other multilateral agencies such as the IMF and the World Bank should emphasize and encourage is the publication of defence white papers by the newly formed ex-Soviet republics. In their absence misperceptions are bound to increase and Confidence and Security Building Measures (CSBMs) will fail to achieve their desired aims. Much more needs to be known about the defence expenditure allocations of Russia and the CIS states.

In 1990, before the price explosion began, official defence spending was 72 billion roubles – less than 8 per cent of GDP. On the other hand, even until 1990/91, Western estimates of Soviet defence spending were around 150 billion roubles – almost double the official estimate. There are many reasons why Soviet military expenditure, particularly procurement spending, appears low as compared to rouble estimates provided by Western intelligence agencies. The most obvious reason given is that prices of weapons systems are kept artificially low to accommodate low budgets. The few prices of individual weapons systems that are available clearly demonstrate the wide divergence between Soviet and Western unit prices of weapons.

There is also the additional question as to whether these Soviet prices paid by the military truly reflect resource cost. It is important to know the economic burden of the military on the economy as well as the benefits of conversion. A cost-benefit analysis can be done by comparing similar US weapons, incorporating an efficiency factor to account for qualitative differences, utilizing a conversion rate to change one currency to another and making estimates about inflation to make the prices consistent for the same year. According to a noted RAND analyst, for tanks and tactical aircraft the unit prices do indeed reflect resource use within a reasonable margin; however, for naval ships and helicopters the prices are vastly lower than what any reasonable comparisons would suggest. Commenting on the wide price differential under appropriate conversion rates between the unit price (cost) of fighting ships, between Soviet and American models of comparable quality, it has been noted that:

First, ships take years to construct and require substantial investments in ship-yards, buildings, and equipment; since interest rates are subsidized by the Soviet state and there is no land rent these "missing costs" could contribute to the underpricing of Soviet ships. In general, the more capital- and land-intensive the means of production, the more these factors would operate. Another possible explanation is that the Soviets could have been comparing the bare ship cost, un-outfitted, as it was completed at the Nikolaev North shipyard, with a fully equipped Ticonderoga, or the level of technology and complexity is considerably lower than estimated by US naval designers, or the efficiency of Soviet shipyards and equipment suppliers is many times greater than that of US producers, or the Soviet navy is stealing the cruiser from the shipyards. Only the first and last explanations are credible. Most likely the price to the shipyard does not cover its costs, and a substantial loss must be covered by the Ministry of Shipbuilding, by the state budget, or by bank loans. (Alexander, 1990)

Grave uncertainty characterizes the future. More transparency will be difficult to achieve simply because disorderly transition will stop the gathering of proper information. If national armies are formed by all the former republics then it will be even more complicated regarding analysis and forecasts of the evolution of defence expenditures. The following issues are potentially important: first, whether a centralized CIS Ministry of Defence will exist and which part of military expenditure will be spent by it; secondly, if a central ministry does exist and a unified army remains, then under what conditions the system will continue and what will be the republics' and new states' budgetary contributions. This is the classic burden-sharing problem and raises the whole issue of "free riders." It should be noted that Russia and Ukraine (the two overwhelmingly dominant CIS military powers) now have their own national armies although Russia has maintained close links with the CIS command structure. The third issue is that each category of defence expenditure may be separately borne out and allocated by the republics, which will increase the confusion even further. Personnel costs could be borne by the budgets of successor states depending on the number of troops stationed in their territory. So also could O&M. Procurement costs could be spent centrally. But since the overwhelming number of defence enterprises are in Russia and Ukraine the prices at which weapons will be "traded" among the ex-republics could be important. If Russia charges high prices will the other states pay for the arms required for common defence? R&D resources are also concentrated and their expenditure allocation could also be controversial. Finally, the costs of weapons destruction (due to arms control agreements) and safe maintenance of strategic and tactical nuclear weapons (due to problems of proliferation) need to be shared equitably since the alternatives could be catastrophic.

The evolution of military expenditure in the last three years of existence of the Soviet state, from 1989 to 1991, exhibits a number of interesting features as well as clues to the future. As mentioned earlier, during 1989 to 1991 military expenditure was substantially reduced. The decline almost certainly exceeded the 14 per cent cut within three years proposed by Gorbachev in his 1989 speech to the USSR Congress of the Peoples Deputies (speech given on 30 May 1989). The proposed reduction in procurement spending, at the same speech, was of the order of 19.5 per cent. This also has been exceeded. Military research and development, relatively protected throughout the 1980s, was slashed in 1991 by apparently 23 per cent in real terms. The first feature of change, therefore, is the decline in aggregate defence spending – the decline accelerating during 1991 and the level falling even faster in 1992.

Secondly, the most interesting change that has taken place is in the composition of the investment part of the budget (procurement, R&D, nuclear defence, military construction) as compared to the operating cost (personnel, O&M, pensions, social services, housing). In 1989 the former took almost 70 per cent of the budget leaving the rest for operational expenditure. In 1991 this share had declined to about 55 per cent. If current trends continue, in 1992 the investment component of the budget will become less than one-fourth of total defence spending – a share not seen since World War II.

It is also reported that since 1989, when the disarmament phase began, there has been a sharp reduction in the acquisition of individual weapons and hardware. By 1991 acquisition of strategic missiles had been reduced by 40 per cent, sea launched ballistic missiles by 54 per cent, tanks by 66 per cent, armoured vehicles by 80 per cent, artillery systems by 59 per cent, combat vehicles by 50 per cent, as well as the total elimination of a whole class of tactical nuclear missiles. According to Western intelligence reports, Soviet procurement declined by 10 per cent per annum each year between 1988 and 1989 and between 1989 and 1990, almost equally distributed between strategic and conventional forces with maximum impact on the army followed by the air force. Naval procurement continued haltingly with the completion in 1991 of a new aircraft carrier. However, with the break-up of the Union the future of shipyards such as the Niko-laev in Ukraine became uncertain. In any case, naval procurement collapsed in 1992 and the respective governments are trying to sell their old stocks.

The third feature of change relates to military R&D. Until the be-ginning of 1991 there were still many reports of weapons moderniza-tion and continuing military R&D. However, information gathered in 1991 indicates that these research activities are being reduced con-siderably and resource transfer towards the civilian sectors is in full swing. The defence R&D sector is expected to bear the full weight of conversion in the future with the emphasis on high technology exports.

Fourthly, as regards manpower, at the beginning of 1991 the Soviet armed forces numbered 3,760,000 and the force reductions of half a million men (announced by Gorbachev in his 1988 UN speech) had been completed. There have been major problems with conscription (around 60 per cent of the army are conscripts) and it is thought that structural decay will force the army to lose more personnel even without disarmament measures. In October 1991 Gorbachev an-nounced a further 700,000 reduction in personnel, which is now con-tinuing. If the central defence apparatus of the CIS totally disin-tegrates then republican armies will probably be smaller than current deployments. Thus the Soviet successor states could in aggregate have far smaller armed forces than the currently envisaged 3 million.

It is well known that there is grave dissatisfaction in the armed forces, about pay and pensions, which were low in the past especially for conscripts. Troop withdrawals from Germany and Central Europe have increased the problems, particularly of housing. Even though German foreign aid has alleviated some of the specific problems, overall grievance remains high and morale is low. The large increase in pensions and other benefits is intended to reduce tension in the army that could create problems of law and order.

The way for the future at least for the medium term seems to be the following for Russia and the CIS states: to utilize the benign in-ternational security climate to restructure the armed forces on a pro-fessional basis; to cut back on costly weaponry, some of it outdated and others exceeding Treaty Limited Items of arms control agree-ments; to reduce O&M by scrapping ancient systems; to restructure military R&D and skip a generation of modernization; to utilize the spin-ins from new civilian research; to begin a new procurement cycle and modernization after the professional army is completed and political stability achieved. The process has already begun in Russia, although there are still formidable obstacles from the military-industrial complex.

Turning now to Europe, West European military expenditures are also falling, but again in slow and steady fashion rather than responding to the dramatic changes in the continent. The mood is one of caution and there is little evidence of any so-called peace dividend. Rather, disarmament is viewed as having initial costs, particularly in micro-economic terms such as for individual companies and regions concentrating in arms production.

Aggregate military expenditure of the European NATO countries, as well as those of the EC, rose consistently from 1980 to 1988/89 and then fell back modestly. In 1991 it exceeded $150 billion (in US dollars; 1988 constant prices and exchange rates) about $10 billion more in real terms compared to 1980. There have been some allocational changes with procurement and investment spending falling faster during the last few years. Total procurement spending by European NATO on major conventional weapons rose from $30 to $35 billion between 1982 and 1988. Since then there has been a fall by 1991 to around $30 billion. Although the decline in procurement expenditure is quite sharp, it is nowhere as unprecedented as commonly believed. The same trends, with minor modifications, hold true for the EC.

By early 1992, very few major weapons acquisition programmes have been totally terminated, although many are to be stretched out. For France and the United Kingdom, major recent cuts are concentrated in the area of nuclear weapons, particularly tactical systems. For Germany, the possible withdrawal from the production stage of the European Fighter Aircraft is an important step towards cutting procurement spending. However, other purchases remain substantially similar. The reorganization of European defence budgets has been more modest compared to those of the United States. In terms of trends, relative to the United States the growth of defence spending has been slower in the early 1980s and the contraction has also been slower in the last five years.

The impact on European defence industries, of military expenditure reductions and procurement cuts, has been painful but hardly traumatic. Clearly restructuring is called for but this would have happened in any case due to economic and technological reasons.

The formation of a single European market, demands for greater competition in public procurement, the growing interdependence between civil and military parts of company activities, the possibilities for spin-in from civilian R&D, increasing popularity of mergers and acquisitions financed by perfect capital mobility, widening interest in privatization and the withdrawal of the government from direct production, as well as the attempts to achieve not only economies of scale but also economies of scope – have all meant that defence industries would be forced to restructure. Indeed, industrial reorganization is far more advanced in other sectors compared to defence, and the transition in say, coal, shipbuilding, or steel industries has been far more painful. Protectionism, the creation of national champions, state subsidies, creation of entry barriers, the use of national security arguments to stop competition and continue with lower competitiveness, are all symptomatic of the European defence industrial base. Recent political changes and the movement towards European integration in other spheres, have acted as catalysts towards the long overdue reorganization of the defence industrial sector. However, the transition has been slow and the macroeconomic costs of adjustment are rather low. Estimates of half to one million job losses in European arms industries alone by the mid-1990s seem to be quite exaggerated.

The one area of military restructuring where dramatic changes are expected is that of personnel. Calculations of armed forces for European NATO are distorted by Turkish and Greek forces since these are based on different threat perceptions. Leaving out these two countries, between 1985 and 1990 military personnel declined by only 1.9 per cent over the whole period. On the other hand, in 1991 alone military personnel numbers in European NATO (except Turkey and Greece) had fallen by 3 per cent and this trend is set to accelerate fast. Germany will have a maximum of 370,000 men by 1994 down from over 520,000 currently in service. The total military personnel of the British Armed Forces dipped below 300,000 in 1991 for the first time. In France, military personnel has come down from over 570,000 in the early 1980s to around 540,000 in the early 1990s. Advances in technology, increase in capital-labour ratios, the requirements for more sophisticated personnel to handle modern military hardware, demographic factors, difficulties with the conscription system, the political problem of selling large standing armies to a sceptical electorate without a clear threat perception – all these factors will contribute to a rapid decline in European armed forces. Indeed it may be

31

argued that the days of large standing armies, permanently ready for war in fixed formations, are becoming outdated. The greater emphasis on rapid deployment forces, and C3I activities to support speed and operational flexibility, means that large armies are becoming less relevant in Europe. In addition, out of area operations, i.e. to engage in conflict or peace-keeping outside the traditional areas of NATO involvement, are becoming more important. This will require more technologically sophisticated mobile units.

In the Eastern part of Europe, among the former members of the WTO, military expenditure reductions have taken place much faster in recent years. Between 1988 and 1991 the following percentage reductions in military expenditures have taken place in real terms among ex-Warsaw Pact countries: Bulgaria, 37 per cent; Czechoslovakia, 58 per cent; Hungary, 42 per cent; Poland, 36 per cent; Romania, 29 per cent. Given the economic crises in these countries it has simply been impossible to maintain defence spending at anything remotely similar to the past. Political changes have broken any inertia and resistance that the establishment could have towards cuts. The speed of the cuts has therefore been phenomenal. As the aggregates have been reduced so has the share of defence procurement, which is now minimal.

Security needs are yet to be properly defined for these countries in Central and Eastern Europe, as are military doctrines and requirements. Defence expenditure is now at a minimum level and further cuts are probably difficult. We could expect therefore a plateau of defence expenditures from now on, with attempts to develop collective security arrangements, which will reduce the needs of the armed forces and make them consistent with low levels of military spending.

## III. Third world military expenditure and arms trade

As mentioned earlier, in 1990 total defence spending internationally was around $950 billion. The total figure was dominated by the United States and the former USSR, which between them spent about 60 per cent of the world total. In general, the developed countries of the world (including the USSR and members of the WTO) spent around $800 billion, while developing nations aggregated about $150 billion in 1990.

Figures 1 and 2 show military expenditure trends over the 1980s for various regions in the third world, in terms of an index with a starting

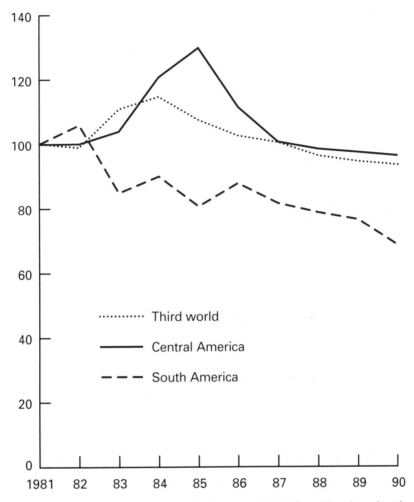

Fig. 1 **Trends in regional military expenditure for the third world, selected regions, 1981–1990**

value of 100 in 1980. These trends contrast significantly with those of the 1970s, which are shown in figures 3 and 4. More specifically, by the mid- to late-1980s all regions of the third world (except significantly the Far East) showed declines in military expenditures. On the other hand, throughout the 1970s, all regions in the third world (particularly the Middle East) showed expanding defence allocations. One important point to note is that the trend rate of change varies considerably making it difficult to draw generalized conclusions.

In table 1 we provide data for the annual percentage decline in

33

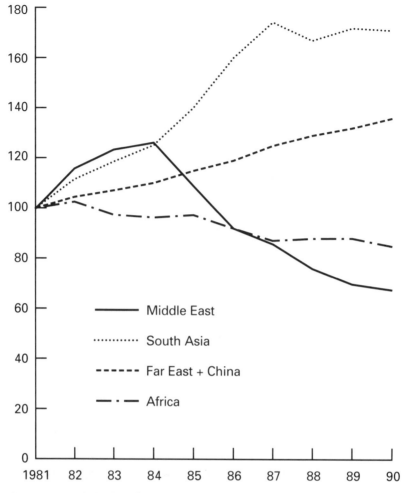

Fig. 2 **Trends in regional military expenditure for the third world, selected regions, 1981–1990**

military expenditures for the various regions of the world starting from the peak year in the 1980s when the U-turn took place. The Middle East shows the largest fall starting around the middle of the decade. However, once again the problem of interpreting the data remains. Part of the fall for this region is attributable to larger military aid (increasingly taking the form of grants and concessional transfers of weapons) and its concentration towards Egypt and Israel following a change in US government policy. Military aid is usually left out of the figures following the NATO/IMF definition of military

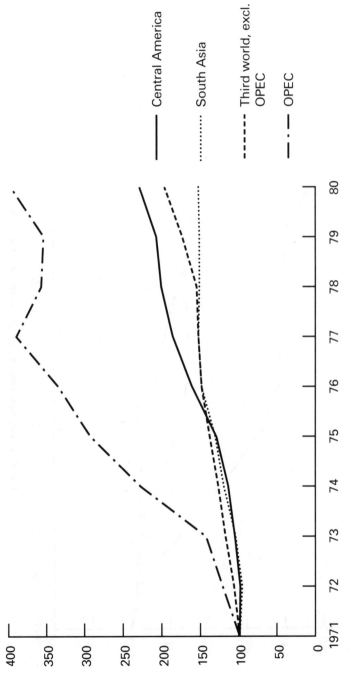

Fig. 3 **Trends in regional military expenditure, selected regions, 1971–1980**

35

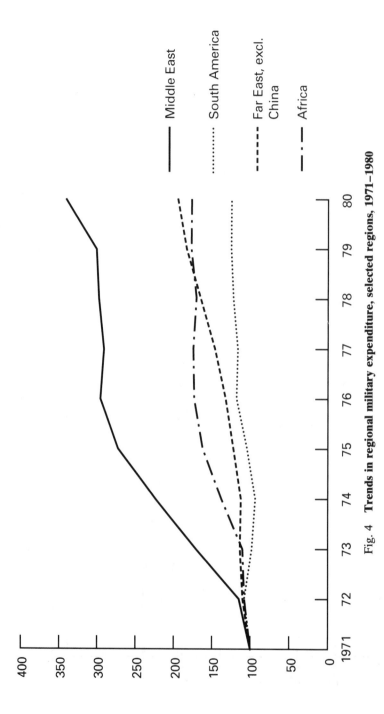

Fig. 4 **Trends in regional military expenditure, selected regions, 1971–1980**

36

Table 1 **Annual percentage decline in military expenditure from respective peak year in the 1980s to 1990, regions in the developing world**

| Regions | Peak year | Annual change until 1990 (%) |
|---|---|---|
| Middle East | 1984 | −9.2 |
| South Asia | 1987 | −1.0 |
| Far East | 1981 | +3.4 |
| Africa | 1982 | −2.3 |
| Central America | 1985 | −6.1 |
| South America | 1982 | −4.9 |
| All developing countries | 1984 | −3.1 |

Source: Author's estimates from *SIPRI Yearbook 1992*, Appendix 7A.
Note: The Far East had military expenditure increases at a rate of 3.4 per cent per annum from 1981 to 1990.

Table 2 **Annual percentage decline in arms trade, from respective peak year in the 1980s to 1990, regions in the developing world**

| Regions | Peak year | Annual change until 1990 (%) |
|---|---|---|
| Middle East | 1987 | −30.5 |
| South Asia | 1987 | −18.6 |
| Far East | 1988 | −30.5 |
| Sub-Saharan Africa | 1984 | −13.8 |
| Central America | 1985 | −12.8 |
| South America | 1984 | −21.8 |
| North Africa | 1986 | −29.6 |
| All developing countries | 1987 | −24.2 |

Source: Author's estimates from *SIPRI Yearbook 1991*, Appendix 7A.

expenditures. Thus the declining trend is overestimated. If total defence spending in the region was considered, through the adding of military aid, the fall would be less significant. However, the underlying trend would still be negative and there is little doubt that military spending in the Middle East has fallen fastest until 1990 out of all regions in the developing world. Again the sharp contrast with the 1970s should be noted when regional spending rose the fastest in the Middle East.

The trend in the trade in arms follows similar patterns although the peak years are somewhat later than for defence spending (see table 2). This suggests that the initial impact of budgetary cuts, which forced this demilitarization in developing countries, fell on domestic defence resources and there was an initial tendency to "protect" the

37

importation of weapons. In addition, the long standing Iran-Iraq war fuelled the demand for imported weapons. By the late 1980s all regions of the third world significantly reduced their arms purchases from abroad. Note also that the falls in imports have been at much higher rates compared to the fall in defence spending in general. This suggests that as the overall downturn proceeded for a long period of time, the domestic content of military resources was reduced less. In a relative sense personnel and operations and maintenance expenditures were protected while procurement fell dramatically in the longer run. Thus, in the short run arms procurement and imports are protected. However, in the long run, during cuts, arms importation is reduced sharply. In addition, domestic production of armaments could have gone up as more countries acquired the means to manufacture at least some forms of weaponry.

One major index of militarization, security requirement, as well as the resource cost of defence, is the ratio of military expenditure to GDP (or GNP) – called the military burden. In table 3 regional military burdens are given for developing countries. There is a substantial regional variation in this index ranging from 2 to 10 per cent on average. For the decade of the 1980s, on average for all developing countries, the burden approaches 5 per cent – somewhat lower than in the 1970s. By the early 1990s it is estimated that the average for the third world is less than 4.5 per cent – reflecting the fall in defence spending discussed earlier. A related index is that the share of defence in total central government expenditures was around 18 per cent for the whole third world.

Table 3 **Share of military expenditure in GDP and central government expenditure for developing countries (all figures in percentages)**

| Regions | Share of military expenditure in GDP, 1980–1990 | Share of military expenditure in central government expenditure, 1980–1988 |
|---|---|---|
| Asia | 4.5 | 21.7 |
| Middle East | 10.1 | 21.0 |
| North Africa | 5.6 | 13.0 |
| Sub-Saharan Africa | 3.1 | 12.2 |
| Latin America and the Caribbean | 2.2 | 8.2 |
| All developing countries | 4.9 | 18.0 |

Sources: Author's estimates from *SIPRI Yearbook 1992*, Appendix 7A; Hewitt (1991).

Table 4  **The levels of military burdens in the 1980s**

| Range of military burdens (%) | Number of countries in each range |
| --- | --- |
| 10 plus | 14 |
| 6–10 | 14 |
| 4–6 | 12 |
| 2–4 | 31 |
| 1–2 | 18 |
| Less than 1 | 12 |

Source: Calculated from *SIPRI Yearbook 1991*, Table Appendix 5A.

For individual developing countries, the military burdens vary enormously from over 20 per cent down to less than 0.5 per cent. However, there are at least 40 countries in the third world whose military burden is higher than the average for advanced industrial countries of the West (i.e. leaving out Eastern Europe). The latter averaged just below 4 per cent on average during the period 1981 to 1989. Although third world countries expended less than 18 per cent of the world total during the decade, the relative burden for many of these countries was higher. On the other hand, over 25 countries averaged 2 per cent or less military burden over the decade – a level considered reasonable by some analysts. In table 4 we provide data for 1981–1989 averages to indicate the number of developing countries falling in each range of the defence burdens.

After reaching a peak around 1987 the arms imports of developing countries have been continuously declining. The largest regional falls have been recorded for Latin America and Africa – again reflecting their economic decline and the consequences of the debt crisis. The former Soviet Union stopped arms delivery except for hard currency in 1991 and this implied a sharp drop in the aggregate import of the third world. Yet even until 1989 the level of arms importation remained quite high, particularly if the value of small arms is accounted for.

In many respects, and in terms of alternative indices, the arms trade is highly concentrated both in terms of demand and supply. One simple measure of concentration is that only five supplier countries exported 87 per cent of total arms sold to the third world between 1987 and 1991. On the demand side, only 15 developing country arms importers bought about 80 per cent of total arms imported by the third world.

In table 5 we show the changes in the share of developing country

Table 5  **Major conventional weapons imports of developing country regions as share of the world total, 1987–1991 (%)**

| Regions | 1987 | 1988 | 1989 | 1990 | 1991 |
|---|---|---|---|---|---|
| Asia | 23.2 | 26.9 | 32.3 | 25.2 | 29.2 |
| Middle East | 34.7 | 25.0 | 15.2 | 23.5 | 21.4 |
| North Africa | 1.4 | 1.3 | 3.9 | 0.5 | 0 |
| Sub-Saharan Africa | 5.5 | 4.8 | 1.2 | 4.0 | 0.5 |
| Central America | 0.9 | 0.5 | 0.8 | 1.2 | 1.0 |
| South America | 4.2 | 2.2 | 3.0 | 2.9 | 3.1 |
| All developing countries | 70.1 | 61.1 | 56.9 | 57.7 | 55.8 |

Source: Author's estimates from *SIPRI Yearbook 1992*; Appendix 8B; totals do not add up due to rounding errors.

regions in the total world arms trade of major conventional weapons. The last row, which gives the share of the third world overall, demonstrates that developing countries in aggregate are buying a lesser proportion of a declining world total of armaments imported. From over two-thirds this share has rapidly fallen towards one-half in the last five years. In particular, Middle Eastern arms import share has fallen dramatically. Whether the new arms contracts after the Gulf War will change these proportions is still a matter of debate.

The chief beneficiary of the arms trade – both from economic motives (making profits) and from political motives (foreign policy influence) – has been ironically the five permanent members of the UN Security Council. Between 1987 and 1991 they sold over 87 per cent of all arms exported to the third world. Table 6 gives the market shares of these countries during these five years. In addition it also provides similar information on the 15 largest arms exporters between 1987 and 1991. Even though the former USSR has stopped selling arms in large quantities it could still be the second largest arms exporter in the world.

What are the motives for arms sales, given that it has negative externalities and could be considered a "public bad" from an international point of view? Until 1990 the position regarding suppliers' motives was relatively clear. The United States and USSR had predominantly political motives and used arms trade as an important foreign policy tool. Then there were the second tier exporters – France, the United Kingdom, Germany, and China – which had predominantly economic motives, although arms are generally not sold to potentially troublesome countries. Table 7 shows the market share of these two groups of exporters plus all others taken together over

Table 6  **Share of arms exports of major conventional weapons to the third world, 1987–1991**

| Country | Share in arms exports to the third world (%) | Share in arms exports to all countries of the world (%) |
|---|---|---|
| USSR | 42.4 | 35.1 |
| USA | 22.1 | 34.4 |
| France | 8.4 | 6.4 |
| China | 7.2 | 4.5 |
| UK | 7.1 | 5.2 |
| Germany | 1.6 | 3.5 |
| Brazil | 1.5 | 0.9 |
| Netherlands | 1.3 | 1.0 |
| Italy | 1.3 | 1.1 |
| Czechoslovakia | 0.8 | 1.9 |
| Israel | 0.8 | 0.7 |
| Spain | 0.7 | 0.7 |
| Sweden | 0.7 | 0.9 |
| Yugoslavia | 0.7 | 0.4 |
| Egypt | 0.6 | 0.4 |
| All others | | 3.0 |

Source: Estimated from *SIPRI Yearbook 1992*, Table 8.1.

Table 7  **Market shares of total arms exports to the third world (%)**

| | 1970–74 | 1975–79 | 1980–84 | 1985–89 | 1990 |
|---|---|---|---|---|---|
| Predominantly political exporter countries | 76.9 | 73.0 | 60.0 | 62.0 | 61.8 |
| Major commercial exporter countries | 18.1 | 19.2 | 24.8 | 26.1 | 31.4 |
| All other exporters | 5.0 | 7.8 | 15.2 | 11.9 | 6.7 |
| Index of market concentration | 1.60 | 1.74 | 2.25 | 2.14 | 2.06 |

Source: Author's estimates from *SIPRI Yearbook* (various years).
Note: The first group consists of the USA and the USSR; the second group consists of France, China, UK, Germany; the third group consists of all others including a few developing country exporters. The index of market concentration is defined in the text.

the last two decades. The long-term trend was that the commercially and economically motivated exporters were gaining in market shares and becoming relatively more important in a shrinking market. Since 1991 the position has become even more extreme since Russia (the second largest exporter) has clearly become a commercial exporter.

The last row of table 7 gives the index of market concentration, defined as the inverse of the squared sum of market shares. For three groups as in the table, when there is no concentration and everybody has an equal share the index would be 3. If one group has the total market, and there is perfect concentration, the index would be unity. The index therefore varies between 1 and 3 and when it rises the concentration in the market declines. From the actual indices in table 7 it is clear that concentration in the 1980s was lower than in the 1970s but has been rising in recent years.

Until now the burden of military expenditure has been shown in terms of its share in GDP or central government expenditure. This is the traditional method. A more non-traditional approach would be to look at the share of defence spending in current government revenue. Such an indicator for the government would conform to the household budget constraint where expenditure shares are taken as proportions of current earnings. In the same way, since governments are the only spenders on the military within any national economy, it may be useful to consider how much the military accounts for in spending the current revenue of the government. In addition, we also consider one of the major burdens of the 1980s, i.e. the servicing of external debts, which for many countries took a far higher share than the prime "unproductive" spending on defence. In table 8 we give the

Table 8  **Military expenditure and external debt service as shares of central government current revenue in 1988 (%)**

| Country | External debt service | Military expenditure | External debt service plus military expenditure |
|---------|------------------------|----------------------|-------------------------------------------------|
| Argentina | 22.3 | 15.2 | 37.5 |
| Colombia | 54.3 | 16.7 | 71.0 |
| Chile | 19.6 | 24.6 | 44.2 |
| Egypt | 10.8 | 18.1 | 28.9 |
| Indonesia | 51.6 | 12.0 | 63.6 |
| Jordan | 67.1 | 51.4 | 118.5 |
| Morocco | 26.2 | 20.5 | 46.7 |
| Pakistan | 20.6 | 41.8 | 62.4 |
| Philippines | 49.0 | 9.1 | 58.1 |
| Sri Lanka | 24.7 | 16.8 | 41.5 |
| Zimbabwe | 22.8 | 18.1 | 40.9 |

Source: Deger and Sen (1992).
Note: Egypt and Philippines military expenditures do not include arms purchases through foreign aid.

**Table 9  Third world long-term debt, financial flows, official development assistance, and arms imports, 1985–1989 (in US$bn)**

| Item | 1985 | 1987 | 1989 |
|---|---|---|---|
| Official development assistance (ODA) | 29.4 | 41.6 | 46.7 |
| Arms imports by third world countries | 32.5 | 43.8 | 39.3 |
| Net transfers from South to North on long-term debt | 19.7 | 32.2 | 42.9 |
| Ratio of arms imports plus net transfer to ODA | 177.5 | 182.7 | 176.0 |

Sources: Author's estimates from OECD (1990); World Bank (1990); ACDA (1990).

data for 1988 of selected developing countries. It is clear that these two ratios alone accounted for a substantial proportion of government earnings. For some countries the ratio exceeded 50 or even 100 per cent leaving very little for developmental expenditures without further borrowing.

We have shown that the burden on the public exchequer of providing for defence and paying interest on debt can be substantial. A similar burden, in terms of foreign exchange and trade, is shown in table 9. Inflows of official development assistance (ODA) are contrasted with "unproductive" outflows of arms importation and net transfers on long-term debt that were moving from the South to the North during the second half of the 1980s. It is seen that during the period 1985 to 1989, the value of arms import plus net transfer payments made by developing countries far exceeded the ODA received by them (from the Development Assistance Committee [DAC] countries of the OECD). Even though the ratio in the last row exaggerates the contribution of outflows, since a large part of arms imports are not paid for, it is still certain that net transfers plus weapons actually paid for would be higher than any ODA received. Once again, debt alleviation as well as arms import reductions are both necessary for the disarmament dividend to have any impact in the long term.

## IV. Causes for the decline

For the industrial countries, reviewed in section 2, there are essentially three sets of causes that prompted the decline in military expenditure. The first can be termed Technological and Economic Structural Disarmament (TESD). The second is domestic political and economic systemic changes. The third set relates to factors specifically concerned with international security. The first set of factors has already affected the Western industrial countries particularly in NATO. The second set is relevant for the CEEC and the post-Soviet states. The third is expected to become increasingly important in the future.

TESD implies that military expenditure cuts, and concomitant demilitarization, depend predominantly on the nature of technology and structural factors rather than on political changes. Essentially, oversophistication of defence technology has reached a situation of overkill. Defence production processes are subject to increasing returns to scale, after a minimum level of output is produced, as well as requiring inordinately high sunk costs. Military R&D, for the major powers, has increased much faster than other components of defence budgets. Unless the numbers of systems produced are large, requiring high levels of procurement demand, average costs cannot be met nor can the gains from increasing returns be realized. Therefore, the relatively new defence technologies of the 1980s (smart weapons, use of robotics and artificial intelligence, stealth weapons, space defence, etc.) require expanding aggregate procurement budgets to become viable. By the late 1980s budget constraints were binding in most Western countries and the economic systems in the socialist economies were near to collapse. This produced a "scissors crisis" where expanding unit costs and shrinking aggregate budgets produced some form of demilitarization. In practice, this was achieved by cancelling major individual programmes (such as the B-2 bomber for the United States, or production of aircraft carriers for Russia, or withdrawal of Germany from the European Fighter Aircraft system).

In the CEEC (including the CIS) the whole systemic collapse has meant that military security has lost its predominance in resource allocation. Economic and environmental security are far more important than building up military power. There are no defined external enemies. Arms control treaties mean that large stocks need to be eliminated. Defence industries are being either run down or converted so that the potential to produce arms is being circumscribed.

The third factor, and possibly the most fundamental change since 1991, has been the demise of the Soviet Union. Thus, for the first time in post-World War II history there exists only one military superpower and the adversarial arms races of the past cannot be rationalized any more. The end of the Soviet state renders the military arsenals of the major powers, built up with high military spending, superfluous. The conflicts of 1991 – in the Middle East and the Balkans – required altered military structures and doctrines and certainly less expenditures. The reduction of defence spending, and the forces, procurement, and military research that it buys, have moved beyond TESD and are subject to a political transformation whereby there exists only one major superpower and the type of military threats that were possible until recently are now no more.

As discussed earlier, for developing countries in general (barring a few exceptions), both defence spending and arms imports are falling. There are many reasons for these fundamental changes: the prolonged economic crisis, particularly in Latin America and sub-Saharan Africa has meant less money for all public goods including that spent on security; the change in the attitude of governments and pressure of multilateral institutions (such as the IMF) have forced aggregate government expenditure cuts, which include military spending reductions; the debt crisis and more general balance of payments problems, which have forced arms importations to be restricted; the end of conflicts say in Central America or in Southern Africa or in South-East Asia; the end of prolonged wars such as that between Iran and Iraq; high weapons stocks between 1975 and 1985 mean fewer requirements before the next replacement cycle; greater arms production in a few large developing countries. All of these factors have contributed to the fall in defence spending as well as in arms importation in the third world. Essentially, resource booms, government expenditure expansion, and the involvement in conflict and war explain the high defence burden in developing countries. On the other hand, the fall in commodity and oil prices, macroeconomic and budgetary austerity, balance of payments and debt problems, as well as conflict cessation and resolution all account for low or declining defence burdens.

So what then is the problem? If peace is breaking out and resource wastage in terms of defence spending and arms imports are rapidly declining then there seems to be no major contradiction between security and development in the third world, as seen in the past. However, this optimistic scenario is not precisely correct although there are some hopeful signs of more security in the future. There are two major problems. First, although military spending and arms trade are falling, economic conditions are not improving rapidly enough and there is little sign of the disarmament dividend. There is still insufficient transfer of resources across the world for developmental purposes (including those in Eastern Europe). Hence disillusionment is spreading and the problems of internal security (related to poverty, civil conflict, human rights violation) may become more important in the future. Secondly, savings from military expenditure reductions may be transferred to internal security spending; in the same way the fall in major weapons imports may be compensated by importation of small arms or dual-use technology to produce weapons at home. Then we could have a "peace penalty" where inter-state security problems may be replaced by "intra-state" security problems. The European example – where the Cold War is over but the war in former Yugoslavia has accelerated – is instructive of future changes in the third world.

There are four major features of the arms trade as it now stands that are relevant for arms control. Since economic crisis has a direct and major impact on third world arms trade it is clear that in the current situation most countries simply cannot afford to purchase weapons in world markets. Military aid is drying up particularly from the previously socialist countries but also from the European nations. However, a rise in economic growth rates will clearly increase demand unless institutional mechanisms are set in place for trade controls. The focus of controls must be on suppliers. Secondly, the share of the world total due to commercially motivated supply is rising. This creates problems for controlling the trade in weapons since economic interests conflict with political motives. Even though governments might wish in the interests of international relations to impose controls there will be commercial and economic pressure against this, making it very difficult to impose sanctions on the trade. The third feature is that market concentration is rising and the small producing countries are falling out of the export market. Thus only a few countries are actively involved in exports and it will be easier to control transfers. It has been noted above that the five permanent members of the Security Council between them supply more than 85 per cent of arms imported by the third world. Hence, control on exports of the final weapons system should be quite simple if there exists the political will. In the aftermath of the Gulf War of 1991 there is greater awareness that controls are essential and the major suppliers are now tightening up procedures and will be more careful about what to sell and to whom. The United Nations will begin a register of arms transfers starting from 1992 and it is hoped that this transparency will help to find out more details of sales and means of stopping them. Fourthly, it will be most problematic to control dual-use technology given that multinationals are involved and that trade restrictions on technology transfer will hurt the developing world. It is also possible that arms production in the third world could increase in the future (through dual-use technology imports) at the same time as trade in final weapons systems are going down. However, demand for weapons is low and it is simply not cost effective to produce arms given the technological characteristics of the production process.

## V. Concluding remarks: The issues for the future

Demilitarization, in the form of military expenditure reductions and decline in arms procurement through imports, is occurring in many countries of the third world. With a few significant exceptions, mostly in the Middle East, most regions of the world are attempting to curb defence spending. The process of demilitarization generally, and military spending falls in particular, will be steady but relatively slow. The first step could be large reductions in personnel numbers (as in China or in war-torn Southern Africa). However, the process of demobilization will be slow and will require additional expenditures. Thus, there will be less proportional reduction in personnel expenditures compared to the fall in the size of the forces, due to an increase in pensions and benefits. Procurement of major weapons systems will be drastically cut while attempting to increase the efficiency of existing systems. Thus procurement expenditure will continue to fall but not spending on Operations and Support. Arms production, certainly for small arms, could continue to exhibit resilience. However, in a declining world market and fiercer competition, developing countries stand little chance of achieving the economies of scale required for advanced weapons manufacture. Conversion efforts are therefore essential with the warning that the "export version" of conversion should be avoided at all costs. For a few large countries, involved in military research and development, there will be much closer integration with civilian research to acquire the benefits of "spin-in."

The central problems will move away from armaments and disarmament to conflicts both within and between nation states. There are fundamental reasons for conflicts both within and between third world countries. A large part of these conflicts is a product of poverty and underdevelopment. But even when resources rise sharply, as after the oil-price boom, countries spend more on the military, creating insecurity for their neighbours and contributing to a regional arms race. Thus the causes of militarization and related conflicts are complex. Often, conflictual societies are prone to have authoritarian leadership and governments. The interplay – of conflicts, dictatorial governments, economic backwardness, attempts to grow at fast rates – can cause human rights violation. There is therefore a symbiotic relationship between democratization, demilitarization, and development. However, getting the right mix of policies, to proceed along the transitional path towards preferred goals, is very difficult to achieve. Military expenditure and the arms trade are neither causes nor solutions to such problems. But they are certainly major catalysts and can contribute to a worsening of the situation as it exists.

The long-term trends in military expenditure and the trade in major conventional weapons point to a structural decline. Now is the time to seize the opportunity to reduce it to the barest minimum. Then, one contributory catalyst to non-democratic and militarized behaviour by third world governments and élites can be eradicated. But this will only remove the symptom and not the disease. Fundamental changes in regional security structures and economic growth are the only long-term permanent solutions. The use of institution building (such as regional variants of the CSCE process) and growth-enhancing wealth transfer from the North to the South are the only ways to achieve disarmament, democracy, and development. Without such a perspective in 3-D the world will not be secure nor will it be stable.

# References

Alexander, A.A. (1990). *Perestroika and Change in Soviet Weapons Acquisition.* RAND Report R-3821-USDP. The RAND Corporation, Santa Monica.

Deger, S. (1991). "World military expenditure." In *SIPRI Yearbook 1991: World Armaments and Disamament.* Oxford University Press, Oxford.

Deger, S., and Sen, S. (1990). *Military Expenditure: The Political Economy of International Security.* Oxford University Press, Oxford.

—— (1992a). "World military expenditure." In *SIPRI Yearbook 1992: World Armaments and Disarmament.* Oxford University Press, Oxford.

—— (1992b). "Military expenditure, aid and economic development." In *Proceedings of the World Bank Annual Conference on Development Economics 1991.* The World Bank, Washington, D.C.

—— (1992c). "Re-orientation and conversion of military R&D towards environmental R&D and protection." In N.P. Gledtisch, ed., *Conversion and the Environment.* PRIO Report, Oslo.

—— (1993). *The Economics of the Arms Trade.* Mimeo.

Hewitt, D. (1991). "Military expenditure trends." IMF Staff Papers. IMF, Washington D.C.

McNamara, R.S. (1992). "The post cold war world: Implications for military expenditure in the developing countries." In *Proceedings of the World Bank Annual Conference on Development Economics 1991.* The World Bank, Washington, D.C.

# Comments on chapter 2

**Daniel P. Hewitt**

Dr. Deger, one of the leading authorities on trends in world military expenditures, has written a very useful and thought-provoking article. She notes a downward trend in military expenditures in the United States, the former Soviet Union, Western Europe, and geographical regions in most of the developing countries. However, she expresses considerable impatience with the modest size of this decrease and the slow implementation of these cuts. For instance, among the former WTO countries, military expenditures remain at the same share of government expenditures and, in general, military restructuring has not kept pace with political developments. In these countries, the FSU, and elsewhere, the short-run costs of demilitarization have proven to be higher than many had previously anticipated. In sum, the peace dividend is not evident. However, the paper points out that arms transfers to developing countries have collapsed and that the decline in military expenditures that is observed appears to be "irreversible."

In explaining the downward trend in military expenditures, Dr. Deger seems to favour a business cycle theory of military spending. After an excessive build-up of arms in the late 1970s and the first half of the 1980s, a reversal was inevitable. Furthermore, the theory of "technical and structural disarmament" implies a kind of cycle due to military weapons becoming more sophisticated and costly over time and extensive economies of scale in the production of weapons. Thus, defence becomes unaffordable. Other reasons cited for the decline is the fact that WTO countries lost their political motivation for military spending; the collapse of the Soviet Union; changes in attitudes and consequent pressures from multinational organizations; the ending of certain prolonged military conflicts between the developing countries; economic and debt crisis; weapons procurement cycles; greater domestic weapons production in developing countries; and a reduction in military aid.

The statistical facts presented in this paper regarding the trends in military spending and arms transfers are well established. The interpretation of the statistics and the reasons behind these trends are open to debate.

The first question that must be raised in analysing trends is what is the proper basis to determine when military spending has risen or fallen: what is a policy-neutral level of military spending? Dr. Deger implies that the real (inflation-adjusted) level of military spending is what counts. In my view, the proper basis for comparison is the share of GDP. Thus, a country that has brisk growth in GDP but maintains real military spending at the same real level should be viewed as decreasing military spending in relative terms.[1] On this basis, the fall in world military spending is much greater. Although real dollar levels of military spending have been approximately constant in the past years, as a share of world GDP, military expenditures have fallen by 20 to 25 per cent from 1985 to 1990.

The second issue is the reasons for the fall in military spending. Is the observed decrease due, as Dr. Deger implies, to long-term factors that happened to coincide with the end of the Cold War? Alternatively, is the end of the Cold War itself the main reason for the observed decline? There is no evidence in the paper that military spending and arms transfers would have fallen in the absence of the political changes brought about by the end of the Cold War. In fact, almost all the reasons cited by Dr. Deger for the decrease in resources allocated to the military are Cold War related. The only possible exceptions are the cycle theory of military spending and the decrease in military tensions in the third world. In fact, many would attribute the decrease in third world tension to the end of the Cold War. Why hasn't the Iran-Iraq war been replaced by similar conflicts?

In fact, one of the major factors behind the fall in military spending in the third world is the decline in military aid, which is clearly attributed to the end of the Cold War. Furthermore, the cycle theory, if it is in fact supported by evidence, could be cited as a cause for the cessation of the Cold War rather than a separate event. Therefore, I think Dr. Deger's discussion actually supports the conclusion that the decreases are primarily Cold War related and therefore likely to be durable.

Finally, regarding Dr. Deger's impatience with the pace of military reform, it is not surprising that political reform has outpaced military restructuring in many countries. In the former Soviet Union and WTO countries, political changes create the impetus for reforming the military and therefore, by necessity, will come later. Furthermore, in retrospect, it is clear that military restructuring is time-consuming, expensive, and likely to be resisted by special interest groups. The economic gains are not immediate but come in the form of a smaller military and less capital tied up in weapons production in the future. Incurring the short-run costs associated with dismantling the military makes medium-term gains possible. Special interest groups vehemently oppose such changes and have been able to retard reform. However, to the extent the changes are irreversible and the trend continues, significant economic gains will be realized in the future.

## Note

1. This analysis is consistent with consumer demand theory of so-called normal goods.

# 3

# Trends in world arms trade and spending and their implications

Daniel Gallik

The extraordinary recent events in the world's political, economic, and military arenas naturally find their reflection in the available statistics the world's military spending and arms trade. It is not surprising that the uncertainty surrounding the direction those events are taking is also encountered when attempting to compile and interpret the statistical data. All the more reason to make the effort.

This paper is based on the statistics prepared for the 1991–1992 edition of the report, *World Military Expenditures and Arms Transfers* or *WMEAT* (pronounced we-meet) issued annually by my agency. This edition adds two years of data instead of the usual one and brings the statistics up through 1991. However, preliminary data for the most recent two full years are available only for the arms trade.[1] Military expenditure data normally require more time to compile and process, mainly because much less effort is made by my government to compile the spending data compared to the trade data. Also, spending data have been especially complicated recently by the volatility in prices, exchange rates, and sources of data for an increasing number of countries. Some observations on military spending are based on the 1990 edition of *WMEAT* and other sources.

## Trends in arms deliveries

The large amount of data compiled on the dollar volume of the arms trade is summarized here in a series of line graphs covering the period 1981 to 1991. These graphs are to be found in figures 1 to 7 below. Figure 1 shows that the world total of arms export deliveries dropped sharply recently, and particularly since 1989, after peaking in 1987. From the all-time 1987 high of $68.7 billion (in 1991 dollars), the

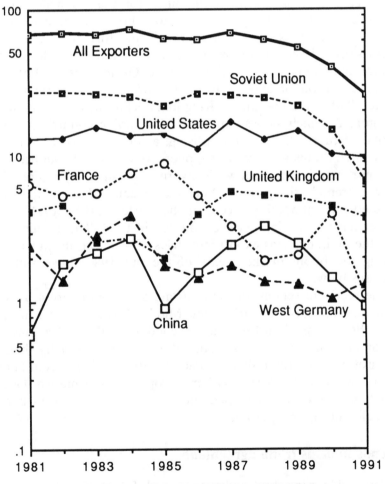

Fig. 1   **Major arms exporters to the world (deliveries)**

53

world level dropped to $25.5 billion in 1991. The rate of decline was a huge 33 per cent annually from 1989 to 1991 and averaged 22 per cent in 1987 to 1991.

A word of caution is needed, however. A similarly sharp decline appeared to have taken place in 1987 to 1989 according to the previous edition, *WMEAT 1990*, but in figure 1 the decline in those years seems much more modest. This represents a recurring phenomenon in these statistics – a tendency for the latest years to rise considerably in subsequent reports. Although this tendency is greater when the trend is a rising one, it occurs with falling trends as well, making interpretation all the more difficult.

Figure 1 also shows the trend lines for the six major supplier countries, which in 1991 accounted for about 92 per cent of total world exports. It is clear that a drop in the former Soviet Union's exports after 1989 was the major reason for the world decline, with France and China also contributing. (The German rise in 1991 is due to the inclusion of exports from the former East Germany.) The United States and the United Kingdom decline was more moderate.

Figure 2, which shows exports to developing countries, carries a similar picture. This is not surprising, as only the Soviet Union and the United States were major suppliers to developed countries.

Other suppliers are shown in figure 3, grouped by region. These show extremely sharp rates of decline. Because these suppliers contributed only about 7 per cent of the world total by 1991, they no longer have much influence on the world total. The trends suggest that the budding arms export industries of which so much was heard during the boom market years of the mid-1980s have suffered a grievous blow.

The recipient regions of the arms are shown in figure 4. It will be seen that the largest market, the Middle East, has been declining since the huge peak in 1984 and a secondary peak in 1987. Since then the annual rate of drop was about 20 per cent. Especially sharp was the drop in the former Warsaw Pact countries – 75 per cent annually from 1989 to 1991. Africa, Other Europe, Latin America, Oceania, and South Asia also dropped on the order of 40 to 50 per cent annually during this period.

## Trends in arms trade agreements

Before addressing the significance and future direction of these trends in deliveries, it is of interest to examine trends in arms trade

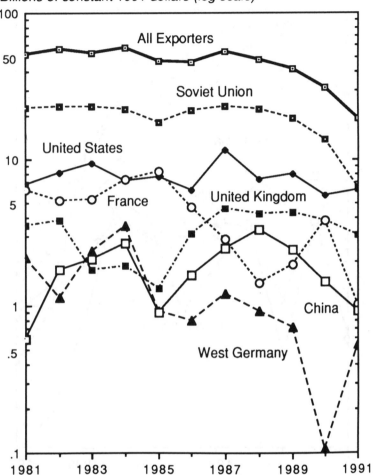

*Billions of constant 1991 dollars (log scale)*

Fig. 2 **Major arms exporters to developing countries (deliveries)**

agreements, even though these data are even more difficult to obtain and are probably less reliable than those on deliveries. By their nature, they also tend to be more erratic, making for interpretation difficulties. Two features stand out in figure 5 – one is the recent rising trend in agreements by the United States and the United Kingdom and the other is the much more severe drop for smaller suppliers – as was the case with deliveries.

Figures 6 and 7 illustrate two divergent trends in arms agreements: first, the moderate drop to stable levels shown in figure 7 for the

55

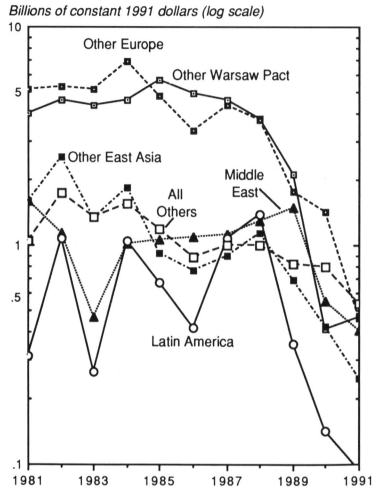

Fig. 3  **Other supplier regions to the world (deliveries)**

Middle East, East Asia, South Asia, NATO Europe and North America (although the South Asian trend is clearly downward since 1989), and the very sharp drop for Africa, Latin America, the former Warsaw Pact countries, Oceania, and Other Europe (figure 7). The first trend is all the more important since it applies to the main importing regions.

## Some observations on military spending

The decline in the arms trade can only partly be attributed to the end of the Cold War, since it appears that the beginning of declines in

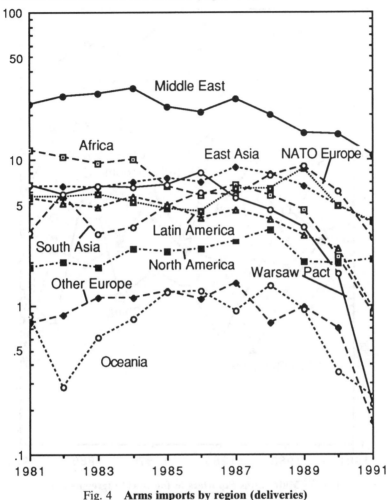

Billions of constant 1991 dollars (log scale)

Fig. 4 **Arms imports by region (deliveries)**

military spending began earlier, as figure 8 indicates. Although world millitary spending peaked in 1987 at $1.21 trillion (in 1991 dollars), falling to $1.04 trillion in 1991, the developing country total declined from a crest of $238 billion in as early as 1983 to $209 billion in 1989, before returning to $242 billion in 1991. This is particularly true in the developing world, especially in the Middle East, Africa, South Asia. Of course, the Middle East decline was from a very high level and reflected in part the end of the Iran–Iraq War. The low growth, stagnation, and even actual declines in the developing countries'

57

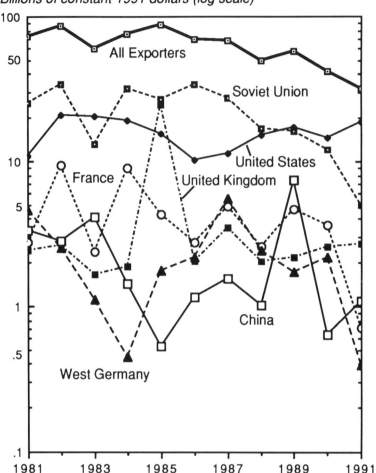

Fig. 5 **Major arms exporters to the world (agreements)**

GNP in the early 1980s must be given due credit for the beginning of military spending declines that came somewhat later.

## Implications and future trends

The recent decline in the arms trade and military spending (as is evident in other sources such as SIPRI and from developments in the major spenders) carry no promise to this observer that the trends will continue. Much depends on perceptions of the capabilities for col-

Billions of constant 1991 dollars (log scale)

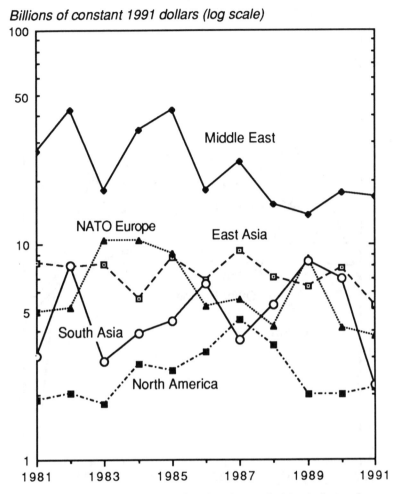

Fig. 6 **Arms imports by region (agreements); (a) steady trend**

lective peace-keeping and peacemaking that are being demonstrated in the many raging areas, and on developments in several potential areas of conflict. The nationalism-releasing effect of the end of the Cold War and a concomitant burgeoning of local conflictual situations could well outweigh the dampening effect of less-than-robust economic performance. Recourse to a build-up of national military establishments could also be spurred by improvement in the economic situation where it is felt that those establishments have been allowed to deteriorate recently.

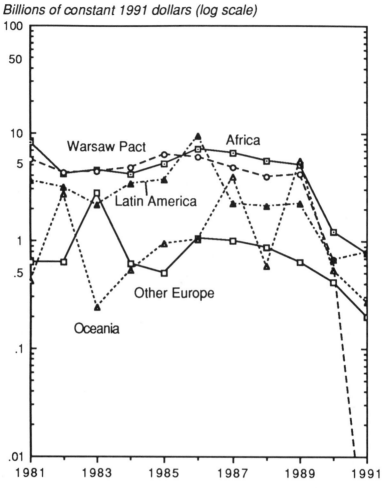

Fig. 7 **Arms imports by region (agreements); (b) declining trend**

Some slackening of worldwide military efforts at the present time could provide an opportunity to solidify and perpetuate such trends, but I believe that the recent benign trends will not continue of their own accord. Some sort of confidence-inspiring substitutes are needed for the present reliance on national means of security assurance, as occasionally supplemented by ad hoc coalitions led by big powers. Positive efforts should be directed towards the creation of improved security mechanisms, whether these be through further development of present types of United Nations' programmes, new regional ar-

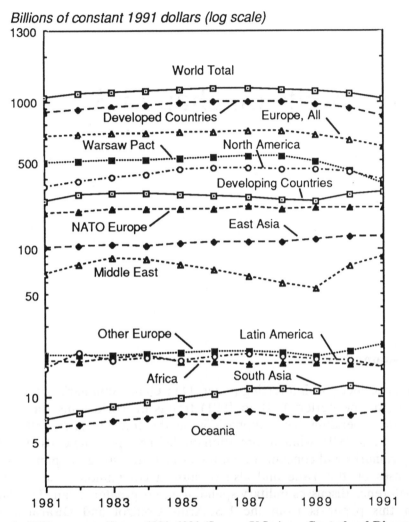

Fig. 8 **Military expenditures, 1981–1991 (Source: U.S. Arms Control and Disarmament Agency [1991].** *World Military Expenditures and Arms Transfers 1991–1992*)

rangements tailored to unique regional conditions, or even some new forms of international peace-keeping and peacemaking mechanisms yet to be devised.

## Note

1. Originally prepared prior to publication of the U.S. Arms Control and Disarmament Agency's *WMEAT 1991–1992* report, this paper has been slightly revised and the graphs redrawn to reflect final data as published and to change current dollars to constant 1991 dollars.

61

# Comments on chapter 3

## 1. Somnath Sen

In a succinct and interesting paper, Dan Gallik summarizes the decade (for the period 1981 to 1991) trends in world arms trade and
military spending. The emphasis is on the trade in arms with data
updated to 1991, while information on defence spending ends at 1989.
My remarks will concentrate on the arms trade, since the paper itself
focuses on this issue and also because a companion paper at this
conference discusses military spending in far greater detail. The data
for this paper is from the US Arms Control and Disarmament
Agency (ACDA), which is one of two international institutions that
provide information on military spending and arms trade on a regular
basis.

It is very clear that the world trade in arms is falling rapidly, and is
probably on the verge of collapse. Since May 1987 there has been a
rapid decline and the pace had accelerated by 1989. Indeed, in 1991
the value of arms trade in *current* dollars has been more than halved
compared to the level in 1989. Clearly, constant dollar indices would
show a more startling fall. The main contributing cause of the fall in
exports is the collapse of the former Soviet Union (FSU) as the
world's leading arms exporter. A corresponding cause on the import

side is the rapid decline in the demand for arms in the developing world – which still accounts for a large part of international trade.

It is also interesting to note the trends in arms agreements (which ACDA tracks), as compared to deliveries or actual sales. The trends are similar, although with greater fluctuations, and a distinct downward movement is discernible. However, the current dollar value of agreements in 1991 seems to be considerably higher than the corresponding value for 1991 deliveries. Further, for the United States, which is currently the world's largest exporter of arms, the value of agreements seems to be rising since the middle of the 1980s (fig. 5). This imparts a cautionary tone to the general story of the possible demise of the arms trade.

Overall however, the implications are clear enough. The economic crises of the 1980s, the disintegration of the Soviet empire, the end of the Cold War, positive changes in international security, and the fall in global arms production, have all caused a rapid decline in arms trade. The central question is whether this favourable trend – so important for both security and development – will continue into the future. The last section of Dan Gallik's paper briefly mentions this issue and reaches a rather pessimistic conclusion. Specifically, he claims that in the absence of positive efforts to increase security and reduce conflicts these trends will be reversed and it is possible that arms expenditures will begin to rise again. I have full sympathy and support for the confidence building measures and the reduction of tensions and conflicts. However, I am more optimistic about the *trends in arms trade*, irrespective of the problems facing international security in the post-Cold War era.

The aggregate value of arms trade is dominated by major conventional weapons – ships, aircrafts, missiles, etc. – and related technology transfers for domestic production. Technological oversophistication has considerably raised unit costs in modern weaponry. Given increasing returns, and the lack of procurement demand at home for the major producers (in the FSU and the OECD), costs will be even higher. In the absence of military assistance (which is also falling fast worldwide), developing countries will simply not be able to afford new generation weapons even after the expected economic upturn during the 1990s. There will be a tendency to postpone modernization, stretching out the lifetime of the weapons in use, retrofitting and upgrading of components rather than buying new platforms, and possibly a shift towards domestic production at lower levels of technology. The 1980s saw arms trade peaking because of a long drawn-out war between two relatively rich countries (Iran and Iraq) with little internal protest about the costs of war. It is very unlikely that such a combination of circumstances are possible in the medium-term future. Import demand, which has traditionally been the major motivating force in weapons trade, is set to stabilize at far lower levels than in the mid-1980s.

Arms trade regulation is also increasing. Transparency in the trade will be helped by the United Nations Register, which will monitor the supply of major conventional weapons. Arms production in the major supplier countries is falling and companies and enterprises are adjusting and restructuring fast. Arms procurement and production in the former Soviet Union, the largest in the world around 1990, has collapsed in the last two years (see Sen, 1992) even though conversion efforts have been generally futile. In the United States and Western Europe, major restructuring and diversification will lead to far more limited capacity compared to the last four decades. In the past, fall in domestic procurement was often compensated by foreign sales, maintaining production capacity, since domestic demand was thought to be cyclical. The current feeling is that the fall in demand is forever and capacity must shrink drastically. The incentive to export is therefore much reduced.

The remaining niggling worry, in this area of arms reduction and economic development, relates to arms production in the developing world. There have been spectacular failures when third world countries have tried to produce a diversified range of weapons (for example Brazil). The sunk costs are prohibitively high and given shrinking world market demand it is difficult to recuperate much of these costs let alone make operating profits. However, taking advantage of civilian industrial growth, reaping the fruits of spin-in and technology transfer from civil to military lines, and restricting production to a narrower range of products, it is possible to have a viable domestic arms industry at least for the NICs and the large developing countries. China, which has both converted large parts of its defence industrial complex and at the same time modernized and streamlined production, emerging as a significant exporter in the process, could be a role model. In addition, the impact of regulation could have significant effect on the number of "varieties" of products produced (Krugman, 1979), which would be increased (although the choices for each country would be limited due to trade restrictions). Thus, the number of arms producing countries might well increase. Our quantitative information on developing country arms production is still an "area of darkness" and much needs to be known before judgement can be passed. This is certainly an area for future research.

## References

Krugman, P.R. (1979). "Increasing returns, monopolistic competition, and international trade." *Journal of International Economics 9.*
Sen, S. (1992). "The Economics of Conversion: Transforming Swords to Ploughshares." In G. Bird, ed., *Economic Reform in Eastern Europe.* Edward Elgar, Aldershot, UK.

## 2. Shinichi Ichimura

Before I make my own specific comments, I would like to say one general thing about discussions on armament and disarmament. Although we are concerned, in this conference, with the importance of disarmament, we must also admit that there are positive aspects of military expenditure such as R&D, investment in human capital (education and discipline), and contributions to maintaining law and order domestically and internationally. Needless to say, there are trade-offs, so we must analyse the alternatives to armament and disarmament. I would like to say, however, that it may cause some ideological biases in our analysis if we pay attention only to the negative aspects of armament and the positive aspects of disarmament. We will not be able to persuade realistic politicians and conscientious scientists who are seeking for a certain balanced middle road to peace and security. Politically speaking, one could not deny that very significant military expenditure of the West, particularly the United States, played a crucial role in ending the Cold War. Such an aspect, which models cannot handle, must be always kept in mind, even if we are merely economists.

It is regrettable that China and Korea are not included in the analysis. An estimate of the military expenditure and trade of these two countries has been given by Mr. Gallik and looks very large. This could become a source of trouble in Asia.

Figure 5 shows the basic response of each national economy to the reduction in arms expenditure. The effects depend on what supplementary policies will accompany the reduction. Is it safe to presume that in a country with a large fiscal deficit like the United States, reduction of military expenditure automatically reduces the deficit and the money supply? We need to make a more careful assessment

65

as to how a reduction in military expenditure can be compensated in the new budget.

As for the conversion model, difficulties involved are in labour mobility, industrial restructuring, particularly in connection with the downward shift, and very special problems in some specific sectors like banking and security sectors in Japan, which is now faced with formidable debt problems.

If we analyse the results of a big reduction of expenditure, the impact on specific firms is likely to be so much that macro models may not be adequate to deal with the issues. We have to pin down a specific number of industries and enterprises.

In handling the effects of some changes in governments' expenditure in general, it is crucial to specify the accompanying fiscal and monetary policies pursued by particular governments and central bank sectors. They are clear in general in the context of the Flow of Funds Account and their stock tables, and should not be forgotten, especially in the light of the present-day international flow of capital funds.

# 4

# Military spending in developing countries and official development assistance

Paul Armington and Jalaleddin Jalali

## I. Introduction

This paper presents data that are relevant to the relationship between Official Development Assistance (ODA) and military spending by developing countries. Developing countries are here defined as those classed Low and Middle Income Countries (LMICs) in the data publications of the World Bank. The paper explores some of the ways in which these data might be used in a process that made access to ODA conditional on a finding that military spending of a developing country was not high compared with some norm.[1] This idea has been explored in a qualitative way in the paper "Military Expenditures of Developing Countries and Aid Policy," prepared for the Ministry of Foreign Affairs, the Government of Japan, by the International Development Center of Japan, March 1992. The present paper attempts to extend the analysis by examining some relevant data, in particular to show how military spending above and below the median for all developing countries has compared in the past with countries receiving ODA above and below the median.

The views expressed here are those of the authors and do not reflect the policies of the World Bank or the views of the Bank's staff generally.

Any attempt to link military spending and economic assistance in any precise way would encounter a number of mundane but important practical questions. What is the universe of countries to which this programme could logically be applied? For which of these countries are data available both for military spending and ODA? What types of military spending data are available? Is military spending on "home" goods and services just as relevant as military spending on imports? How important are gaps in the data? Is there evidence that extreme values are suppressed or underreported? Are time series sufficiently long or complete to permit analysis of persistence of features over time? What is the most appropriate definition of ODA in this context?

Once these basic data issues are handled, the issue of what constitutes high military spending naturally arises. It is well understood that there can be no simple rule for this, since legitimate needs vary with all sorts of circumstances that influence national security. But as a first and partial step toward a more complete analysis, we interpret the median of the population as the "norm," measuring "high" and "low" military spending relative to that norm.

The next question is: what is the correlation between high/low military spending and ODA? Did the big spenders get much of ODA, historically? Was the total ODA that they received large or small relative to their military spending, or relative to ODA flows to all developing countries? Would the amounts resulting from cutting off ODA to high military spenders have been significant from the donors' standpoint? If these amounts had been redeployed as additional economic aid to low military spenders, which countries would have gained, and would these gains have been of significant magnitudes for them? The answer to the latter question seems to be yes. While relatively few countries with high military spending were major recipients of ODA, they nevertheless accounted for a large percentage of total ODA in the period. A redistribution of ODA according to military conditions could, in principle, have more than doubled ODA flows to a large number of countries that had low military spending in the period.

These calculations cannot tell us how useful the introduction of such a regime of ODA conditionality might be in the future. That would depend in large part on the scale of future ODA, on the future trends in international tensions that will motivate military spending in the developing countries, and on the tendency for donors (in the absence of military conditionality) to direct their aid toward these areas of military tension.

One fundamental issue is clear: systematic links of any kind between military spending and assistance would benefit from – and possibly require – much improved data-reporting systems for military transactions, especially international transactions. During the Cold War, international data-reporting systems tended to exclude or cover up military transactions. Such totals as were reported could generally not be checked against components or verified by reference to partner-country records. Data resources are still being affected by this mantel of secrecy and lack of sufficient corroborating evidence. Use of data on military transactions as a "negative linkage" to ODA could create incentives that would tend to weaken further their accuracy and completeness. Thus, international cooperation (of *all* countries) to strengthen these data would be needed, starting with the international trade statistics. The World Bank, with many other international organizations of the broader UN system, is working to improve the reporting, auditing, and gap-filling of basic international trade data. Its weakest link may well be the military sector.

## II. Data issues

The sample group of countries includes those designated by the World Bank as LMICs, whether or not they have received ODA in recent years. Data on military expenditures and on imports of arms are far from complete. Our estimates of these variables have been taken from the two latest annual publications of *World Military Expenditures and Arms Transfers*, published by the US Arms Control and Disarmament Agency. While this publication is widely considered as authoritative in its field, we have not been able to assess the accuracy of these series. A note about these data is included in the "Note on military data" below. Other sources of military data include the *SIPRI Yearbook: World Armaments and Disarmament* issued by the Stockholm International Peace Research Institute; *The Military Balance* issued by the International Institute for Strategic Studies, and *The World Factbook* produced annually by the Central Intelligence Agency.

The period covered in the present paper is 1978 to 1989, a period limited by our access to military estimates. Even so, estimates are not available for every country in every year. As table 1 shows, the countries covered include 114 of the Bank's LMICs.

To assess the macroeconomic significance of military information, statistics on GNP, total merchandise imports, and total government

Table 1  **Coverage of military data***[a]*

| Region | Number of LMICs included in the study*[b]* | Number for which military data complete for 1978–1989 |
|---|---|---|
| Sub-Saharan Africa | 43 | 16 |
| Asia | 19 | 15 |
| Europe and Central Asia*[c]* | 12 | 10 |
| Middle East and North Africa*[d]* | 15 | 8 |
| Americas | 25 | 13 |
| All regions | 114 | 62 |

*a.* Military data here refer both to government military expenditure and to arms imports.
*b.* Countries are included if some data exist, even though incomplete.
*c.* Former Soviet Union constitutes one country.
*d.* Republic of Yemen, consisting of formerly independent countries of Yemen Arab Republic and PDR Yemen, accounts for two countries.

expenditures are needed. World Bank sources have been used for these series whenever available. The countries for which the Bank does not have sufficient data on these variables are Afghanistan, Albania, Cuba, Cambodia, Lao PDR, Lebanon, Libya, Mongolia, Mozambique, and Viet Nam. For these countries, the Agency's estimates were used for the sake of completeness (although appropriate qualifications as to their accuracy need to be borne in mind).

For purposes of this study ODA has been defined as the sum of grants (excluding technical assistance) and disbursements of long-term concessional loans from both multilateral and bilateral sources, as reported in the World Bank's *World Debt Tables*. For countries that have not reported such data to the Bank, data from the OECD's *Geographical Distribution of Financial Flows to Developing Countries* have been used. These countries include Afghanistan, Barbados, Cambodia, Cuba, Greece, Iraq, PDR Korea, Libya, Mongolia, Saudi Arabia, and Viet Nam. An alternative definition of ODA, net of repayments of long-term concessional loans, was also tried, but discarded. Net ODA is sometimes negative, which created a problem in some of the calculations to be performed with these data. More generally, in so far as (historical) ODA is functioning in our analysis as an indicator of current need for external development assistance, repayments of loans made much earlier are not relevant.

## III. Who were the high military spenders?

In order to analyse the macroeconomic significance of military expenditures and arms imports, three statistics have been computed for each country, using the database for 114 countries described above: military expenditures as a percentage of GNP (ME/GNP), military expenditures as a percentage of general government expenditures (ME/GE), and military imports as a percentage of total merchandise imports (MM/TM).

ME/GNP signifies the share of the country's overall productive resources that its total military spending accounts for. The country's resource envelope is measured by its GNP, and military spending represents a call on that capacity. Even if that spending is directly on imports, there is a cost in terms of GNP, since exports (part of GNP) are eventually required to pay for imports. ME/GE adds pertinent information to the extent that the government's budget itself is limited (e.g., by the power to tax). High ME/GE may thus indicate that military spending is "crowding out" other important public-sector activities. And this "crowding out" may extend to private-sector activities, too, through the credit rationing, high interest rates, or inflation that typically is engendered by deficit spending. MM/TM adds still more information to the analysis, to the extent that the "balance-of-payments constraint" limits the pace of economic development – commonly the case in developing countries. Arms imports effectively compete for scarce foreign exchange, and may crowd out imports of capital goods and other items essential for economic development. Lifting the balance of payments restraint in the long run means raising the capacity to export, and many developing countries lack sufficient flexibility on the supply side to shift resources quickly into production for export (without additional imports to smooth the process).

The three ratios, taken together, thus provide quite a lot of information about whether military spending is high from the standpoint of furthering economic development.[2] While these indicators obviously overlap, they also complement each other and can be seen as a package, especially for purposes of identifying extreme cases. The extent of overlap is indicated by the fact that the correlation coefficient between ME/GNP and ME/GE has been about 0.73 in every year of the sample period, while the correlation coefficient between each of these variables and MM/TM has been less than 0.45.

The three ratios have been computed for averages of the entire 12-year period of 1978 to 1989. The ratios have also been computed for its two 6-year sub-periods, 1978 to 1983 and 1984 to 1989, in order to give some idea of their persistence. When the data were not available for the entire period of 6 or 12 years, averages were obtained on the basis of the available years. (Therefore, some period averages have been obtained on the basis of data for as little as one year.) If there were no observations for a country/variable over a given 6-year period, that country/variable was dropped out of the sample for purposes of any further analysis of that period. Countries were ranked in decreasing order of magnitude of each of the three ratios in each period. The complete list of countries included in this study and their ranks according to each of these ratios in each period are presented in table A1 of the Statistical Annex. This table thus lays out the basic information that is subsequently summarized in the following analysis.

As a crude, preliminary way to address the question of who the high military spenders were, in any given period, we here define high military spenders as those that ranked among the top 50 per cent of countries in the sample (i.e., the top 57 countries) according to *all three* rankings. Our reasoning is simply that if this "test" is passed, the case for spending to be construed as high is relatively clear. However, as already noted, this "test" may be both too stringent (in cases of threat to national security from large neighbours, for example) and too lax. There can be no substitute, in the final analysis, for comprehensive study of each country's situation on a case-by-case basis.

Countries in the top 25 per cent according to *all three* criteria (i.e., ranked 1 to 28) have been designated as the A list (very high) and the rest as the B list. The A and B lists for each of the three periods are presented in tables 2 to 4. Looking at the results for the full period of 12 years in table 2, we can note that 34 countries qualify on this basis as having had high military spending over that period. That is, 30 per cent of all LMICs covered by our database fell in the top 50 per cent on all three tests. Of these, 13 countries (or 11 per cent of all LMICs) fell in the top 25 per cent of countries on all three tests. Of these, eight countries, Angola, Egypt, Ethiopia, Jordan, Libya, Mozambique, Syria and (former) Yemen Arab Republic appear in the A lists for all three periods, indicating very high and persistent military spending for these countries. More complete data would add to this

**Table 2  High military spenders in 1978–1989 (countries that fall in the top 50% of the sample by all the three criteria)**

| | Military expen./GNP (ME/GNP) | | | | | | Military expen./govt. expen. (ME/GE) | | | | | | Military imports/total imports (MM/TM) | | | | | |
| --- | --- | --- | --- | --- | --- | --- | --- | --- | --- | --- | --- | --- | --- | --- | --- | --- | --- | --- |
| | 1978–1989 | | 1978–1983 | | 1984–1989 | | 1978–1989 | | 1978–1983 | | 1984–1989 | | 1978–1989 | | 1978–1983 | | 1984–1989 | |
| | Ratio | Rank | Ratio | Rank | Ratio | Rank | Ratio | Rank | Ratio | Rank | Ratio | Rank | Ratio | Rank | Ratio | Rank | Ratio | Rank |
| **The A list** | | | | | | | | | | | | | | | | | | |
| Angola | 15.2 | 13 | 10.4 | 16 | 20.1 | 5 | 49.3 | 8 | 35.7 | 14 | 62.8 | 8 | 59.0 | 7 | 62.6 | 7 | 56.7 | 7 |
| Egypt | 18.8 | 8 | 19.7 | 6 | 17.8 | 11 | 67.3 | 5 | 64.2 | 5 | 70.3 | 4 | 13.6 | 24 | 13.2 | 21 | 14.0 | 23 |
| Ethiopia | 7.7 | 21 | 6.8 | 22 | 8.8 | 20 | 26.6 | 21 | 26.8 | 21 | 26.3 | 20 | 102.2 | 5 | 123.1 | 3 | 81.3 | 5 |
| Iran | 8.9 | 19 | 8.9 | 18 | NA | 999 | 24.4 | 24 | 24.4 | 25 | NA | 999 | 14.0 | 22 | 9.8 | 29 | 19.1 | 19 |
| Iraq | 24.9 | 3 | 24.9 | 2 | NA | 999 | 64.2 | 6 | 64.2 | 4 | NA | 999 | 45.3 | 9 | 37.7 | 18 | 53.0 | 8 |
| Jordan | 12.0 | 16 | 12.5 | 14 | 11.4 | 15 | 25.2 | 22 | 25.4 | 23 | 25.0 | 21 | 17.6 | 19 | 20.7 | 18 | 14.4 | 22 |
| Lao PDR | 10.5 | 17 | NA | 999 | 10.5 | 17 | 25.2 | 23 | 29.1 | 19 | 21.3 | 27 | 218.8 | 2 | 364.8 | 1 | 72.8 | 6 |
| Libya | 14.3 | 15 | 13.3 | 12 | 15.8 | 14 | 34.9 | 17 | 35.0 | 15 | 34.6 | 17 | 31.8 | 13 | 42.6 | 10 | 21.0 | 16 |
| Mozambique | 7.4 | 22 | 6.4 | 23 | 8.7 | 21 | 32.7 | 19 | 28.9 | 20 | 37.8 | 15 | 30.5 | 14 | 27.2 | 15 | 35.4 | 12 |
| Saudi Arabia | 18.5 | 9 | 15.9 | 8 | 21.0 | 3 | 44.4 | 11 | 42.9 | 8 | 46.0 | 11 | 13.8 | 23 | 7.0 | 42 | 20.5 | 17 |
| Syria | 17.0 | 10 | 14.4 | 10 | 19.6 | 8 | 50.1 | 7 | 37.0 | 11 | 63.2 | 7 | 54.6 | 8 | 64.0 | 6 | 45.3 | 10 |
| Viet Nam | 19.4 | 6 | NA | 999 | 19.4 | 9 | 40.8 | 14 | NA | 999 | 40.8 | 14 | 105.7 | 4 | 115.0 | 4 | 91.7 | 3 |
| Yemen Arab Rep. | 9.6 | 18 | 10.8 | 15 | 8.4 | 22 | 29.8 | 20 | 31.8 | 18 | 27.7 | 19 | 28.2 | 15 | 31.2 | 13 | 24.7 | 14 |
| **The B list** | | | | | | | | | | | | | | | | | | |
| Afghanistan | 5.7 | 30 | 5.1 | 34 | 9.1 | 19 | 40.6 | 15 | 36.6 | 12 | 64.6 | 6 | 126.4 | 3 | 71.9 | 5 | 180.9 | 2 |
| Argentina | 3.0 | 55 | 3.4 | 43 | 2.7 | 61 | 16.0 | 37 | 15.1 | 36 | 17.0 | 30 | 6.5 | 44 | 8.7 | 35 | 4.3 | 53 |
| Bulgaria | 26.1 | 2 | 23.8 | 3 | 28.4 | 2 | 73.8 | 3 | 70.5 | 3 | 77.1 | 3 | 4.4 | 53 | 4.0 | 54 | 4.9 | 47 |
| Cape Verde | 7.1 | 24 | 7.1 | 20 | NA | 999 | 18.0 | 33 | 18.0 | 33 | NA | 999 | 17.2 | 21 | 30.6 | 14 | 6.6 | 35 |
| Cuba | 5.3 | 33 | 6.3 | 25 | 4.3 | 41 | 10.2 | 56 | NA | 999 | 10.2 | 63 | 19.0 | 18 | 17.4 | 19 | 20.5 | 18 |
| El Salvador | 4.9 | 37 | 3.9 | 38 | 5.9 | 25 | 22.4 | 27 | 16.8 | 34 | 28.1 | 18 | 5.3 | 48 | 2.9 | 58 | 7.2 | 32 |
| Greece | 6.5 | 26 | 5.8 | 28 | 7.2 | 23 | 22.7 | 26 | 22.5 | 25 | 23.0 | 24 | 4.3 | 55 | 4.1 | 53 | 4.4 | 48 |
| Guinea | 4.3 | 39 | 5.5 | 30 | 3.0 | 56 | 19.4 | 31 | 24.8 | 24 | 14.0 | 39 | 9.3 | 29 | 7.4 | 39 | 9.8 | 26 |
| Mauritania | 7.2 | 23 | 8.6 | 19 | 5.2 | 33 | 19.8 | 30 | 20.2 | 30 | 19.1 | 28 | 6.2 | 45 | 6.1 | 46 | 6.3 | 37 |
| Morocco | 5.4 | 32 | 5.2 | 33 | 5.6 | 29 | 13.2 | 42 | 11.5 | 43 | 15.7 | 33 | 6.9 | 41 | 9.8 | 27 | 4.0 | 55 |
| Myanmar | 5.6 | 31 | 6.0 | 27 | 5.3 | 32 | 21.4 | 28 | 20.9 | 28 | 22.0 | 25 | 9.5 | 28 | 8.0 | 37 | 10.9 | 24 |

Table 2 (*cont.*)

| | Military expen./GNP (ME/GNP) | | | | | | Military expen./govt. expen. (ME/GE) | | | | | | Military imports/total imports (MM/TM) | | | | | |
|---|---|---|---|---|---|---|---|---|---|---|---|---|---|---|---|---|---|---|
| | 1978–1989 | | 1978–1983 | | 1984–1989 | | 1978–1989 | | 1978–1983 | | 1984–1989 | | 1978–1989 | | 1978–1983 | | 1984–1989 | |
| | Ratio | Rank | Ratio | Rank | Ratio | Rank | Ratio | Rank | Ratio | Rank | Ratio | Rank | Ratio | Rank | Ratio | Rank | Ratio | Rank |
| Oman | 20.1 | 4 | 20.4 | 4 | 19.8 | 7 | 43.0 | 13 | 43.5 | 7 | 42.5 | 12 | 7.4 | 39 | 9.7 | 30 | 5.1 | 46 |
| Pakistan | 4.8 | 38 | 3.7 | 40 | 5.8 | 26 | 18.7 | 32 | 15.5 | 35 | 21.8 | 26 | 7.3 | 40 | 7.5 | 38 | 7.1 | 33 |
| Peru | 8.7 | 20 | 6.9 | 21 | 11.3 | 16 | 48.8 | 10 | 36.4 | 13 | 67.3 | 5 | 7.8 | 38 | 9.3 | 32 | 6.3 | 38 |
| Poland | 18.8 | 7 | 16.8 | 7 | 20.8 | 4 | 71.1 | 4 | 62.5 | 6 | 79.7 | 2 | 4.0 | 56 | 3.8 | 55 | 4.1 | 54 |
| Somalia | 4.9 | 35 | 5.5 | 31 | 3.3 | 51 | 16.0 | 38 | 18.2 | 32 | 9.3 | 65 | 42.3 | 10 | 49.0 | 8 | 34.4 | 13 |
| Sudan | 3.1 | 52 | 3.8 | 39 | 2.4 | 69 | 16.2 | 35 | 19.0 | 31 | 13.3 | 43 | 8.7 | 32 | 10.2 | 24 | 7.3 | 31 |
| Turkey | 3.9 | 42 | 3.3 | 45 | 4.5 | 37 | 16.0 | 36 | 13.5 | 39 | 18.5 | 29 | 5.2 | 49 | 4.6 | 50 | 5.8 | 40 |
| Yemen PDR | 3.6 | 46 | 3.7 | 41 | 3.5 | 47 | 10.2 | 57 | 10.0 | 50 | 10.4 | 59 | 41.7 | 11 | 44.0 | 9 | 39.0 | 11 |
| Zambia | 7.1 | 25 | 9.2 | 17 | 4.3 | 39 | 17.6 | 34 | 20.7 | 29 | 13.6 | 41 | 4.6 | 52 | 7.0 | 41 | 2.2 | 70 |
| Zimbabwe | 4.9 | 36 | 4.0 | 35 | 5.8 | 27 | 14.2 | 41 | 13.2 | 40 | 15.2 | 35 | 4.8 | 50 | 3.4 | 56 | 7.6 | 29 |

Source: Table A1.
1. The A list includes countries in top 25% of the sample by every one of the three criteria; the B list includes the rest in the top 50% by all three criteria.
2. A ranking of 999 indicates that the required data have been unavailable for that ranking.

Table 3  High military spenders in 1978–1983 (countries that fall in the top 50% of the sample by all the three criteria)

| | Military expen./GNP (ME/GNP) | | | | | | Military expen./govt. expen. (ME/GE) | | | | | | Military imports/total imports (MM/TM) | | | | | |
|---|---|---|---|---|---|---|---|---|---|---|---|---|---|---|---|---|---|---|
| | 1978–1989 | | 1978–1983 | | 1984–1989 | | 1978–1989 | | 1978–1983 | | 1984–1989 | | 1978–1989 | | 1978–1983 | | 1984–1989 | |
| | Ratio | Rank | Ratio | Rank | Ratio | Rank | Ratio | Rank | Ratio | Rank | Ratio | Rank | Ratio | Rank | Ratio | Rank | Ratio | Rank |
| **The A list** | | | | | | | | | | | | | | | | | | |
| Angola | 15.2 | 13 | 10.4 | 16 | 20.1 | 5 | 49.3 | 8 | 35.7 | 14 | 62.8 | 8 | 59.0 | 7 | 62.6 | 7 | 56.7 | 7 |
| Egypt | 18.8 | 8 | 19.7 | 6 | 17.8 | 11 | 67.3 | 5 | 64.2 | 5 | 70.3 | 4 | 13.6 | 24 | 13.2 | 21 | 14.0 | 23 |
| Ethiopia | 7.7 | 21 | 6.8 | 22 | 8.8 | 20 | 26.6 | 21 | 26.8 | 21 | 26.3 | 20 | 102.2 | 5 | 123.1 | 3 | 81.3 | 5 |
| Iraq | 24.9 | 3 | 24.9 | 2 | NA | 999 | 64.2 | 6 | 64.2 | 4 | NA | 999 | 45.3 | 9 | 37.7 | 12 | 53.0 | 8 |
| Jordan | 12.0 | 16 | 12.5 | 14 | 11.4 | 15 | 25.2 | 22 | 25.4 | 23 | 25.0 | 21 | 17.6 | 19 | 20.7 | 18 | 14.4 | 22 |
| Libya | 14.3 | 15 | 13.3 | 12 | 15.8 | 14 | 34.9 | 17 | 35.0 | 15 | 34.6 | 17 | 31.8 | 13 | 42.6 | 10 | 21.0 | 16 |
| Mozambique | 7.4 | 22 | 6.4 | 23 | 8.7 | 21 | 32.7 | 19 | 28.9 | 20 | 37.8 | 15 | 30.5 | 14 | 27.2 | 15 | 35.4 | 12 |
| Syria | 17.0 | 10 | 14.4 | 10 | 19.6 | 8 | 50.1 | 7 | 37.0 | 11 | 63.2 | 7 | 54.6 | 8 | 64.0 | 6 | 45.3 | 10 |
| Yemen Arab Rep. | 9.6 | 18 | 10.8 | 15 | 8.4 | 22 | 29.8 | 20 | 31.8 | 18 | 27.7 | 19 | 28.2 | 15 | 31.2 | 13 | 24.7 | 14 |
| **The B list** | | | | | | | | | | | | | | | | | | |
| Afghanistan | 5.7 | 30 | 5.1 | 34 | 9.1 | 19 | 40.6 | 15 | 36.6 | 12 | 64.4 | 6 | 126.4 | 3 | 71.9 | 5 | 180.9 | 2 |
| Argentina | 3.0 | 55 | 3.4 | 43 | 2.7 | 61 | 16.0 | 37 | 15.1 | 36 | 17.0 | 30 | 6.5 | 44 | 8.7 | 35 | 4.3 | 53 |
| Bulgaria | 26.1 | 2 | 23.8 | 3 | 28.4 | 2 | 73.8 | 3 | 70.5 | 3 | 77.1 | 3 | 4.4 | 53 | 4.0 | 54 | 4.9 | 47 |
| Cape Verde | 7.1 | 24 | 7.1 | 20 | NA | 999 | 18.0 | 33 | 18.0 | 33 | NA | 999 | 17.2 | 21 | 30.6 | 14 | 6.6 | 35 |
| Greece | 6.5 | 26 | 5.8 | 28 | 7.2 | 23 | 22.7 | 26 | 22.5 | 26 | 23.0 | 24 | 4.3 | 55 | 4.1 | 53 | 4.4 | 48 |
| Guinea | 4.3 | 39 | 5.5 | 30 | 3.0 | 56 | 19.4 | 31 | 24.8 | 24 | 14.0 | 39 | 9.3 | 29 | 7.4 | 39 | 9.8 | 26 |
| India | 2.8 | 60 | 2.5 | 57 | 3.1 | 53 | 11.5 | 49 | 11.4 | 44 | 11.6 | 51 | 12.8 | 26 | 8.5 | 36 | 17.0 | 20 |
| Iran | 8.9 | 19 | 8.9 | 18 | NA | 999 | 24.4 | 24 | 24.4 | 25 | NA | 999 | 14.0 | 22 | 9.8 | 29 | 19.1 | 19 |
| Mauritania | 7.2 | 23 | 8.6 | 19 | 5.2 | 33 | 19.8 | 30 | 20.2 | 30 | 19.1 | 28 | 6.2 | 45 | 6.1 | 46 | 6.3 | 37 |
| Morocco | 5.4 | 32 | 5.2 | 33 | 5.6 | 29 | 13.2 | 42 | 11.5 | 43 | 15.7 | 33 | 6.9 | 41 | 9.8 | 27 | 4.0 | 55 |
| Myanmar | 5.6 | 31 | 6.0 | 27 | 5.3 | 32 | 21.4 | 28 | 20.9 | 28 | 22.0 | 25 | 9.5 | 28 | 8.0 | 37 | 10.9 | 24 |
| Oman | 20.1 | 4 | 20.4 | 4 | 19.8 | 7 | 43.0 | 13 | 43.5 | 7 | 42.5 | 12 | 7.4 | 39 | 9.7 | 30 | 5.1 | 46 |
| Pakistan | 4.8 | 38 | 3.7 | 40 | 5.8 | 26 | 18.7 | 32 | 15.5 | 35 | 21.8 | 26 | 7.3 | 40 | 7.5 | 38 | 7.1 | 33 |
| Peru | 8.7 | 20 | 6.9 | 21 | 11.3 | 16 | 48.8 | 10 | 36.4 | 13 | 67.3 | 5 | 7.8 | 38 | 9.3 | 32 | 6.3 | 38 |
| Poland | 18.8 | 7 | 16.8 | 7 | 20.8 | 4 | 71.1 | 4 | 62.5 | 6 | 79.7 | 2 | 4.0 | 56 | 3.8 | 55 | 4.1 | 54 |

Table 3 (*cont.*)

| | Military expen./GNP (ME/GNP) | | | | | | Military expen./govt. expen. (ME/GE) | | | | | | Military imports/total imports (MM/TM) | | | | | |
|---|---|---|---|---|---|---|---|---|---|---|---|---|---|---|---|---|---|---|
| | 1978–1989 | | 1978–1983 | | 1984–1989 | | 1978–1989 | | 1978–1983 | | 1984–1989 | | 1978–1989 | | 1978–1983 | | 1984–1989 | |
| | Ratio | Rank | Ratio | Rank | Ratio | Rank | Ratio | Rank | Ratio | Rank | Ratio | Rank | Ratio | Rank | Ratio | Rank | Ratio | Rank |
| Sao Tome and Principe | 2.9 | 58 | 2.9 | 49 | NA | 999 | 10.9 | 53 | 10.9 | 47 | NA | 999 | 64.3 | 6 | 26.3 | 16 | 83.4 | 4 |
| Saudi Arabia | 18.5 | 9 | 15.9 | 8 | 21.0 | 3 | 44.4 | 11 | 42.9 | 8 | 46.0 | 11 | 13.8 | 23 | 7.0 | 42 | 20.5 | 17 |
| Somalia | 4.9 | 35 | 5.5 | 31 | 3.3 | 51 | 16.0 | 38 | 18.2 | 32 | 9.3 | 65 | 42.3 | 10 | 49.0 | 8 | 34.4 | 13 |
| Sudan | 3.1 | 52 | 3.8 | 39 | 2.4 | 69 | 16.2 | 35 | 19.0 | 31 | 13.3 | 43 | 8.7 | 32 | 10.2 | 24 | 7.3 | 31 |
| Turkey | 3.9 | 42 | 3.3 | 45 | 4.5 | 37 | 16.0 | 36 | 13.5 | 39 | 18.5 | 29 | 5.2 | 49 | 4.6 | 50 | 5.8 | 40 |
| Uganda | 2.4 | 70 | 2.8 | 52 | 1.9 | 75 | 326.9 | 1 | 535.6 | 1 | 13.9 | 40 | 8.8 | 31 | 11.9 | 23 | 5.6 | 42 |
| Yemen PDR | 3.6 | 46 | 3.7 | 41 | 3.5 | 47 | 10.2 | 57 | 10.0 | 50 | 10.4 | 59 | 41.7 | 11 | 44.0 | 9 | 39.0 | 11 |
| Zambia | 7.1 | 25 | 9.2 | 17 | 4.3 | 39 | 17.6 | 34 | 20.7 | 29 | 13.6 | 41 | 4.6 | 52 | 7.0 | 41 | 2.2 | 70 |
| Zimbabwe | 4.9 | 36 | 4.0 | 35 | 5.8 | 27 | 14.2 | 41 | 13.2 | 40 | 15.2 | 35 | 4.8 | 50 | 3.4 | 56 | 7.6 | 29 |

Source: Table A1.
1. The A list includes countries in top 25% of the sample by every one of the three criteria; the B list includes the rest in the top 50% by all three criteria.
2. A ranking of 999 indicates that the required data have been unavailable for that ranking.

**Table 4  High military spenders in 1984–1989 (countries that fall in the top 50% of the sample by all the three criteria)**

| | Military expen./GNP (ME/GNP) | | | | | | Military expen./govt. expen. (ME/GE) | | | | | | Military imports/total imports (MM/TM) | | | | | |
|---|---|---|---|---|---|---|---|---|---|---|---|---|---|---|---|---|---|---|
| | 1978–1989 | | 1978–1983 | | 1984–1989 | | 1978–1989 | | 1978–1983 | | 1984–1989 | | 1978–1989 | | 1978–1983 | | 1984–1989 | |
| | Ratio | Rank | Ratio | Rank | Ratio | Rank | Ratio | Rank | Ratio | Rank | Ratio | Rank | Ratio | Rank | Ratio | Rank | Ratio | Rank |
| **The A list** | | | | | | | | | | | | | | | | | | |
| Afghanistan | 5.7 | 30 | 5.1 | 34 | 9.1 | 19 | 40.6 | 15 | 36.6 | 12 | 64.4 | 6 | 126.4 | 3 | 71.9 | 5 | 180.9 | 2 |
| Angola | 15.2 | 13 | 10.4 | 16 | 20.1 | 5 | 49.3 | 8 | 35.7 | 14 | 62.8 | 8 | 59.0 | 7 | 62.6 | 7 | 56.7 | 7 |
| Egypt | 18.8 | 8 | 19.7 | 6 | 17.8 | 11 | 67.3 | 5 | 64.2 | 5 | 70.3 | 4 | 13.6 | 24 | 13.2 | 21 | 14.0 | 23 |
| Ethiopia | 7.7 | 21 | 6.8 | 22 | 8.8 | 20 | 26.6 | 21 | 26.8 | 21 | 26.3 | 20 | 102.2 | 5 | 123.1 | 3 | 81.3 | 5 |
| Jordan | 12.0 | 16 | 12.5 | 14 | 11.4 | 15 | 25.2 | 22 | 25.4 | 23 | 25.0 | 21 | 17.6 | 19 | 20.7 | 18 | 14.4 | 22 |
| Lao PDR | 10.5 | 17 | NA | 999 | 10.5 | 17 | 25.2 | 23 | 29.1 | 19 | 21.3 | 27 | 218.8 | 2 | 364.8 | 1 | 72.8 | 6 |
| Libya | 14.3 | 15 | 13.3 | 12 | 15.8 | 14 | 34.9 | 17 | 35.0 | 15 | 34.6 | 17 | 31.8 | 13 | 42.6 | 10 | 21.0 | 16 |
| Mozambique | 7.4 | 22 | 6.4 | 23 | 8.7 | 21 | 32.7 | 19 | 28.9 | 20 | 37.8 | 15 | 30.5 | 14 | 27.2 | 15 | 35.4 | 12 |
| Saudi Arabia | 18.5 | 9 | 15.9 | 8 | 21.0 | 3 | 44.4 | 11 | 42.9 | 8 | 46.0 | 11 | 13.8 | 23 | 7.0 | 42 | 20.5 | 17 |
| Syria | 17.0 | 10 | 14.4 | 10 | 19.6 | 8 | 50.1 | 7 | 37.0 | 11 | 63.2 | 7 | 54.6 | 8 | 64.0 | 6 | 45.3 | 10 |
| Viet Nam | 19.4 | 6 | NA | 999 | 19.4 | 9 | 40.8 | 14 | NA | 999 | 40.8 | 14 | 105.7 | 4 | 115.0 | 4 | 91.7 | 3 |
| Yemen Arab Rep. | 9.6 | 18 | 10.8 | 15 | 8.4 | 22 | 29.8 | 20 | 31.8 | 18 | 27.7 | 19 | 28.2 | 15 | 31.2 | 13 | 24.7 | 14 |
| **The B list** | | | | | | | | | | | | | | | | | | |
| Bulgaria | 26.1 | 2 | 23.8 | 3 | 28.4 | 2 | 73.8 | 3 | 70.5 | 3 | 77.1 | 3 | 4.4 | 53 | 4.0 | 54 | 4.9 | 47 |
| Congo | 3.4 | 49 | 2.8 | 53 | 4.6 | 35 | 9.3 | 62 | 7.9 | 64 | 11.7 | 50 | 8.2 | 34 | 9.9 | 26 | 6.5 | 36 |
| El Salvador | 4.9 | 37 | 3.9 | 38 | 5.9 | 25 | 22.4 | 27 | 16.8 | 34 | 28.1 | 18 | 5.3 | 48 | 2.9 | 58 | 7.2 | 32 |
| Gabon | 2.6 | 66 | 1.8 | 75 | 3.3 | 49 | 9.3 | 63 | 6.7 | 78 | 12.0 | 47 | 3.8 | 58 | 2.9 | 62 | 5.6 | 43 |
| Greece | 6.5 | 26 | 5.8 | 28 | 7.2 | 23 | 22.7 | 26 | 22.5 | 26 | 23.0 | 24 | 4.3 | 55 | 4.1 | 53 | 4.4 | 48 |
| Guinea | 4.3 | 39 | 5.5 | 30 | 3.0 | 56 | 19.4 | 31 | 24.8 | 24 | 14.0 | 39 | 9.3 | 29 | 7.4 | 39 | 9.8 | 26 |
| Honduras | 3.0 | 56 | 2.3 | 63 | 3.7 | 43 | 11.0 | 51 | 9.1 | 56 | 13.0 | 44 | 3.8 | 59 | 1.0 | 94 | 5.6 | 44 |
| India | 2.8 | 60 | 2.5 | 57 | 3.1 | 53 | 11.5 | 49 | 11.4 | 44 | 11.6 | 51 | 12.8 | 26 | 8.5 | 36 | 17.0 | 20 |
| Mauritania | 7.2 | 23 | 8.6 | 19 | 5.2 | 33 | 19.8 | 30 | 20.2 | 30 | 19.1 | 28 | 6.2 | 45 | 6.1 | 46 | 6.3 | 37 |
| Morocco | 5.4 | 32 | 5.2 | 33 | 5.6 | 29 | 13.2 | 42 | 11.5 | 43 | 15.7 | 33 | 6.9 | 41 | 9.8 | 27 | 4.0 | 55 |
| Myanmar | 5.6 | 31 | 6.0 | 27 | 5.3 | 32 | 21.4 | 28 | 20.9 | 28 | 22.0 | 25 | 9.5 | 28 | 8.0 | 37 | 10.9 | 24 |
| Oman | 20.1 | 4 | 20.4 | 4 | 19.8 | 7 | 43.0 | 13 | 43.5 | 7 | 42.5 | 12 | 7.4 | 39 | 9.7 | 30 | 5.1 | 46 |
| Pakistan | 4.8 | 38 | 3.7 | 40 | 5.8 | 26 | 18.7 | 32 | 15.5 | 35 | 21.8 | 26 | 7.3 | 40 | 7.5 | 38 | 7.1 | 33 |
| Peru | 8.7 | 20 | 6.9 | 21 | 11.3 | 16 | 48.8 | 10 | 36.4 | 13 | 67.3 | 5 | 7.8 | 38 | 9.3 | 32 | 6.3 | 38 |
| Poland | 18.8 | 7 | 16.8 | 7 | 20.8 | 4 | 71.1 | 4 | 62.5 | 6 | 79.7 | 2 | 4.0 | 56 | 3.8 | 55 | 4.1 | 54 |
| Turkey | 3.9 | 42 | 3.3 | 45 | 4.5 | 37 | 16.0 | 36 | 13.5 | 39 | 18.5 | 29 | 5.2 | 49 | 4.6 | 50 | 5.8 | 40 |
| Zimbabwe | 4.9 | 36 | 4.0 | 35 | 5.8 | 27 | 14.2 | 41 | 13.2 | 40 | 15.2 | 35 | 4.8 | 50 | 3.4 | 56 | 7.6 | 29 |

Source: Table A1.

1. The A list includes countries in top 25% of the sample by every one of the three criteria; the B list includes the rest in the top 50% by all three criteria.

2. A ranking of 999 indicates that the required data have been unavailable for that ranking.

list. For example, Iraq appears in the lists for 1978 to 1989 and 1978 to 1983, but not 1984 to 1989, even though Iraq's military expenditures undoubtedly continued at a high rate over the latter period.

## IV. High military spenders and ODA

To what extent has ODA flowed to countries that were high military spenders? Table A2 presents average annual ODA disbursements to all the countries in our study over each of the three time periods. The table also shows the countries' ranks in decreasing order of ODA. These countries received $24.9 billion ODA funds per year during the 12-year period 1978 to 1989 (dollars are US dollars). The amount has been increasing over time, from an annual average of $21.7 billion during the years 1978 to 1983 to $28.1 billion during years 1984 to 1989. For the 12-year period, India and Syria were at the top of the rank in ODA, with average annual ODA receipts of just over $2 billion, followed by Egypt ($1.4 billion), Bangladesh ($1.3 billion) and Indonesia ($1.1 billion).

ODA ranks for A list and B list countries are set out in table 5. Of the top five ODA recipients, receiving over $1 billion a year in ODA funds, Egypt and Syria are in the A list in all periods. Over the 12-year period, Egypt spent an average of $5.1 billion a year on the military, amounting to 19 per cent of its GNP or 67 per cent of its general government expenditures (see table 2). Syria spent $2.3 billion annually on the military, amounting to 17 per cent of its GNP or 50 per cent of its general government expenditures. Military imports accounted for 14 per cent of the total imports bill in the case of Egypt and 55 per cent in the case of Syria. These two countries received 14 per cent of total ODA in the sample period. In the aggregate, A list countries received about $6 billion of ODA per year during the period 1978 to 1989.

On the other hand, in the period under review, there was only a slight *overall* tendency for the high military spenders to be high-ranked as ODA recipients. Eight out of 13 A list countries, and 13 out of 21 B list countries ranked in the top half of ODA recipients (i.e., not much over half). But the major factor reducing the positive relationship between military spending and ODA is the fact that our sample includes countries that were militarily aligned with the Soviet Union during the period, and receipts of ODA by these countries may well be underreported in our data. If countries that were mili-

Table 5  **High military spenders, ODA, and ODA ranks in 1978–1989**

|  | Average annual ODA (US$m) for 1978–1989 | ODA rank for 1978–1989 |
|---|---|---|
| *A list countries for 1978–1989* | | |
| Angola | 67 | 69 |
| Egypt, Arab Republic of | 1,446 | 3 |
| Ethiopia | 445 | 15 |
| Iran | 9 | 100 |
| Iraq | 20 | 93 |
| Jordan | 801 | 7 |
| Lao PDR | 94 | 60 |
| Libya | 1 | 106 |
| Mozambique | 319 | 20 |
| Saudi Arabia | 11 | 99 |
| Syrian Arab Republic | 2,053 | 2 |
| Viet Nam | 126 | 50 |
| Yemen Arab Republic | 533 | 12 |
| Total | 5,925 | – |
| | | |
| *B list countries for 1978–1989* | | |
| Afghanistan | 30 | 88 |
| Argentina | 33 | 87 |
| Bulgaria | 0 | 108 |
| Cape Verde | 52 | 78 |
| Cuba | 17 | 95 |
| El Salvador | 232 | 30 |
| Greece | 16 | 97 |
| Guinea | 154 | 42 |
| Mauritania | 194 | 34 |
| Morocco | 518 | 13 |
| Myanmar | 322 | 19 |
| Oman | 113 | 54 |
| Pakistan | 926 | 6 |
| Peru | 240 | 29 |
| Poland | 52 | 79 |
| Somalia | 295 | 23 |
| Sudan | 719 | 8 |
| Turkey | 561 | 11 |
| Yemen PDR | 0 | 114 |
| Zambia | 244 | 26 |
| Zimbabwe | 158 | 41 |
| Total | 4,876 | – |

Sources: Tables 2 and A2.

tarily dependent on the Soviet Union were excluded from table 5, the bulk of the remaining countries would have high ODA rankings (that is, low numbers in the last column of the table). A list countries that did *not* rank in the top half of ODA recipients according to the available data, were: Angola, Iran, Iraq, Lao PDR, Libya, and Saudi Arabia (clearly an exceptional case).

Countries that were low military spenders, defined symmetrically as those LMICs for which all three military ratios were below the median in 1978/89, are shown in table 6. These 35 countries together received $5.3 billion per annum of ODA from 1978 to 1989, which is less than what the A list countries received during the same period ($5.9 billion [see table 5]). In other words, if the ODA received by the top military spenders had been received instead by the low military spenders (table 6), the latter's ODA would have more than doubled. This illustrates how a system of linkage might have quantitatively significant effects on incentives, both through penalizing high military spending and through rewarding low military spending, within a given constraint on total ODA flows.

It must be emphasized again, however, that what constitutes "high" or "low" military spending cannot realistically be measured solely by reference to the spending ratios used in this illustration; that no simple formula can sort out all cases in a fair and reasonable way; and that the practical difficulties of implementing any such system of incentives would be immense.

## Note on military data[3]

### Military expenditures

For non-socialist countries, military expenditures are generally taken to be the expenditures of the ministry of defence with appropriate adjustments to remove the cost of internal security when the data are known to include them. These data are of uneven accuracy and completeness as, for example, military expenditures reported by some countries consist mainly or entirely of recurring or operating expenditures and omit all or most capital expenditures, including arms purchases. In some of these cases, total military expenditures have been estimated as the sum of nominal military expenditures and the value of arms imports. This method, however, introduces over or underestimation of the actual expenditures in a given year due to the fact that payment for arms may not coincide in time with deliveries. For countries that have major clandestine nuclear or other military weapon development programmes, estimates of total military expenditures are particularly subject to errors.

Particular problems arise in estimating the military expenditures of socialist countries due to exceptional scarcity and ambiguity of released information. These data for the former Soviet Union are based on the Central Intelligence Agency's (CIA) estimates. For most of the series, these are estimates of what it would cost in the United States in dollars to develop, procure, staff, and operate a military force similar to that of the Soviet Union. Estimates of this kind, based entirely on one country's price pattern, generally overstate the relative size of the second country's expenditures in inter-country comparisons. Nevertheless, the basic CIA estimates are the best available.

For other former Warsaw Pact countries, estimates of military expenditures refer only to the officially announced state budget expenditures on national defence. Because of defence outlays by non-defence agencies of the central government, local governments, and economic enterprises, these figures understate total military expenditures. Possible subsidization of military procurement may also cause understatement. The dollar estimates were derived by calculating pay and allowances at the current full US average rates for officers and for lower ranks. After subtraction of pay and allowances, the remainder of the official defence budgets in national currencies was converted into dollars at overall rates based on comparisons of the various countries' GNPs expressed in dollars and in national currencies. The rates are based in part on the purchasing power parities estimated by the International Comparison Project of the United Nations. These conversion rates are not as specific as might be desired and, when the problems mentioned above are taken into account, the resulting estimates must be considered subject to limitations. Another omission in all Warsaw Pact data is that the non-personnel component of military assistance is not covered.

Data used here for China are based on US government estimates of the yuan costs of Chinese forces, weapons, programmes and activities. Due to the exceptional difficulties in both estimating yuan costs and converting them to dollars, comparisons of Chinese military spending with other data should be treated as having a wide margin of error.

Table 6 Low military spenders and their average annual ODA in 1978–1989 (countries that fall in the bottom 50% of the sample by all the three criteria)

| | Military expend./GNP (ME/GNP) | | | | | | Military expend./govt. expen. (ME/GE) | | | | | |
|---|---|---|---|---|---|---|---|---|---|---|---|---|
| | 1978–1989 | | 1978–1983 | | 1984–1989 | | 1978–1989 | | 1978–1983 | | 1984–1989 | |
| | Ratio | Rank | Ratio | Rank | Ratio | Rank | Ratio | Rank | Ratio | Rank | Ratio | Rank |
| Barbados | 0.8 | 102 | 0.9 | 92 | 0.8 | 100 | 3.5 | 103 | 3.6 | 92 | 3.4 | 101 |
| Brazil | 1.1 | 94 | 0.9 | 93 | 1.4 | 90 | 6.8 | 86 | 5.4 | 82 | 8.6 | 71 |
| Cameroon | 1.6 | 86 | 1.3 | 83 | 1.9 | 76 | 6.5 | 89 | 5.3 | 84 | 7.7 | 79 |
| Colombia | 1.0 | 98 | 0.7 | 97 | 1.4 | 91 | 3.7 | 100 | 3.1 | 96 | 4.4 | 98 |
| Costa Rica | 0.6 | 106 | 0.6 | 101 | 0.5 | 104 | 2.0 | 108 | 1.9 | 104 | 2.1 | 104 |
| Côte D'Ivoire | 1.3 | 89 | 1.3 | 84 | 1.4 | 89 | 4.8 | 92 | 4.1 | 88 | 5.6 | 90 |
| Dominican Republic | 1.0 | 97 | 0.8 | 94 | 1.2 | 95 | 5.9 | 90 | 5.5 | 81 | 6.2 | 87 |
| Fiji | 1.1 | 92 | 0.7 | 96 | 1.6 | 85 | 4.0 | 99 | 2.2 | 101 | 5.8 | 88 |
| Gabon | 2.6 | 66 | 1.8 | 75 | 3.3 | 49 | 9.3 | 63 | 6.7 | 78 | 12.0 | 47 |
| Ghana | 0.5 | 108 | 0.4 | 105 | 0.6 | 101 | 3.5 | 102 | 3.6 | 93 | 3.5 | 100 |
| Guatemala | 1.2 | 91 | 1.0 | 88 | 1.4 | 88 | 9.0 | 66 | 6.9 | 74 | 11.0 | 57 |
| Haiti | 1.9 | 79 | 1.9 | 71 | 1.8 | 81 | 8.8 | 68 | 8.8 | 57 | 8.8 | 70 |
| Indonesia | 1.6 | 84 | 1.6 | 78 | 1.7 | 82 | 7.2 | 85 | 7.0 | 72 | 7.4 | 81 |
| Jamaica | 1.0 | 100 | 0.9 | 91 | 1.0 | 97 | 3.2 | 105 | 2.7 | 99 | 3.7 | 99 |
| Kenya | 2.4 | 68 | 2.5 | 59 | 2.4 | 68 | 7.8 | 77 | 7.8 | 65 | 7.9 | 77 |
| Liberia | 2.7 | 63 | 2.1 | 64 | 3.3 | 50 | 9.6 | 61 | 6.7 | 79 | 12.5 | 45 |
| Malawi | 2.3 | 71 | 2.4 | 60 | 2.2 | 72 | 6.8 | 87 | 6.7 | 76 | 6.9 | 85 |
| Malta | 1.1 | 93 | 0.9 | 90 | 1.3 | 93 | 4.7 | 93 | 3.8 | 89 | 5.4 | 92 |
| Mauritius | 0.2 | 111 | 0.2 | 108 | 0.2 | 107 | 1.0 | 110 | 0.9 | 107 | 1.0 | 105 |
| Mexico | 0.5 | 109 | 0.3 | 107 | 0.6 | 103 | 2.1 | 106 | 1.5 | 105 | 2.8 | 102 |
| Mongolia | NA | 999 | NA | 999 | NA | 999 | NA | 999 | NA | 999 | NA | 999 |
| Nepal | 0.8 | 103 | 0.6 | 98 | 1.0 | 98 | 4.4 | 95 | 4.2 | 87 | 4.6 | 96 |
| Niger | 0.7 | 104 | 0.5 | 103 | 0.9 | 99 | 4.0 | 98 | 2.8 | 98 | 5.5 | 91 |
| Nigeria | 0.5 | 107 | 0.6 | 100 | 0.5 | 105 | 2.1 | 107 | 2.0 | 103 | 2.1 | 103 |

| | | | | | | | | | | | | |
|---|---|---|---|---|---|---|---|---|---|---|---|---|
| Panama | 1.7 | 82 | 1.2 | 86 | 2.2 | 73 | 5.3 | 91 | 3.1 | 95 | 7.1 | 84 |
| Papua New Guinea | 1.4 | 88 | 1.3 | 82 | 1.5 | 86 | 4.2 | 97 | 3.7 | 91 | 4.6 | 95 |
| Paraguay | 1.1 | 96 | 1.0 | 89 | 1.2 | 94 | 8.3 | 69 | 7.5 | 69 | 9.3 | 66 |
| Philippines | 1.7 | 83 | 1.6 | 77 | 1.8 | 80 | 9.2 | 65 | 8.4 | 61 | 10.0 | 64 |
| Sierra Leone | 0.6 | 105 | 0.5 | 102 | 0.6 | 102 | 4.3 | 96 | 3.3 | 94 | 5.6 | 89 |
| Sri Lanka | 2.0 | 76 | 1.2 | 87 | 2.7 | 60 | 7.9 | 76 | 4.6 | 85 | 11.1 | 55 |
| Swaziland | 1.6 | 87 | 1.4 | 80 | 1.7 | 83 | 4.4 | 94 | 3.7 | 90 | 5.2 | 93 |
| Togo | 2.8 | 61 | 2.5 | 58 | 3.2 | 52 | 7.2 | 84 | 5.8 | 80 | 9.0 | 68 |
| Trinidad and Tobago | 1.0 | 99 | 0.8 | 95 | 1.5 | 87 | 3.3 | 104 | 2.8 | 97 | 4.6 | 97 |
| Tunisia | 2.7 | 64 | 2.5 | 56 | 2.9 | 57 | 7.8 | 78 | 7.0 | 73 | 8.6 | 72 |
| Venezuela | 0.9 | 101 | 0.6 | 99 | 1.1 | 96 | 3.6 | 101 | 2.2 | 102 | 5.1 | 94 |

Total

Source: Tables A1 and A2.
Note: The list also includes countries that, because of data unavailability, could not be ranked and thus placed at the bottom (they are assigned rank 999).

Table 6  (cont.)

| | Military imports/total imports (MM/TM) | | | | | | Average annual ODA (in US$m) in 1978–1989 |
| | 1978–1989 | | 1978–1983 | | 1984–1989 | | |
| | Ratio | Rank | Ratio | Rank | Ratio | Rank | |
|---|---|---|---|---|---|---|---|
| Barbados | 2.2 | 75 | 1.8 | 76 | 2.4 | 67 | 9 |
| Brazil | 0.8 | 103 | 0.6 | 105 | 1.0 | 93 | 91 |
| Cameroon | 2.2 | 74 | 2.6 | 67 | 1.9 | 74 | 153 |
| Colombia | 2.3 | 73 | 1.1 | 93 | 3.6 | 57 | 56 |
| Costa Rica | 1.1 | 97 | NA | 999 | 1.1 | 92 | 129 |
| Côte D'Ivoire | 2.0 | 80 | 2.5 | 68 | 0.9 | 95 | 122 |
| Dominican Republic | 0.4 | 111 | 0.5 | 106 | 0.4 | 104 | 114 |
| Fiji | 1.1 | 96 | 1.1 | 92 | NA | 999 | 19 |
| Gabon | 3.8 | 58 | 2.9 | 62 | 5.6 | 43 | 38 |
| Ghana | 2.6 | 70 | 2.9 | 60 | 2.2 | 69 | 229 |
| Guatemala | 1.0 | 98 | 0.6 | 102 | 1.4 | 82 | 96 |
| Haiti | 1.7 | 86 | 1.7 | 81 | 1.8 | 78 | 104 |
| Indonesia | 1.6 | 88 | 2.1 | 72 | 1.2 | 89 | 1,064 |
| Jamaica | 0.5 | 108 | NA | 999 | 0.5 | 99 | 145 |
| Kenya | 3.0 | 65 | 4.3 | 52 | 1.7 | 79 | 385 |
| Liberia | 2.8 | 69 | 1.7 | 82 | 3.3 | 62 | 64 |
| Malawi | 2.1 | 77 | 2.9 | 59 | 1.5 | 80 | 153 |
| Malta | 0.6 | 105 | 0.9 | 98 | 0.4 | 102 | 22 |
| Mauritius | 0.6 | 106 | 0.8 | 99 | 0.4 | 101 | 40 |
| Mexico | 0.5 | 110 | 0.4 | 108 | 0.6 | 98 | 78 |
| Mongolia | 0.5 | 109 | NA | 999 | 0.5 | 100 | 0 |
| Nepal | 1.6 | 89 | 1.2 | 91 | 2.0 | 73 | 182 |
| Niger | 2.0 | 79 | 2.0 | 75 | NA | 999 | 191 |
| Nigeria | 2.4 | 72 | 1.4 | 88 | 3.4 | 61 | 46 |

| | | | | | | | |
|---|---|---|---|---|---|---|---|
| Panama | 0.9 | 99 | 1.0 | 95 | 0.9 | 94 | 34 |
| Papua New Guinea | 1.8 | 84 | 1.7 | 80 | 1.9 | 76 | 308 |
| Paraguay | 3.3 | 63 | 2.9 | 57 | 3.6 | 58 | 54 |
| Philippines | 0.7 | 104 | 0.8 | 101 | 0.6 | 97 | 512 |
| Sierra Leone | 3.9 | 57 | 2.2 | 71 | 7.3 | 30 | 55 |
| Sri Lanka | 1.1 | 95 | 0.6 | 103 | 1.3 | 86 | 422 |
| Swaziland | NA | 999 | NA | 999 | NA | 999 | 21 |
| Togo | 3.0 | 66 | 2.9 | 61 | 3.2 | 63 | 98 |
| Trinidad and Tobago | 0.6 | 107 | 0.6 | 104 | NA | 999 | 8 |
| Tunisia | 2.8 | 67 | 2.1 | 73 | 3.5 | 59 | 241 |
| Venezuela | 2.0 | 78 | 1.2 | 90 | 2.8 | 65 | 6 |
| Total | | | | | | | 5,289 |

## Arms imports

Arms imports represent the international transfers (under terms of grant, credit, barter, or cash) of military equipment, usually referred to as "conventional," including weapons of war, parts thereof, ammunition, support equipment, and other commodities designed for military use. Among the items included are tactical guided missiles and rockets, military aircraft, naval vessels, armoured and non-armoured military vehicles, communications and electronic equipment, artillery, infantry weapons, small arms, ammunition, other ordnance, parachutes, and uniforms. Dual-use equipment, which can have application in both military and civilian sectors, is included when its primary mission is identified as military. The building of defence production facilities and licensing fees paid as royalties for the production of military equipment are included when they are contained in military transfer agreements. There have been no international transfers of purely strategic weaponry. Excluded are food-stuffs, medical equipment, petroleum products, and other supplies. Data on military services, which are normally of small magnitudes, are included when available.

The statistics are estimates of the value of goods actually delivered during the reference year, in contrast both to the value of programmes, agreements, contracts, or orders which may result in future deliveries, and to payments made during the period. Both deliveries and agreements data represent arms transfers to governments and do not include the value of arms obtained by subnational groups.

Data estimates are generally from US government sources. Arms imports data for the Soviet Union and other socialist countries are approximations based on limited information.

## Notes

1. At least as far as the World Bank is concerned, a linkage between military expenditures and assistance is ruled out by the Articles of Agreement. More generally, the present paper must not be construed as Bank advocacy of such a linkage.
2. However, they can be incomplete, or even misleading, as indicators of whether spending is high or low relative to what is needed to deal with issues of national security. For instance, to assess whether a given external military threat is being adequately countered, the *absolute* level of military spending, not the ratios suggested here, may be the pertinent indicators.
3. Quoted, with minor alterations, from the U.S. Arms Control and Disarmament Agency's *World Military Expenditures and Arms Transfers, 1990.*

**Table A1  Average share of military expenditures in GNP and government expenditures, and that of military imports in total imports**

| | Military expen./GNP (ME/GNP) | | | | | | Military expen./govt. expen. (ME/GE) | | | | | | Military imports/total imports (MM/TM) | | | | | |
|---|---|---|---|---|---|---|---|---|---|---|---|---|---|---|---|---|---|---|
| | 1978–1989 | | 1978–1983 | | 1984–1989 | | 1978–1989 | | 1978–1983 | | 1984–1989 | | 1978–1989 | | 1978–1983 | | 1984–1989 | |
| | Ratio | Rank | Ratio | Rank | Ratio | Rank | Ratio | Rank | Ratio | Rank | Ratio | Rank | Ratio | Rank | Ratio | Rank | Ratio | Rank |
| AFGHANISTAN | 5.7 | 30 | 5.1 | 34 | 9.1 | 19 | 40.6 | 15 | 36.6 | 12 | 64.4 | 6 | 126.4 | 3 | 71.9 | 5 | 810.9 | 2 |
| ALBANIA | 5.0 | 34 | 5.5 | 32 | 4.9 | 34 | 11.0 | 52 | 10.9 | 48 | 11.1 | 56 | NA | 999 | NA | 999 | NA | 999 |
| Algeria | 2.6 | 65 | 2.6 | 54 | 2.5 | 64 | 8.0 | 74 | 8.7 | 59 | 7.2 | 83 | 8.3 | 33 | 8.8 | 34 | 7.9 | 28 |
| Angola | 15.2 | 13 | 10.4 | 16 | 20.1 | 5 | 49.3 | 8 | 35.7 | 14 | 62.8 | 8 | 59.0 | 7 | 62.6 | 7 | 56.7 | 7 |
| Argentina | 3.0 | 55 | 3.4 | 43 | 2.7 | 61 | 16.0 | 37 | 15.1 | 36 | 17.0 | 30 | 6.5 | 44 | 8.7 | 35 | 4.3 | 53 |
| Bangladesh | 1.6 | 85 | 1.5 | 79 | 1.8 | 79 | 11.6 | 47 | 11.3 | 45 | 11.9 | 48 | 1.8 | 82 | 1.4 | 86 | 2.2 | 71 |
| Barbados | 0.8 | 102 | 0.9 | 92 | 0.8 | 100 | 3.5 | 103 | 3.6 | 92 | 3.4 | 101 | 2.2 | 75 | 1.8 | 76 | 2.4 | 67 |
| Benin | 2.2 | 74 | 1.9 | 72 | 2.5 | 65 | 10.1 | 58 | 8.7 | 58 | 11.8 | 49 | 7.9 | 37 | 10.2 | 25 | 3.4 | 60 |
| Bolivia | 2.8 | 62 | 2.3 | 62 | 3.3 | 48 | 11.3 | 50 | 8.6 | 60 | 14.6 | 36 | 3.7 | 60 | 6.0 | 47 | 1.5 | 81 |
| Botswana | 3.7 | 45 | 2.9 | 50 | 4.5 | 38 | 10.3 | 55 | 7.2 | 71 | 13.4 | 42 | 1.8 | 83 | 1.7 | 79 | 1.9 | 75 |
| Brazil | 1.1 | 94 | 0.9 | 93 | 1.4 | 90 | 6.8 | 86 | 5.4 | 82 | 8.6 | 71 | 0.8 | 103 | 0.6 | 105 | 1.0 | 93 |
| Bulgaria | 26.1 | 2 | 23.8 | 3 | 28.4 | 2 | 73.8 | 3 | 70.5 | 3 | 77.1 | 3 | 4.4 | 53 | 4.0 | 54 | 4.9 | 47 |
| Burkina Faso | 2.0 | 75 | 1.8 | 74 | 2.3 | 70 | 8.0 | 73 | 7.7 | 67 | 8.4 | 73 | 4.3 | 54 | 2.3 | 69 | 6.3 | 39 |
| Burundi | 2.3 | 72 | 2.1 | 65 | 2.4 | 67 | 7.9 | 75 | 7.6 | 68 | 8.4 | 74 | 6.0 | 46 | 6.7 | 43 | 5.4 | 45 |
| CAMBODIA | NA | 999 | NA | 999 | NA | 999 | NA | 999 | NA | 999 | NA | 999 | 640.9 | 1 | 333.4 | 2 | 948.5 | 1 |
| Cameroon | 1.6 | 86 | 1.3 | 83 | 1.9 | 76 | 6.5 | 89 | 5.3 | 84 | 7.7 | 79 | 2.2 | 74 | 2.6 | 67 | 1.9 | 74 |
| Cape Verde | 7.1 | 24 | 7.1 | 20 | NA | 999 | 18.0 | 33 | 18.0 | 33 | NA | 999 | 17.2 | 21 | 30.6 | 14 | 6.6 | 35 |
| Central African Rep. | 1.9 | 78 | 2.0 | 68 | 1.6 | 84 | 8.8 | 67 | 9.6 | 54 | 6.4 | 86 | 9.8 | 27 | 9.8 | 28 | NA | 999 |
| Chad | 2.4 | 69 | 1.8 | 73 | 2.8 | 58 | 9.9 | 60 | 9.3 | 55 | 10.3 | 61 | 13.5 | 25 | 5.5 | 48 | 16.7 | 21 |
| Chile | 2.8 | 59 | 2.1 | 66 | 3.6 | 45 | 12.2 | 44 | 9.9 | 51 | 14.6 | 37 | 3.7 | 61 | 4.4 | 51 | 3.0 | 64 |
| China | 6.4 | 28 | 6.4 | 24 | 6.3 | 24 | 24.4 | 25 | 25.7 | 22 | 23.0 | 22 | 0.9 | 100 | 0.8 | 100 | 1.1 | 91 |
| Colombia | 1.0 | 98 | 0.7 | 97 | 1.4 | 91 | 3.7 | 100 | 3.1 | 96 | 4.4 | 98 | 2.3 | 73 | 1.1 | 93 | 3.6 | 57 |
| Congo | 3.4 | 49 | 2.8 | 53 | 4.6 | 35 | 9.3 | 62 | 7.9 | 64 | 11.7 | 50 | 8.2 | 34 | 9.9 | 26 | 6.5 | 36 |
| Costa Rica | 0.6 | 106 | 0.6 | 101 | 0.5 | 104 | 2.0 | 108 | 1.9 | 104 | 2.1 | 104 | 1.1 | 97 | NA | 999 | 1.1 | 92 |
| Côte d'Ivoire | 1.3 | 89 | 1.3 | 84 | 1.4 | 89 | 4.8 | 92 | 4.1 | 88 | 5.6 | 90 | 2.0 | 80 | 2.5 | 68 | 0.9 | 95 |
| CUBA | 5.3 | 33 | 6.3 | 25 | 4.3 | 41 | 10.2 | 56 | NA | 999 | 10.2 | 63 | 19.0 | 18 | 17.4 | 19 | 20.5 | 18 |
| Czechoslovkia | 16.0 | 11 | 13.7 | 11 | 18.2 | 10 | 38.2 | 16 | 34.1 | 16 | 42.4 | 13 | 2.8 | 68 | 2.9 | 63 | 2.6 | 66 |

Table A1  *(cont.)*

| | Military expen./GNP (ME/GNP) | | | | | | Military expen./govt. expen. (ME/GE) | | | | | | Military imports/total imports (MM/TM) | | | | | |
|---|---|---|---|---|---|---|---|---|---|---|---|---|---|---|---|---|---|---|
| | 1978–1989 | | 1978–1983 | | 1984–1989 | | 1978–1989 | | 1978–1983 | | 1984–1989 | | 1978–1989 | | 1978–1983 | | 1984–1989 | |
| | Ratio | Rank | Ratio | Rank | Ratio | Rank | Ratio | Rank | Ratio | Rank | Ratio | Rank | Ratio | Rank | Ratio | Rank | Ratio | Rank |
| Dominican Republic | 1.0 | 97 | 0.8 | 94 | 1.2 | 95 | 5.9 | 90 | 5.5 | 81 | 6.2 | 87 | 0.4 | 111 | 0.5 | 106 | 0.4 | 104 |
| Ecuador | 1.8 | 80 | 1.7 | 76 | 1.9 | 77 | 7.3 | 83 | 6.7 | 77 | 7.8 | 78 | 6.8 | 42 | 9.2 | 33 | 4.4 | 52 |
| Egypt | 18.8 | 8 | 19.7 | 6 | 17.8 | 11 | 67.3 | 5 | 64.2 | 5 | 70.3 | 4 | 13.6 | 24 | 13.2 | 21 | 14.0 | 23 |
| El Salvador | 4.9 | 37 | 3.9 | 38 | 5.9 | 25 | 22.4 | 27 | 16.8 | 34 | 28.1 | 18 | 5.3 | 48 | 2.9 | 58 | 7.2 | 32 |
| Equatorial Guinea | NA | 999 | NA | 999 | NA | 999 | NA | 999 | NA | 999 | NA | 999 | 40.9 | 12 | 40.9 | 11 | NA | 999 |
| Ethiopia | 7.7 | 21 | 6.8 | 22 | 8.8 | 20 | 26.6 | 21 | 26.8 | 21 | 26.3 | 20 | 102.2 | 5 | 123.1 | 3 | 81.3 | 5 |
| Fiji | 1.1 | 92 | 0.7 | 96 | 1.6 | 85 | 4.0 | 99 | 2.2 | 101 | 5.8 | 88 | 1.1 | 96 | 1.1 | 92 | NA | 999 |
| Gabon | 2.6 | 66 | 1.8 | 75 | 3.3 | 49 | 9.3 | 63 | 6.7 | 78 | 12.0 | 47 | 3.8 | 58 | 2.9 | 62 | 5.6 | 43 |
| Gambia, The | 0.4 | 110 | 0.5 | 104 | 0.4 | 106 | 1.0 | 109 | 1.2 | 106 | 1.0 | 106 | 9.1 | 30 | NA | 999 | 9.1 | 27 |
| Ghana | 0.5 | 108 | 0.4 | 105 | 0.6 | 101 | 3.5 | 102 | 3.6 | 93 | 3.5 | 100 | 2.6 | 70 | 2.9 | 60 | 2.2 | 69 |
| Greece | 6.5 | 26 | 5.8 | 28 | 7.2 | 23 | 22.7 | 26 | 22.5 | 26 | 23.0 | 24 | 4.3 | 55 | 4.1 | 53 | 4.4 | 48 |
| Guatemala | 1.2 | 91 | 1.0 | 88 | 1.4 | 88 | 9.0 | 66 | 6.9 | 74 | 11.0 | 57 | 1.0 | 98 | 0.6 | 102 | 1.4 | 82 |
| Guinea | 4.3 | 39 | 5.5 | 30 | 3.0 | 56 | 19.4 | 31 | 24.8 | 24 | 14.0 | 39 | 9.3 | 29 | 7.4 | 39 | 9.8 | 26 |
| Guinea-Bissau | 3.1 | 51 | 3.3 | 46 | 2.8 | 59 | 8.3 | 70 | 8.3 | 62 | 8.3 | 75 | 22.7 | 17 | 22.7 | 17 | NA | 999 |
| Guyana | 4.2 | 40 | 4.0 | 37 | 4.6 | 36 | 7.4 | 81 | 6.8 | 75 | 8.1 | 76 | 3.4 | 62 | 2.9 | 64 | 4.4 | 49 |
| Haiti | 1.9 | 79 | 1.9 | 71 | 1.8 | 81 | 8.8 | 68 | 8.8 | 57 | 8.8 | 70 | 1.7 | 86 | 1.7 | 81 | 1.8 | 78 |
| Honduras | 3.0 | 56 | 2.3 | 63 | 3.7 | 43 | 11.0 | 51 | 9.1 | 56 | 13.0 | 44 | 3.8 | 59 | 1.0 | 94 | 5.6 | 44 |
| Hungary | 15.3 | 12 | 14.4 | 9 | 16.3 | 13 | 43.2 | 12 | 37.7 | 10 | 48.6 | 10 | 1.9 | 81 | 2.6 | 66 | 1.2 | 90 |
| India | 2.8 | 60 | 2.5 | 57 | 3.1 | 53 | 11.5 | 49 | 11.4 | 44 | 11.6 | 51 | 12.8 | 26 | 8.5 | 36 | 17.0 | 20 |
| Indonesia | 1.6 | 84 | 1.6 | 78 | 1.7 | 82 | 7.2 | 85 | 7.0 | 72 | 7.4 | 81 | 1.6 | 88 | 2.1 | 72 | 1.2 | 89 |
| Iran | 8.9 | 19 | 8.9 | 18 | NA | 999 | 24.4 | 24 | 24.4 | 25 | NA | 999 | 14.0 | 22 | 9.8 | 29 | 19.1 | 19 |
| Iraq | 24.9 | 3 | 24.9 | 2 | NA | 999 | 64.2 | 6 | 64.2 | 4 | NA | 999 | 45.3 | 9 | 37.7 | 12 | 53.0 | 8 |
| Jamaica | 1.0 | 100 | 0.9 | 91 | 1.0 | 97 | 3.2 | 105 | 2.7 | 99 | 3.7 | 99 | 0.5 | 108 | NA | 999 | 0.5 | 99 |
| Jordan | 12.0 | 16 | 12.5 | 14 | 11.4 | 15 | 25.2 | 22 | 25.4 | 23 | 25.0 | 21 | 17.6 | 19 | 20.7 | 18 | 14.4 | 22 |
| Kenya | 2.4 | 68 | 2.5 | 59 | 2.4 | 68 | 7.8 | 77 | 7.8 | 65 | 7.9 | 77 | 3.0 | 65 | 4.3 | 52 | 1.7 | 79 |
| KOREA, PDR | 20.0 | 5 | 20.0 | 5 | 20.0 | 6 | NA | 999 | NA | 999 | NA | 999 | 17.3 | 20 | 14.3 | 20 | 21.1 | 15 |
| Korea, Rep. of | 5.8 | 29 | 6.1 | 26 | 5.6 | 30 | 34.7 | 18 | 33.5 | 17 | 35.8 | 16 | 1.7 | 85 | 2.2 | 70 | 1.3 | 85 |
| LAO PDR | 10.5 | 17 | NA | 999 | 10.5 | 17 | 25.2 | 23 | 29.1 | 19 | 21.3 | 27 | 218.8 | 2 | 364.8 | 1 | 72.8 | 6 |

| | | | | | | | | | | | | | | | | | | |
|---|---|---|---|---|---|---|---|---|---|---|---|---|---|---|---|---|---|---|
| LEBANON | 6.4 | 27 | 5.8 | 29 | 10.1 | 18 | 21.3 | 29 | 21.1 | 27 | 23.0 | 23 | 2.1 | 76 | 2.0 | 74 | 2.3 | 68 |
| Lesotho | 3.7 | 44 | 2.1 | 67 | 5.3 | 31 | 7.4 | 80 | 4.3 | 86 | 10.4 | 60 | 0.9 | 101 | 0.9 | 96 | NA | 999 |
| Liberia | 2.7 | 63 | 2.1 | 64 | 3.3 | 50 | 9.6 | 61 | 6.7 | 79 | 12.5 | 45 | 2.8 | 69 | 1.7 | 82 | 3.3 | 62 |
| LIBYA | 14.3 | 15 | 13.3 | 12 | 15.8 | 14 | 34.9 | 17 | 35.0 | 15 | 34.6 | 17 | 31.8 | 13 | 42.6 | 10 | 21.0 | 16 |
| Madagascar | 1.3 | 90 | 1.3 | 85 | 1.3 | 92 | 7.7 | 79 | 7.7 | 66 | 7.6 | 80 | 6.6 | 43 | 7.4 | 40 | 5.7 | 41 |
| Malawi | 2.3 | 71 | 2.4 | 60 | 2.2 | 72 | 6.8 | 87 | 6.7 | 76 | 6.9 | 85 | 2.1 | 77 | 2.9 | 59 | 1.5 | 80 |
| Malaysia | 3.2 | 50 | 3.3 | 44 | 3.1 | 54 | 9.3 | 64 | 9.6 | 53 | 8.9 | 69 | 1.4 | 92 | 1.4 | 85 | 1.4 | 83 |
| Mali | 2.2 | 73 | 2.0 | 70 | 2.5 | 66 | 11.7 | 46 | 11.1 | 46 | 12.3 | 46 | 7.9 | 36 | 6.2 | 45 | 10.5 | 25 |
| Malta | 1.1 | 93 | 0.9 | 90 | 1.3 | 93 | 4.7 | 93 | 3.8 | 89 | 5.4 | 92 | 0.6 | 105 | 0.9 | 98 | 0.4 | 102 |
| Mauritania | 7.2 | 23 | 8.6 | 19 | 5.2 | 33 | 19.8 | 30 | 20.2 | 30 | 19.1 | 28 | 6.2 | 45 | 6.1 | 46 | 6.3 | 37 |
| Mauritius | 0.2 | 111 | 0.2 | 108 | 0.2 | 107 | 1.0 | 110 | 0.9 | 107 | 1.0 | 105 | 0.6 | 106 | 0.8 | 99 | 0.4 | 101 |
| Mexico | 0.5 | 109 | 0.3 | 107 | 0.6 | 103 | 2.1 | 106 | 1.5 | 105 | 2.8 | 102 | 0.5 | 110 | 0.4 | 108 | 0.6 | 98 |
| MONGOLIA | NA | 999 | NA | 999 | NA | 999 | NA | 999 | NA | 999 | NA | 999 | 0.5 | 109 | NA | 999 | 0.5 | 100 |
| Morocco | 5.4 | 32 | 5.2 | 33 | 5.6 | 29 | 13.2 | 42 | 11.5 | 43 | 15.7 | 33 | 6.9 | 41 | 9.8 | 27 | 4.0 | 55 |
| MOZAMBIQUE | 7.4 | 22 | 6.4 | 23 | 8.7 | 21 | 32.7 | 19 | 28.9 | 20 | 37.8 | 15 | 30.5 | 14 | 27.2 | 15 | 35.4 | 12 |
| Myanmar | 5.6 | 31 | 6.0 | 27 | 5.3 | 32 | 21.4 | 28 | 20.9 | 28 | 22.0 | 25 | 9.5 | 28 | 8.0 | 37 | 10.9 | 24 |
| Nepal | 0.8 | 103 | 0.6 | 98 | 1.0 | 98 | 4.4 | 95 | 4.2 | 87 | 4.6 | 96 | 1.6 | 89 | 1.2 | 91 | 2.0 | 73 |
| Nicaragua | 3.5 | 47 | 2.8 | 51 | 5.7 | 28 | 8.1 | 71 | 7.4 | 70 | 10.2 | 62 | 26.9 | 16 | 12.4 | 22 | 48.6 | 9 |
| Niger | 0.7 | 104 | 0.5 | 103 | 0.9 | 99 | 4.0 | 98 | 2.8 | 98 | 5.5 | 91 | 2.0 | 79 | 2.0 | 75 | NA | 999 |
| Nigeria | 0.5 | 107 | 0.6 | 100 | 0.5 | 105 | 2.1 | 107 | 2.0 | 103 | 2.1 | 103 | 2.4 | 72 | 1.4 | 88 | 3.4 | 61 |
| Oman | 20.1 | 4 | 20.4 | 4 | 19.8 | 7 | 43.0 | 13 | 43.5 | 7 | 42.5 | 12 | 7.4 | 39 | 9.7 | 30 | 5.1 | 46 |
| Pakistan | 4.8 | 38 | 3.7 | 40 | 5.8 | 26 | 18.7 | 32 | 15.5 | 35 | 21.8 | 26 | 7.3 | 40 | 7.5 | 38 | 7.1 | 33 |
| Panama | 1.7 | 82 | 1.2 | 86 | 2.2 | 73 | 5.3 | 91 | 3.1 | 95 | 7.1 | 84 | 0.9 | 99 | 1.0 | 95 | 0.9 | 94 |
| Papua New Guinea | 1.4 | 88 | 1.3 | 82 | 1.5 | 86 | 4.2 | 97 | 3.7 | 91 | 4.6 | 95 | 1.8 | 84 | 1.7 | 80 | 1.9 | 76 |
| Paraguay | 1.1 | 96 | 1.0 | 89 | 1.2 | 94 | 8.3 | 69 | 7.5 | 69 | 9.3 | 66 | 3.3 | 63 | 2.9 | 57 | 3.6 | 58 |
| Peru | 8.7 | 20 | 6.9 | 21 | 11.3 | 16 | 48.8 | 10 | 36.4 | 13 | 67.3 | 5 | 7.8 | 38 | 9.3 | 32 | 6.3 | 38 |
| Philippines | 1.7 | 83 | 1.6 | 77 | 1.8 | 80 | 9.2 | 65 | 8.4 | 61 | 10.0 | 64 | 0.7 | 104 | 0.8 | 101 | 0.6 | 97 |
| Poland | 18.8 | 7 | 16.8 | 7 | 20.8 | 4 | 71.1 | 4 | 62.5 | 6 | 79.7 | 2 | 4.0 | 56 | 3.8 | 55 | 4.1 | 54 |
| Portugal | 4.0 | 41 | 4.0 | 36 | 4.0 | 42 | 15.1 | 39 | 14.3 | 37 | 16.0 | 32 | 0.8 | 102 | 0.9 | 97 | 0.8 | 96 |
| Romania | 14.7 | 14 | 12.9 | 13 | 16.4 | 12 | 48.9 | 9 | 40.9 | 9 | 56.9 | 9 | 1.7 | 87 | 1.6 | 83 | 1.9 | 77 |
| Rwanda | 2.0 | 77 | 2.0 | 69 | 1.8 | 78 | 10.0 | 59 | 10.5 | 49 | 9.1 | 67 | 4.8 | 51 | 5.4 | 49 | 3.9 | 56 |
| Sao Tome and Principe | 2.9 | 58 | 2.9 | 49 | NA | 999 | 10.9 | 53 | 10.9 | 47 | NA | 999 | 64.3 | 6 | 26.3 | 16 | 83.4 | 4 |
| Saudi Arabia | 18.5 | 9 | 15.9 | 8 | 21.0 | 3 | 44.4 | 11 | 42.9 | 8 | 46.0 | 11 | 13.8 | 23 | 7.0 | 42 | 20.5 | 17 |
| Senegal | 3.0 | 57 | 3.3 | 47 | 2.6 | 63 | 11.5 | 48 | 12.4 | 41 | 10.7 | 58 | 1.3 | 93 | 1.4 | 87 | 1.2 | 87 |
| Sierra Leone | 0.6 | 105 | 0.5 | 102 | 0.6 | 102 | 4.3 | 96 | 3.3 | 94 | 5.6 | 89 | 3.9 | 57 | 2.2 | 71 | 7.3 | 30 |
| Somalia | 4.9 | 35 | 5.5 | 31 | 3.3 | 51 | 16.0 | 38 | 18.2 | 32 | 9.3 | 65 | 42.3 | 10 | 49.0 | 8 | 34.4 | 13 |
| South Africa | 3.8 | 43 | 3.4 | 42 | 4.3 | 40 | 12.9 | 43 | 11.7 | 42 | 14.1 | 38 | 0.3 | 112 | 0.5 | 107 | 0.2 | 105 |

Table A1 *(cont.)*

| | Military expen./GNP (ME/GNP) | | | | | | Military expen./govt. expen. (ME/GE) | | | | | | Military imports/total imports (MM/TM) | | | | | |
|---|---|---|---|---|---|---|---|---|---|---|---|---|---|---|---|---|---|---|
| | 1978–1989 | | 1978–1983 | | 1984–1989 | | 1978–1989 | | 1978–1983 | | 1984–1989 | | 1978–1989 | | 1978–1983 | | 1984–1989 | |
| | Ratio | Rank | Ratio | Rank | Ratio | Rank | Ratio | Rank | Ratio | Rank | Ratio | Rank | Ratio | Rank | Ratio | Rank | Ratio | Rank |
| Sri Lanka | 2.0 | 76 | 1.2 | 87 | 2.7 | 60 | 7.9 | 76 | 4.6 | 85 | 11.1 | 55 | 1.1 | 95 | 0.6 | 103 | 1.3 | 86 |
| Sudan | 3.1 | 52 | 3.8 | 39 | 2.4 | 69 | 16.2 | 35 | 19.0 | 31 | 13.3 | 43 | 8.7 | 32 | 10.2 | 24 | 7.3 | 31 |
| Suriname | 3.1 | 54 | NA | 999 | 3.1 | 55 | 7.3 | 82 | NA | 999 | 7.3 | 82 | 3.2 | 64 | 1.5 | 84 | 4.4 | 50 |
| Swaziland | 1.6 | 87 | 1.4 | 80 | 1.7 | 83 | 4.4 | 94 | 3.7 | 90 | 5.2 | 93 | NA | 999 | NA | 999 | NA | 999 |
| Syria | 17.0 | 10 | 14.4 | 10 | 19.6 | 8 | 50.1 | 7 | 37.0 | 11 | 63.2 | 7 | 54.6 | 8 | 64.0 | 6 | 45.3 | 10 |
| Tanzania | 1.8 | 81 | 1.4 | 81 | 2.2 | 71 | 8.1 | 72 | 5.3 | 83 | 11.4 | 54 | 8.0 | 35 | 9.4 | 31 | 6.6 | 34 |
| Thailand | 3.4 | 48 | 3.2 | 48 | 3.6 | 44 | 15.1 | 40 | 13.9 | 38 | 16.3 | 31 | 2.4 | 71 | 2.7 | 65 | 2.1 | 72 |
| Togo | 2.8 | 61 | 2.5 | 58 | 3.2 | 52 | 7.2 | 84 | 5.8 | 80 | 9.0 | 68 | 3.0 | 66 | 2.9 | 61 | 3.2 | 63 |
| Trinidad and Tobago | 1.0 | 99 | 0.8 | 95 | 1.5 | 87 | 3.3 | 104 | 2.8 | 97 | 4.6 | 97 | 0.6 | 107 | 0.6 | 104 | NA | 999 |
| Tunisia | 2.7 | 64 | 2.5 | 56 | 2.9 | 57 | 7.8 | 78 | 7.0 | 73 | 8.6 | 72 | 2.8 | 67 | 2.1 | 73 | 3.5 | 59 |
| Turkey | 3.9 | 42 | 3.3 | 45 | 4.5 | 37 | 16.0 | 36 | 13.5 | 39 | 18.5 | 29 | 5.2 | 49 | 4.6 | 50 | 5.8 | 40 |
| Uganda | 2.4 | 70 | 2.8 | 52 | 1.9 | 75 | 326.9 | 1 | 535.6 | 1 | 13.9 | 40 | 8.8 | 31 | 11.9 | 23 | 5.6 | 42 |
| Uruguay | 2.5 | 67 | 2.3 | 61 | 2.7 | 62 | 10.5 | 54 | 9.7 | 52 | 11.6 | 53 | 1.5 | 90 | 1.7 | 78 | 0.4 | 103 |
| USSR | 42.7 | 1 | 33.7 | 1 | 51.8 | 1 | 100.6 | 2 | 77.0 | 2 | 124.2 | 1 | 1.5 | 91 | 1.7 | 77 | 1.3 | 84 |
| Venezuela | 0.9 | 101 | 0.6 | 99 | 1.1 | 96 | 3.6 | 101 | 2.2 | 102 | 5.1 | 94 | 2.0 | 78 | 1.2 | 90 | 2.8 | 65 |
| VIET NAM | 19.4 | 6 | NA | 999 | 19.4 | 9 | 40.8 | 14 | NA | 999 | 40.8 | 14 | 105.7 | 4 | 115.0 | 4 | 91.7 | 3 |
| YEMEN ARAB REP. | 9.6 | 18 | 10.8 | 15 | 8.4 | 22 | 29.8 | 20 | 31.8 | 18 | 27.7 | 19 | 28.2 | 15 | 31.2 | 13 | 24.7 | 14 |
| Yemen PDR | 3.6 | 46 | 3.7 | 41 | 3.5 | 47 | 10.2 | 57 | 10.0 | 50 | 10.4 | 59 | 41.7 | 11 | 44.0 | 9 | 39.0 | 11 |
| Yugoslavia | 3.1 | 53 | 2.6 | 55 | 3.6 | 46 | 11.9 | 45 | 8.1 | 63 | 15.7 | 34 | 1.3 | 94 | 1.3 | 89 | 1.2 | 88 |
| Zaire | 1.1 | 95 | 0.4 | 106 | 2.0 | 74 | 6.5 | 88 | 2.4 | 100 | 11.6 | 52 | 5.6 | 47 | 6.7 | 44 | 4.4 | 51 |
| Zambia | 7.1 | 25 | 9.2 | 17 | 4.3 | 39 | 17.6 | 34 | 20.7 | 29 | 13.6 | 41 | 4.6 | 52 | 7.0 | 41 | 2.2 | 70 |
| Zimbabwe | 4.9 | 36 | 4.0 | 35 | 5.8 | 27 | 14.2 | 41 | 13.2 | 40 | 15.2 | 35 | 4.8 | 50 | 3.4 | 56 | 7.6 | 29 |

Source: Data on military expenditures and military imports as share of total imports are from the 1989 and 1990 issues of "World military expenditures and arms transfers." Data on GNP and general government expenditures are from the World Bank's "Economic and social database" except for countries in upper case letters whose data are from the first source. Government expenditures in the case of countries in upper case letters refer to the "central" government expenditures.

Note: A ranking of 999 has been assigned to countries for which data were unavailable.

Table A2  Average annual grants and concessional loan disbursments, and countries' ranks during 1978–1989, 1978–1983, and 1984–1989

| | Average annual ODA (US$m) | | | Rank | | |
| --- | --- | --- | --- | --- | --- | --- |
| | 1978–1989 | 1978–1983 | 1984–1989 | 1978–1989 | 1978–1983 | 1984–1989 |
| TOTAL | 24,931 | 21,721 | 28,141 | | | |
| AFGHANISTAN | 30 | 31 | 29 | 88 | 88 | 85 |
| ALBANIA | NA | NA | NA | 111 | 111 | 111 |
| Algeria | 128 | 115 | 140 | 48 | 42 | 52 |
| Angola | 67 | 33 | 100 | 69 | 85 | 63 |
| Argentina | 33 | 51 | 15 | 87 | 76 | 93 |
| Bangladesh | 1,314 | 1,187 | 1,442 | 4 | 4 | 3 |
| BARBADOS | 9 | 12 | 6 | 101 | 96 | 101 |
| Benin | 85 | 66 | 104 | 64 | 65 | 62 |
| Bolivia | 200 | 122 | 279 | 33 | 41 | 30 |
| Botswana | 74 | 63 | 86 | 68 | 68 | 65 |
| Brazil | 91 | 85 | 96 | 61 | 56 | 64 |
| Bulgaria | 0 | 0 | 0 | 108 | 106 | 107 |
| Burkina Faso | 159 | 139 | 180 | 40 | 39 | 43 |
| Burundi | 109 | 79 | 139 | 55 | 59 | 53 |
| CAMBODIA | 27 | 45 | 8 | 90 | 77 | 100 |
| Cameroon | 153 | 144 | 162 | 43 | 36 | 46 |
| Cape Verde | 52 | 39 | 65 | 78 | 80 | 70 |
| Central African Republic | 86 | 57 | 115 | 62 | 71 | 60 |
| Chad | 107 | 60 | 154 | 56 | 69 | 50 |
| Chile | 28 | 25 | 30 | 89 | 90 | 84 |
| China | 660 | 176 | 1,145 | 9 | 31 | 6 |
| Colombia | 56 | 54 | 57 | 73 | 74 | 78 |
| Congo, People's Republic of | 85 | 93 | 76 | 65 | 50 | 67 |

Table A2 (cont.)

| | Average annual ODA (US$m) | | | Rank | | |
|---|---|---|---|---|---|---|
| | 1978–1989 | 1978–1983 | 1984–1989 | 1978–1989 | 1978–1983 | 1984–1989 |
| Costa Rica | 129 | 81 | 177 | 47 | 57 | 44 |
| Côte d'Ivoire | 122 | 80 | 165 | 51 | 58 | 45 |
| CUBA | 17 | 21 | 13 | 95 | 93 | 94 |
| Czechoslovakia | 0 | 0 | 0 | 109 | 107 | 108 |
| Dominican Republic | 114 | 92 | 136 | 53 | 52 | 54 |
| Ecuador | 77 | 32 | 123 | 67 | 87 | 59 |
| Egypt, Arab Republic of | 1,446 | 1,487 | 1,404 | 3 | 3 | 5 |
| El Salvador | 232 | 141 | 323 | 30 | 38 | 25 |
| Equatorial Guinea | 17 | 8 | 26 | 96 | 101 | 87 |
| Ethiopia | 445 | 233 | 658 | 15 | 21 | 11 |
| Fiji | 19 | 19 | 18 | 94 | 94 | 91 |
| Gabon | 38 | 24 | 51 | 85 | 91 | 79 |
| Gambia, The | 50 | 39 | 61 | 80 | 81 | 74 |
| Ghana | 229 | 109 | 350 | 31 | 45 | 22 |
| GREECE | 16 | 29 | 2 | 97 | 89 | 103 |
| Guatemala | 96 | 58 | 134 | 59 | 70 | 55 |
| Guinea | 154 | 85 | 223 | 42 | 54 | 38 |
| Guinea-Bissau | 62 | 55 | 68 | 72 | 73 | 69 |
| Guyana | 43 | 54 | 32 | 83 | 75 | 82 |
| Haiti | 104 | 76 | 132 | 57 | 62 | 56 |
| Honduras | 167 | 108 | 225 | 39 | 46 | 37 |
| Hungary | 86 | 147 | 25 | 63 | 35 | 88 |
| India | 2,058 | 1,889 | 2,227 | 1 | 2 | 1 |
| Indonesia | 1,064 | 718 | 1,410 | 5 | 7 | 4 |

| | | | | | | |
|---|---|---|---|---|---|---|
| Iran | 9 | 9 | 9 | 100 | 98 | 98 |
| IRAQ | 20 | 12 | 28 | 93 | 97 | 86 |
| Jamaica | 145 | 134 | 156 | 45 | 40 | 48 |
| Jordan | 801 | 942 | 660 | 7 | 5 | 10 |
| Kenya | 385 | 283 | 488 | 17 | 18 | 16 |
| KOREA PDR | 5 | 8 | 1 | 105 | 100 | 104 |
| Korea, Republic of | 183 | 215 | 151 | 36 | 24 | 51 |
| Lao PDR | 94 | 63 | 125 | 60 | 67 | 58 |
| Lebanon | 45 | 192 | (102) | 82 | 25 | 110 |
| Lesotho | 64 | 56 | 72 | 70 | 72 | 68 |
| Liberia | 64 | 68 | 60 | 71 | 64 | 75 |
| LIBYA | 1 | 2 | 1 | 106 | 104 | 105 |
| Madagascar | 206 | 163 | 249 | 32 | 33 | 33 |
| Malawi | 153 | 109 | 196 | 44 | 44 | 42 |
| Malaysia | 144 | 85 | 204 | 46 | 55 | 41 |
| Mali | 244 | 187 | 300 | 27 | 28 | 29 |
| Malta | 22 | 39 | 5 | 91 | 82 | 102 |
| Mauritania | 194 | 178 | 209 | 34 | 30 | 40 |
| Mauritius | 40 | 32 | 48 | 84 | 86 | 80 |
| Mexico | 78 | 73 | 82 | 66 | 63 | 66 |
| MONGOLIA | 0 | 0 | 0 | 107 | 108 | 106 |
| Morocco | 518 | 604 | 433 | 13 | 10 | 20 |
| Mozambique | 319 | 89 | 549 | 20 | 53 | 13 |
| Myanmar | 322 | 298 | 346 | 19 | 15 | 23 |
| Nepal | 182 | 114 | 251 | 37 | 43 | 32 |
| Nicaragua | 258 | 149 | 367 | 25 | 34 | 21 |
| Niger | 191 | 144 | 238 | 35 | 37 | 36 |
| Nigeria | 46 | 35 | 58 | 81 | 84 | 77 |
| Oman | 113 | 167 | 59 | 54 | 32 | 76 |
| Pakistan | 926 | 868 | 985 | 6 | 6 | 7 |

Table A2  (cont.)

| | Average annual ODA (US$m) | | | Rank | | |
|---|---|---|---|---|---|---|
| | 1978–1989 | 1978–1983 | 1984–1989 | 1978–1989 | 1978–1983 | 1984–1989 |
| Panama | 34 | 35 | 33 | 86 | 83 | 81 |
| Papua New Guinea | 308 | 305 | 311 | 22 | 14 | 26 |
| Paraguay | 54 | 43 | 64 | 77 | 79 | 73 |
| Peru | 240 | 240 | 241 | 29 | 20 | 35 |
| Philippines | 512 | 290 | 734 | 14 | 16 | 9 |
| Poland | 52 | 0 | 104 | 79 | 109 | 61 |
| Portugal | 119 | 78 | 160 | 52 | 61 | 47 |
| Romania | 0 | 0 | 0 | 110 | 110 | 109 |
| Rwanda | 127 | 99 | 155 | 49 | 48 | 49 |
| Sao Tome & Principe | 14 | 9 | 18 | 98 | 99 | 90 |
| SAUDI ARABIA | 11 | 14 | 8 | 99 | 95 | 99 |
| Senegal | 312 | 190 | 434 | 21 | 26 | 19 |
| Sierra Leone | 55 | 44 | 65 | 75 | 78 | 72 |
| Somalia | 295 | 283 | 307 | 23 | 17 | 27 |
| SOUTH AFRICA | NA | NA | NA | 112 | 112 | 112 |
| Sri Lanka | 422 | 339 | 505 | 16 | 13 | 15 |
| Sudan | 719 | 674 | 764 | 8 | 8 | 8 |
| Suriname | 55 | 92 | 17 | 76 | 51 | 92 |
| Swaziland | 21 | 22 | 21 | 92 | 92 | 89 |
| Syrian Arab Republic | 2,053 | 2,204 | 1,901 | 2 | 1 | 2 |
| Tanzania | 582 | 541 | 624 | 10 | 12 | 12 |
| Thailand | 351 | 258 | 445 | 18 | 19 | 18 |
| Togo | 98 | 65 | 132 | 58 | 66 | 57 |
| Trinidad & Tobago | 8 | 4 | 13 | 102 | 103 | 95 |

| | | | | | | |
|---|---|---|---|---|---|---|
| Tunisia | 241 | 220 | 262 | 28 | 23 | 31 |
| Turkey | 561 | 616 | 507 | 11 | 9 | 14 |
| Uganda | 173 | 103 | 243 | 38 | 47 | 34 |
| Uruguay | 7 | 5 | 9 | 103 | 102 | 97 |
| USSR | NA | NA | NA | 113 | 113 | 113 |
| Venezuela | 6 | 1 | 10 | 104 | 105 | 96 |
| VIET NAM | 126 | 186 | 65 | 50 | 29 | 71 |
| Yemen Arab Republic | 533 | 593 | 473 | 12 | 11 | 17 |
| YEMEN PDR | NA | NA | NA | 114 | 114 | 114 |
| Yugoslavia | 55 | 79 | 31 | 74 | 60 | 83 |
| Zaire | 277 | 223 | 331 | 24 | 22 | 24 |
| Zambia | 244 | 188 | 300 | 26 | 27 | 28 |
| Zimbabwe | 158 | 98 | 218 | 41 | 49 | 39 |

Source: Data for countries in lower case are from the World Bank's "World debt tables," and those for for countries in upper case are from the OECD's "Geographical distribution of financial flows to developing countries."
Note: Unavailable data are taken as 0 for the purpose of adding the data up.

# Part 2
# Economic and social consequences of military conversion

# 5

# The economics of arms reduction

Lawrence R. Klein

There can be no doubt that military spending will be reduced during the next several years. At the end of 1989, US defence expenditure (1987 US dollars) was estimated to be \$281.5 billion. During "Desert Storm" it reached \$291.8 billion and has now (1992 dollars) receded to \$263.1 billion. In nominal terms there has been no decline – a slight increase.

The American figures are well documented and publicized although it is always hard to classify many borderline expenditures as defence or non-defence use. The US Administration has baseline plans, which do involve reductions, and indirect evidence such as labour force statistics or employment in well-known defence enterprises shows that the decline is actually taking place. During the last 12 months there have been fairly steady month-by-month reductions in resident armed force personnel. Force strength is between 150,000 and 200,000 below the peak levels reached in 1986.

The steps towards arms reduction seem to be assured because of the demise of the Soviet Union and the end of the Cold War. Russian statistics of all sorts are weak, and defence expenditures are particularly elusive; therefore it is difficult to be very precise about the magnitude of cut-backs in Russia and even more so about such figures for other republics that were formerly in the USSR. We can simply assume that there will be very large reductions, as all members of the former WTO concentrate more on civilian production and the overall reorientation of their entire economies.

At the beginning of the restructuring process in the entire WTO, many bold statements were made about demobilization and about reduced production of arms, but now that the countries involved are struggling with their economic reforms, it is evident that there has been considerable reconsideration of their economic activities.

Take the case of Czechoslovakia (or the Czech Republic and Slovakia). A high-principled statement was made by the new President, Havel, that Czechoslovakia would stop providing arms for export to developing countries. Czechoslovakia had built and maintained a formidable arms industry that earned a great deal of precious foreign exchange. It was not long before economic necessity triumphed, and a pragmatic decision was made to honour existing contracts. By now, even more pragmatism has prevailed, and Czechoslovakia is back in production for arms trade. The breakaway state in Slovakia had great arms production capability and great need for foreign exchange; so they made a predictable choice.

Stockpiles of weaponry in former Soviet republics and production of new weapons are major earners of foreign exchange for some governments. Arms exports were a principal export of the USSR. New republics want to have their own defence forces, as well as to earn foreign exchange; so the world still confronts a dangerous situation with regard to arms production and arms trade in the WTO area. There is a reduction in arms, but there are still arms use, arms production, and arms trade associated with the former Soviet bloc.

The ethnic battles raging in the former Yugoslavia are supplied partly from existing inventories of the Yugoslav military. Some of the combatants, however, are being supplied from producing units that one might have hoped had vanished. In total, military activity has declined in Eastern Europe and the republics of the CIS, but it is still present, and old policy problems remain. The conflict situation, active or potential, is still a threat, but the gain, so far, is that the possibility of World War III is more remote than ever since 1945.

The major reductions in military spending and production will take place in the United States and the former Soviet Union, and some quantitative idea about possible economic effects can best be understood by examination of the American cut-backs. US strategy is based on being prepared to deal with threats posed by limited regions or by individual countries, instead of facing World War III and fighting a ground war in Europe. Capability of handling two limited wars simultaneously is a strategic target of US defence planners. This calls for more reliance on highly mobile tactical forces that can be readied on short notice to fight in distant parts. In terms of personnel, the Administration has proposed a downsizing of a base force that is 20 per cent lower than 1990 levels. This view is still maintained by the Administration, but there have been some recommendations by others for even greater reductions. Active and reserve forces would thus be estimated at about 1.6 and 0.9 million, respectively.

In terms of expenditures (1990 prices), the Administration's 1991 plan amounts to an annual reduction of 3 per cent. The budget level would be reduced by 26 per cent at the end of the period 1993 to 1997. The Congressional Budget Office (CBO) has analysed much larger reductions, amounting to 7 per cent annually and 40 per cent under 1990 levels by 1997. The total savings come to $143 billion in a five-year period.

Plans have changed and Congressional committees and outside experts have considered a wide range of expenditure options, some that reduce national defence spending by more than 50 per cent at some date in this decade. For purposes of analysis, however, the CBO figures (not recommendations – simply illustrations) seem to me to be more realistic; therefore the Administration's 1991 plan and the CBO figures will form the basis of comparison in this paper for examination of economic implications.

Instead of 400,000 people being separated from duty by the Administration plan (a reduction of 20 per cent), the CBO estimates are for an extra 18 per cent reduction in active forces (2 Army wings, 2 carrier battle groups, 80 Navy ships, 3 Air Force fighter wings, 1 Marine Corps brigade). There could be many components of such a reduction in defence spending – cut-backs or elimination of B-2 bombers, retirement of Minuteman II missiles, reductions in SDI activities, cancellation of the F-22 aircraft programme, reduced procurements of carriers or destroyers, etc. The CBO have computed savings on 47 different options.

There can be a peace dividend. Under the Administration's programme it would amount to approximately $100 billion in 1997, while the larger figure for a peace dividend estimated by the CBO would provide an additional $55 billion in 1997. The former represents a cut of 26 per cent, while the latter amounts to 40 per cent. Both are fairly large amounts even if not the largest being talked about. A reduction of $100 billion is double what many economists are presently arguing for, an infrastructure programme to get the economy on a better recovery path. A peace dividend of this size would even permit some deficit reduction and some contribution to neglected items of infrastructure that are desperately in need of support. If the larger CBO alternative were implemented, the dividend would be more than $150 billion by 1997, more than enough to contribute towards the two objectives, infrastructure repair and deficit reduction.

Of course, these are 1997 estimates, but the savings from phased-in programmes would build up over the five-year period and a large fraction of the dividend could be used for needy civilian expenditures at the beginning, with an understanding that deficit reduction would be started soon. Also, there are other ways of getting at deficit reduction besides the peace dividend, and these, too, could be gradually put in place.

There are people with a long "laundry list" of excellent causes for consumption of the peace dividend of $100 billion or more per year. They are such things as infant children's programmes, education reform (K–12 – kindergarten through twelfth grade – and higher studies), employment training, civilian R&D, and repair or improvement of fixed capital facilities in the public sector. The ploughing of a dividend into expenditures such as these improve or create both human and fixed capital. Given enough time, they pay for themselves by generating a productive return. This is the main economic difference between defence spending and the formation of non-defence capital. The former goods do not generate future income streams, while the latter do. Also, a good infrastructure eventually contributes to better performance in the private business sector of the economy.

If the peace dividend is used for the purpose of repaying debt, a similar capital expansion can be realized, provided that monetary authorities *accommodate* the reduction of public liabilities. In that case, a drop in unit capital costs should lead to capital formation, as judged by market needs or perceptions, but we have been seeing how uncertain markets are these days about responding to lower capital costs; therefore we should have enough flowing immediately into public capital expenditure in order to stimulate aggregate demand and help the economy pull out of the slump more vigorously. A judicious mixture of fiscal and monetary policy should have been started much earlier in 1991; then there would have been more room for manoeuvrability, especially in moving markets, when interest rates were higher.

Another potential source of gain from arms reduction is the *conversion* of abandoned defence facilities into civilian capital use. This is in addition to the use of released funds when the military sector is reduced. One of the most successful conversions occurred in the United States after the end of World War II. By 1950, most of the capital that had previously been converted to wartime objectives, or that had been built during the war, was producing consumer and producer durables along trend paths that were established before the war. In retrospect, this seems to have been a fast conversion. People were impatient at the time, but five years is not a long time to wait for something as favourable as that conversion process. The five-year period represented the total maturity of the process, and goods/services were forthcoming in some increasing amount, year by year, since 1945.

The reconversion of 1945 to 1950 cannot automatically be repeated because there were some special factors at work. The country was united in spirit; the veterans' educational programme was working very well; and, most of all, there was a large pent-up demand, backed by purchasing power from wartime savings.

Conversion was good after the Korean and Viet Nam Wars, too. At the present time, following the end of the Cold War, we can find some interesting cases of individual firms that have successfully converted or diversified, but it is too early to find general statistical confirmation such as that which is evident from the production figures of 1945 to 1950. There are cases of failure and of success; so individual stories do not settle the matter.

In Eastern Europe and the former Soviet Union, there are some examples of conversion, but also stories of outmoded capital that is not suited for use in either military or civilian production under modern conditions and standards. After World War II, there were some good examples of conversion, but new cases are not visible on an outstanding scale at the present time.

Studies of Soviet production before World War II have established the point that the extreme emphasis on heavy industry (a code word for military activity) held back the economy; therefore by analogous reasoning, one would expect that the process could now be reversed and a de-emphasis on the military sector could pave the way for more civilian output.

Apart from the conversion of enterprises, there is the possibility of conversion of military facilities. The US Department of Defense has compiled an interesting record of Civilian Re-Use of Military Facilities – arsenals, camps, air fields, naval yards, and similar facilities. Nearly 100 such facilities have been converted during the past 30 or more years. More civilian jobs have been created than existed under military use of the facilities. The average conversion time has been three to five years. The new facilities are used for civilian airports, public office buildings, commercial/industrial parks, community colleges, training schools, and other productive activities. If people are patient, significant gains can be realized. These gains come only after some losses. It is almost inevitable that the closing of a base or other military installation will have an adverse economic impact on the surrounding region. Once the facility has been restructured for civilian use, however, it can produce useful economic output for a long period of time.

The most important thing that public authorities can do to soften the effects of loss of jobs in defence-related enterprises that are having fewer orders, the effects of troop reductions, or the effects of base closings is to educate or retrain the people who are directly affected. The educational grants for demobilized service personnel after World War II were extremely effective in building human capital. A cost was involved, but an excellent return was realized on the cost of the investment in people. The same can be said of retraining and educational grants that could be made available in the present situation because there will be an immediate rise in unemployment. If the overall economy were more prosperous and growing at a healthy rate now, placement of separated personnel would occur more rapidly than we are presently finding. Stimulative policy for economic advancement should be in order regardless of the issue of arms reduction. Unfortunately remedial action is not being taken vigorously enough now in the United States.

As for the former Soviet Union, the steps being taken to restructure the economy create unemployment and business disturbance by their very nature; therefore arms reduction there has little chance of being offset by overall expansion of the economy. One can only try to minimize the economic hardship that is happening and wait as patiently as possible for expansion to take place in the civilian economy.

If we shift attention from arms reduction in the two superpowers to worldwide arms reduction we face an entirely different set of circumstances and issues. The UNDP, in their *Human Development Report 1992*, have estimated a cumulative peace dividend for the world over the time span 1987 to 2000 at $1.5 trillion. The greater part, by far, of this stupendous sum is attributed to arms reduction in the United

States and the former USSR. Together, they account for $1,236 trillion, divided fairly even between the two countries. NATO countries and the advanced industrial countries have cut back very little and show little inclination to make future arms reductions. In fact, countries in Western Europe and Japan may be expanding their defence outlays to fill a void if US withdrawals continue at a more rapid pace. It is interesting that the arms race associated with the Cold War was so heavily concentrated in the two superpowers.

There is, however, another dimension to the arms race. It still goes on in the developing world. Arms reduction programmes could produce a peace dividend of some $279 billion, 1987–2000, most of it associated with arms for the Middle East. Iraq, for example, was one of the most heavily armed nations of the Middle East, and it remains a question about their present defence situation. While they were building up arms prior to the invasion of Kuwait, they had ample oil revenues that could have been used for general economic development. Now, these revenues have been cut off (temporarily), and the means for development continue to be unmet. This is a general problem – not one of Iraq alone, or the Middle East; it is a problem for the entire developing world.

For a number of years some governments, in particular the US government, did not admit that a linkage existed between disarmament and development. Officials admitted that each subject was worthy of consideration and investigation in its own right but not together in a relationship. There are relationships, but the matter is complicated; it is not simply a matter of finding a bivariate relation and certainly not a linear equation indicating that a given level of defence spending is (correctly) associated with a particular rate of economic growth.

There are some countries that spend very little to support a military establishment, say Costa Rica, which has civil and rural guards but not an army. Costa Rica has enjoyed a good rate of economic advancement, not the best in Latin America, but very good. Many social indicators of health, education, and other population characteristics are favourable. This is a good example of low military expenditures and high socio-economic performance. Consider, however, the South Koreans. They have quite significant defence expenditures, yet they have achieved extremely impressive economic goals. They grow fast, they have avoided high inflation; they have managed their external accounts admirably. They have been star performers on the world scene, and are prominent in the restructuring of Russia. South Korea received strategic support from the

105

United States after the Korean War, and the United States covers a great deal of their large defence needs; nevertheless they have managed their defences and their economic development extremely well. One might say the same thing about Taiwan and Israel, but the latter received a great deal of external assistance, especially from Jews in the Diaspora.

There are also many examples of countries with high defence expenditures and poor economic conditions, such as Nicaragua, and also countries which spend little on defence and which have also not managed to experience good economic development. Ivory Coast is such a case.

If a country enjoys a peaceful existence over a long period of time (three or more decades), has good natural endowments, spends little on defence, and puts funding into human capital and other social infrastructure projects, then it is highly likely that such a country will have a good phase of economic development. Many countries aspire to be another "Japan." That is a very different thing to duplicate, but it is a challenging objective, and it is evident that officials of multinational institutions are thinking along the lines of small defence spending leading to improved economic development when they have fixed conditional guidelines on the ratio of defence spending to GDP or similar statistical indicators in order for developing countries to qualify for financial aid or other assistance. The conditionality criterion essentially confirms that there is linkage between arms outlays and development.

It is also interesting to consider conditionality imposed by Japan on its overseas development assistance (ODA). Japan, among all countries, is presently the largest ODA donor and imposes such conditions on recipients as limits on the shares of national expenditure going to defence, trade in armament (exports or imports), and development of weapons of mass destruction. These conditions, set out in a White Paper for ODA activity in the fiscal year 1991, are not the only ones imposed by Japan, but they are the most relevant for arms limitations and peace. In terms of US dollars, Japan's ODA grants totalled $11,024 billion during the last fiscal year.

Environmental protection is another matter of concern for arms reduction activities, not only in developing countries but in all countries where there are large stocks of weapons, especially those of biological, chemical, or nuclear composition. Accidents with reactors or in manufacturing plants have already shown the environmental damage that can be inflicted. Safeguards are expensive to install and maintain; therefore they are likely to be inferior in poorer developing

106

countries. If some developing countries are able, one way or another, to secure some of the stockpiles from republics of the former USSR, they may not have the necessary know-how to provide adequate environmental safeguards.

If would be far better for the main industrial countries to acquire and destroy existing stockpiles that made up the Soviet and entire WTO arsenal. This would be expensive yet highly productive in protecting conditions of production for the future. It should be regarded as an economic investment, considering the alternatives (opportunity costs) involved. It is probably one way of getting some economic assistance for the restructuring of the economies of Eastern Europe, Russia, Ukraine, and other states that shared the Soviet arsenal.

The United States has provided some figures about disposal and environmental protection.[1] In the 1960s, many waste materials from military sites were dumped at sea, but this was quite unsatisfactory, and now more modern methods are used. For chemical warfare material incineration is being used, and the United States has established a disposal system facility on the Johnson Atoll in the Pacific Ocean.

There are some 17,500 sites for clean-up in US military facilities, a significant portion of which involves dealing with nuclear materials. Approximately 11,000 sites require restoration work. For the fiscal year 1993, the sum allocated to pollution clean-up at military bases was $3.7 billion and an additional $5.5 billion was requested for cleaning up pollution from the Department of Energy's nuclear weapons programmes. It has been estimated that 30 years will be required to deal with contamination and that the cost could be as much as $400 billion. These figures, as are most of those associated with environmental protection, subject to error. Often, actual costs turn out to be much larger than estimates. Uncertainty is introduced further because of the unsettled conditions in Russia and other WTO areas. Whatever final resolution is reached between Russia and the United States, the number of nuclear weapons to be destroyed will be in the thousands on each side.

It is evident that the costs of winding down the Cold War in a proper way that observes all safeguards will be substantial. The realization of a peace dividend does not come about easily.

## Note

1. (1992). *World Economic Survey*. UN, New York, pp. 121–137.

# 6

# Defence reductions in the United States in the 1990s

Murray Weidenbaum

## Introduction

The end of the Cold War has provided an unparalleled opportunity for the United States to reduce its defence budget and shift resources from military to civilian uses.[1] However, the early euphoria about a large peace dividend has been replaced by greater realism concerning the many restraints and obstacles facing policy makers in both the public and private sectors.

To begin with, American national security policy must acknowledge that the world continues to be a dangerous place. The Cold War is over, but the Middle East and the Balkans are constant reminders of the dangers of armed hostilities. Famine in Africa reflects the social and political instability in many regions. The image of the heavily armed republics of the former Soviet Union conjures up potential threats of nuclear conflict. And then there are the terrorist groups active in every hemisphere.

This is precisely why the declines now taking place in the US military budget are far more moderate than the precipitous reductions that followed the end of World War II.[2] Also, there is not yet an agreement between Congress and the President as to the specific

Table 1  **Savings from alternative defence paths compared with the CBO baseline (fiscal years, in US$bn)**

| Category of spending | 1991 | 1992 | 1993 | 1994 | 1995 | Total 1991–1995 |
|---|---|---|---|---|---|---|
| 2% annual real decline in budget authority | | | | | | |
| Change in defence spending | $−4 | $−9 | $−15 | $−22 | $−30 | $−80 |
| Change in interest spending | *a* | −1 | −2 | −3 | −5 | −11 |
| Total change in deficit | $−4 | $−10 | $−17 | $−25 | $−35 | $−91 |
| 4% annual real decline in budget authority | | | | | | |
| Change in defence spending | $−8 | $−18 | $−30 | $−44 | $−58 | $−158 |
| Change in interest spending | *a* | −1 | −3 | −6 | −10 | −20 |
| Total change in deficit | $−8 | $−19 | $−33 | $−50 | $−68 | $−178 |

Source: Compiled from Congressional Budget Office data.
Note: *a* = less than $500 million.

weapon systems and military missions to be cut. There is always conflict between these two independent branches of our national government. Nevertheless, the outlook is clear: military spending in the United States will be reduced significantly and steadily. (See table 1 for an illustration.)

In real terms (after an allowance for inflation), the military budget five years from now likely will be one-fourth to one-third lower than it now is. That means an aggregate reduction equal to 2 to 3 per cent of the nation's gross domestic product. Even in a $6 trillion (US dollars) economy, a reduction of $200 billion or more in military demand generates problems as well as opportunities.

A further complication is the fact that the reductions in defence spending are not uniform across all categories. Production of weapon systems is being reduced more than operations. Operating costs are being cut more than research and development. Within the key category of production, the percentage decreases also vary. Some weapon systems are being eliminated, others are being scaled back, still others stretched out, while some remain unscathed.

As a result, the regional and economic impacts are uneven. That is a topic to which we will soon return. One other thought: great uncertainty always attaches to defence planning. The most brilliant defence officials can only guess which, if any, of the numerous potential threats to the national security will materialize. There is always a

109

vigorous competition between military leaders and civilian administrators. The Irish economist, C.F. Bastable, accurately described the basic situation a century ago, "To maintain a due balance between the excessive demands of alarmists and military officials, and the undue reductions in outlay sought by the advocates of economy, is one of the difficult tasks of the statesman."[3]

## Economic impacts

Large changes in defence outlays can be strategic for the US economy. Although other factors were involved, recessions occurred after the end of the Korean War, after the Viet Nam War, and most recently following the end of the Cold War. Nevertheless, economists generally agree that the long-term prosperity of an economy such as that of the United States does not depend on high levels of military demand.[4] However, the shift from military to civilian production does not occur instantly. A lengthy period of transition is to be expected and often occurs.[5]

The serious problems of economic adjustment to defence changes arise because of the specialized resources that are used. Few of these companies serve civilian markets in major ways. If defence demand were distributed equally across all industries, the transition to a more civilian-oriented society would be far easier. But the reverse is more the case. Large portions of military outlay go to companies in a handful of high-tech industries, companies that tend to specialize in meeting the esoteric needs of modern military establishments. Moreover, these companies – or at least their defence-oriented divisions – cluster in a relatively few regions of the country.

In 1988, for example, four industry groups won the lion's share of defence contracts: aerospace, machinery and instrumentation, electronics and communication, and miscellaneous transportation equipment (especially shipbuilding). In that year, one-half of the value of all defence contracts went to 25 companies in those four industries. Few of those firms cater to consumer or civilian-industrial markets in a major way. The defence production leaders include such specialized companies as McDonnell Douglas, General Dynamics, Tenneco, Raytheon, Martin Marietta, Hughes Aircraft, Lockheed, United Technologies, and Boeing (see table 2). Moreover, the defence-industry relationship has tended to be long lasting. Of the top 25 defence contractors in 1971, 20 of them or 80 per cent were still in that category 17 years later, in 1988 (see table 3).

Table 2　**Major defence contractors in 1988**

| Rank company | Military awards (in US$bn) | Key products |
|---|---|---|
| 1. McDonnell Douglas | 8.0 | F-18, F-15, Apache, and Harrier aircraft, R&D for missile/space systems |
| 2. General Dynamics | 6.5 | F-16 fighter aircraft, nuclear sub-marines, M-1 tank, Tomahawk, Stinger, Sparrow missiles |
| 3. General Electric | 5.7 | Jet engines, nuclear reactors for submarines, communication equipment |
| 4. Tenneco | 5.1 | Nuclear aircraft carriers, sub-marines |
| 5. Raytheon | 4.1 | Patriot, Aegis, and Phoenix missiles, underwater sound equipment |
| 6. Martin Marietta | 3.7 | Titan missile, Apache aircraft, ammunition |
| 7. General Motors | 3.6 | Amraam, Maverick, Phoenix, and Tow missiles |
| 8. Lockheed | 3.5 | Trident missile, C-130 and P-3 aircraft, R&D for missile/space systems |
| 9. United Technologies | 3.5 | Aircraft engines, helicopters, R&D for aircraft |
| 10. Boeing | 3.0 | C-135 and E-3A aircraft, Chinook helicopters, R&D for aircraft and missiles |

Source: U.S. Department of Defense.

Table 3　**Turnover among the 100 major defence contractors, 1971–1988**

| Top 100 contractors in 1988 | Ranking in 1971 | | | | | |
|---|---|---|---|---|---|---|
| | 1 to 25 | 26 to 50 | 51 to 75 | 76 to 100 | Below 100 | Total |
| 1 to 25 | 20 | 5 | 0 | 0 | 0 | 25 |
| 26 to 50 | 2 | 7 | 3 | 3 | 10 | 25 |
| 51 to 75 | 0 | 5 | 2 | 4 | 14 | 25 |
| 76 to 100 | 0 | 1 | 2 | 1 | 21 | 25 |
| Total | 22 | 18 | 7 | 8 | 45 | 100 |

Source: U.S. Department of Defense

The regional concentration of defence employment is equally striking. Of the estimated 3.4 million people employed in defence jobs in 1988, over 2.2 million or 66 per cent resided in 10 of the 50

Table 4   **Major centres of defence employment in 1988**

| State | Number of defence jobs |
| --- | --- |
| 1. California | 657,868 |
| 2. Texas | 246,473 |
| 3. New York | 236,421 |
| 4. Massachusetts | 214,299 |
| 5. Virginia | 203,307 |
| 6. Missouri | 147,417 |
| 7. Florida | 145,219 |
| 8. Connecticut | 134,018 |
| 9. Ohio | 127,916 |
| 10. Maryland | 117,206 |
| Subtotal | 2,230,144 |
| Other 40 states | 1,169,856 |
| Total | 3,400,000 |

Source: Joseph V. Cartwright, *Potential Defense Work Force Dislocations and U.S. Defense Budget Cuts*, U.S. Department of Defense, Office of Economic Adjustment, Washington, D.C., 1990.

states (see table 4). However, the size of these states varies substantially, from giant California on the West Coast to Maryland on the East Coast.

Another way of looking at the data reveals that only six states depended on military outlays for 5 per cent or more of their jobs in 1988. In descending order of defence dependence, they are Connecticut (7.9 per cent), Massachusetts (7.0 per cent), Virginia (6.8 per cent), Missouri (6.0 per cent), Alaska (5.9 per cent), and Maryland (5.0 per cent). However, in many of these states, defence employment is clustered in a few metropolitan areas.

The future of defence activity in many regions will depend on decisions on individual weapon systems. Defence employment in Connecticut is primarily shipbuilding (General Dynamics Corporation) and aeroplane engine production (United Technologies). Missile-producing Raytheon is a key Massachusetts contractor. Fighter aircraft production at McDonnell Douglas accounts for the bulk of Missouri's defence employment.

In contrast, Virginia, Alaska, and Maryland are the locations for a great number of Defense Department installations, bases, and offices. Large shifts in their defence-generated employment will result from substantial changes in the size and composition of the armed forces.

## Repercussions and responses

Great pressures exist in the United States, especially from the larger centres of defence activity, to convert the production of the major contractors from military to civilian work. That sounds so eminently sensible that people may wonder what all the fuss is about. Reality, of course, is quite complicated.

To be sure, the providers of standard equipment used by both the armed forces and civilians – gasoline, office supplies, and medical equipment are good examples – suffer no great adjustments. Their economic health depends primarily on maintaining high levels of aggregate demand. The fortunes of individual companies will vary with their ability to maintain market share.

### Conversion and diversification

The specialized contractors are quite another matter. Of course, it was relatively easy for the motor manufacturers after World War II to stop making tanks and planes and reconvert. In striking contrast, the specialized defence contractors of today never had to convert in the first place. History shows that each of them has tried repeatedly to use its capabilities in civilian markets – to convert or diversify away from military work. However, the results generally have been very disappointing, especially among the larger firms. Each has lost money on its conversion efforts. Although this painful experience is well known in the US defence industry, many of the participants in the current debate on defence conversion do not seem to be aware of the many past efforts.

Ever since the end of World War II, defence contractors have been trying to use their special talents in other areas of the economy. They have been extremely successful in diversifying into several large but very narrowly defined markets.

For example, the expansion from aircraft to missiles and space systems was a natural but noteworthy progression. Because it happened without a great degree of economic disruption, few appreciate the tremendous transformation of the airframe manufacturers into aerospace designers and producers. Several large aerospace companies too, have developed and manufactured substantial numbers of civilian passenger aircraft but, except for Boeing, profitability has been illusive.

113

However, the numerous attempts on the part of the larger, specialized defence contractors to penetrate civilian non-aerospace markets have not met with similar success. Their failed attempts literally range from canoes to coffins.[6]

Most of the diversification ventures outside of the defence/aerospace markets have been abandoned or sold off. The remainder generally operate at marginal levels. These negative experiences have been so frequent – and many of them have so drained the companies – that they now constitute a major obstacle to further diversification efforts. A recent survey of defence firms by the Center for Strategic and International Studies confirms this. A majority of the companies reported that they believe a reorientation to civilian production is "neither feasible nor desirable." Most of the remainder are focusing on civilian government opportunities.[7]

In 1983, Grumman introduced the Kubvan, hoping to open a new market for aluminum truck bodies. It abandoned the effort two years later. It sold its solar energy division in 1985 and Pearson Yacht in 1986. From 1983 to 1985, the company experienced a cumulative net loss in its non-aerospace commercial production of $15 million (since then this category has been merged in its financial reports with other more profitable items). Other major defence contractors report very similar experiences.

In 1983, McDonnell Douglas purchased Computer Sharing Services for $69 million. In 1985, it announced the objective of making its information service group a major segment of the corporation by the 1990s. Nevertheless, the information systems sector reported annual losses from 1983 to 1989. After losing $333 million in 1989, McDonnell Douglas reduced the size of the commercial part of the information systems operation and narrowed its focus. In 1990, the company sold its computer maintenance and hardware distribution subsidiary in Santa Ana, California.

In 1989, General Dynamics announced that it had "decided to stick to the defense business" and pursue only those new programmes for which the government need is "strong and valid." That statement can be appreciated by examining the accompanying financial report, which showed a substantial cumulative loss in the company's non-governmental programmes over the previous eight years.

Even Boeing – the most successful builder of commercial jet airliners – has reported a cumulative deficit in its non-aerospace, non-government sales. Boeing had entered the mass transit business in the 1970s to offset the decline in its helicopter business. After encountering much grief in dealing with the Department of Transportation, several large cities, and union restrictions, it left the business. At its peak, Boeing's transit production employed only 550 workers compared to 9,000 employees laid off by its helicopter division.

Curtiss-Wright provides the most extreme example of the short-comings of naive conversion efforts. This pioneering aviation firm – which built more aircraft during World War II than any other US company – acted on the assumption that the military market would never recover from its post-World War II lows. The company diversified with a vengeance into a host of miscellaneous industrial product areas. Curtiss-Wright never recovered to its previous height. While its former competitors now enjoy annual sales of aircraft, missiles, and space vehicles measured in the billions, the company's revenues from its assortment of parts and components now total a modest $200 million a year.

The actual numbers on the aerospace industry's diversification look much better than would be expected from its experiences, but that is deceptive. By 1975, the non-aerospace sales by the major aerospace companies rose to $4 billion, or 15 per cent of their revenues. The 1980 total of non-aerospace sales, $11 billion, came to 19 per cent of the industry's aggregate volume. In 1990, the aerospace industry reported non-aerospace sales of $22 billion, or 17 per cent of its total volume for the year, a smaller ratio than a decade earlier.

Even these modest figures on the ability to diversify turn out to be misleading (see table 5). For example, Rockwell International, a major defence contractor, reports that its civilian sales rose from 55 per cent of its total revenues in 1987 to more than 75 per cent in 1989. However, the company was formed as the result of a merger between Rockwell-Standard (an established company in civilian markets) and North American Aviation, a mainstay defence supplier. The recent growth in the corporation's civilian business came about mainly from expansion in the Rockwell-Standard divisions, rather than from diversification of the aviation divisions.

The Rockwell form of expansion in civilian production surely is helpful from the viewpoint of the shareholder interest in diversification of risk. However, it furnishes little indication of the ability to use the factories, people, and other defence industry resources in civilian markets. The company's 1985 purchase of Allen-Bradley, a leading producer of electronic and electrical controls for industrial automation, was probably a wise move for the shareholders, but it did not represent conversion of defence capabilities.

115

Table 5  **Aerospace industry sales by customer calendar year 1975–1990 (US$bn)**

| Year | Aerospace products and service | | | | Other products and services | Grand total |
|---|---|---|---|---|---|---|
| | U.S. Dept. of Defense | NASA and other govt. agencies | Other customers | Total aerospace | | |
| 1975 | $13.1 | $2.8 | $8.9 | $24.9 | $4.8 | 29.7 |
| 1976 | 13.4 | 2.9 | 8.2 | 24.5 | 5.3 | 29.8 |
| 1977 | 14.4 | 3.0 | 8.7 | 26.1 | 6.1 | 32.2 |
| 1978 | 15.5 | 3.2 | 12.2 | 30.9 | 6.8 | 37.7 |
| 1979 | 18.9 | 3.5 | 15.3 | 37.7 | 7.7 | 45.4 |
| 1980 | 22.8 | 4.1 | 19.0 | 45.9 | 8.8 | 54.7 |
| 1981 | 27.2 | 4.7 | 21.1 | 53.1 | 10.9 | 64.0 |
| 1982 | 34.0 | 4.9 | 17.5 | 56.4 | 11.4 | 67.8 |
| 1983 | 41.6 | 5.9 | 19.2 | 66.6 | 13.3 | 80.0 |
| 1984 | 46.0 | 6.1 | 17.5 | 69.6 | 11.4 | 83.5 |
| 1985 | 53.2 | 6.3 | 21.0 | 80.5 | 16.1 | 96.6 |
| 1986 | 59.2 | 6.2 | 23.0 | 88.5 | 18.3 | 106.2 |
| 1987 | 61.8 | 6.8 | 23.0 | 91.7 | 18.3 | 110.0 |
| 1988 | 61.3 | 7.9 | 26.2 | 95.5 | 19.1 | 114.6 |
| 1989 | 58.5 | 9.6 | 29.9 | 98.0 | 19.6 | 117.6 |
| 1990 | 56.8 | 12.0 | 40.8 | 109.5 | 21.9 | 131.4 |

Source: Aerospace Industries Association.

The Rockwell experience is not unique among defence contractors, although others were less successful even in "stockholder diversification." After several decades of trying to penetrate the electronics market through internal product diversification, Lockheed purchased Sanders Associates in 1986. Three years later, the company closed down the main plant of its older electronics division. Only about 15 per cent of the employees there were moved to New Hampshire to work at Lockheed Sanders.

## Why did diversification fail?

A common set of themes arises from studying the diversification experiences of military contractors. The major defence companies are very special business organizations. They are outstanding at what they are set up to do – to design and produce state-of-the-art weapons. But to do so, they differ from typical commercial companies in fundamental ways.

Compared with commercially oriented companies, US defence

firms have very highly specialized technology, relatively low capitalization, little if any commercial marketing capabilities, and limited experience in producing at high volume and low unit cost. Moreover, their entire administrative structure is geared to the unique reporting and control requirements of the governmental customer. Those defence firms that do operate in civilian markets maintain operationally separated, insulated divisions that have little contact with each other, merely reporting to the same top management.

The lack of commercial marketing experience is another familiar refrain in defence industry circles. Grumman developed and tried to sell a mini-van years before Chrysler popularized the vehicle. The project failed because of the lack of a distribution system.

It is not hard to understand why defence company managements have become so reluctant to move from fields they have mastered into lines of business quite alien to them. Their lack of knowledge of non-defence industries is pervasive. It includes ignorance of products, production methods, advertising and distribution, financial arrangements, funding of research and development, contracting forms, and the very nature of the private customer's demands.

Clearly, the type of company that can successfully design and build a new multibillion dollar ICBM network or space exploration system has a very different capability from that of the soap, steel, toy, or other typical cost-conscious but low-technology company operating in the commercial economy.

The point made here was underscored recently when the chief executive of Martin Marietta, a large and successful defence contractor, was asked by the Russians how to convert a tank-producing facility into a refrigerator factory. His response was to tear down the tank plant and build a new refrigerator factory.

## R&D resources

As conventionally measured, there will be no peace dividend for the United States to enjoy as a result of the end of the Cold War. After all, the military build-up of the 1980s was financed out of borrowed funds. To argue about the different civilian uses of the defence savings is an exercise in futility. Because of the rising budget deficit, there is no excess cash sitting in the Federal Treasury and available to be spent on all sorts of worthy civilian endeavours.

But, in a more fundamental sense, there is a potential peace dividend which ultimately may be very substantial. It is in the form of the scientists, engineers, skilled craftsmen, and the special equipment they use which are becoming available as a result of the substantial reduction in defence production. If these valuable resources can be put to productive use in the civilian sectors of the economy, the benefit will be great – in the form of a quickened pace of innovation and enhanced industrial productivity and competitiveness, and ultimately a higher living standard of the society.

As shown in the previous section, the obstacles to the direct conversion from defence to civilian production are very great. However, over its history, the United States has been a very mobile society. Indeed, many of the people leaving defence work originally came from civilian employment. Increases in civilian demand for research and development are vital to that transition.

Indeed, many people advocate large-scale direct subsidies to high-tech civilian companies. Such measures are undesirable for many reasons. They politicize the technological choices. As has been demonstrated so frequently, government financing often goes to the project with the strongest political support, rather than the proposal with the most compelling scientific justification. Moreover, in a period of budget stringency, it is difficult to rationalize financial support to business when benefits to other parts of the society are being squeezed.

Yet the most basic reason to oppose expenditure subsidies for technology (as opposed to research) is that government is not very good at choosing among technological alternatives. A better approach is to put the onus on private institutions to select the technological undertakings and to risk their own capital. The result is far more likely to meet the needs of the market-place.

There are important roles for government in advancing technology and thus in assisting the transfer of R&D resources from military to civilian pursuits. First of all, because of the powerful externalities generated by basic research, no individual business firm has incentive to devote much of its resources to this portion of R&D. However, precisely because of the large benefits to society – many in the form of applied technology – government has a major responsibility for ensuring adequate financing of basic research.

In addition, government should reduce the large array of statutory and administrative roadblocks that it has erected, albeit often without meaning to reduce technological progress. In the case of some of the most important high-tech industries – chemicals, pharmaceuticals, and biotechnology – the major constraints on commercializing the advances in technology arise from burdensome government regula-

118

tion. Many regulatory agencies exempt existing facilities, product, and processes from their directives. As a result, the main burden of rapidly expanding environmental and safety regulations falls on new enterprises, new undertakings, and new technology. The sensible answer is not to provide offsetting subsidies but to streamline the government's elaborate rulemaking apparatus.

Other reforms in government policies and practices would help develop civilian technology. A simpler and more effective patent system would encourage the creation and diffusion of new product ideas. Such a change would ensure that smaller inventors are not overwhelmed by the cost of obtaining patents. Also, larger firms would be encouraged to seek patents rather than protecting their new products and processes by maintaining secrecy.[8]

In addition, revisions in the antitrust laws would help. The current statutes impede the formation of joint ventures to develop new technology. However, the capital requirements to develop generic technology are often beyond the financial capability of a single firm. Waiving or amending the antitrust laws would be a far more sensible – and economical – approach than providing governmental financial support.

## Outlook

An extended period of slow growth – which characterizes the American economy at present – is a difficult time to deal with the problems of transferring defence resources to civilian uses. The difficulty is compounded by a massive and rising deficit in the federal budget, which inhibits the government from taking strong anticyclical tax and spending measures to stimulate production and employment.

Under the circumstances, there is an opportunity for economic concerns to feed back into decisions on national defence policy – and not always necessarily in a constructive way. The most obvious example is the pressure to increase sales of armaments to third world nations. As a general proposition, requests from the less developed nations to buy the latest US weapon systems are weighed against the desire to avoid contributing to a renewed arms race in those regions.

Nevertheless, the present weakened condition of the US defence industry – plus the concern with maintaining an adequate supporting industrial base – is increasing the likelihood of a go-ahead for multibillion dollar sales of supersonic fighter jet aeroplanes to Saudi Arabia and Taiwan.[9] To be effective, restraints that have been proposed on these sales must be multilateral, not unilateral.

Barring a new and unforeseen threat to the US national security, the major US defence firms will look significantly different by the mid-1990s than they do today. They will be much smaller and there will be fewer of them. But the need for a ready defence industrial base will continue. The existing inventory of weapons will be depleted by wear and tear, training accidents, and technological obsolescence. Thus, if they can minimize "conversion" attempts which drain their finances and instead streamline their operations, they can survive in the smaller military market without special subsidies.

Surely no great unmet commercial needs exist and, to the extent that they do, they are being adequately met by those commercial companies which are highly experienced in those markets. An indication of the future of the defence industry was Lockheed's painful decision in early 1990 to close down all its aircraft production at Burbank, the city where it was founded. Honeywell spun off its torpedo and munitions business to its shareholders after trying unsuccessfully to sell it to other companies. Emerson Electric also spun off its defence divisions. Varian Associates dropped most of its defence operations to focus on more profitable lines of electronic equipment.

On the positive side, defence contractors can be expected to continue to search for new applications of their existing product lines, especially in markets close to the ones they now dominate. Grumman is working on a $1 billion contract with the US Postal Service to build over 99,000 delivery trucks by 1993. The Sikorsky Division of United Technologies produced $206 million's worth of helicopters for the Coast Guard for intercepting drug smugglers. Lockheed sold two radar planes to the Customs Service for $58 million. Boeing has sold some of its Vertol helicopters to oil companies to service offshore drilling platforms.

Also, Martin Marietta won a $900 million contract from the Federal Aviation Administration to help overhaul the nation's air traffic control system. The list goes on. But, in the aggregate, these close civilian applications of military products are a minor fraction of the government market. The $1 billion being spent annually for drug interdiction equipment is dwarfed by the $120 billion allocation each year to the development and acquisition of weapon systems. Moreover, it is too soon to say whether these new diversification efforts will be any more successful financially than the poor record of the past.

It is ironic that the strongest support for the "conversion" of defence companies comes from those who had most vehemently attacked the wasteful, inefficient, cost-plus operating environment of the "military-industrial complex." On the contrary, it should be expected that the critics would welcome the rare opportunity to move resources out of those "wasteful, inefficient" companies to more efficiency-minded civilian-oriented enterprises.

It is wrong to concentrate national policy on how to keep large defence companies large. That is the wrong question. It makes much more sense to focus on generating higher levels of demand for technological advance and for doing and using research and development in the public and private sectors. That approach shifts the debate on defence conversion away from government planning and control and to encouraging innovative civil entrepreneurship, and that is a very different public policy agenda.

## Notes

1. This paper draws heavily on Murray Weidenbaum (1992), *Small Wars, Big Defense: Paying for the Military After the Cold War*. Oxford University Press, Oxford. (1992).
2. See Joint Chiefs of Staff (1992), *National Military Strategy, 1992*. Department of Defense, Washington, D.C.
3. C.F. Bastable (1895), *Public Finance*. Macmillan, New York, pp. 67–68.
4. There is also widespread agreement that, if necessary, for high priority national security purposes, the economy could support increases in defence outlays. See Murray Weidenbaum (1990), "Defense Spending and the American Economy." *Defence Economics*, April, pp. 233–242.
5. See Lawrence R. Klein and Kei Mori (1973), "The Impact of Disarmament on Aggregate Economic Activity." In Bernard Udis, ed., *The Economic Consequences of Reduced Military Spending*. Lexington Books, Lexington, Mass., pp. 76–77.
6. *Economic Adjustment/Conversion (1985)*. President's Economic Adjustment Committee; John E. Lynch, ed. Washington, D.C. (1987). *Economic Adjustment and Conversion of Defense Industries*. Westview Press Boulder, Colo.; Suzanne Gordon and Dave McFadden, eds. (1984), *Economic Conversion*. Ballinger Publishing, Cambridge, Mass.
7. Leo Reddy (1991), *How U.S. Defense Industries View Diversification*. Center for Strategic and International Studies, Washington, D.C., pp. 5–6.
8. Murray Weidenbaum (1992), "Sponsoring Research and Development." *Society*, July/August, pp. 39–47.
9. Eric Schmitt (1992), "Jet Sales to Saudis and Taiwan Weighed." *New York Times*, 25 August, p. A8.

# Comments on chapter 6

## 1. Takashi Inoguchi

Professor Weidenbaum portrays in his excellent paper the picture of defence reductions and their impacts on the US economic and technological development in the intermediate term of 5 to 20 years. He is basically optimistic about the positive impacts of defence reductions. In the short term, he opines that there may be some difficulties in the process of substantially reducing the size of defence production, as the United States does not see any major military threat except for small regionally confined conflicts immediately appearing on the horizon and slightly converting it into civilian-oriented production, as many defence production firms are not accustomed to civilian-oriented production and marketing. Defence reductions are painful to most defence producers especially when the US economy has not been performing very well recently.

Yet in immediate terms, he argues, the prospects for the US economy reinvigorating itself and for defence reductions to take place without creating more pain, are encouraging. Even if defence production facilities are hard to convert into civilian-oriented production in the short term, the prospect for a greater pool of scientists and engineers released from defence-related work to civilian-related work in science and technology means that the American economy

122

will have greater chances of utilizing new invention and innovation for more efficiently run civilian-oriented enterprises.

Furthermore, it seems to me that he is saying two important things about the nature of defence spending. First, he assumes that, because of the end of the Cold War more continuity is discerned than discontinuity. Despite substantial reductions in 5 to 10 years from now, the world will remain as dangerous as before even if the nature of the danger may have changed somewhat. As long as no candidate can be seen to be coming forward to take over the United States' position as leading military power, it will continue to assume that role even if the scale and mode of exercising power may differ somewhat. And once the current slow growth of the US economy is replaced by a more vigorous growth, which is more likely from the late 1990s into the 2000s, not only for the US economy but also the world economy as a whole, then the substantial defence reductions that have been taking place since the late 1980s are likely to be less accentuated towards 2000. In other words, defence spending may be invigorated again in tandem with the reinvigorated economic growth. After all, it is not easy to find a number of cases in which military spending is not basically proportional to economic growth rate in the longer term.

Secondly, the negative impacts of US current defence reductions seem to be somewhat offset by the military build-up in most parts of Pacific Asia, which have started to purchase an alarmingly large volume of military weapons from the United States as well as other suppliers. Since Pacific Asia has been registering the highest economic growth rate in the world, it may not be surprising. But what is alarming is that Pacific Asia has been moving very rapidly into being an excessively heavily armed area without any scheme of moderating its military build-up. If defence reductions in the United States can be achieved more smoothly by arms exports to Pacific Asia, the urgent need exists for the process of regional security regime formation in Pacific Asia to be encouraged by the United States and all countries in the region.

Taking this opportunity, I would like to raise three general points on arms reductions in the United States as portrayed by Professor Weidenbaum. Since I have not had the opportunity to read his latest book entitled *Small Wars, Big Defense* (1992), I may ask for his pardon if my points have already been elaborated there.

First, all politics is local, as Tip O'Neill of Massachusetts puts it. As Gordon Adams notes, "Congress is caught between a rock and a hard place. The rock is the desire for a peace dividend. The hard place is jobs in your district."[1] Professor Weidenbaum seems more than mildly optimistic about this aspect of the politics of defence reductions.

Secondly, all politics are partisan. Bill Clinton has won in the US Presidential election. Democrats will assume power in 1993. Thus, for instance, the Bush-Cheney revised Five-Year Defense Plan put forward by Secretary of Defense Dick Cheney in late 1991 and early 1992 will be altered. Instead, the idea that constituted William Kaufmann's and John Steinbrunner's criticisms of the revised Bush-Cheney Plan may be incorporated in the Clinton defence policy. Their idea is "to rethink and restructure US defense planning on the basis of a collective arrangement among many national governments around the globe, rather than trying to use the defense budget to perpetuate US military preponderance unilaterally."[2]

Thirdly, all politics are international. As I have touched on already, Pacific Asia has been quite energetic in making a defence build-up. What is alarming is that Pacific Asia has been moving very rapidly to a heavily armed area without any scheme of moderating its moves.

## 2. Jean-Claude Berthélemy

The fact that a good deal of the peace dividend could be lost as a result of the many difficulties brought about by the transition process should certainly be an important matter of concern for a number of OECD governments. In this regard, Professor Weidenbaum affords a valuable contribution, in particular by recalling the several cases of unsuccessful attempts of conversion in the military industry. On the other hand, it is undeniable that in the long run a reduction in arms expenditures should be beneficial to the economy as a whole, by releasing scarce resources; a point on which I have no disagreement. *Transition difficulties could threaten the whole process of military expenditure reduction*, for obvious political economic reasons, as has been observed during the presidential campaign in the United States, even though the election of President Clinton has shown that people are ready to vote for a candidate in favour of significant military expenditure reductions. It is, therefore, important to set up policies to facilitate the reallocation of resources from military to civilian industries. Professor Weidenbaum's paper is also useful in providing some ideas to support this transition process.

Opinions expressed here are those of Jean-Claude Berthélemy and should not be attributed to the OECD Secretariat.

## Difficulties of conversion

I will not challenge the assertion that direct conversion in the military industry might be difficult, even though the size of the military reduction is much smaller than after World War II or after the Viet Nam War. Such difficulties are noticeable not only in the United States, but also in European countries like France. I would tend, however, to think that *using past experience on this matter is not totally convincing*; denying on this ground any gain in future direct conversion efforts is to my mind a bit too extreme. Also, a successful conversion requires a *corporate culture* of defence contractors, which might have been impossible to obtain when this business was profitable. However, now that military budgets are being cut down, there might be something to be gained in conversion, and the experience of the past 15 years cannot tell us much about these opportunities.

The arguments given by Professor Weidenbaum to explain the inability of specialized defence contractor firms to transform their activities are not necessarily all convincing. In particular, he argues that the lack of commercial marketing experience and knowledge of non-defence industries is an obstacle to direct conversion. But these assets can be purchased in the market, through hiring experts from the civilian industry. Also, arguing that the transition is difficult because one cannot turn a high-tech company into a low-technology company is a bit partial: I presume that we all agree about that, but there are also other high-tech activities besides the defence industry.

Therefore, I would tend to put less emphasis on direct conversion difficulties than Professor Weidenbaum has. As a matter of fact, Professor Klein gave us, earlier in this conference, examples of successful conversion attempts in the case of the American military industry. This having been said, it seems reasonable to think that a significant cut in military equipment budgets will imply transition costs, due to existing obstacles to *direct conversion*.

## Policies

Three different kinds of costs should be identified, corresponding to the primary factors involved in military production: employees, equipment, and intangible assets of the firms. *Labour is certainly the most important of these factors*, due to the high content of skilled labour in the military industry. It is also the more mobile, at least in the United States, so that potential transition difficulties should not

125

be overestimated. However, policies oriented towards promoting a move of these workers to civilian industries could be worthwhile, and in some cases necessary, and in this sense the idea of supporting basic research activities might be relevant: scientists previously working in the high-tech military industry should be most useful in this basic research. One could add that, in the United States, some of the skilled former defence workers could be usefully employed in the education sector, in which investments are badly needed.

With respect to equipment and intangible assets, some losses are probably unavoidable, but some of these assets are still of some value, for instance, patents on dual technologies, specifically designed for weapons production but usable in civilian production. In sum, if as asserted by Professor Weidenbaum, a direct conversion is almost impossible, a partial one should be attempted anyway, through the sale of those assets which are of some value to the civilian industry. Facilitating this partial conversion should be a policy objective in developed countries involved in defence expenditure reduction.

At present, the federal funds allocated to conversion assistance are of a limited size in the United States ($1.5 billion in 1993). One may wonder whether these investments are sufficient to avoid, in particular, skilled workers released from the military industry remaining unemployed.

Finally, I would like to say that promoting this transition process is not only important from the point of view of improving economic conditions in developed countries. At present, an important side effect of cuts in military budgets in the United States and in Western and Eastern Europe is increased competition in the selling of weapons to developing countries. Paradoxically, as a consequence, these countries are offered a new incentive to buy more and more sophisticated military equipment, as we have seen for instance in the case of Taiwanese jet fighters. Therefore, efforts oriented towards limiting our military expenditures should be combined with an improved control of arms sales.

## Notes

1. Quoted by Helen Dewar, "With the Cold War won, jobs are being lost," *Washington Post*, 14 February 1992, which is in turn cited in Michael Ward and David Davis (1992), "Sizing up the peace dividend: Economic growth and military spending in the United States, 1948–1986." *American Political Science Review* 86 (3), pp. 748–755.
2. Ward and Davis, *op. cit.*

# Part 3
# Global economic consequences of reductions in military spending

# 7

# The impact on the world economy of reductions in military expenditures and military arms exports

Warwick J. McKibbin and Stephan Thurman

## Abstract

The end of the Cold War has reduced global military requirements over the foreseeable future. The Persian Gulf War has graphically illustrated the problem of allowing developing nations to arm themselves in the global market for military equipment. These wars have raised the probability of substantial reductions in the production of military arms in the industrial countries and a reduction of arms trade between these countries and developing countries.

This paper attempts to quantify the likely impact on the world economy of possible cut-backs in both production and trade of military arms over the next two decades. We base our analysis on an empirical general equilibrium multi-country model with forward-looking production sectors, and careful treatment of production

This paper reflects work in progress on a project sponsored under Brookings' Network Program for Encouraging Empirical Research in International Macroeconomics (NERIM), which is supported in part by the Ford Foundation and the John D. and Catherine T. MacArthur Foundation. The authors thank Ralph Bryant, Susan Collins, and other colleagues at the Brookings Institution and the Congressional Budget Office for helpful discussions on the topic of this paper. Tomas Bok provided excellent technical assistance. The views expressed are those of the authors and do not necessarily reflect the views of the staff or Trustees of the Brookings Institution, the OECD, or the US Congressional Budget Office.

and the interaction of trade and asset flows between countries. This model, which is called the McKibbin-Sachs Global model, is used to simulate a number of scenarios. We do not address the problems of implementation of the policies but focus on the economic consequences of these policies.

We find that the effects of gradually cutting back military production and directly limiting military exports may be stimulative in the short run if the cuts are credibly announced in advance and the revenue is used for permanent reduction in future fiscal deficits. As the cuts are implemented between 1993 and 1996, there is an inevitable period of unemployed resources but over time these resources are re-employed and the world economy experiences higher income levels by the end of the current decade.

## I. Introduction

The end of the Cold War has important implications for the future direction of the world economy. There are many immediate aspects of this change such as the reunification of Germany, and the collapse and restructuring of the economies of Eastern Europe and the former Soviet Union (hereafter referred to as EFSU) which have already had dramatic effects on the world economy.[1] In this paper we focus on another aspect of the end of the cold war; that is the possible path of future military expenditures within the industrialized economies and the likely implication of this for the world economy into the next century. McNamara (1991) and Kaufmann and Steinbruner (1991) amongst others argue that it is feasible to reduce US military expenditure by 50 per cent from the level in 1990 to a level of around 3 per cent of GDP by the end of this decade. Other members of the Organization for Economic Co-operation and Development (OECD) are also likely to be cutting defence budgets given the decline in the threat of Soviet military activity although to date the response of NATO members in Europe has been cautious.[2] We explore the implications of a cut in US defence expenditures where these expenditures are limited to 3.2 per cent of GDP after 1997 and of moderate cuts in European countries which hold defence expenditures to 2 per cent of GDP by 1997. The likelihood of these cuts given political considerations is debatable although military budgets as a share of GDP have already begun to fall gradually in many of these countries. Despite the considerable uncertainty about likely scenarios, a sizeable cut-back in European military expenditure (although

130

substantially less than in the United States) provides a useful benchmark for evaluating other scenarios.

It is likely that a substantial reduction in military expenditures will have negative short-run impacts on OECD countries but over time the gains of freeing up the resources used for defence may be positive. The timing and magnitude of the effects are important for policy makers given that other policies may need to adjust during the transition phase. The first part of this paper focuses on these issues.

The shape of the new world order is still unclear although the Iraqi invasion of Kuwait and subsequent Persian Gulf War in 1991 illustrates that it is quite possible that the Cold War between the two superpowers could be replaced by a number of regional conflicts. Some of these conflicts could be the direct consequence of the transition from a high level of military expenditure to a low level of military expenditure in industrialized countries, as weapons are recycled to developing countries. Indeed in the recent CFE (Conventional Armed Forces in Europe) treaty there is no restriction on exporting either new or second-hand weapons to other countries. This leaves open the possibility that the military equipment that is removed from the conventional forces of the signatory countries will be recycled to other countries.[3] It seems that a reasonable response to this is to seek to cut substantially the exports of military arms by industrial countries to developing countries. The second focus of this paper is to explore the key aspects and magnitude of a policy of cutting arms exports from the OECD and EFSU countries to developing countries.

Because of the global nature of the issues outlined above and the need for quantifying the various scenarios we turn to a global simulation model as the basis for this study. The model is a new version of the McKibbin-Sachs Global (MSG) model[4] which has been extended to give country detail for Canada, France, Italy, and the United Kingdom.[5] This model without the disaggregation of Europe has recently been used for two related studies of defence and arms trade policy by the U.S. Congressional Budget Office.[6]

A number of important features make the MSG model useful for considering the consequences of changes in future paths of military expenditures and arms trade. First, the flows of goods and capital between each country and region in the model are explicitly treated in the model. Secondly, announcements of future policies have important effects through forward-looking behaviour by firms, households, and financial markets. Other important features include a well-defined long run of the world economy based on a Solow-Swan neoclassical growth model,[7] with exogenous underlying technical progress and population growth in different economies. In the short run, however, the dynamics of the global economy towards this growth path are determined by a mix of Keynesian-style rigidities in the goods and labour markets and optimal decisions by households and firms, conditional on expected future paths of the global economy. In addition, important stock-flow relations are imposed within the model: investment leads to physical capital accumulation; fiscal deficits lead to accumulation of government debt; and current account deficits lead to the accumulation of foreign claims against domestic production. Asset prices are forward looking and are consistent with the imposition of intertemporal budget constraints; all outstanding stocks of assets are ultimately serviced. In addition to providing a well-defined theoretical framework, it is shown in McKibbin and Sachs (1991) that this model does reasonably well in accounting for the global experience of the 1980s.

The paper proceeds as follows. In section 2 we give an overview of the historical experience of military expenditures and arms trade in the world for the last ten years. The MSG model is introduced briefly and the simulation approach is outlined in section 3. In section 4, we consider the global impacts of a reduction in military expenditure in the industrial regions announced in 1993 under the assumption that the fiscal resources which become available are used to cut budget deficits in each country. We start with a baseline which assumes the US gradually cuts the defence budget from 5.2 per cent in 1992 to 4.8 per cent of GDP from 1993 forever. We then assume that in 1993 it is announced that, commencing in 1994, the US defence budget will be cut further to 3.2 per cent of GDP by 1997. It then stays at that per cent of GDP forever. We also assume that other OECD countries or regions with military expenditures in excess of 2 per cent of GDP in 1991 gradually cut their military budgets commencing in 1993 to 2 per cent of GDP by 1997. These policies are announced in 1993 and are assumed to be completely credible.

In section 5 we focus on arms trade. We present a scenario in which there is a reduction in total arms exports from OECD countries and EFSU of $26 billion in 1992 US dollars, commencing in 1993. This reduction is then kept constant as a share of US GDP forever. Each OECD and EFSU exporting country cuts back its exports in proportion to that country's share in total arms trade. For example, the United States cuts back exports by $6.5 billion in 1993. We then make two assumptions about foreign assistance which accompanies this reduction in arms shipments. The first assumption is that transfers from each OECD and EFSU region to the developing countries are also cut by 50 per cent of the cut in arms exports. The second assumption is that transfers from the industrialized countries to the developing regions are unaffected by the cut in arms exports and this aid is channelled into demand for non-military goods and services.

A summary and conclusion are contained in section 6.

## II. Military expenditure and arms trade

In this section we give an overview of recent trends in military expenditure and military arms trade. A number of data sources are available including the U.S. Arms Control and Disarmament Agency (ACDA) and the Stockholm Institute for Peace Research (SIPRI). Before presenting this data, we should stress that there are problems with using data on military expenditure and arms trade. Problems with reporting and other problems are discussed in a variety of places including ACDA (1990), CBO (1992c, appendix A), SIPRI (1991 and 1992), and Sen (1990). We rely on data from ACDA except where noted that we have used more up to date SIPRI data.

## (a) Military expenditures

Military spending by industrialized regions and developing regions for the period from 1979 to 1989 are shown in figures 1a and 1b. We also show data for selected OECD countries from 1987 to 1991 in figure 1c. The data for each region or country is scaled by the Gross National Product (GNP) of that country or region. This gives a measure of the proportion of the country's resources devoted to military expenditure.

The data show that there was a gradual rise in the ratio of world military spending to GNP from the beginning of the period through to 1983 which peaked at 5.7 per cent of GNP. Spending as a share of GNP then declined gradually to 4.9 per cent of GNP by 1989. This pattern of build-up and subsequent decline is consistent across each region shown except perhaps the South Asia region which peaked in 1987. Although there are similar trends in the data, the shares of resources devoted to military expenditures differ substantially across regions. In figure 1b it is clear that countries in the Middle East spent by far the largest proportion of GNP on military outlays. At 17.2 per cent of GNP in 1983 this was almost three times the world average.

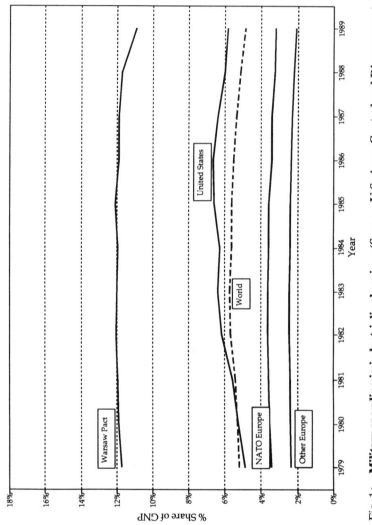

Fig. 1a    **Military spending in industrialized regions (Source: U.S. Arms Control and Disarmament Agency [1990].** *World Military Expenditures and Arms Transfers*)

134

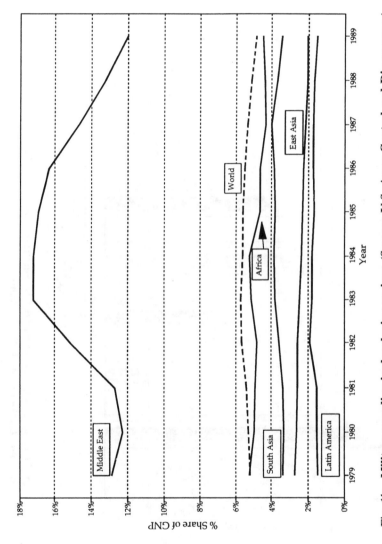

Fig. 1b  **Military spending in developing regions (Source: U.S. Arms Control and Disarmament Agency [1990].** *World Military Expenditures and Arms Transfers)*

135

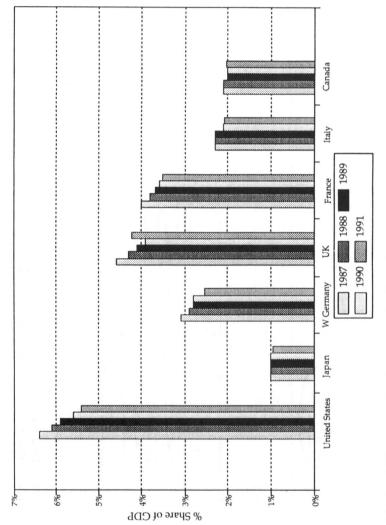

Fig. 1c **Military spending in selected OECD countries (Source: *SIPRI Yearbook 1992; OECD World Economic Outlook* [1992]. No. 51, June**

136

The next highest regional spending was the Warsaw Pact countries which spent close to 12 per cent of GNP in the same year. The only other country which allocated more than the world average to military expenditures was the United States which peaked at 6.6 per cent of GNP in 1986.

Although only shown for OECD countries, the trend decline in military outlays has continued through 1990 and 1991 for most regions.[8] The U.S. Congressional Budget Office projects discretionary defence spending in the United States to be down to 4.8 per cent of GDP by 1993 from 5.7 per cent of GDP in 1991, under the assumption that the discretionary spending caps of the Budget Enforcement Act of 1990 are binding.[9] By 1997 this figure is projected to be down to 4.3 per cent of GDP (around $335 billion in 1992 dollars) under the assumption of binding spending caps and a minimal cut-back in resources devoted to defence (source CBO [1992c] table 11 and authors' calculations). With the proposals in the President's 1993 budget, this ratio would still be 3.8 per cent of GDP (around $292 billion in 1992 dollars) by 1997.

Under these scenarios the share of US resources devoted to military spending would still be larger than those in other major OECD countries. A comparison for the years 1987 through 1991 in figure 1c illustrates this. The United Kingdom spent just over 4 per cent of GDP on military equipment in 1991 followed by France (3.5 per cent) and West Germany (2.5 per cent).

## (b) Arms trade

Total world exports of arms in constant and current dollars continued to rise through 1989. The data for the exports of the six largest exporters from 1979 to 1989 are shown in figure 2. These are the former Soviet Union, United States, France, West Germany, United Kingdom, and China. The figures are in billions of constant 1989 dollars. The late 1980s sees declines in exports of each country (despite a rise in global arms trade). New data from SIPRI (1992) for 1990 and 1991 (not shown) suggest a decline in global arms exports by 25 per cent in 1991 relative to 1990. The composition is also quite different due to the impact of the Gulf War and the arms embargo against Iraq which had a particularly large impact on French exports of military arms.[10] SIPRI data also suggest that German exports rose substantially in 1990 and 1991.

Arms imports in billions of 1989 constant dollars by major devel-

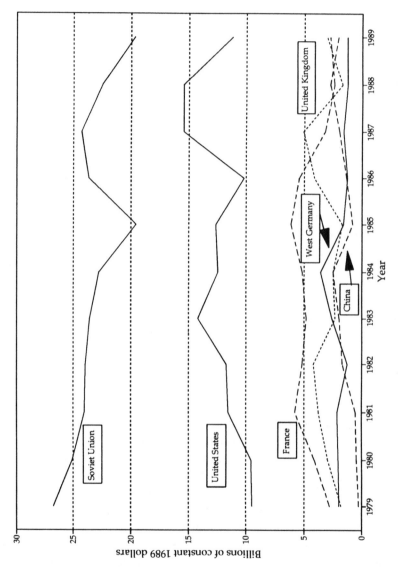

Fig. 2  **Arms exports, by country (Source: U.S. Arms Control and Disarmament Agency [1990].** *World Military Expenditures and Arms Transfers)*

138

oping country regions from 1979 to 1989 are shown next in figure 3. Absolute imports of arms by these regions fell from 1987 through to 1989 although the share of South Asia has grown whereas the shares of the Middle East and Africa have shrunk. These same data are presented again in figure 4 although this time they are scaled by regional GNP. The trend declines in African and Middle Eastern arms imports are accentuated in this case.

According to SIPRI (1992) data, the import picture for 1990 and 1991 is dominated by the United Nations Arms Embargo against Iraq. In addition imports by Israel in 1991 increased significantly which tends to offset the decline in Middle East imports. The SIPRI data for South Asia show a decline in imports which is dominated by reductions in military imports by India and Pakistan in 1990 and 1991 relative to 1989. Imports by East Asia also tend to fall over 1990 and 1991, although within this overall trend imports of major weapons by Thailand more than doubled in 1991 relative to 1989.

## III. The framework for analysing the implications of alternative policies

We have outlined trends in world military expenditures and arms trade over the past decade and highlighted recent developments. In this section we will set out the framework that will be used to analyse alternative assumptions about future policies. The approach that we will follow here is to use a conceptual and empirical framework provided by a simulation model of the world economy which includes the key empirical linkages between major countries and regions in the world. We acknowledge that a plethora of possible problems can occur when using a specific model. But it is inevitable that a question such as cuts in budget deficits and changes in trading patterns needs a broader yet consistent framework that simple rules of thumb are incapable of providing. We choose for this purpose a new version of the McKibbin-Sachs Global model. This model has a number of attractive theoretical features, it has a good track record in explaining the world economy of the 1980s and has been useful projecting the problems facing Germany in the process of reunification.[11] Our goal in this paper is to use the insights from the model to highlight the major issues facing the world from possible scenarios.

The reader should refer to the cited references to the MSG model in this paper. The main reference is a recent book by McKibbin and Sachs (1991) which lays out the theoretical and empirical basis of the

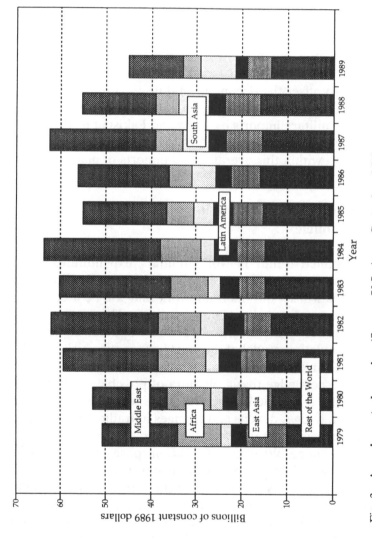

Fig. 3 **Arms imports, by region (Source: U.S. Arms Control and Disarmament Agency [1990].**
***World Military Expenditures and Arms Transfers)***

140

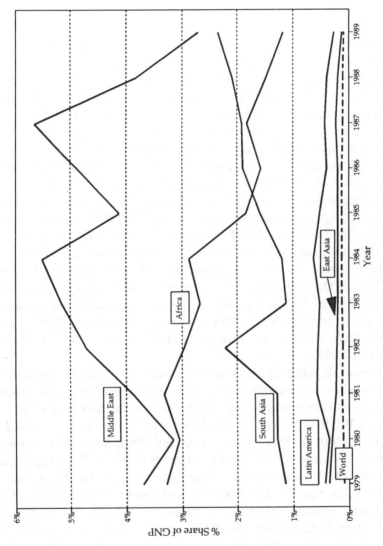

Fig. 4   **Arms imports in developing regions (Source: U.S. Arms Control and Disarmament Agency [1990].** *World Military Expenditures and Arms Transfers***)**

141

model as well as evaluating the tracking ability of the model over the 1980s. As already outlined in the introduction, a number of important features make the MSG model useful as a backdrop to our paper. First, it is a fully specified dynamic general equilibrium model with careful treatment of stock-flow relations such as the cumulation of investment into capital stocks, the cumulation of fiscal deficits into net asset stocks and the cumulation of current account deficits into foreign claims against domestic production. Secondly, the short run demand and supply sides of the major economies are incorporated. In the long run, supply is determined by neoclassical growth theory. Thirdly, the model incorporates a number of financial markets such as share markets and markets for short and long bonds in each of the industrial regions where prices are determined by intertemporal arbitrage relations as well as long-run sustainability conditions on fiscal deficits and current account positions. The modelling of forward looking expectations in these financial markets as well as some forward-looking behaviour in real spending decisions ensures that the effects of anticipated policy changes are well handled by this model. Finally the model has a global coverage. In the version used in this paper, the model contains separate country and regional models of the United States, Japan, Germany, the United Kingdom, France, Italy, Canada, the rest of the EMS (hereafter REMS), the rest of the OECD (hereafter ROECD), non-oil developing countries (hereafter LDCs), oil exporting developing countries (hereafter OPEC), and the economies of Eastern Europe and the former Soviet Union (hereafter EFSU).

The approach taken in this study is to use the model to simulate a number of alternative paths for military expenditure and arms trade. Each of these is considered separately so that the key issues can be drawn out. We first consider a simulation in which there is an OECD-wide reduction in defence expenditure credibly announced beginning from 1992. We start with a baseline consistent with CBO projections out to 1993 which assumes that military spending in the US gradually falls from 5.2 per cent of GDP in 1992 to 4.8 per cent of GDP in 1993. The baseline assumes that military spending remains at 4.8 per cent of GDP after 1993 forever. Similarly in other OECD countries we assume that baseline military expenditures remain at their 1991 shares of GDP from 1992 forever. For the shock simulation we assume an announcement of a fall in US defence spending beginning in 1994. The new path for defence expenditures is 4.4 per cent of GDP in 1994, 4.0 per cent of GDP in 1995, 3.6 per cent of GDP in 1996 and

3.2 per cent of GDP in 1997 and thereafter. The change in spending relative to baseline is therefore 0.4 per cent of GDP in 1994, 0.8 per cent of GDP in 1995, 1.2 per cent of GDP in 1996, and 1.6 per cent of GDP from 1997 onwards. In other OECD countries we assume that from 1992, all OECD countries with military expenditure above 2 per cent of GDP in the baseline cut this back smoothly to be at 2 per cent of GDP by 1997. Countries, such as Japan, that are well below 2 per cent of GDP do not alter their military outlays relative to baseline. These policies are announced in 1992 and are completely credible.

We next use the original baseline and then present a second scenario where there is a reduction in total arms exports from OECD countries and Eastern Europe and the former Soviet Union (EFSU) to developing countries of $26 billion in 1992 US dollars commencing in 1992.[12] This reduction is then kept constant as a share of US GDP forever. Each OECD and EFSU exporting country cuts back its exports in proportion to that country's share in total arms trade (based on 1989 ACDA data). For example, the United States cuts back exports by $6.5 billion in 1992 (25 per cent of the total). We then make two assumptions about foreign assistance which accompanies this change in exports. The first assumption is that transfers from the industrialized countries to the developing regions are cut by 50 per cent of the cut in military exports. The second assumption is that transfers from each country to the developing countries are unaffected by the cut in arms exports and this aid is channelled into non-military areas.

## IV. A reduction in OECD military expenditures

We now consider the first scenario. That is a policy announced in 1993 and completely credible to all participants in the financial markets and the real economy of each country that there is to be a further reduction in government military expenditures in most OECD countries, phased in during 1994 to 1997. As already outlined above, in the United States the cut-back is a reduction from 4.8 per cent of GDP in 1993 to 3.2 per cent of GDP by 1997. The timing is very important because of the forward-looking expectations in the model. Some cuts in military expenditure in 1993 are already built into the baseline. Hence the new information is an additional cut relative to where military spending would otherwise have been. In the other OECD countries we cut spending so that all countries that spend more than 2 per cent of GDP on military outlays in 1991 (e.g. France, Germany, the United Kingdom, Belgium, the Netherlands, and Norway) cut the level of military spending smoothly to 2 per cent of GDP by 1997.

The results for several key variables are presented in figures 5 to 9. These figures show the deviation from baseline of variables as a result of the policy changes. These variables are scaled so that real GDP is measured as a percentage deviation from base; the trade balance is measured as per cent of baseline GDP deviation from base (i.e. 0.5 per cent is 0.5 per cent of US GDP in the year indicated); the interest rate on 10-year bonds is measured as percentage point deviation (i.e. −1 on the vertical axis is a fall of 1 per cent or 100 basis points); and the nominal effective exchange rate is percentage deviation from base where a rise of 1 per cent is an appreciation of that country's exchange rate relative to an export weighted basket of other currencies. Results are presented for a subgroup of countries in the model to focus on some key results. These countries are the United States, Japan, Germany, the United Kingdom, and France.

Before examining the results, it is important to be clear about the policy regimes in place in each country. In analytical exercises studying a change in fiscal policy it is common to assume for monetary policy either that the stock of money is fixed or the nominal interest rate is fixed. As is well known, the simulation results for a fiscal shock can be very different under alternative assumptions about monetary policy. For members of the European Monetary System (EMS) we assume that monetary policy in each country is tied to targeting the exchange rate. In the results presented here we assume that France, Italy, the United Kingdom, and the REMS countries maintain parities within the EMS. The assumptions for Japan, Germany, and the United States are more problematic. To illustrate the importance of assumptions about monetary policy, the first set of results assume that the money supply is held at its baseline path in each of these three countries. The EMS members adjust monetary policies within the constraints of the EMS.

We only present results for real GDP in this case. These results are then followed by a complete set of results for the case in which monetary policy is adjusted in response to the shock. This second set of results is more plausible and will be the focus of our attention. However, it is useful to start with the case we present in figure 5 to separate the effects of the shock from the effects of the change in monetary policy.

Referring to figure 5, we find an interesting result. In 1993, when the reductions in defence expenditure over the period 1994 to 1997

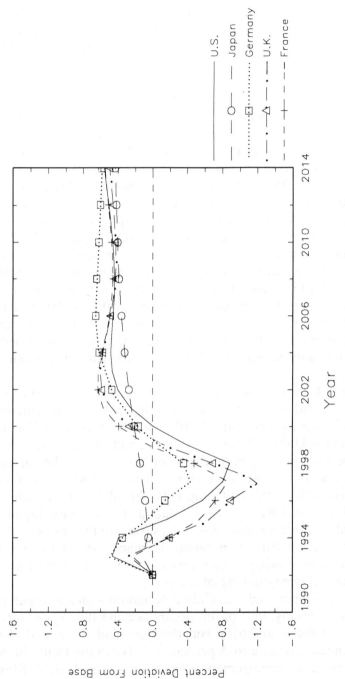

Fig. 5   Real GDP in selected countries: Simulated cut in military expenditures

are announced, the expected cut in fiscal expenditures actually raises GDP in each region reported (and indeed in all regions in the model). The essential reason is that no spending cuts are made in the United States in 1993 relative to those already expected in 1993 and the cuts in Europe are small relative to what had been expected for 1993 and relative to the new future cuts announced in 1993. In this special set of circumstances, current demand by government in 1993 is not affected but long-term real interest rates fall by around 200 basis points on impact because of the future increase in government saving which is credibly expected for 1994 to 1997. For the United States this cut in future military expenditure which is assumed to also be a cut in future fiscal deficits is 1.6 per cent of GDP relative to what would have occurred without the incremental defence cuts. For other countries the future reduction in military expenditures and fiscal deficits are between zero and 2 per cent of GDP. In the United States, this decline in interest rates is sufficient to stimulate private investment directly and other components of demand through multiplier effects, so that GDP rises in 1993 by over 0.4 per cent. This result is directly reflecting the role of expectations in the model used in this paper. In more conventional models that do not allow for expectations of future events this particular mechanism would be absent and there would only be effects when the actual cuts in spending take place.

The short-term stimulus due to anticipation of future deficit cuts is quickly reversed when the real spending cuts are implemented in 1994 and in subsequent years. GDP then falls through to 1997 by 0.8 per cent in the United States and to lesser and greater extent in other European countries. Japan on the other hand escapes the contraction in GDP. This is because there is no cut in government spending in Japan. Also with global capital mobility, the fall in fiscal deficits in the United States and Europe causes capital to flow into Japan. This capital inflow reduces Japanese long-term interest rates and stimulates private investment in Japan. Demand for Japanese exports falls because of slowing foreign economies and because of a capital inflow induced strengthening of the yen.

Note that France and the United Kingdom suffer a larger fall in GDP than Germany. Part of this occurs because the expenditure cuts are larger in these countries. But the franc and the pound also are under incipient pressure to depreciate relative to the Deutsche Mark. Because of EMS arrangements, France and the United Kingdom tighten monetary policy to strengthen their currencies (preventing the depreciation that would otherwise have occurred). This monetary tightening further exacerbates the output loss.

Another feature of figure 5 which is important is the longer run consequence of the shock. The level of output is permanently higher by around 0.5 per cent in all countries shown. This should not be confused with a rise in the growth rate. This is a higher level of output (at each point in time) relative to the baseline level. The rise in government saving resulting from the lower path of military expenditure leads to a permanent fall in real interest rates relative to baseline. This lowers the marginal product of capital in all countries with open capital markets. Given full employment of labour in the long run this implies a rise in the capital-output ratio in all countries. As capital accumulates, output rises until the new capital-output ratio is reached. Investment is higher in this new steady state to support the higher capital stock but the rate of growth of each economy returns to the rate given by population of exogenous productivity growth rates. This result about output and the capital stock in the long run has nothing to do with any assumption that might be made about how productive defence spending is relative to other government spending. It is purely the result of higher government saving and would hold whether it was a cut in defence spending or a cut in some other government spending that leads to a rise in government saving.

As already mentioned, the monetary policy assumption in figure 5 is that the United States, Japan, and Germany maintain a fixed stock of money. This is not the most likely policy response in these regions, and so figures 6 to 10 present the same defence cut-backs as in figure 5 but with alternative assumptions about monetary policy in these three regions. Japan and Germany are assumed to target inflation at the baseline level whereas the United States adjusts monetary policy to target nominal income growth in the United States.[13]

It is clear comparing figures 6 and 5 that the United States and the European economies are able to smooth fluctuations in real GDP by changing monetary policies. The initial stimulus occurring in 1993 is postponed into future periods and the later recovery can be brought forward. The peak loss to US GDP is more than 0.8 per cent in 1998 without a response of monetary policy (fig. 5) whereas the loss in GDP is more than cut in half to 0.35 per cent in the same year with an adjustment of monetary policy (fig. 6). In Germany the output loss can be completely offset with an adjustment of monetary policy. Fortunately for France and the United Kingdom, the German res-

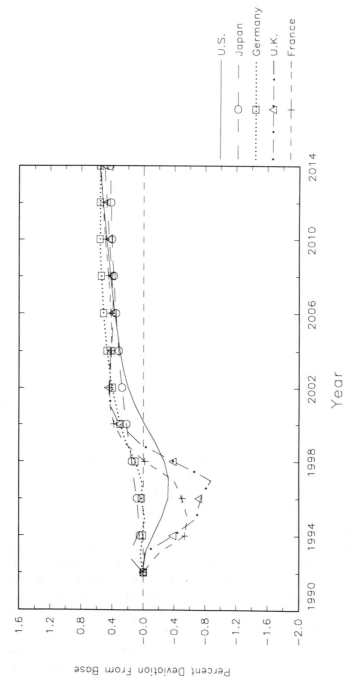

Fig. 6  **Real GDP in selected countries: Simulated cut in military expenditures with policy response**

148

ponse is a relaxation of monetary policy, which also allows France and the United Kingdom to relax their monetary policies and partially stimulate output. Unfortunately the restrictions imposed by the EMS prevent these countries from relaxing monetary policy by as much as required to further offset the loss in GDP. The fact that the shock is an asymmetric real shock, in that it is much larger in France and the United Kingdom than in Germany, illustrates one of the drawbacks of a regime of fixed nominal exchange rates when wages are sticky, as they are in these countries.

As would be expected the long-run results are independent of the assumptions about national monetary policies. It should be added that the explicit assumption in each set of results is that the target of policy is the baseline path. However given the slow recovery in the world economy in 1992, there may not be any reason to smooth out the initial rise in output that would accompany a credible defence cut-back with national money stocks unchanged.

Figure 7 presents results for trade balances as a result of the defence cut-backs with the same adjustments of monetary policies assumed for figure 6.[14] Over time the trade balances in the countries that cut government spending improve. The Japanese trade balance worsens, reflecting the flow of capital into Japan, which appreciates the yen as shown in figure 9. The global fall in nominal long-term interest rates is shown in figure 8. This fall in nominal interest rates is also a fall in real interest rates, because the rate of inflation eventually returns to baseline by assumption. In the group of European countries, interest rates move in unison. The reason why interest rates in other countries do not move exactly equally is because exchange rates are changing in the simulation as shown in figure 9. The expected return from holding assets in different currencies is equalized by assumption in this model. US interest rates fall by more than in other countries and, as seen in figure 9, the US dollar after 1998 gradually appreciates (following the initial depreciation), consistent with the movement in interest rates. The dollar weakens as a result of the policy, the yen strengthens and in effective terms the European currencies remain almost unchanged.

In summary these results show that in the short run a credible cut in defence expenditures can actually be expansionary as firms begin to move resources into the private sector in response to falls in long-term real and nominal interest rates resulting from a credible future rise in government saving. However, there is no medium-term free lunch. As actual government spending is cut, there is a fall in ag-

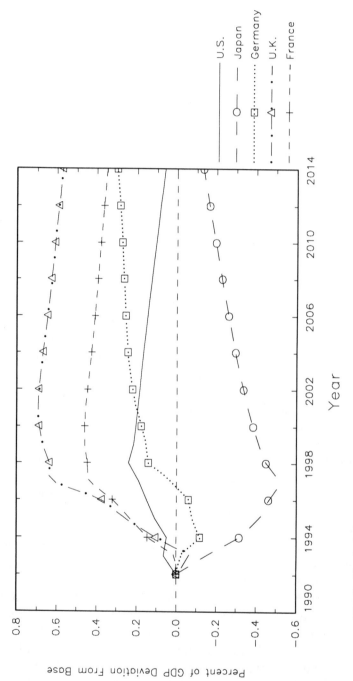

Fig. 7 Trade balances of selected countries: Simulated cut in military expenditures with policy response

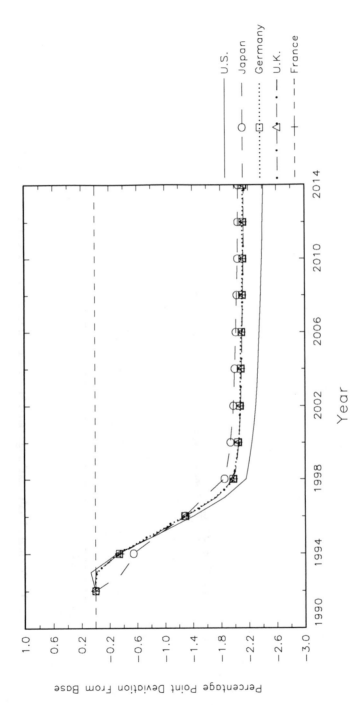

Fig. 8  10-year bond rates of selected countries: Simulated cut in military expenditures with policy response

151

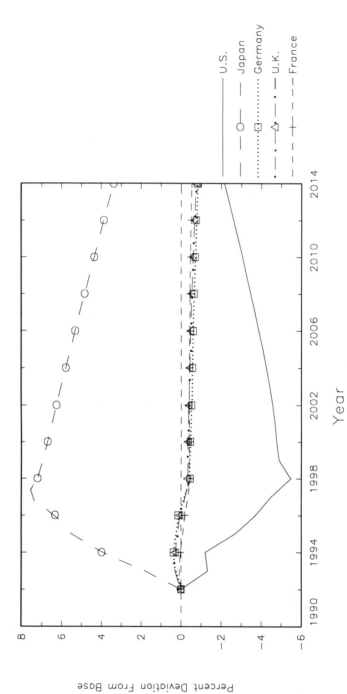

Fig. 9  **Nominal effective exchange rates: Simulated cut in military expenditures with policy response**

gregate demand in the countries cutting their defence budgets. More than half of this can be offset by suitable adjustments of monetary policies. The result for the United States is a reduction of GDP by up to 0.5 per cent below baseline by 1997. In Germany the output loss is completely offset although at the cost of a smaller offset in the rest of Europe where for example French GDP is 0.5 per cent below baseline by 1995 and the United Kingdom close to 1 per cent below baseline by 1997. In addition to the output consequences for these countries, there is a generalized fall in long-term real interest rates that is beneficial to countries not cutting defence budgets (such as Canada and Japan) as well as to indebted developing countries. The cuts in military expenditures and resulting changes in savings and investment balances act to narrow the Japanese current account and trade surpluses. In practice this would be helpful for reducing future trade tensions resulting from continued high Japanese surpluses.

## V. Substantial cut in arms exports to developing countries

We now consider the implication of an embargo on arms exports from the OECD and EFSU to developing countries. The details of this simulation were already given in section 3. The embargo is implemented relative to the baseline outlined above. That is that the simulation is independent of the cuts in military expenditures that were discussed in the previous section. Our assumptions amount to a complete cessation in exports of military arms to the developing countries. In one case we assume that a proportion of the imports of military equipment by developing countries is financed from assistance loans and grants to those countries. We first assume that the cut in arms exports is accompanied by a partial cut in this financial assistance to these countries. The reduction in financial assistance is scaled to be half the cut in exports of arms. We then consider the results without any change in financial assistance to these countries.

Before presenting the results in detail, it is important to be clear how this policy of an arms embargo is implemented in the model. We assume that the total quantity of imports by developing countries from each industrial country is cut by the baseline value of the shares of arms imports by the developing countries from each OECD and EFSU region. Without any change in the current account balance (i.e. without any change in foreign assistance, loans, or grants through the capital account) developing countries could take the money saved from not buying arms and reallocate the funds across a basket of foreign goods according to the initial trade shares in the database. This allocation would then be adjusted by any change in relative prices that occur as a result of the shock. With a cut in foreign assistance, loans, or grants, however, inflows through the capital account would decline and therefore the current account balance would also have to decline. The amount of money that is available to be reallocated across the basket of foreign non-military imports would be reduced in total by the cut in aid.

We first consider the case where financial assistance is partly cut, as we feel this is the more likely scenario. We then re-examine the outcome when financial assistance is not cut.

## (a) Arms reduction with a reduction in aid

As with the results for the cut in military spending, the assumptions about the reaction of monetary policy is crucial to the results for the industrial economies. In figures 10 through 13 we present results under the assumption that arms shipments are halted and aid is partly cut. We assume that monetary polices can adjust in the United States to maintain nominal income growth at baseline and in Japan and Germany to maintain inflation at baseline.

Referring to figure 10, it is clear that GDP rises in all industrial countries shown, although by small amounts. The small size of the result is to be expected given that arms exports are a small share of GDP in most countries. The positive effect on GDP in OECD economies is perhaps surprising given that the exports of these economies have been cut. For the United States, the cut in arms exports tends to reduce nominal GDP. This leads to a relaxation of monetary policy in the United States that more than offsets the negative impact of the arms embargo. For Germany, the fall in demand reduces domestic price inflation, which leads to a relaxation of monetary policy in Germany. For France the results are perhaps more surprising given the relative importance of arms exports to French GDP. Again the constraints on policy imposed by participation in the EMS are playing a crucial role here. To illustrate this, figure 11 shows the path for French GDP under the assumption that France adjusts monetary policy to maintain the franc parity within the EMS (the same as in figure 10) compared to the assumption that France is outside the EMS. With France outside the EMS and hence a fixed supply of money in France, GDP falls as you would expect from a cut in French exports. The EMS imposes a very different monetary res-

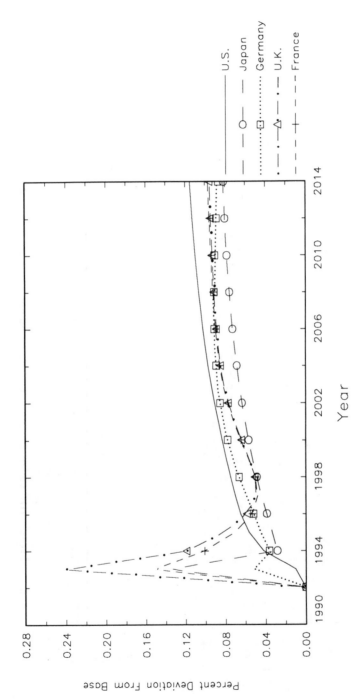

Fig. 10   **Real GDP in selected countries: Simulated arms embargo and aid cut with policy response**

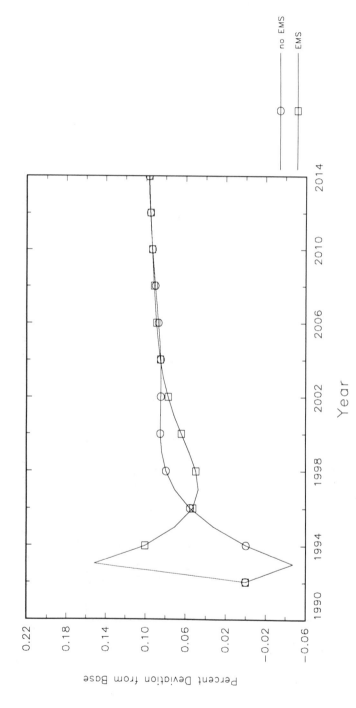

Fig. 11  French GDP under alternative EMS assumptions: Simulated arms embargo and aid cut

ponse in France. The relaxation of monetary policy in Germany leads to a tendency for a depreciation of the Deutsche Mark relative to the franc, which requires France to relax monetary policy.[15] This relaxation in monetary policy and the resulting stimulus to aggregate demand is more than enough to absorb the unemployed resources from the French arms industry.

A similar point is made in figure 12 where a comparison is presented of the paths for US real GDP under the assumption of a fixed path for money in the United States versus the case where monetary policy targets nominal income growth. Again with a fixed stock of money, we find the expected result that GDP falls in 1993 when exports are cut. Over time GDP recovers as the resources freed up from the military export industries are re-employed in other industries. With US monetary policy targeting nominal income, the negative output loss from the fall in exports can be completely offset by a relaxation of monetary policy.

For the assumptions where national monetary policies are adjusted (figure 10) it is clear that the long-run response of GDP is positive in all countries shown. This is also true throughout the world. The explanation for this result can be traced in a crucial assumption in the model. This assumption is that the arms imported by developing countries are consumed by these countries. When exports of military arms to developing countries are halted, the factors of production in the OECD are reallocated over time towards producing non-military goods. These are then partly used for consumption and partly for investment purposes within the OECD. The additional investment raises the capital stock and therefore the level of output over time. In the long run the result is a higher level of output relative to the baseline. This result would be different if it was assumed that the arms shipments were somehow used for investment purposes in the developing countries.

Figure 13 presents results for changes in the trade balances of the major OECD countries and the developing country region. The trade balance of the developing countries improves because their imports are exogenously cut while their current account balance is only partly cut through the reduction in aid. The result is an improvement in the trade balance in these countries with a trade balance deterioration in the industrial countries, ranging from 0.14 per cent of GDP for Germany to 0.8 per cent of GDP for Japan. The Japanese trade balance deteriorates because even though developing countries reallocate their demand away from military arms to non-military imports, the

157

158

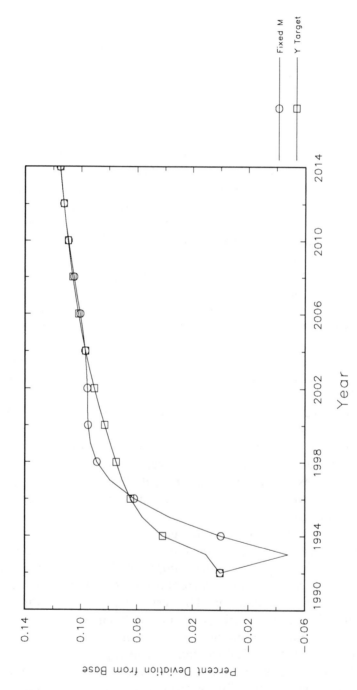

Fig. 12 US GDP under alternative policy rules: Simulated arms embargo and aid cut

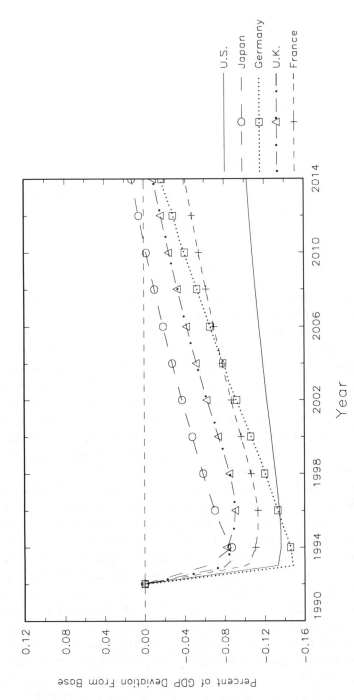

**Fig. 13  Trade balances of selected countries: Simulated arms embargo and aid cut with policy response**

overall level of imports is cut due to the reduction in direct financial assistance.

The results for 10-year bond rates are shown in figure 14. Interest rates fall in each OECD country due primarily to the cut in financial assistance. The forced increase in world saving reduces world interest rates including those facing developing countries. This is also consistent with the fall in the marginal product of capital resulting from a rise in the capital-output ratio in each country.

Finally nominal exchange rate paths are shown in figure 15. The yen appreciates in effective terms due to the relative rise in demand for Japanese goods as developing countries substitute into non-military goods. The European currencies depreciate in effective terms because of the relatively greater reliance on arms exports in these countries.

## (b) Arms reduction with no reduction in financial assistance

The above scenario of cuts in arms exports together with a cut in foreign aid was presented as a plausible scenario. It is also worth attempting to isolate the effects of the arms cuts from the cut in aid. This is done in figures 16 to 19, where results are presented for an arms embargo without any change in foreign aid to the developing countries. This simulation is not strictly comparable to the previous simulation because we continue to assume that monetary policies in the United States, Japan, and Germany do respond to the change in shocks. Thus the response of monetary policy is different for different shocks. However, a comparison of results does improve our understanding of the earlier results.

The cut in military exports to developing countries is offset by a reallocation of the spending power of the developing countries towards non-military goods. The allocation is determined by the initial trade shares between the developing countries and each OECD country adjusted by any changes in relative prices due to the shock. By keeping the same amount of financing of the current account balance, the developing countries have the same amount of foreign exchange to spend on a new basket of goods that does not include military equipment. This simulation therefore is dominated by the substitution of demand by developing countries away from military goods towards non-military goods. Countries that export a relatively small share of military goods will lose the exports of military goods but will more than offset this loss by an increase in demand for non-

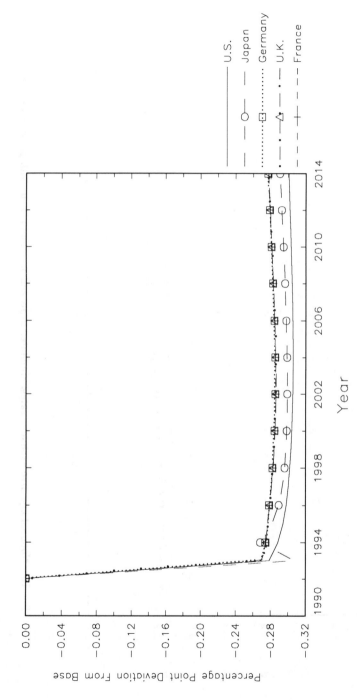

Fig. 14  **10-year bond rates of selected countries: Simulated arms embargo and aid cut with policy response**

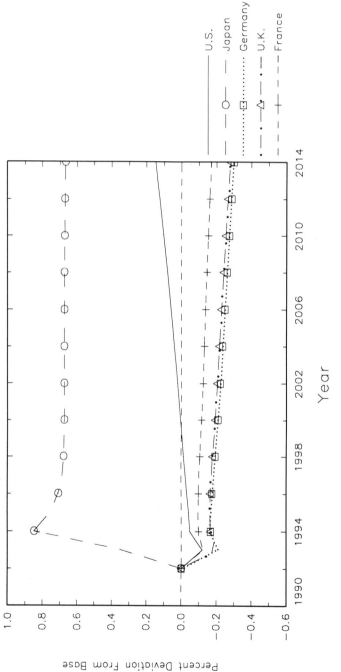

Fig. 15 **Nominal effective exchange rates: Simulated arms embargo and aid cut with policy response**

military goods. Similarly countries that rely proportionately more on military exports relative to non-military exports will tend to experience a fall in overall exports as only some of the lost military exports will be made up for by exports of non-military equipment. The composition of trade is based on the shares of trade in the database (based on 1987 trade shares).

Figure 16 contains the result for real GDP in each of the major industrial countries. The arms embargo alone tends to raise GDP even more in the short run in all countries except Germany. This outcome occurs because there is no reduction in overall demand for imports by developing countries. All that is changed is the relative demands across the bundles of foreign goods. In the longer run the output gains, although still positive, are smaller than when aid is also cut. Again this reflects the assumption that the foreign assistance is consumed by developing countries rather than used for investment purposes in these countries. Thus, by redirecting these financial resources back to OECD economies, part of these resources are used for investment purposes. Therefore the long-run level of output is higher. The assumption about how foreign assistance is used by developing countries may be plausible for the 1980s but may be less plausible in the future. It is also crucial to the results because if we assume that the share of investment out of foreign financial assistance is the same as the share that would be invested if the funds were redirected back to the OECD economies, then the long-run effects of the level of output would be minimal and the only consequences of the shock would be the short-run consequences of a reallocation of demand.

The difference made by the assumption about foreign assistance is clearer in figure 17. This figure shows the consequence of the arms embargo for trade balances, when there is no change in financial assistance to developing countries. Countries that experience a substitution towards their goods, such as Japan and the United Kingdom, experience an improvement in their trade balances. Germany experiences a noticeable deterioration in its trade balance as the result of substitution away from German goods. Note however that the magnitude of the results is very small.

Figures 18 and 19 show the implications for world interest rates and key exchange rates. In this case, the fall in interest rates and changes in exchange rates are negligible. It is not surprising that the yen appreciates given that there is no cut in military exports from

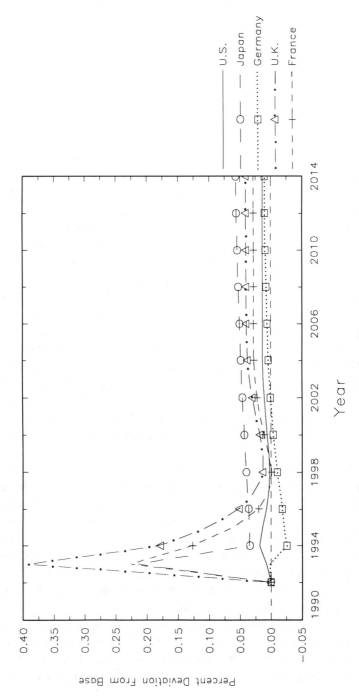

Fig. 16  **Real GDP in selected countries: Simulated arms embargo with policy response**

164

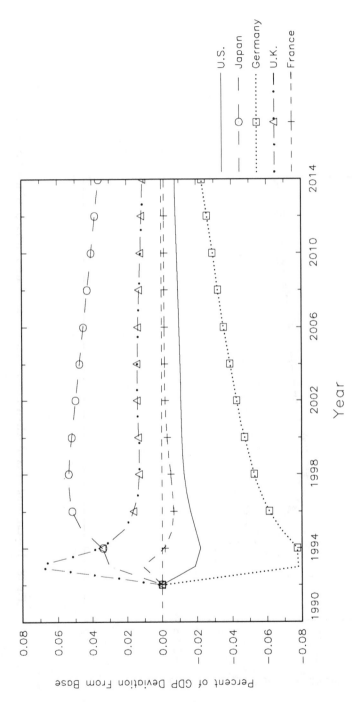

Fig. 17 **Trade balances of selected countries: Simulated arms embargo with policy response**

165

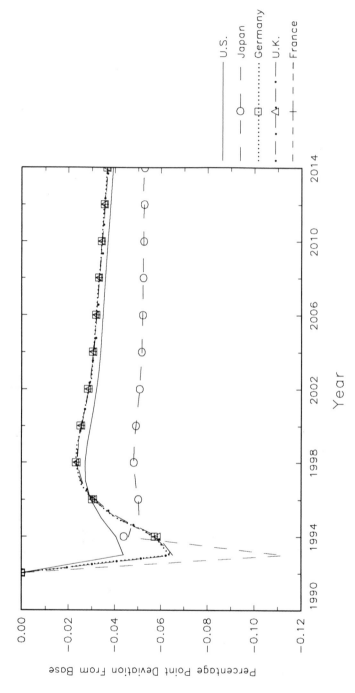

Fig 18  **10-year bond rates of selected countries: Simulated arms embargo with policy response**

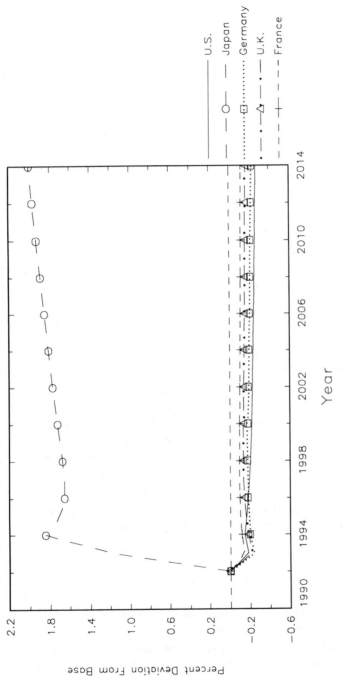

Fig. 19  Nominal effective exchange rates: Simulated arms embargo with policy response

167

Japan and there is a rise in demand for Japanese goods by developing countries.

## VI. Summary and conclusions

This paper has given an overview of recent trends in military expenditures and arms trade in the world and then projected the possible consequences of a number of scenarios involving reductions in military expenditures and arms exports by the OECD economies. Each scenario was considered separately, not because they are likely to be independent events, but because by separating the scenarios, we were better able to isolate the key aspects of each. Combinations of scenarios can be assembled by the interested reader by simply adding the results of scenarios together. However, the results cannot be simply modified by the reader to adjust for alternative paths for future policies. Changing the timing of policies in a model with rational expectations can change results in a way that is not a simple algebraic transformation of the results presented.

Several points that emerge from the analysis should be stressed. The first is that a credible reduction in future government expenditures on defence in OECD countries could have a significant short-run stimulative impact on the world economy. However, as cuts are implemented, there is a negative impact on GDP over time that cannot be completely offset by adjustments to monetary policy. The reallocation of resources from defence-related to other industries will inevitably involve short-run unemployment of these resources. In the long run, using the revenue gain from the defence cut-backs to reduce fiscal deficits permanently raises real GDP through higher global saving. In contrast to most popular debate on the issue of defence cut-backs, which argues that there would be short-run losses followed by long-run gains, this paper has shown that it is possible, by credibly announcing substantial cuts in advance, for there to be a short-run gain, medium-term loss, and then long-run gain from cutting defence expenditures.

The second point is that a large reduction in exports of arms to developing countries has a small impact on the exporting countries in the OECD. Indeed these countries can offset this loss in the short run by changes in monetary policy.

This paper has concentrated on the macroeconomic adjustments in OECD economies to several scenarios about military spending and arms exports. Far less has been said about the implications for developing countries of these policies, partly because the model forming the basis of this study has rudimentary internal detail for these regions. Despite the lack of focus on developing countries, the model does capture the external linkages between these developing regions and the OECD. The paper has also ignored the complex issues of the relationship between economic development and military transfers.[16] However, the analysis does provide some crucial insights that would not be rendered irrelevant by ignoring the possible links between development and military outlays. The above results show that in the case of a substantial cut in OECD military budgets, developing countries gain through lower world interest rates. In the case of cuts in arms shipments, developing countries clearly lose if financial assistance that previously accompanied these shipments is also cut. In the case where financial assistance to developing countries is not cut, but military arms are replaced by non-military goods, the size of gains or losses suggested by our analysis is small.

With the end of the Cold War and a possibility of increased regional conflicts involving developing countries, the results in this paper suggest that an ending of arms exports to the developing world would have a negligible effect on growth in the industrialized economies. In addition, with the world economy in a global recession, using defence cut-backs as part of credible deficit-reduction packages in a number of countries could contribute towards increasing short-run world growth by lowering long-term real interest rates. However, policy makers should be aware that the process of shifting factors of production out of defence-related industries will involve a period of slower growth until these factors are reabsorbed by non-defence industries. By the end of this decade the long-run gains from defence cuts are realized. However, to realize these gains it is crucial that the savings from smaller defence outlays be part of a credible deficit reduction programme.

## Notes

1. For an analysis of these issues see for example Collins and Rodrick (1991). Also see McKibbin (1992a) and CBO (1990), which use a version of the same model underlying this study.
2. See Kirby and Hooper (1991). Deger and Sen (1992, p. 190) suggest that in reality despite the expectation and the need for cuts, these are unlikely in Europe for a long period.
3. See the discussion in Anthony et al. (1991).
4. See McKibbin and Sachs (1991) for a complete description of the model and applications to the issues of interdependence and policy coordination in the world economy using an earlier version of the model.

5. The new European version of the model is described in McKibbin and Bok (1992).
6. See CBO (1992a) for a study of impact of defence cut-backs in the United States, and CBO (1992c) for a study of a cut in US arms exports to the Middle East.
7. See Solow (1970) and Swan (1956).
8. See Deger and Sen (1992). According to SIPRI's data, military expenditure in the Middle East increased in 1991 due to the Gulf War. Also there was a significant rise in Chinese defence expenditure in 1990 and 1991.
9. See CBO (1991c), table 8, p. 35.
10. See Anthony et al. (1992). According to SIPRI's data, global trade in arms fells by 25 per cent in 1991 relative to 1990, primarily due to the collapse in arms exports by the former Soviet Union, whose exports in 1991 were 22 per cent of the value in 1987.
11. See McKibbin and Sachs (1991) for a study of the evolution of the world economy during the 1980s and McKibbin (1992a) for German unification.
12. See CBO (1992c) table 5, which has an estimate by the Congressional Research Service of total exports of arms to the third world in 1991 of $25.4 billion (1992 prices).
13. An evaluation of alternative policy rules under a range of shocks can be found in Bryant et al. (1992). Nominal income targeting works well as an intermediate target in the range of multi-country models used in that study, which included the MSG model.
14. These results are very similar to those without a monetary response because monetary policy has very little effect on the trade balance in this model even though it has significant effects on real output. See McKibbin and Sachs (1991) for a full discussion of this issue.
15. Note that without any change in German monetary policy there is a tendency for the real value of the franc to decline relative to the Deutsche Mark. This occurs because of a shift in demand away from French goods that is larger than the shift in demand away from German goods.
16. See the literature review in Bayoumi et al. (1992) for an overview.

# References

ACDA (1991). *World Military Expenditures and Arms Transfers 1990*. U.S. Arms Control and Disarmament Agency, Washington D.C.

Anthony I., Allebeck A., Hagmeyer-Gaverus G., Miggiano P., and H. Wulf (1991). "The Trade in Major Conventional Weapons." In *SIPRI (1991)*, chap. 7.

Anthony I., Allebeck A., Miggiano P., Skons E., and H. Wulf (1991). "The Trade in Major Conventional Weapons." In *SIPRI (1992)*, chap. 8.

Bayoumi T, Hewitt, D., and J. Schiff (1992). "Economic Consequences of Lower Military Spending: Some Simulation Results." Paper presented to the United Nations University. Tokyo Conference on Arms Reduction and Economic Development in the Post-Cold War Era, November.

Bryant, R., Henderson D., Holtham, G., Hooper, P., and S. Symansky (eds.) (1988). *Empirical Macroeconomics for Open Economies*. The Brookings Institution, Washington, D.C.

Bryant R., Hooper P., and C. Mann (eds.) (1993). *Evaluating Policy Regimes: New Research in Empirical Macroeconomics*. The Brookings Institution, Washington, D.C.

Collins S., and D. Rodrick (1991). *Eastern Europe and the Soviet Union in the World Economy*. Policy Analyses in International Economics no. 32. Institute for International Economics.

Congressional Budget Office (CBO) (1990). *How the Economic Transformations in Europe Will Affect the United States*. Washington D.C., December.

—— (1992a). *The Economic Effects of Reduced Defense Spending*. Washington D.C., February.

—— (1992b). *The Economic and Budget Outlook: An Update*. Washington D.C., August.

—— (1992c). *Limiting Conventional Arms Exports to the Middle East*. Washington D.C., September.

Deger, S. (1991). "World Military Expenditure." In *SIPRI (1991)*, chap. 5.

Deger S., and S. Sen (1991). "Defense Expenditures, Aid, and Economic Development." Paper presented to the World Bank Annual Conference on Development Economics 1991.

—— (1992) "World Military Expenditure." In *SIPRI (1992)*, chap. 7.

Fleming J.M. (1962). "Domestic Financial Policies Under Fixed and Floating Exchange Rates." *International Monetary Fund, Staff Papers* 9(3), pp. 369–379.

Kaufmann W.W., and J. Steinbruner (1991). *Decisions for Defense: Prospects for a New Order*. Studies in Defense Policy. The Brookings Institution, Washington, D.C.

Kirby S., and N Hooper (eds.) (1991). *The Cost of Peace: Assessing Europe's Security Options*. Harwood, Switzerland.

McKibbin W. (1992a). "The New European Economy and its Economic Implications for the World Economy." Brookings Discussion Paper in International Economics no. 89, *Economic and Financial Computing* 2(3).

—— (1992b). *The MSG Multi-Country Model: European Version (no. 33)*. Computer Manual, McKibbin Software Group Inc., Arlington, Va.

McKibbin W.J., and T. Bok (1992). "An Empirical Evaluation of Alternative Policy Regimes for Europe." The Brookings Institution, Washington, D.C.

McKibbin W.J., and J. Sachs (1991). *Global Linkages: Macroeconomic Interdependence and Co-operation in the World Economy*. The Brookings Institution, Washington, D.C.

McNamara R. (1991) "The Post-Cold War World and Its Implications for Military Expenditures in the Developing Countries." Paper presented to the World Bank Annual Conference on Development Economics 1991.

Mundell R. (1963). "Capital Mobility and Stabilization Policy Under Fixed and Flexible Exchange Rates." *Canadian Journal of Economic and Political Science* 29(4), pp. 475–485.

SIPRI (1991). *SIPRI Yearbook 1991: World Armaments and Disarmament*, Stockholm International Peace Research Institute, Oxford University Press.

—— (1992). *SIPRI Yearbook 1992: World Armaments and Disarmament*, Stockholm International Peace Research Institute, Oxford University Press.

Sen S. (1990). "Military Expenditure Data for Developing Countries: Methods and Measurement." Paper presented at World Bank Symposium.

Solow R. (1970). *Growth Theory: An Exposition*. Oxford University Press, Oxford.

Swan T. (1956). "Economic Growth and Capital Accumulation." *Economic Record* 32(63), pp. 334–361.

171

# 8

# Economic consequences of lower military spending: Some simulation results

Tamim Bayoumi, Daniel P. Hewitt, and Jerald Schiff

**Abstract**

The IMF MULTIMOD model is used to trace the economic impact of a 20 per cent reduction in world military expenditures. GDP falls in the short run, however, private consumption and investment rise, leading to an increase in GDP in the medium and long run. The estimated gains to economic welfare are substantial, particularly for developing countries, although most of these gains are realized in the long run. A positive international economic externality is found to exist, implying that for any given country the economic gains from a coordinated reduction in military expenditures exceeds the gains from a unilateral reduction.

**Summary**

Recent changes in international politics offer the possibility of general reductions in military expenditures – the so-called "peace dividend." This paper reports the results from simulations designed to

The authors would like to thank Ke-young Chu, Peter Clark, and Steve Symansky for their assistance with this paper. The views expressed in the paper do not necessarily reflect those of the International Monetary Fund.

172

estimate the economic and financial impact of a 20 per cent decrease in worldwide military expenditures. No attempt is made to measure the impact on security of lowering military expenditures or to estimate its associated welfare impact.

The initial impact of lowering military spending is a modest reduction in the growth of GDP, with those countries whose military expenditures (in proportion to their GDP) are above the world average experiencing greater losses. At the same time, lower government spending reduces interest rates and allows governments to lower taxes, which raises private sector consumption and investment. In the medium and long run, GDP rises significantly above baseline values. Hence, while in the short run military spending creates jobs and stimulates the economy, in the long run military expenditures lower economic growth by crowding out investment.

Tracing the movements of GDP provides insight into changes in total output and employment; it is not, however, appropriate as a measure of economic welfare in the present case. The correct measure of *economic* welfare is the gain in current and future non-military consumption. A 20 per cent cut in military spending is estimated to produce long-run increases in both private consumption and investment in industrial countries, raising economic welfare by an estimated 48 per cent of 1992 GDP, with those countries that implement the largest cuts having proportionally higher benefits. Less developed countries could experience gains in economic welfare that are significantly larger than those of the industrial countries (79 per cent of 1992 GDP).

Since most of the gains in economic welfare come in the longer run, these results are relatively insensitive to short-term factors such as the timing of the tax cuts associated with lower government expenditures and the speed of the cuts in spending, although they are affected by the size of the government spending multipliers and percentage of military spending that is assumed to represent productive investment. In all cases, however, the simulations indicate a substantial gain to economic welfare.

Another result that emerges from the simulations is a positive international economic externality. The economic benefits to all countries are found to be greater when a coordinated reduction in military expenditures is carried out than when a nation undertakes a unilateral decrease in military expenditures. This externality results from lower world interest rates and increased volumes of international trade. The external benefits to developing countries appear to be particularly pronounced, and the externality implies that there are economic, as well as security, reasons for coordinating expenditure cut-backs.

## I. Introduction

Recent changes in international politics, and in particular the easing of East-West tensions, offer many new challenges to the world economy. One of the most clear and tangible is the possibility of general reductions in military expenditures, the so-called "peace dividend." Lower military spending, by reducing the resources allocated to this sector of the economy, should expand the resources available for non-military consumption and investment, providing more rapid growth and higher standards of living in both industrial and developing countries.

While there is widespread agreement that such economic benefits would result from reductions in military spending, there is uncertainty as to the likely size and distribution of these benefits, both over time and across countries. Reductions in government spending on the military will have significant macroeconomic effects, particularly upon interest rates, exchange rates, and trade patterns, all of which will influence the size and distribution of gains from cuts in military expenditures. Furthermore, there is considerable concern, often expressed in the popular press, regarding short-term increases in unemployment and a lowering of economic growth that might result from decreasing military expenditures. Particularly in industrial countries, it is widely acknowledged that decreasing military outlays will force military contractors to shrink their labour force in response to reductions in government contracts.

This paper reports the results from simulations designed to estimate the economic and financial impact of a broad-based decrease in world military expenditures using the IMF MULTIMOD computer simulation model. The model, which simulates the financial interactions between countries based upon economic principles and observed data, is used to trace the potential effects of lower military spending on economic growth, international trade, and world capital markets for the major industrial countries as well as country groups. Due to the nature of the analysis, the simulations necessarily reflect a number of underlying assumptions on both the nature of the cuts and the responses of the government and the private sector. Thus, sensitivity analysis will be carried out in order to determine the robustness of our results to changes in these assumptions.

This study concentrates on the economic impact of military expenditures and accordingly traces the effect of alternative military expenditure levels on private consumption and investment. The primary impact of military expenditures is on security rather than on the economy. However, the allocation of resources to the military has indirect economic effects and untangling the economic consequences provides an important input into overall policy decisions.

The study makes no attempt to measure the impact on security of lowering military expenditures or to estimate the associated welfare impact since such an analysis is outside the scope of economic analysis. Economic theory does, however, provide a rationale for government provision of security, since security displays the classic features of a public good. Additionally, from an international perspective, military expenditures by one nation impose a negative externality on other nations that feel threatened.[1] Thus, the security impact of a coordinated decrease in military expenditures is quite different from a unilateral reduction by one nation. While a unilateral decrease in military expenditures almost certainly decreases national security, a coordinated decrease in military spending has an uncertain impact on security since the reductions in security caused by domestic military cuts are counterbalanced by the greater security provided by lower military spending in rival countries.[2]

The paper also focuses on the economic consequences when each and every country reduces military expenditures by 20 per cent over a five-year period. The initial impact of lowering military spending is a general reduction in the growth of GDP, with those countries whose military expenditures (in proportion to their GDP) are above the world average experiencing greater losses. These losses stem from the short-term fall in aggregate demand caused by reducing government spending, and support the popular notion that decreasing military expenditures will have negative macroeconomic consequences in the short run.

At the same time, however, lower government spending reduces interest rates and allows governments to lower taxes or the fiscal deficit. This sets in motion a sequence of events that induces higher private sector investment and consumption. Lower business taxes and long-term interest rates raise private sector investments, which in turn increase the rate of growth of the capital stock and potential output, while the anticipation of higher future disposable income raises private consumption. This increase in private sector activity overcomes the initial set-back to output, and GDP rises significantly above baseline values in the medium and long run. Thus, after an initial fall, reduced military spending produces significant longer-run increases in GDP.

Tracing the movements of GDP provides insight into changes in total output, employment, and perhaps the distributional consequences of lowering military expenditures. However, GDP is not an appropriate measure of economic welfare in the present case. GDP incorporates a crude measure of the benefits of government expenditures; government non-transfer expenditures, and therefore military expenditures, are automatically recorded as part of GDP. Clearly, when a coordinated decrease occurs, changes in the level of military spending by one country do not necessarily coincide with changes in security.[3] Therefore, this analysis concentrates exclusively on measuring changes in *economic welfare*, or the gain in current and future non-military spending, which can be easily estimated in the MULTIMOD framework.[4] Any economic benefits provided by the military will eventually be transmitted through increases in civilian economic activity.

The economic welfare effects of a coordinated decrease in military spending can be quite different from the impact on total output. The initial fall in GDP compared to baseline values described above may obscure a rise in economic welfare in the short term. To the extent that cuts in military expenditures lead to immediate increases in non-military consumption, the immediate impact on economic welfare will be positive, even if GDP falls. The notion that "military expenditures are good for the economy" can only be true to the extent that they induce higher overall private sector activity. The results from the simulations in this study indicate that in the longer term there is little question that military spending crowds out private consumption, and, in many cases this crowding out of private sector activity holds even in the short run.

Another interesting result that emerges from the simulations is that a positive international economic externality is found to exist. The economic benefits to all countries are found to be greater when a coordinated reduction in military expenditures is carried out than when a nation undertakes a unilateral decrease in military expenditures. This externality results from lower world interest rates and increased volumes of international trade. The external benefits to developing countries appear to be particularly pronounced.

The remainder of this paper is organized in the following manner. Section 2 provides background information on related research and the data. Section 3 describes the MULTIMOD model and summarizes the results for the industrial countries, developing countries, and the United States. Section 4 discusses the results in other industrial countries. Section 5 analyses the results for developing countries. Section 6 concludes.

## II. Literature review and background

### (a) Military expenditures and economic growth

The question of whether military expenditures promote economic growth or are detrimental to growth remains largely unsettled. Some people believe that the military creates jobs and is generally good for the economy. The case of the US recovery from the depression during World War II and the high economic growth following the war is often offered as an example. Alternatively, the simple theory of opportunity costs implies that military expenditures will crowd out other types of expenditures, including private investment, with negative consequences for growth. The post-World War II economic successes of Germany, Japan, and Italy are often cited as counter examples.

At a more academic level, studies inspired by Benoit (1973) have found a positive correlation between military expenditures and the rate of economic growth in empirical studies using a cross-section of countries. The explanation of the mechanism through which this comes about has always been somewhat weak. Followers of the Benoit thesis seem to subscribe to two views. First, military expenditures provide a beneficial macroeconomic stimulus to an economy. Secondly, the military can be a force for modernization, technological advancement, and training in developing countries, and a source of technological innovation in industrialized countries. An alternative thesis is offered in Kohler (1988) who finds that the level of capital formation is positively associated with expenditures on military equipment and negatively associated with expenditures on military personnel in African countries. The conclusion offered is that the former promotes security, which induces more private investment, while the latter does not.

Deger (1986), on the other hand, offers evidence that military expenditures are detrimental to growth in a cross-section of countries. In a simultaneous equations system, the direct impact of military expenditures on economic growth is indeed found to be positive. However, high military expenditures are associated with low savings ratios, which in turn leads to low economic growth; this effect turns out to be larger than the direct effect of military expenditures. These results suggest two opposing effects. On the one hand, a short-term positive relationship exists between military expenditures and economic growth due to macroeconomic stimulus of increasing government spending. In the long term, military spending lowers the savings rate and therefore causes the steady state rate of economic growth to fall.

A new generation of studies investigates the direction of causality. Chowdhury (1991), Joerding (1986), and LaCivita and Frederiksen (1991) use Granger causality tests to investigate the connection between military spending and economic growth. All three find a feedback relationship for at least some countries, which suggests a complicated interaction between military spending and economic growth. Furthermore, the results provide clear evidence that higher military spending leads to lower growth, but that higher growth induces higher military spending. In Chowdhury's study, although no significant relationship is found for 55 per cent of the 55 countries covered in the study, military spending is found to lower economic growth in 35 per cent, and economic growth causes higher military spending in 15 per cent.[5] LaCivita and Frederiksen find that among 21 countries investigated no significant relationship was found for 19 per cent, in 38 per cent military expenditures were found to have a negative impact on economic growth, and in 43 per cent high growth was found to have a positive impact on military expenditures.[6] Hewitt (1992) finds clear evidence that economic prosperity leads to higher military expenditures among developing countries. Thus, a simple correlation between high growth rates and high military expenditures could be interpreted as evidence that military expenditures are a "superior good."

In recent years, a number of simulation studies of the economic effects of reducing military expenditures have been published. Leontief and Dutchin (1983) conduct simulations in an input-output framework which confirm the long-run economic gains from cuts in military expenditures. They note, however, that even if a substantial portion of the savings to the industrial countries were transferred to

178

LDCs (less developed countries) in the form of increased aid, the LDCs would be unable to close the economic gap appreciably unless substantial structural changes were made. Atesoglu and Mueller (1990) find that military expenditures have a positive short-run effect on economic growth, but conclude that the impact is relatively small. Thomas et al. (1991) use a macroeconomic model to simulate the effects of reducing military expenditures and find that there is a negative short-run effect on real output, employment, and the price level.

The simulation results herein differ substantially from those listed above mainly due to the use of the MULTIMOD framework. First, the short-run macroeconomic effects of changes in the pattern of government expenditures can be distinguished from the long-term economic growth effects. Secondly, the international trade effects are examined in detail, which provides insight into international linkages in the impact of military spending cuts. Thirdly, this study provides estimates of the present value of the economic benefits from reducing military expenditures and thereby more fully analyses the long-run implications. Two other simulation studies have recently been published that use a similar model, the McKibbin-Sachs Global model, to examine the economic impact of decreased military expenditures. Congressional Budget Office (1992) investigates the impact of a cut-back of US military expenditures, and analyses the differential regional/state impact and the effects on specific industries. McKibbin and Thurman (1992) carry out a simulation of a decrease in military expenditures by OECD countries, focusing on the differential impact of the timing of the cuts and of alternative monetary regimes. The results in these two papers are in many ways complementary with those in this one, which concentrates on the impact of cuts in military spending on international economic linkages and economic welfare.

## (b) Military expenditures, imports, and exports

The simulations are based upon average levels of military expenditures, military exports, and military imports during the years 1987 to 1989, as shown in table 1. The data on military expenditures comes from the Stockholm International Peace Research Institute (SIPRI), which are generally believed to be the most accurate estimates of levels of military spending available.[7] Trade data were taken from the U.S. Arms Control and Disarmament Agency (ACDA), which is widely regarded as the best available source for this data.

Table 1 **Military expenditure, arms exports, and arms imports, 1987–1989 average**

| | (% GDP) | | | ($USbn) | | | (% total country) | |
|---|---|---|---|---|---|---|---|---|
| | Military expenditures | Arms exports | Arms imports | Military expenditures | Arms exports | Arms imports | Arms exports | Arms imports |
| Industrial countries, average | 3.68 | 0.17 | 0.07 | 503.0 | 22.7 | 8.1 | 1.18 | 0.42 |
| United States | 6.07 | 0.28 | 0.04 | 296.1 | 13.4 | 2.1 | 4.29 | 0.57 |
| Japan | 1.00 | 0.00 | 0.04 | 26.8 | 0.1 | 1.2 | 0.04 | 0.52 |
| Germany, Federal Republic | 2.96 | 0.11 | 0.07 | 34.3 | 1.3 | 0.9 | 0.41 | 0.29 |
| France | 3.78 | 0.29 | 0.02 | 35.4 | 2.7 | 0.2 | 1.62 | 0.13 |
| Italy | 2.32 | 0.04 | 0.03 | 19.8 | 0.3 | 0.3 | 0.25 | 0.20 |
| United Kingdom | 4.25 | 0.41 | 0.08 | 33.2 | 3.1 | 0.6 | 2.17 | 0.41 |
| Canada | 2.03 | 0.12 | 0.04 | 9.8 | 0.6 | 0.2 | 0.49 | 0.17 |
| Smaller industrial countries[1] | 2.30 | 0.08 | 0.25 | 47.6 | 1.2 | 2.7 | 0.25 | 0.55 |
| Eastern Europe and USSR | 14.35 | 1.31 | 0.22 | 269.0 | 24.3 | 3.9 | 9.80 | 1.60 |
| Developing Countries | 4.15 | 0.14 | 1.03 | 125.0 | 5.4 | 40.3 | 0.85 | 6.38 |
| Net creditor countries[2] | 7.05 | 0.02 | 2.03 | 30.9 | 0.1 | 9.0 | 0.07 | 8.98 |
| Net debtor countries[3] | 3.70 | 0.16 | 0.87 | 94.1 | 5.3 | 31.3 | 1.05 | 5.66 |

Source: ACDA, SIPRI, IFS, Steinberg.
1. Australia, Austria, Belgium, Denmark, Finland, Greece, Iceland, Ireland, Luxembourg, Netherlands, New Zealand, Norway, Portugal, Spain, Sweden, and Switzerland.
2. Iran, Kuwait, Libya, Oman, Qatar, Saudi Arabia, Taiwan Province of China, United Arab Emirates.
3. See Masson et al. (1990) for a list of countries incorporated in the analysis.

The majority of world military expenditures are associated with industrialized countries, which account for 56 per cent of total world military expenditures (3.7 per cent of GDP). Within this group, the United States accounts for one-third of world military expenditures (6.1 per cent of GDP), while other industrialized nations spend considerably less, both in absolute value and as a share of GDP. The United States holds a similarly dominant position with respect to exports. Arms exports represent only 1.2 per cent of total industrial country exports, with one-third of these exports going to other industrial countries and two-thirds to the rest of the world. For the United States, however, arms exports are more significant, representing 4.3 per cent of total exports. Arms exports are also relatively high in the United Kingdom (2.2 per cent of total exports) and France (1.6 per cent of total exports). These three countries are also those which tend to provide various forms of military assistance. For instance, direct US military assistance was $5 billion annually during this time period (dollars are US dollars). In addition, trade credit is also regularly provided for military purchases. As a consequence, the level of net earnings from the sale of arms is relatively insignificant for these economies in question; relatively little income is gained from purely non-domestic financing of military goods.

Although Eastern Europe and the USSR are not included in the simulation analysis, examination of their data is important to any analysis of worldwide military expenditures and trade in arms. Further, they provide an interesting perspective on the military policies of other countries. These countries spent about $269 billion on the military (14.4 per cent of GDP) in 1987–1989.[8] Net military exports, presumably to developing countries, are estimated to be 8.2 per cent of total exports. This clearly would represent a significant source of income, to the extent that the recipients actually paid for the military goods that they received. However, it is likely actual receipts were only a fraction of the value assessed by ACDA.

The data on developing countries indicate that in total, they spent $125 billion on the military, 4.2 per cent of GDP on average. However, the eight *net creditor nations*[9] accounted for one-quarter of this total with military expenditures to GDP of over 7 per cent. The other developing countries (the net debtor developing countries) had a ratio of military expenditure to GDP that matched that of the industrialized nations, 3.7 per cent. The net creditor countries also accounted for about one quarter of arms imports by developing countries (9 per cent of total imports). Furthermore, for the most part

181

these countries are known to have paid full price for the arms they received without the assistance of concessionary financing.

The arms imports of the *net debtor countries* are estimated at $31 billion, 5.7 per cent of total imports. This is quite significant compared to the estimate of official development assistance of about $50 billion in 1988. However, these countries also received considerable amounts of military aid in the form of grants and concessionary loans associated with arms imports from the industrialized countries and discounts from the USSR. Through examining related data, Hewitt (1992) estimates that as much as 80 per cent of the assessed value of military imports by net debtor developing countries could have been aid financed. This implies that domestically financed payments for military imports were probably a less significant part of overall domestic expenditures than the total figures would suggest. It is also worth noting that a good deal of the imports of arms is carried out by middle income developing countries. For instance, 40 per cent of the imports of net debtor countries is accounted for by Middle East and North Africa.

## III. Simulation results

The simulations below use MULTIMOD, a multi-region econometric model designed to analyse the economic interactions among industrial and developing countries. The main linkages among the regions are through trade, exchange rates, and interest rates. Imports of the industrial and capital-exporting developing countries are functions of relative prices and aggregate demand, while imports by other developing countries depend upon the amount of available foreign exchange. Short-term interest rates depend on monetary policy through the money demand equations, while long-term interest rates are a moving average of current and expected future short-term rates. Nominal exchange rates are determined by relative interest rates.[10]

For the purposes of this paper three features of the model are particularly important. It is a rational expectations model, which means that in those markets where future expectations are particularly important (in particular exchange rate and bond markets), future behaviour feeds back into current prices. It has a well-defined supply side based on a production function, so that changes in investment feed through into higher potential output in the future. Finally, the trade equations take account of the geographic distribution of trade across different economies.

At the same time the limitations of the highly aggregated MULTI-MOD framework should be recognized. It combines all government spending, which limits the extent to which the simulations can be used to analyse the impact of changing the composition of government spending. The structure of the model also limits the extent to which issues related to the conversion from military to civilian production can be explicitly analysed. While the initial decline in output reflects the implicit assumption that capital and labour are less than perfectly mobile, the aggregate production functions take no account of the fact that some capital currently used in the production of military output may not be convertible to civilian production.[11] To the extent that this is the case, the capital stock, and hence output, will tend to be smaller than suggested by the simulations. However, this effect is unlikely to be large. The percentage of the world's capital stock engaged in military production is small, and will depreciate over time, allowing the capital stock in this sector to return to equilibrium.

The simulations are all expressed relative to a scenario corresponding to the projections of MULTIMOD for each country and country group published in the May 1992 *World Economic Outlook*. Thus, each result reported in the tables represents a deviation from the baseline caused by the policy changes associated with each simulation. In the primary policy change considered here, the "main case," all countries simultaneously carry out a 20 per cent reduction in military expenditures in equal increments over five years. Each nation is assumed to lower its military aid, military imports, and military exports as well by the same percentage over the same period, so the cut can be thought of as a phased reduction in all types of military spending. In terms of MULTIMOD, government consumption was lowered by 20 per cent of the average value of military spending from 1987 to 1989 (as a percentage of GDP).[12] The residuals on the trade equations were changed so that the first round effects on trade corresponded to the data on military trade, and the assistance to capital importing developing countries was also reduced. Since trade connected with military spending is relatively small, the initial fall in trade is smaller than would be predicted by a standard simulation. This produces responses which are significantly different from a standard government spending simulation. In particular, countries with relatively high military spending require larger devaluations of their exchange rate in order to bring their trade back into balance, as the relatively domestically orientated military spending is replaced by more import intensive consumption and investment.

183

The results from several other simulations are reported. In the first two, it is assumed that all nations simultaneously decrease their military spending by 20 per cent as in the main case. In the Accelerator Model, the possibility that investment will be adversely effected by the fall in military spending is accounted for. In the Investment Model, the possibility that military spending has a positive impact on civilian productive capacity is taken into account. As far as government policy is concerned, it is assumed that governments adjust taxes (or government transfers, which are equivalent to negative taxes in the model) in order to keep the fiscal deficit unchanged. Alternative scenarios indicate that if instead the deficit is lowered (i.e., tax cuts are delayed), the short-term output losses are larger but the long-run economic gains are similar. On monetary policy, it is assumed that the monetary authorities in most of the industrial countries follow a target path for the money supply, which, in the face of cuts in government consumption and hence downward pressure on the price level, leads to a fall in interest rates.[13]

The simulation results in table 2 show the percent change from the baseline caused by the policy shift for the two major country groups and a sample of major countries (see table A1 for more details). The cut in military expenditures is recorded as a fall in real government spending. The movements in other variables will be discussed below. Table 3 lists the dollar values of the changes in military spending, GDP, and consumption for the main simulation and the alternative simulations. Table 4 lists the present value of the benefits.

## (a) Aggregate world results

The long-run reduction in world military expenditures among industrial countries is about $160 billion.[14] The developing countries are assumed to decrease military spending by $50 billion.[15] Most of the countries in Eastern Europe and the former Soviet Union are not covered in the simulations. The long-run reduction in military expenditures in both industrial and net debtor developing countries is equivalent to 0.75 per cent of GDP, with decreases occurring in increments of 0.15 per cent of GDP in each of the first five years.

For *industrial countries* the simulation results show a decrease in GDP in 1993 of $12 billion, less than 0.1 per cent of GDP, compared to a cut in military spending of $27 billion. This reflects the boost to private sector spending caused by current and future reductions in taxes and interest rates. Private consumption rises by $1 billion in the

Table 2  **Sample simulation results: Main case[1] (% deviation from baseline)**

| | Government consumption | GDP | Private consumption | Private investment | Short-term interest | Long-term interest | Exchange rate | Exports | Imports |
|---|---|---|---|---|---|---|---|---|---|
| Industrial countries | | | | | | | | | |
| Year 1 | −0.8 | −0.1 | 0.0 | 0.5 | 0.1 | 0.1 | 0.1 | −0.0 | −0.0 |
| Year 5 | −4.0 | −0.0 | 0.6 | 1.7 | −0.0 | −0.3 | 0.0 | 0.1 | 0.0 |
| Year 8 | −4.0 | 0.3 | 1.0 | 2.0 | −0.3 | −0.2 | 0.0 | 0.6 | 0.2 |
| United States | | | | | | | | | |
| Year 1 | −1.4 | −0.1 | 0.0 | 0.5 | 0.1 | 0.1 | −1.7 | 0.3 | −0.6 |
| Year 5 | −7.4 | −0.0 | 0.8 | 1.8 | −0.0 | −0.3 | −2.2 | 0.7 | −1.4 |
| Year 8 | −7.4 | 0.3 | 1.2 | 2.2 | −0.4 | −0.2 | −1.9 | 1.5 | −1.2 |
| Japan | | | | | | | | | |
| Year 1 | −0.3 | −0.0 | 0.0 | 0.4 | 0.0 | −0.1 | 2.5 | −0.4 | 0.8 |
| Year 5 | −1.5 | 0.1 | 0.4 | 1.2 | −0.1 | −0.2 | 2.9 | −0.9 | 1.4 |
| Year 8 | −1.5 | 0.2 | 0.6 | 1.3 | −0.2 | −0.1 | 2.6 | −0.4 | 1.7 |
| France | | | | | | | | | |
| Year 1 | −0.7 | −0.1 | −0.0 | 0.2 | −0.0 | 0.3 | 0.2 | −0.0 | 0.0 |
| Year 5 | −3.6 | −0.1 | 0.5 | 1.9 | −0.2 | −0.4 | 0.3 | 0.4 | 0.2 |
| Year 8 | −3.6 | 0.4 | 1.0 | 2.4 | −0.2 | −0.3 | 0.2 | 0.9 | 0.2 |
| Net debtor developing countries | | | | | | | | | |
| Year 1 | −0.8 | −0.1 | 0.0 | −0.5 | NA | NA | 0.0 | 0.0 | −0.6 |
| Year 5 | −3.9 | −0.1 | 0.0 | 0.4 | NA | NA | 0.2 | 0.3 | −1.5 |
| Year 8 | −3.9 | 1.1 | 1.1 | 3.5 | NA | NA | 0.2 | 0.5 | −0.4 |

Source: Table A1.
1. Assumes a 20% reduction in military expenditures, military exports, and military imports phased in over 5 years.

Table 3  Sample simulation results: Alternative simulations (in 1992 $USbn)

| | Military spending | Main case (GDP | consumption) | | Accelerator model[1] (GDP | consumption) | | Investment model[2] (GDP | consumption) | | US only[3] (GDP | consumption) | |
|---|---|---|---|---|---|---|---|---|---|---|
| Industrial countries | | | | | | | | | | |
| Year 1 | −27.2 | −11.6 | 1.2 | −20.9 | −0.6 | −8.8 | 2.1 | 2.8 | 4.5 |
| Year 5 | −153.2 | −0.6 | 80.1 | 1.2 | 71.9 | −4.5 | 54.7 | 8.1 | 58.8 |
| Year 8 | −164.9 | 76.5 | 135.0 | 52.3 | 112.7 | 40.9 | 87.6 | 37.1 | 85.9 |
| United States | | | | | | | | | | |
| Year 1 | −12.4 | −3.8 | 0.2 | −9.0 | −1.1 | −3.5 | 0.6 | −2.4 | −0.2 |
| Year 5 | −70.0 | −3.4 | 38.8 | −4.0 | 35.6 | 0.0 | 30.0 | −6.4 | 31.6 |
| Year 8 | −75.3 | 25.9 | 61.7 | 18.4 | 54.0 | 15.4 | 45.5 | 18.5 | 50.1 |
| Japan | | | | | | | | | | |
| Year 1 | −1.4 | −0.8 | 0.8 | −1.7 | 0.8 | 0.0 | 0.8 | 0.0 | 0.8 |
| Year 5 | −7.6 | 5.9 | 11.7 | 5.0 | 10.0 | 3.3 | 6.7 | 4.2 | 6.7 |
| Year 8 | −8.3 | 12.5 | 17.6 | 10.0 | 14.2 | 6.7 | 10.0 | 7.5 | 9.2 |
| France | | | | | | | | | | |
| Year 1 | −1.1 | −1.3 | −0.2 | −1.5 | −0.2 | −0.9 | −0.1 | −0.1 | 0.4 |
| Year 5 | −6.3 | −0.6 | 3.2 | −0.3 | 2.9 | −0.6 | 2.1 | 0.7 | 1.7 |
| Year 8 | −6.7 | 5.2 | 6.6 | 3.8 | 5.4 | 3.1 | 4.2 | 0.9 | 2.2 |
| Net debtor developing countries | | | | | | | | | | |
| Year 1 | −6.4 | −5.8 | 0.0 | −8.8 | −0.8 | −6.1 | 0.4 | −0.2 | 0.7 |
| Year 5 | −39.5 | −5.7 | 1.2 | −9.9 | −4.9 | −13.4 | −3.9 | −0.7 | 0.6 |
| Year 8 | −42.5 | 76.0 | 45.6 | 66.7 | 29.4 | 56.1 | 25.7 | 4.4 | 4.5 |

Source: Table A2.
1. Assumes investment is more responsive to short-term fluctuations in output.
2. Assumes 20% military expenditure represents productive investment.
3. Assumes that the US unilaterally reduces military spending by 20%.

Table 4  **Present value of costs and benefits of reducing military spending (1992 US$bn)**[1]

| | US$ 1992 | | | % 1992 GDP | | |
|---|---|---|---|---|---|---|
| | 1993 to 2000 | Beyond 2000 | Total gain | 1993 to 2000 | Beyond 2000 | Total gain |
| **Industrial countries** | | | | | | |
| Military spending | −750 | −6025 | −6775 | −4.3 | −34.2 | −38.5 |
| Main case[2] | 446 | 8024 | 8469 | 2.5 | 45.6 | 48.1 |
| Accelerator model | 384 | 6503 | 6887 | 2.2 | 37.0 | 39.1 |
| Investment model | 299 | 4916 | 5215 | 1.7 | 27.9 | 29.6 |
| US only | 319 | 4841 | 5159 | 1.8 | 27.5 | 29.3 |
| **United States** | | | | | | |
| Military spending | −415 | −3329 | −3744 | −7.0 | −55.8 | −62.8 |
| Main case | 211 | 3267 | 3478 | 3.5 | 54.8 | 58.3 |
| Accelerator model | 188 | 2807 | 2995 | 3.1 | 47.1 | 50.2 |
| Investment model | 161 | 2299 | 2460 | 2.7 | 38.6 | 41.3 |
| US only | 170 | 2595 | 2764 | 2.8 | 43.5 | 46.4 |
| **Japan** | | | | | | |
| Military spending | −46 | −367 | −413 | −1.2 | −9.3 | −10.4 |
| Main case | 65 | 1192 | 1257 | 1.6 | 30.1 | 31.8 |
| Accelerator model | 54 | 978 | 1032 | 1.4 | 24.7 | 26.1 |
| Investment model | 38 | 672 | 710 | 0.9 | 17.0 | 17.9 |
| US only | 36 | 642 | 678 | 0.9 | 16.2 | 17.1 |
| **France** | | | | | | |
| Military spending | −37 | −297 | −334 | −3.0 | −24.1 | −27.1 |
| Main case | 18 | 407 | 425 | 1.5 | 33.0 | 34.5 |
| Accelerator model | 16 | 325 | 341 | 1.3 | 26.4 | 27.6 |
| Investment model | 12 | 307 | 318 | 1.0 | 24.9 | 25.8 |
| US only | 10 | 137 | 146 | 0.8 | 11.1 | 11.9 |
| **Net debtor developing countries** | | | | | | |
| Military spending | −230 | −1879 | −2109 | −4.6 | −37.3 | −41.8 |
| Main case | 57 | 3913 | 3970 | 1.1 | 77.6 | 78.7 |
| Accelerator model | 15 | 4169 | 4184 | 0.3 | 82.7 | 83.0 |
| Investment model | 17 | 3776 | 3793 | 0.3 | 74.9 | 75.2 |
| US only | 11 | 181 | 192 | 0.2 | 3.6 | 3.8 |

Source: Table A3.
1. See table 3 and the text for a description of the different simulations.
2. In each case, total benefits: consumption plus investment gains.

first year and investment increases by $16 billion (see discussion be-
low). Over the next four years, as military spending continues to fall,
the output losses become smaller as private consumption and investment rise steadily to $80 billion and $65 billion above baseline, respectively.[16] By the sixth year of the simulation, after all decreases in

military expenditures have stopped, the economic performance of industrial countries is considerably improved. In the main case, GDP is up $38 billion (0.1 per cent), consumption is up $104 billion (0.8 per cent), and investment is up $78 billion (1.9 per cent).

From the sixth year onward, economic growth begins to accelerate, and by the year 2000 GDP is 0.3 per cent higher than would have been expected ($77 billion). Consumption is 1 per cent higher than the baseline ($135 billion), and investment remains about 2 per cent higher. Thus, due to the increased investment in the intervening years, the annual level of consumption increases by almost the full amount of the original decrease in military expenditures.

The long-run change in economic welfare can be estimated by calculating the present value of the rise in private consumption over time.[17] Over the period 1993 to 2000 this can be calculated directly, using the results from the simulation. From the year 2000 onwards, however, it was necessary to calculate the gains assuming that the values of consumption and investment as a share of GDP in the year 2000 represented the new long-run levels. The overall gains to consumption implied by permanently higher consumption, and by the increased growth implied by higher investment, were then calculated. The gains to economic welfare, based on a discount rate of 4 per cent and underlying economic growth of 2 per cent (see appendix II for more details), can be split into three parts: (i) the rise in consumption between 1993 and 2000, estimated at $446 billion; (ii) the long-term gains in consumption based on the level reached in the year 2000, estimated at $4,933 billion; and (iii) the increased consumption associated with the higher long-term level of investment, estimated at $3,090 billion. The estimated present discounted value of the total long-run gains for industrial countries sums to $8.4 trillion, 48 per cent of 1992 GDP.[18]

The long-run gains in proportion to GDP are larger in those countries with a large military sector, in particular the United States, and smallest in those with a small military, such as Japan. However, because of positive international economic externalities, these differences are significantly smaller than the differences in the underlying cuts. For instance, relative to GDP, the military cuts in Japan are assumed to be only one-sixth of those in the United States, while the economic gains are over half of the US value.

For the *net debtor developing countries*, the simulation results indicate that GDP falls by between 0.1 and 0.2 per cent over the first five years, an accumulated loss of $50 billion. However, the loss in output is considerably smaller than the accumulated reductions in military expenditure, which total $134 billion over the same period. In the longer run GDP rises by 1.1 per cent, with much of this offset coming from private sector investment, which is 3.5 per cent ($61 billion) higher by the year 2000. For the net debtor nations, the decrease in worldwide military expenditures has a more pronounced economic impact than for industrial countries. The initial GDP decrease is larger, however, the impact on investment is also greater, so that the long-term gains are commensurately higher. These countries benefit considerably from the international economic externality.

## (b) US results

In order to fully explain the derivation of the simulation results, the economic impact on individual economies must be traced. For expositional ease, the analysis will trace the impact on one economy, the United States, in some detail, and then discuss the results in other countries in comparison to this country. This will enable a combined discussion of the economic linkages in MULTIMOD along with a detailed description of the results.

The United States was chosen because it is the largest economy, has the largest level of military spending (30 per cent of total world military expenditure), and allocates an above average share of GDP to the military. During the years 1987 to 1989 military spending in the United States represented 6 per cent of GDP. A 20 per cent reduction implies a total cut of $75 billion per annum (7.4 per cent of government expenditure), assumed to be phased in evenly over five years. As might be expected, the short-term impact of this is to reduce GDP below baseline values. This fall in GDP reflects a drop in aggregate demand from shifting expenditures from the public sector to the private sector via the cut in taxes – the opposite of the balanced budget multiplier. Since the cuts in military expenditure are spread out over five years, real GDP is still below baseline in the fifth year, before rebounding from 1998 onwards.

These losses in output are, however, relatively small; over the first five years the cumulative loss in real GDP is some $9 billion (less than 0.03 per cent of GDP) compared to cumulative expenditure cuts of $245 billion.[19] The small initial losses reflect the stimulation to private consumption and investment caused by lower interest rates and taxes. Given that agents are forward looking, these expenditures are stimulated by both current and by anticipated future reductions in these variables. Since the cuts are phased in over several years, the short-run stimulus to these variables is relatively large in comparison to the initial expenditure cuts, and the short-term losses to GDP correspondingly smaller. Private consumption increases slightly in the first year and continues to increase over the simulation, reaching $62 billion above baseline by the year 2000, a rise of 1.2 per cent. Overall, the present value of the increase in consumption is $211 billion over the course of the first eight years (1993–2000). Investment expenditures rise initially by 0.5 per cent, and by over 2 per cent ($28 billion) by the year 2000.

Over time, the increase in the capital stock caused by higher investment leads to a more than full recovery of GDP. The impact of military spending cuts on GDP turns positive after six years and from there onward rises quite substantially. By the year 2000, GDP is 0.3 per cent higher than it otherwise would have been. Hence, while in the short term there is a trade-off between military expenditures and the level of the GDP, in the medium term no such trade-off exists because the higher level of investment expenditure causes an increase in the GDP growth rate. Eventually, the GDP level surpasses the level that it would have attained without the change in military spending.

The present value of the consumption gains are calculated in three parts (see appendix II for a full explanation). The short and medium-term consumption gains (up to the year 2000) are estimated at $211 billion. The long-term direct consumption gains are estimated at $2,255 billion, while the future consumption gains associated with the higher level of investment are estimated at $1,012 billion. Thus the total economic welfare gain is $3,500 billion (58 per cent of 1992 GDP).[20] It should be stressed that most of the gains accrue in the very long term. By the year 2000 the overall gain to consumption is only 3.5 per cent of GDP, less than 7 per cent of the eventual total.

## (c) Trade and financial flows: the positive international externality

The basic effect of cutting military expenditure is to lower US interest rates due to the reduction in government spending. In the medium term, as the price level falls, the fixed monetary target implies lower interest rates. By the year 2000 short and long rates are 0.4 and 0.3

percentage points lower than in the baseline, respectively. In the short run, however, interest rates rise. The reason for this is that there is an initial depreciation in the currency, which causes a rise in inflation. The increase in the price level raises nominal demand, which raises interest rates; in countries such as Japan, where the exchange rate appreciates, interest rates fall immediately.

The exchange rate depreciation (the real effective exchange rate falls by 1.2 per cent in the first year) reflects the fact that the United States implements the largest cuts in military spending. Since it spends more on the military than other countries, the long-run fall in its interest rates is larger than in its competitors. Future falls in interest differentials result in a depreciation in the current nominal exchange rate, reflecting expectations of future appreciations in the rate.[21] It also reverses the negative initial impact on net exports caused by the replacement of military spending by relatively import-intensive private sector consumption and investment. The depreciation of the US dollar leads to a boost to net exports and an improvement in the current account; by 2000 real exports are 1.5 per cent higher and imports 1.2 per cent lower than in the baseline, while the current account improves by $11 billion. More generally, countries with a large military budget (in particular the United States) experience a depreciation in their exchange rate, while those with a small military budget (such as Japan and Canada) experience an appreciation. This real exchange rate effect means that part of the aggregate consumption gains from countries with relatively large cuts in military spending benefits economies whose cuts are smaller. These external benefits are quite significant; real net exports represent almost a quarter of the rise in US non-military output by the year 2000, although, since the United States would be running a current account surplus, some of the rise in net exports reflects an accumulation of international assets.

An implication of this external factor is that the economic welfare gains for any one country are larger when military expenditure cuts are carried out in conjunction with other countries, rather than unilaterally. This can be confirmed by comparing the results from the main case with a simulation in which only the United States cuts its military spending (table 3). It suffers greater short-run losses in output, as downward pressure on world interest rates is weaker. In the long-run, US welfare gains are about 20 per cent lower than when all countries cut simultaneously.

## IV. Other industrial countries

In Japan, military expenditures represent approximately 1 per cent of GDP, the smallest ratio of all of the G7 countries. Because of Japan's relatively low military expenditures in proportion to GDP, two very different results occur. First, the initial fall in output is short lived and mild in comparison to the United States; real GDP growth is reduced in the first year, by $1 billion, but already by the second year it is above the baseline and continues to increase thereafter. Secondly, the long-run gains are also smaller in Japan than in the United States relative to GDP, although the terms of trade effect means that they are larger than might initially be expected. By the year 2000, real GDP is predicted to be $13 billion higher annually. Because the yen appreciates by 3 per cent, real net exports fall and real consumption and real investment both rise by about $17 billion, significantly larger than the gain to output, and produced by military expenditure cuts of just $8 billion per annum.

The total increase in the present value of consumption is $1.3 trillion, or 32 per cent of 1992 GDP. Hence, in relative terms, the Japanese gain is slightly over half of that of the United States. As might be expected given the small size of the military sector in Japan, much of the economic gains are attributable to positive externalities from cuts in military spending in other countries, transmitted through international trade, rather than the domestic cuts themselves. Comparing the results from a global reduction in military spending with those from a unilateral cut by the United States alone, it appears that approximately half of the economic gains to Japan are attributable to the US decreases in military expenditures alone.

Germany holds an intermediate position between the United States and Japan, with military expenditures of 3 per cent of GDP during years 1987 to 1989. The results also fall between those of the United States and Japan. The exchange rate appreciates relative to the dollar, but remains largely unchanged in effective terms, and exports and imports both rise by around 0.5 per cent. As in Japan, output is already higher than in the baseline by 1994, reflecting the positive response of output to lower interest rates and the impact of the exchange rate mechanism (ERM), as discussed below. Long-run gains are sizeable; by the year 2000 GDP is $6 billion higher, and consumption and investment $9 billion higher (with military spending $12 billion lower). The present value of consumption rises by 42 per cent of GDP, larger than the gains to Japan but somewhat lower than the United States. The positive international economic externality is also apparent in the case of Germany and appears to account for approximately half the gains.

Among the other EC countries, the short-term effect of the cutbacks in military spending is magnified by the assumption that they are in the ERM (if these countries are not assumed to be in the ERM then the overall results can be inferred from those of the non-ERM countries). Because the currencies of these countries are in the ERM, and hence assumed to be pegged to the German mark, fiscal policy in general has a greater impact in these countries than in those countries operating under a floating exchange rate regime. The impact of the spending cuts on those countries in the ERM depends in large part on the size of these cuts compared with those made in Germany. For instance, in France and the United Kingdom, in which military spending is a larger proportion of GDP than in Germany, short-term output losses are relatively large. Indeed, in relative terms, they are significantly larger than in the United States. The long-term gains, which are largely unaffected by the ERM, are similar to those of Germany; by 2000, consumption increases by around 1 per cent in both countries, while investment rises by between 2 per cent and 3 per cent. In Italy and the smaller industrial countries (which, for simplicity, are all assumed to be members of the ERM) military spending is less important than in Germany, and results are correspondingly more favourable. Italy, for instance, experiences almost no short-run output loss. The long-term gains for both Italy and the smaller industrial countries are very similar to those of Germany. The positive international economic externality appears to account for somewhat less than half the total gains for Italy.

## V. Developing countries

For developing countries, the MULTIMOD simulation is not as sophisticated as with the industrial countries. In the first place, only two categories exist: net creditor and net debtor countries.[22] Secondly, the variables are more aggregated within the two developing countries' groups, and the behavioural equations are less well developed. Nevertheless, a broad overview of the impact on these countries can be outlined and some suggestive findings observed.

For net creditor countries, primarily oil exporters, military expenditures are a relatively high 7.1 per cent of GDP. Military imports represent a major share of total imports for this group, and for the most part these countries pay for these imports themselves without the use of military aid.[23] Since a large portion of military expenditures represents imports, costs of conversion would be low since non-military imports can be easily substituted for military ones. As a result, cuts in military spending are immediately replaced by higher private consumption and investment. For these countries the reduction in military spending of about 1.4 per cent of GDP is replaced approximately one-for-one by consumption and investment. The present value of this rise in private sector expenditures is 80 per cent of 1992 GDP ($569 billion), significantly greater in relative terms than the effect in the United States, reflecting the high level of initial military expenditures.

For the net debtor developing countries, total military expenditures represented 3.7 per cent of GDP on average. Imports accounted for 0.9 per cent of GDP or 23 per cent of total military expenditures. However, very few countries actually pay for their military imports.[24] In order to account for this factor, in addition to reducing exports and imports by 20 per cent of the value of military trade, foreign assistance was lowered by 80 per cent of the value of the fall in military imports. In MULTIMOD, these countries are assumed to be finance constrained, so that their ability to import and invest is limited by their ability to attract foreign financing. This, in turn, depends on the ratio of interest payments on foreign debt to exports. Lower interest rates imply lower debt servicing and increased access to foreign capital inflows. In addition, the shift in resources from military spending to private sector consumption and investment increases the demand in the industrial countries for exports of LDCs, in particular primary commodities and oil. This shift in the composition of demand also increases the ability of developing countries, both debtors and oil exporters, to access foreign loans.

Unfortunately, the domestic sector of these economies is modelled in an extremely rudimentary way in MULTIMOD. In particular, falls in domestic consumption are assumed to reflect falls in domestic supply potential. As a result it was not possible to use the unadjusted model in the simulations. Two alterations were made affecting the short- and long-run responses of output. In the short run it was assumed that the multiplier effects from cuts in military spending lead to lower output of non-tradable goods by the full amount of the spending decline in the first year, and half the amount in the second year. These multipliers are somewhat larger than those found for industrial countries, reflecting the less developed financial and labour markets in these countries. In the long run, as in the industrial countries, the level of potential output is made independent of the cuts in military spending.

The simulation results indicate that GDP falls by between 0.1 and 0.2 per cent over the first five years, an accumulated loss of $50 billion, largely reflecting the multiplier effects of reducing military spending. However, the loss in output is considerably smaller than the reductions in military expenditure, which total $134 billion over the same period, with much of the offset coming in the form of higher private sector investment. This rise in investment reflects the lessening of the constraint on imports and the increase in domestic savings. Higher export prices for primary goods, again aided by the demand shift from military to other consumption and investment, and lower worldwide interest rates both increase the ability of the net debtors to access international financial markets. By the year 2000 investment is 3.5 per cent above the baseline value.

This rise in investment leads to a substantial increase in GDP in the medium to long term. By the year 2000, GDP is projected to be 1.1 per cent higher, over $70 billion. This increase continues to rise to over 7 per cent in future years. Therefore, while it appears that net debtor countries as a whole will experience a larger and longer negative impact on output than industrial countries, the positive impact on domestic investment is more pronounced, leading to more dramatic GDP gains in the medium to long term. The gains to economic welfare can be calculated in the same manner as in the industrial countries. The results indicate that developing countries gain $4 trillion in present value terms, 79 per cent of their 1992 GDP.

The large gains reflect the fact that most of the gains from the cuts in military expenditure come in the form of productive investment. This provides a significant boost to the capital stock which in turn raises the growth of potential output in these countries. It is also reflected in the time profile of consumption. There is almost no net cumulative gain to private consumption until the year 2000.

An interesting feature of the results for the net debtor countries is that the overall impact of cuts on military spending appears to depend on the speed at which the cuts are implemented. This can be illustrated by discussing the results from an alternative scenario where the military cuts were assumed to be phased in over three years, rather than five years. It might be expected that this would cause larger short-term losses in output and similar long-run gains, as is the case for the industrial countries. However for the net debtor developing countries there are several offsetting effects. First, as industrial countries shift more quickly from military spending to other consumption and investment, the demand for oil and other commodities experiences a larger increase in the first two years. In addition, world interest rates are lower in the initial years under this scenario. Both of these factors allow LDCs to increase foreign borrowing and, so, imports and investment. The decline in output is actually lower than the base case in the first three years, while higher investment leads to higher real GDP in the medium term.

## VI. Industrial country variations

In order to test the sensitivity of the results to changes in the assumptions used in the main case, two further variations of the main case were simulated, in addition to the variants on the simulations discussed above. In the first, the investment function was augmented to make investment more sensitive to short-term change in output. In the second, the implicit assumption that military spending does not enhance civilian economic productivity is dropped. Instead, it is assumed that one-fifth of military spending is equivalent to productive investment.

## (a) Accelerator effect on investment

In this variant, the investment equation was augmented by a term which linked changes in private investment to changes in overall output. One possible justification for this is that military spending, being relatively geographically concentrated, may have larger short-run negative economic effects than other types of government spending. The major impact of the larger accelerator effect is to exacerbate the initial fall in output. In the industrial countries, real GDP declines by more in the first four years, reflecting both lower investment and, as a consequence of this, lower private consumption. The long-run gains to consumption and investment are also lower, and, at 39 per cent of GDP, the gain to economic welfare is some 20 per cent lower than in the main case. The short-run impact on developing countries is similar. Real growth declines more in the short run as exports and investment are somewhat lower. However, by 2000, investment is actually higher, as is the gain in economic welfare.

The primary conclusion from this simulation is that there is considerable uncertainty about the size of the initial output losses, since they depend crucially upon the extent to which reducing military expenditures inhibits business and consumer expectations. There has been considerable publicity associated with decreasing military expenditures. The initial negative impact could be larger than the relatively mild results obtained in the main case. It is entirely possible that the cuts in military spending could induce an initial reduction in private sector investment, rather than the increase which is predicted in the main case. However, the long-term gains from military spending cuts continue to be large.

## (b) Military spending as productive investment

Perhaps a more troubling issue is the extent to which military expenditures increase the productive capacity of a nation. It is now well established both theoretically and empirically that certain types of government expenditures promote civilian productivity. For instance, a direct positive relationship has been established between private capital and the level of public services (e.g. transportation), and between the quality of human capital and labour productivity. A question that has been hotly debated is the extent to which military activities enhance productivity. Here, a distinction must be established between the GDP and civilian output. Military expenditures enhance GDP in an accounting sense since they are counted as part of the GDP. The possible macroeconomic and trade benefits from military spending have already been explicitly considered in the simulation model. The question raised here is the extent to which the military provides positive spin-offs to civilian production. The spin-offs could come from military related research that has civilian applications, training given to demobilized military personnel, or possibly from infrastructure constructed by the military that is used by civilian producers. The scope for these is obviously more limited in the developing countries, which import most of their military equipment.

In order to determine the potential impact of this assumption, a simulation was produced under the assumption that one-fifth of the reduction in military spending in the industrial countries constitutes a cut in productive investment. Thus, four-fifths of the spending cuts were assumed to be from government consumption and one-fifth from productive government investment. The factor of one-fifth is not supposed to be an accurate estimate of the usefulness of military spending to civilian production.[25] Rather, the object is to get a sense of the impact of different assumptions about the usefulness of military spending for the civilian economy on the simulation results.

The main effect of the simulation is to reduce the long-run welfare gains from cutting military spending. In this scenario, part of the increase in investment brought about by lower taxes and interest rates is offset. While the short-run output declines are similar to the main case, the longer-term gains are smaller. By the year 2000 consumption and investment have increased by 0.6 and 1.1 per cent, compared to 1 and 2 per cent under the main case scenario. Hence, while the overall path of consumption and investment is similar, the level of benefits is considerably lower. The present value calculation indicates that the economic welfare of industrial countries rises by $5.2 trillion, 30 per cent of 1992 GDP, about a third lower than in the main case. The distribution of benefits also changes, with the United States losing proportionately less than Japan. As a result, the benefits are closer to the initial distribution of military cuts than was true in the main case scenario.

At 75 per cent of 1992 GDP, the economic welfare benefits accruing to developing countries are very similar to those found in the main case, partly reflecting the fact that none of the developing countries' spending was assumed to be investment. Lower growth in the industrial countries does, however, tilt the mix in non-military demand towards investment rather than consumption. By the year 2000 private sector consumption is 0.5 per cent above the baseline, only about half of that in the main case. However, almost all of this shortfall is made up for by higher investment. One implication of this switch to investment is that, while the overall increase in consumption is similar, these gains take longer to materialize.

Overall, the results indicate that the positive economic externality gained from reducing world military expenditures continues to exist even if the military proves to enhance civilian production substantially. However, the size of the overall benefits for the industrial countries are lowered somewhat.

## VII. Conclusions

This paper reports the results of a number of simulations using MULTIMOD, a macroeconomic model, to investigate the impact of lowering military expenditures on the world economy. Such a model makes it possible to investigate the implications of a complicated set of assumptions whose interactions are too complex to be traced theoretically. As with any set of simulations, the results reflect the structure and parameter values in the model. There are many factors, particularly of a micro-economic type, that have not been considered in the relatively simple approach pursued in this paper. Possibly the most important of these being that in the main case military expenditures are treated as entirely unproductive expenditure. Despite these caveats, the results provide several insights into the economic effects of military expenditures, as well as a useful benchmark of the potential economic welfare gains.

While there are substantial gains from cutting military spending, these gains are mainly generated in the longer run. Indeed, in the short run output is generally somewhat lower than it would have been otherwise, reflecting the negative impact on demand of cutting government spending. This pattern provides a reconciliation of the different views on the economic impact of military expenditures. In the short run, military spending does create jobs and stimulate the economy. However, military expenditures crowd out both private consumption and private investment and thus in the long term diminish economic growth.

Cutting military spending by 20 per cent worldwide could produce a long-run increase in private consumption and investment in industrial countries of 1 per cent and 2 per cent, respectively. These gains in turn produce the lion's share of the rise in economic welfare, which is estimated to be 48 per cent of current output. Those countries that implement the largest cuts have largest longer-term gains in consumption and investment (as well as the largest short-term losses in output). The long-run impact on less developed countries is also large, since these countries benefit both directly from the direct downsizing of their military and indirectly from lower interest rates and increased demand for their exports. Non-military consumption is estimated to rise by some 1 per cent and investment by 3.5 per cent, producing overall gains in economic welfare that, on a proportionate basis, could be around double those of the industrial countries (78 per cent of current GDP), reflecting the larger positive externalities experienced by these countries.

Since most of the gains in economic welfare come in the longer run, these results are relatively insensitive to short-term factors such as the timing of the tax cuts associated with lower government expenditures and the speed of the cuts in spending (the latter may have some effect on the developing country results), although these factors do have an impact on the size of the short-term losses to output. Two factors, however, do appear to lower the economic welfare gains, namely increasing the government spending multipliers and incorporating the assumption that part of the cut in military spending in the industrial countries represents a fall in productive investment. Even in these cases, however, the simulations indicate there would be substantial gains to economic welfare from cutting military spending. Finally, it should be stressed that all of these estimates of the change in economic welfare are extremely uncertain. They depend upon many assumptions, both in the MULTIMOD model and in the way the simulations were calculated, and should be seen as preliminary attempts to look at the magnitudes involved, rather than precise estimates of the exact benefits that will accrue.

Military expenditure cuts in any one country produce significant positive externalities for the rest of the world, both through lower interest rates and real exchange rates. As a result, the distribution of the economic benefits is considerably more even than the distribution of the cuts. For example, in the base case the cuts in spending in Japan are, as a ratio to GDP, only one-sixth of those in the United States, while the economic welfare gains are over half of those achieved by the United States. This implies that there are economic, as well as security, reasons for coordinating expenditure cut-backs.

## Notes

1. Alternatively, higher military expenditure of an alliance will have a negative impact on the security of rival alliances.
2. In theory, the means of correcting for the negative security externality would be to impose a military expenditure tax on all countries. Theoretically the tax would be proportional to the negative externality imposed on other nations and would induce each country to reduce their military expenditures in proportion to their price elasticity of demand for the military. Since neither the information required to calculate such a solution nor the institutional framework is available, an alternative policy is examined in the paper.
3. Even in the case of a unilateral decrease in military spending, GDP will only provide an accurate measure of the welfare when the spending on the military is at the social optimum and if other countries do not react to the changes.
4. Since non-military government spending is assumed to be unchanged in the simulations, the gain to private sector consumption is used to measure the gain in welfare.
5. For 16 countries military expenditure is found to cause lower economic growth, in six countries higher growth is found to cause higher military spending, in two countries both effects are present, and in two countries higher growth is found to cause lower military spending.
6. The study itself provides no data on the direction of the causality, however the authors provide details in personal correspondence. In eight countries military spending is found to cause lower growth while in five countries the opposite effect is found. In nine countries

higher growth is found to cause higher military spending and the reverse effect is found in five countries. The authors caution that when a feedback relationship exists, causality should be determined in a simultaneous equations framework.

7. SIPRI does not provide estimates for the USSR and China; Steinberg (1992) and ACDA were used for these two countries.

8. All the estimates related to these countries suffer from valuation problems. Even if a reasonably accurate rouble estimate exists, the conversion factor into US dollars is relatively arbitrary. In the data used in table 1, the conversion for military expenditures is based on official exchange rates. Those for military trade, which come from a different source, are based upon valuation methods employed by the US government.

9. Iran, Kuwait, Libya, Oman, Qatar, Saudi Arabia, Taiwan, and the United Arab Emirates.

10. A more extensive description of the properties of the model is contained in appendix 1. Masson et al. (1990) provide a detailed description of the model.

11. The argument that military spending provides technological spin-offs for civilian industries suggests that conversion may not be particularly difficult.

12. The baseline used in these simulations was based on the projections in the May 1992 World Economic Outlook produced by the IMF.

13. France, Italy, the United Kingdom, and the smaller industrial countries are assumed to participate in the exchange rate mechanism (ERM) in Europe, and hence to keep their exchange rates fixed to the Deutsche Mark. See McKibbin and Thurman (1992) for a fuller discussion of the effect of how different assumptions about monetary policy might affect the results.

14. Throughout the text, all the dollar figures are in 1992 real dollars.

15. This includes some of the countries of Eastern Europe.

16. This result is, however, sensitive to the assumptions in the simulation. Alternative simulations that incorporate a delayed reduction in tax rates, or longer accelerative effects in the investment equation, produce larger falls in economic activity. Indeed, both private consumption and investment could fall in the short run. The long-run gains are, however, similar in these simulations.

17. No analysis is made of the distributional effects of a decline in military spending across different sectors and regions, an issue of clear economic as well as political significance. The conversion from military to civilian production would inevitably lead to increased unemployment in the short run, which would be concentrated in particular geographic regions and industries within countries. For this reason changes in GDP, which likely mirror trends in unemployment, are also important for a full understanding of the impact of cuts in military spending. See CBO (1992) for a discussion of these factors in the US context.

18. The present discounted value of the foregone military expenditures is estimated to be $6.8 trillion, 38 per cent of 1992 GDP.

19. If military expenditures were cut more rapidly, the decrease in GDP relative to the baseline estimates would be shorter but steeper ($16 billion lost in three years).

20. By contrast, the present value of the rise in overall output is only 14 per cent of 1992 GDP, reflecting the cuts in military spending. This highlights the importance of recognizing that the welfare gain is based upon the gains in consumption, not the change in GDP.

21. This is the effect highlighted in the overshooting exchange rate model of Dornbusch (1976).

22. A satellite model exists that estimates the impact of policies on the major developing countries. The authors plan to investigate this question in more detail in a subsequent research paper.

23. If the entire Middle East is considered, their imports in 1987 were $21.9 billion or 24 per cent of their total imports. A large portion of these imports are financed through aid and other military credits, particularly for such countries as Egypt, Israel, Jordan, and Syria. Total military expenditures in 1987 in the Middle East are estimated at $57 billion, however it is uncertain to what extent this includes military imports. If it does include the imports, military imports would represent as much as 40 per cent of military spending.

24. Military aid of the United States alone equalled US$5 billion that year and major clients such as Israel and Egypt made no net payments for their arms imports; even their military loans were subsequently forgiven.
25. In this regard, it should be noted that personnel, operations, and maintenance make up between one-half and three-quarters of military spending in most industrial countries.

# References

Alexander, W. Robert (1990). "The Impact of Defence Spending on Economic Growth." *Defence Economics* 2, pp. 39–55.

Atesoglu, H. Somnetz, and Michael Mueller (1990). "Defence Spending and Economic Growth." *Defence Economics* 2, pp. 19–27.

Benoit, Emile (1973). *Defense Spending and Economic Growth in Developing Countries*. D.C. Heath and Co., Boston, Mass.

Brzoska, Michael (1990). "Military Trade, Aid and Developing Country Debt." World Bank working paper.

Chowdhury, Abdur (1991). "A Causal Analysis of Defense Spending and Economic Growth." *Journal of Conflict Resolution* 35 (1), pp. 80–97, 1991.

Congressional Budget Office (CBO) (1992). *The Economics Effects of Reduced Defense Spending*, February.

Deger, Saadet (1986). *Military Expenditure in Third World Countries*. Routledge and Kegan Paul, London.

Dornbusch, Rudiger (1976). "Expectations and Exchange Rate Dynamics." *Journal of Political Economy* 84, pp. 1161–1176.

Hewitt, Daniel (1992). "Military Expenditures Worldwide: Determinants and Trends, 1972–1988." *Journal of Public Policy*.

International Monetary Fund (1992). *International Financial Statistics Yearbook*. International Monetary Fund, Washington D.C.

Joerding, W. (1986). "Economic Growth and Defense Spending: Granger Causality." *Journal of Development Economics* 18, pp. 1–12.

Kohler, Daniel (1988). "The Effects of Defense and Security on Capital Formation in Africa: An Empirical Investigation." Rand Working Paper N-2653-USDP.

LaCivita, Charles, and Peter Frederiksen (1991). "Defense Spending and Economic Growth: An Alternative Approach to the Causality Issue." *Journal of Development Economics* 35, pp. 117–126.

Leontief, W. and F. Dutchin (1983). *Military Spending: Facts and Figures*. Oxford University Press, New York.

Masson, Paul, Steven Symansky, and Guy Meredith (1990). "MULTIMOD Mark II: A Revised and Extended Model." International Monetary Fund, Occasional Paper No. 71, July.

McKibbin, Warwick and Stephan Thurman (1992). "The Impact on the World Economy of Reductions in Military Expenditures and Military Arms Exports." Paper presented at the United Nations University Conference on "Arms Reduction and Economic Development in the Post Cold War Era." Tokyo, November.

Steinberg, Dimitri (1992). "Soviet Defense Burden: Estimating Hidden Defense Costs." *Soviet Studies*, March.

Stockholm International Peace Research Institute (SIPRI), *SIPRI Yearbook 1992*. Oxford University Press, Oxford.

Thomas, R. William, H.O. Stekler, and G. Wayne Glass (1991). "The Economic Effects of Reducing U.S. Defence Spending." *Defence Economics* 2 (2) pp. 183–197.

U.S. Arms Control and Disarmament Agency (ACDA) (1991). *World Military Expenditures and Arms Transfers 1990*. ACDA, Washington, D.C.

# Appendix I. A short description of MULTIMOD

MULTIMOD[1] is a system of linked models designed to analyse the interactions of economic policies and developments among the industrial countries, as well as to examine how changes in economic conditions in the industrial world affect developing countries as a group. The system presently contains econometric models (estimated on the basis of annual data) for each of the G7 countries (the United States, Canada, Japan, Germany, France, Italy, and the United Kingdom), the smaller industrial countries as a group, high-income (capital-exporting) developing countries as a group, and other (capital-importing) developing countries as a group.

The main linkages among the regions are the endogenous determination of prices and volumes of trade in goods and of exchange rates and interest rates. Each of the countries and regions produces manufactured goods which are imperfect substitutes. Imports of manufactured goods by the industrial countries (and capital-exporting developing countries) are functions of relative prices and absorption. Imports by other developing countries depend upon the amount of available foreign exchange (which depends, in turn, on export earnings and borrowing from other regions, as discussed further below). Each country's (or region's) imports of manufactured goods are allocated as exports across the other countries and regions through a trade matrix, with the initial pattern based on historical trading patterns. Trade shares adjust in response to changes in relative prices. It is assumed that all countries demand oil and that oil is homogeneous. Production and exports of oil by the industrial countries are assumed exogenous, and they adjust their imports to satisfy demand. The developing countries as a group are the residual suppliers. Non-oil primary commodities are produced by the developing countries and the price of this aggregate good adjusts in the short run to clear the market with production and supply eventually responding to changes in relative prices.

The prices of domestically-produced goods are determined in a price mark-up Phillips curve relationship that incorporates overlapping contracts, so that prices are sticky. Current wage contracts are forward looking, incorporating anticipated future rates of inflation. Export prices are assumed to move with the domestic output price in the long run, but respond in the short run to price movements in the export markets. Import prices are a weighted average of the export prices of other countries.

MULTIMOD models the demand for base money, rather than for a broader aggregate. It is assumed that the monetary authorities in most industrial countries set a target path for the monetary base. The actual path of the money supply is determined by an interest rate reaction function, which smooths interest rate changes in the short run. In the long run, however, the actual money supply converges to the target path. A fixed exchange rate system is imposed on the model for those countries of the European Monetary System (EMS) that participate in the exchange rate mechanism (ERM). Italy, France, the United Kingdom, and the smaller industrial countries as a group are assumed to peg their currencies to the German Deutsche

Mark by changing their interest rates (and, of course, money supplies). This policy regime results in a loss of independent monetary actions by all the ERM countries except Germany.

Financial assets of the industrial countries are assumed to be perfect substitutes, and nominal exchange rates are determined by open interest parity. Long-term interest rates are specified as a moving average of current and expected future short-term rates. An important feature of the model is that expectations about interest rates and exchange rates, as well as prices, are forward looking and consistent with the model's solution in future periods (i.e., expectations are "rational"). This means, for example, that the effects of future policy changes announced today, but implemented sometime in the future, can have an immediate effect on exchange rates, interest rates, and inflation rates, and thereby, on other macroeconomic variables.

Another key feature of the model is the financial link between industrial countries and the capital-importing developing countries. The flow of credit to developing countries is assumed to depend upon a forward-looking measure of their ability to service their external debt. If current, past, or future events lead to increased developing country export earnings in the future (and to an expected decline in the ratio of their debt service payment to exports), industrial countries will be encouraged to increase their lending to the developing countries in the current period. As noted above, imports of these developing countries are determined residually, by the availability of foreign exchange.

## Note

1. A more detailed description of the model is given in Masson et al. (1990).

## Appendix II. Calculation of present value of long-term welfare gains

The benefits obtained in any country from reducing military expenditure are equivalent to the increase in private consumption realized in current and future years. The cost to the country of this policy is the decrease in security due to lower military expenditures. If a coordinated decrease in military spending occurs, the decrease in the level of military spending by a given country will not necessarily be reflected in a fall in security. Each country will benefit from the decreased military expenditures by neighbouring countries and others, to the extent that they feel threatened. Theoretically, countries could experience an increase in security with a coordinated decrease in military expenditures as the capability of all countries to wage an attack would be diminished.

The present value of the consumption flows consists of a number of different steps. The underlying macroeconomic assumptions behind the calculations are that the baseline real rate of interest is 4 per cent and that the world level of economic growth is 2 per cent per annum. The short- and medium-term costs and benefits can be calculated directly from the simulation results using the discount rate of 4 per cent. For instance, for net debtor developing countries in the main case simulation, the increase in consumption from 1993 to 2000 is estimated to be $57 billion while military expenditures fall by $230 billion.

The long-term gains in consumption consist of two parts. First, there is a higher level of consumption relative to the base case in the year 2000. This will continue to increase as the economy grows. Therefore, in order to calculate the present value of these future increases in consumption, the discount factor is the real interest rate less the rate of growth or 2 per cent. For net debtor developing countries this is estimated to be $1,667 billion.

The increased level of investment from the year 2000 onward will also result in consumption gains. In a well-functioning market economy in equilibrium, the present value of future consumption from each project should be equal to the cost of capital investment (with distortions, the present value of future consumption associated with investment projects may differ from unity). Therefore, the consumption value of investment was calculated at the level of investment expenditures in the year 2000 discounted at the real rate of interest less the growth rate. For the net debtor developing countries this level is estimated at $2,246 billion. The total benefits are $3,970 billion, while the decrease in military spending (using the same discount factors) is $2,109 billion. In the case of the net debtor developing countries, the future consumption increase is considerably above the decrease in military spending. This is due in part to the international economic externality. For instance, with the United States the gains are estimated to be $3,477 billion compared to lower military spending valued at $3,744 billion.

Table A1  **Reducing military expenditures: Main case simulation results**

|  | 1993 | 1994 | 1995 | 1996 | 1997 | 1998 | 1999 | 2000 |
|---|---|---|---|---|---|---|---|---|
|  |  |  |  | (% deviation from baseline) |  |  |  |  |
| **Industrial countries** |  |  |  |  |  |  |  |  |
| Real government spending | −0.8 | −1.6 | −2.4 | −3.2 | −4.0 | −4.0 | −4.0 | −4.0 |
| Real GDP | −0.1 | −0.0 | −0.0 | −0.0 | −0.0 | 0.1 | 0.3 | 0.3 |
| Real consumption | +0.0 | 0.2 | 0.3 | 0.5 | 0.6 | 0.8 | 0.9 | 1.0 |
| Real investment | 0.5 | 0.9 | 1.1 | 1.4 | 1.7 | 1.9 | 2.0 | 2.0 |
| **Developing countries (net debtor)** |  |  |  |  |  |  |  |  |
| Real government spending | −0.8 | −1.6 | −2.3 | −3.1 | −3.9 | −3.9 | −3.9 | −3.9 |
| Real GDP | −0.1 | −0.2 | −0.2 | −0.2 | −0.1 | 0.3 | 0.7 | 1.1 |
| Total consumption[2] | +0.2 | −0.4 | −0.6 | −0.8 | −1.0 | −0.8 | −0.5 | −0.1 |
| Real consumption | 0.0 | 0.0 | −0.1 | −0.1 | 0.0 | 0.2 | 0.6 | 1.1 |
| Real investment | −0.5 | −0.4 | −0.1 | 0.1 | 0.4 | 1.7 | 2.8 | 3.5 |
| **United States** |  |  |  |  |  |  |  |  |
| Real government spending | −1.4 | −2.9 | −4.3 | −5.9 | −7.4 | −7.4 | −7.4 | −7.4 |
| Real GDP | −0.1 | 0.0 | −0.0 | −0.0 | −0.0 | 0.2 | 0.3 | 0.3 |
| Real consumption | 0.0 | 0.2 | 0.4 | 0.6 | 0.8 | 1.0 | 1.2 | 1.2 |
| Real investment | 0.5 | 0.9 | 1.1 | 1.4 | 1.8 | 2.1 | 2.2 | 2.2 |
| Real short-term interest rate[1] | 0.1 | 0.2 | 0.3 | 0.2 | −0.0 | −0.3 | −0.4 | −0.4 |
| Real long-term interest rate[1] | 0.0 | −0.1 | −0.2 | −0.3 | −0.3 | −0.3 | −0.3 | −0.3 |
| Exchange rate (effective) | −1.7 | −1.8 | −2.0 | −2.1 | −2.2 | −2.2 | −2.0 | −1.9 |
| Real exports | 0.3 | 0.6 | 0.8 | 0.7 | 0.7 | 1.2 | 1.4 | 1.5 |
| Real imports | −0.6 | −1.1 | −1.2 | −1.3 | −1.4 | −1.4 | −1.3 | −1.2 |

**Japan**

| | | | | | | | | |
|---|---|---|---|---|---|---|---|---|
| Real government spending | −0.3 | −0.6 | −0.9 | −1.2 | −1.5 | −1.5 | −1.5 | −1.5 |
| Real GDP | −0.0 | 0.1 | 0.1 | 0.1 | 0.1 | 0.2 | 0.2 | 0.2 |
| Real consumption | 0.0 | 0.2 | 0.3 | 0.3 | 0.4 | 0.5 | 0.5 | 0.6 |
| Real investment | 0.4 | 0.8 | 0.9 | 1.0 | 1.1 | 1.2 | 1.2 | 1.2 |
| Real short-term interest rate[1] | 0.0 | −0.0 | −0.1 | −0.1 | −0.1 | −0.2 | −0.2 | −0.2 |
| Real long-term interest rate[1] | −0.1 | −0.1 | −0.1 | −0.2 | −0.2 | −0.2 | −0.2 | −0.1 |
| Exchange rate (effective) | 2.5 | 2.6 | 2.8 | 2.9 | 2.9 | 2.9 | 2.8 | 2.6 |
| Real exports | −0.4 | −0.6 | −0.6 | −0.8 | −0.9 | −0.6 | −0.4 | −0.4 |
| Real imports | 0.8 | 1.2 | 1.4 | 1.4 | 1.4 | 1.7 | 1.7 | 1.7 |

**Germany**

| | | | | | | | | |
|---|---|---|---|---|---|---|---|---|
| Real government spending | −0.5 | −1.0 | −1.6 | −2.1 | −2.6 | −2.6 | −2.6 | −2.6 |
| Real GDP | −0.0 | 0.0 | 0.0 | 0.0 | −0.0 | 0.1 | 0.1 | 0.2 |
| Real consumption | 0.0 | 0.2 | 0.4 | 0.5 | 0.6 | 0.8 | 0.9 | 1.0 |
| Real investment | 0.6 | 1.1 | 1.3 | 1.5 | 1.7 | 2.0 | 2.1 | 2.1 |
| Real short-term interest rate[1] | 0.0 | 0.0 | 0.1 | 0.1 | −0.0 | −0.2 | −0.3 | −0.3 |
| Real long-term interest rate[1] | 0.0 | −0.0 | −0.1 | −0.2 | −0.2 | −0.3 | −0.3 | −0.2 |
| Exchange rate (effective) | −0.0 | −0.0 | −0.0 | −0.0 | −0.0 | −0.0 | 0.0 | 0.1 |
| Real exports | 0.0 | 0.1 | 0.2 | 0.2 | 0.2 | 0.4 | 0.5 | 0.5 |
| Real imports | 0.1 | 0.3 | 0.4 | 0.3 | 0.3 | 0.5 | 0.6 | 0.5 |

**France**

| | | | | | | | | |
|---|---|---|---|---|---|---|---|---|
| Real government spending | −0.7 | −1.4 | −2.1 | −2.9 | −3.6 | −3.6 | −3.6 | −3.6 |
| Real GDP | −0.1 | −0.2 | −0.2 | −0.1 | −0.1 | 0.2 | 0.4 | 0.5 |
| Real consumption | −0.0 | 0.1 | 0.2 | 0.4 | 0.5 | 0.8 | 0.9 | 1.0 |
| Real investment | 0.2 | 0.6 | 1.0 | 1.4 | 1.9 | 2.3 | 2.4 | 2.4 |
| Real short-term interest rate[1] | 0.3 | 0.4 | 0.4 | 0.2 | 0.0 | −0.3 | −0.5 | −0.5 |
| Real long-term interest rate[1] | 0.3 | 0.1 | −0.0 | −0.2 | −0.4 | −0.4 | −0.4 | −0.3 |
| Exchange rate (effective) | 0.2 | 0.2 | 0.2 | 0.3 | 0.3 | 0.3 | 0.2 | 0.2 |
| Real exports | −0.0 | 0.1 | 0.3 | 0.3 | 0.4 | 0.7 | 0.9 | 0.9 |
| Real imports | −0.0 | 0.2 | 0.3 | 0.3 | 0.2 | 0.3 | 0.3 | 0.2 |

Table A1  *(cont.)*

| | 1993 | 1994 | 1995 | 1996 | 1997 | 1998 | 1999 | 2000 |
|---|---|---|---|---|---|---|---|---|
| | | | | (% deviation from baseline) | | | | |
| **United Kingdom** | | | | | | | | |
| Real government spending | −0.7 | −1.5 | −2.2 | −3.0 | −3.7 | −3.7 | −3.7 | −3.7 |
| Real GDP | −0.2 | −0.3 | −0.3 | −0.2 | −0.2 | 0.1 | 0.3 | 0.5 |
| Real consumption | −0.1 | −0.0 | 0.1 | 0.2 | 0.4 | 0.6 | 0.8 | 0.9 |
| Real investment | 0.1 | 0.4 | 1.0 | 1.6 | 2.2 | 2.6 | 2.9 | 2.8 |
| Real short-term interest rate[1] | 0.4 | 0.5 | 0.5 | 0.3 | 0.1 | −0.2 | −0.4 | −0.5 |
| Real long-term interest rate[1] | 0.4 | 0.2 | 0.1 | −0.1 | −0.3 | −0.4 | −0.4 | −0.3 |
| Exchange rate (effective) | 0.2 | 0.2 | 0.2 | 0.2 | 0.2 | 0.2 | 0.2 | 0.1 |
| Real exports | −0.1 | 0.0 | 0.2 | 0.3 | 0.4 | 0.8 | 1.1 | 1.2 |
| Real imports | −0.1 | −0.0 | 0.1 | 0.1 | 0.1 | 0.2 | 0.3 | 0.2 |
| **Italy** | | | | | | | | |
| Real government spending | −0.5 | −0.9 | −1.4 | −1.8 | −2.3 | −2.3 | −2.3 | −2.3 |
| Real GDP | −0.0 | 0.0 | 0.1 | 0.1 | 0.1 | 0.2 | 0.4 | 0.4 |
| Real consumption | 0.0 | 0.2 | 0.4 | 0.5 | 0.7 | 0.9 | 1.0 | 1.1 |
| Real investment | 0.6 | 1.1 | 1.3 | 0.6 | 1.8 | 2.1 | 2.2 | 2.2 |
| Real short-term interest rate[1] | 0.1 | 0.1 | 0.1 | 0.1 | −0.1 | −0.3 | −0.4 | −0.4 |
| Real long-term interest rate[1] | −0.1 | −0.1 | −0.2 | −0.2 | −0.3 | −0.3 | −0.3 | −0.2 |
| Exchange rate (effective) | 0.2 | 0.2 | 0.2 | 0.2 | 0.2 | 0.2 | 0.2 | 0.1 |
| Real exports | −0.1 | 0.0 | 0.1 | 0.1 | −0.0 | 0.2 | 0.3 | 0.3 |
| Real imports | 0.2 | 0.5 | 0.7 | 0.8 | 0.9 | 1.1 | 1.2 | 1.1 |

**Canada**

| | | | | | | | | |
|---|---|---|---|---|---|---|---|---|
| Real government spending | -0.4 | -0.7 | -1.2 | -1.6 | -2.0 | -2.0 | -2.0 | -2.0 |
| Real GDP | -0.0 | 0.1 | 0.1 | 0.1 | 0.1 | 0.2 | 0.3 | 0.3 |
| Real consumption | 0.0 | 0.2 | 0.4 | 0.5 | 0.6 | 0.7 | 0.8 | 0.9 |
| Real investment | 0.6 | 1.1 | 1.3 | 1.4 | 1.6 | 1.8 | 2.0 | 1.9 |
| Real short-term interest rate[1] | -0.0 | 0.0 | 0.1 | 0.0 | -0.1 | -0.3 | -0.3 | -0.3 |
| Real long-term interest rate[1] | -0.0 | -0.1 | -0.1 | -0.2 | -0.3 | -0.3 | -0.2 | -0.2 |
| Exchange rate (effective) | 0.2 | 0.3 | 0.4 | 0.5 | 0.6 | 0.7 | 0.7 | 0.7 |
| Real exports | -0.0 | 0.2 | 0.3 | 0.3 | 0.1 | 0.3 | 0.3 | 0.3 |
| Real imports | 0.3 | 0.6 | 0.8 | 0.9 | 1.0 | 1.2 | 1.2 | 1.1 |

**Smaller industrial countries**

| | | | | | | | | |
|---|---|---|---|---|---|---|---|---|
| Real government spending | -0.4 | -0.9 | -1.3 | -1.8 | -2.3 | -2.3 | -2.3 | -2.3 |
| Real GDP | -0.1 | 0.0 | 0.0 | 0.1 | 0.0 | 0.2 | 0.2 | 0.3 |
| Real consumption | 0.0 | 0.2 | 0.3 | 0.4 | 0.5 | 0.6 | 0.7 | 0.8 |
| Real investment | 0.6 | 1.1 | 1.2 | 1.4 | 1.6 | 1.8 | 1.9 | 1.9 |
| Real short-term interest rate[1] | 0.0 | 0.0 | 0.1 | 0.0 | -0.1 | -0.2 | -0.2 | -0.2 |
| Real long-term interest rate[1] | 0.0 | -0.0 | -0.1 | -0.2 | -0.2 | -0.3 | -0.3 | -0.2 |
| Exchange rate (effective) | 0.3 | 0.3 | 0.4 | 0.4 | 0.4 | 0.4 | 0.3 | 0.3 |
| Real exports | -0.1 | -0.1 | 0.0 | -0.1 | -0.3 | -0.0 | 0.1 | 0.1 |
| Real imports | 0.2 | 0.3 | 0.3 | 0.2 | 0.2 | 0.4 | 0.5 | 0.4 |

1. % point change.

Table A2  Reducing military spending: Alternative simulations (1992 US$bn)

| | 1993 | 1994 | 1995 | 1996 | 1997 | 1998 | 1999 | 2000 |
|---|---|---|---|---|---|---|---|---|
| **Industrial countries** | | | | | | | | |
| Military spending | −27.2 | −56.3 | −87.0 | −118.7 | −153.2 | −156.9 | −160.9 | −164.9 |
| Main case | | | | | | | | |
| Real GDP | −11.6 | −2.1 | −0.8 | −1.2 | −0.6 | 38.1 | 64.4 | 76.5 |
| Real consumption | 1.2 | 20.8 | 39.2 | 59.0 | 80.1 | 103.9 | 122.8 | 135.0 |
| Accelerator model | | | | | | | | |
| Real GDP | −20.9 | −7.9 | −5.9 | −2.3 | 1.2 | 26.7 | 43.1 | 52.3 |
| Real consumption | −0.6 | 19.0 | 35.8 | 53.8 | 71.9 | 88.9 | 102.6 | 112.7 |
| Investment model | | | | | | | | |
| Real GDP | −8.8 | −4.2 | −7.1 | −6.7 | −4.5 | 20.4 | 33.6 | 40.9 |
| Real consumption | 2.1 | 15.5 | 27.1 | 40.4 | 54.7 | 69.0 | 79.6 | 87.6 |
| US only | | | | | | | | |
| Real GDP | 2.8 | 12.8 | 10.2 | 8.7 | 8.1 | 22.6 | 32.4 | 37.1 |
| Real consumption | 4.5 | 20.2 | 32.5 | 45.6 | 58.8 | 70.7 | 79.9 | 85.9 |
| **Developing countries (net debtors)** | | | | | | | | |
| Military spending | −7.7 | −16.3 | −25.9 | −36.3 | −47.8 | −49.0 | −50.2 | −51.4 |
| Main case | | | | | | | | |
| Real GDP | −5.8 | −10.6 | −13.7 | −12.6 | −5.7 | 16.6 | 45.4 | 76.0 |
| Real consumption | 0.0 | −0.9 | −2.2 | −2.2 | 1.2 | 9.9 | 25.4 | 45.6 |
| Accelerator model | | | | | | | | |
| Real GDP | −8.8 | −13.4 | −16.7 | −15.9 | −9.9 | 10.5 | 37.4 | 66.7 |
| Real consumption | −0.8 | −2.6 | −5.0 | −6.2 | −4.9 | 0.8 | 12.7 | 29.4 |
| Investment model | | | | | | | | |
| Real GDP | −6.1 | −12.0 | −16.5 | −17.4 | −13.4 | 5.1 | 29.4 | 56.1 |
| Real consumption | 0.4 | −0.7 | −2.9 | −4.5 | −3.9 | 0.4 | 10.7 | 25.7 |

| | | | | | | | | |
|---|---|---|---|---|---|---|---|---|
| **US only** | | | | | | | | |
| Real GDP | −0.2 | 0.7 | 0.1 | −0.4 | −0.7 | 1.6 | 3.4 | 4.4 |
| Real consumption | 0.7 | 1.5 | 1.3 | 0.8 | 0.6 | 1.3 | 2.9 | 4.5 |
| **United States** | | | | | | | | |
| Military spending | −15.0 | −31.2 | −48.3 | −66.1 | −84.7 | −86.8 | −88.9 | −91.1 |
| **Main case** | | | | | | | | |
| Real GDP | −3.8 | 1.7 | −0.4 | −2.3 | −3.4 | 12.6 | 22.4 | 25.9 |
| Real consumption | 0.2 | 10.8 | 19.4 | 28.8 | 38.8 | 49.0 | 56.7 | 61.7 |
| **Accelerator model** | | | | | | | | |
| Real GDP | −9.0 | −1.6 | −2.8 | −3.5 | −4.0 | 8.5 | 15.4 | 18.4 |
| Real consumption | −1.1 | 9.7 | 18.0 | 26.7 | 35.6 | 43.6 | 49.6 | 54.0 |
| **Investment model** | | | | | | | | |
| Real GDP | −3.5 | 0.7 | −2.2 | −3.9 | −4.7 | 7.5 | 12.9 | 15.4 |
| Real consumption | 0.6 | 9.1 | 15.5 | 22.5 | 30.0 | 37.1 | 42.0 | 45.5 |
| **US only** | | | | | | | | |
| Real GDP | −2.4 | 1.0 | −3.8 | −5.9 | −6.4 | 6.5 | 15.0 | 18.5 |
| Real consumption | −0.2 | 8.6 | 15.2 | 23.0 | 31.6 | 39.4 | 45.9 | 50.1 |
| **Japan** | | | | | | | | |
| Military spending | −1.7 | −3.3 | −5.0 | −7.5 | −9.2 | −10.0 | −10.0 | −10.0 |
| **Main case** | | | | | | | | |
| Real GDP | −0.8 | 3.3 | 4.2 | 5.0 | 5.9 | 9.2 | 11.7 | 12.5 |
| Real consumption | 0.8 | 4.2 | 6.7 | 9.2 | 11.7 | 14.2 | 16.6 | 17.6 |
| **Accelerator model** | | | | | | | | |
| Real GDP | −1.7 | 2.5 | 3.3 | 4.2 | 5.0 | 7.5 | 8.4 | 10.0 |
| Real consumption | 0.8 | 3.3 | 5.9 | 8.4 | 10.0 | 11.7 | 13.4 | 14.2 |
| **Investment model** | | | | | | | | |
| Real GDP | 0.0 | 1.7 | 1.7 | 2.5 | 3.3 | 5.0 | 5.9 | 6.7 |
| Real consumption | 0.8 | 2.5 | 4.2 | 5.0 | 6.7 | 8.4 | 9.2 | 10.0 |
| **US only** | | | | | | | | |
| Real GDP | 0.0 | 2.5 | 3.3 | 4.2 | 4.2 | 5.9 | 6.7 | 7.5 |
| Real consumption | 0.8 | 2.5 | 4.2 | 5.0 | 6.7 | 7.5 | 8.4 | 9.2 |

Table A2  (cont.)

| | 1993 | 1994 | 1995 | 1996 | 1997 | 1998 | 1999 | 2000 |
|---|---|---|---|---|---|---|---|---|
| **Germany** | | | | | | | | |
| Military spending | -2.0 | -4.0 | -6.2 | -8.5 | -11.0 | -11.3 | -11.6 | -11.8 |
| Main case | | | | | | | | |
|   Real GDP | -0.4 | 0.7 | 0.7 | 0.3 | -0.1 | 3.1 | 5.2 | 6.1 |
|   Real consumption | 0.3 | 1.6 | 2.7 | 3.8 | 4.8 | 6.5 | 7.8 | 8.8 |
| Accelerator model | | | | | | | | |
|   Real GDP | -1.3 | 0.1 | 0.2 | 0.2 | 0.3 | 1.7 | 3.0 | 4.0 |
|   Real consumption | 0.2 | 1.5 | 2.4 | 3.4 | 4.2 | 5.2 | 6.3 | 7.1 |
| Investment model | | | | | | | | |
|   Real GDP | -0.3 | 0.1 | -0.2 | -0.3 | -0.2 | 1.3 | 2.3 | 3.1 |
|   Real consumption | 0.4 | 1.1 | 1.7 | 2.4 | 3.0 | 3.9 | 4.6 | 5.4 |
| US only | | | | | | | | |
|   Real GDP | 0.5 | 1.4 | 1.6 | 1.7 | 1.7 | 2.2 | 2.7 | 3.0 |
|   Real consumption | 0.4 | 1.1 | 1.7 | 2.2 | 2.8 | 3.4 | 4.0 | 4.5 |
| **France** | | | | | | | | |
| Military spending | -1.3 | -2.8 | -4.3 | -5.9 | -7.6 | -7.7 | -7.9 | -8.1 |
| Main case | | | | | | | | |
|   Real GDP | -1.3 | -1.7 | -1.5 | -1.2 | -0.6 | 2.3 | 4.2 | 5.2 |
|   Real consumption | -0.2 | 0.3 | 1.1 | 2.0 | 3.2 | 4.7 | 5.9 | 6.6 |
| Accelerator model | | | | | | | | |
|   Real GDP | -1.5 | -1.9 | -1.8 | -1.2 | -0.3 | 1.7 | 3.1 | 3.8 |
|   Real consumption | -0.2 | 0.3 | 0.9 | 1.8 | 2.9 | 4.0 | 4.8 | 5.4 |
| Investment model | | | | | | | | |
|   Real GDP | -0.9 | -1.5 | -1.6 | -1.2 | -0.6 | 1.4 | 2.6 | 3.1 |
|   Real consumption | -0.1 | 0.2 | 0.6 | 1.3 | 2.1 | 3.0 | 3.7 | 4.2 |

| | | | | | | | | |
|---|---|---|---|---|---|---|---|---|
| **United Kingdom** | | | | | | | | |
| US only | | | | | | | | |
| Real GDP | 0.9 | 1.1 | 1.0 | 0.9 | 0.7 | 0.6 | 0.7 | 0.9 |
| Real consumption | 0.4 | 0.9 | 1.2 | 1.4 | 1.7 | 1.9 | 2.1 | 2.2 |
| Military spending | −1.6 | −3.2 | −5.0 | −6.9 | −8.7 | −8.9 | −9.3 | −9.5 |
| Main case | | | | | | | | |
| Real GDP | −1.8 | −2.6 | −2.6 | −2.4 | −1.8 | 13.9 | 3.8 | 5.0 |
| Real consumption | −0.4 | 0.0 | 0.0 | 1.6 | 2.8 | 4.4 | 5.6 | 6.3 |
| Accelerator model | | | | | | | | |
| Real GDP | −2.4 | −3.0 | −2.8 | −2.2 | −1.4 | 0.8 | 2.6 | 3.6 |
| Real consumption | −0.4 | −0.2 | 0.6 | 1.4 | 2.4 | 3.6 | 4.4 | 5.2 |
| Investment model | | | | | | | | |
| Real GDP | −1.4 | −2.4 | −2.6 | −2.2 | −1.6 | 0.6 | 2.0 | 2.8 |
| Real consumption | −0.2 | −0.2 | 0.2 | 0.8 | 1.6 | 2.6 | 3.2 | 3.8 |
| US only | | | | | | | | |
| Real GDP | 1.4 | 1.8 | 1.6 | 1.4 | 1.0 | 1.0 | 0.8 | 0.8 |
| Real consumption | 0.8 | 1.4 | 2.0 | 2.4 | 2.6 | 2.8 | 3.0 | 3.0 |
| **Italy** | | | | | | | | |
| Military spending | −0.9 | −2.0 | −3.1 | −4.2 | −5.4 | −5.5 | −5.6 | −5.8 |
| Main case | | | | | | | | |
| Real GDP | −0.5 | 0.2 | 0.7 | 0.8 | 0.9 | 3.0 | 4.4 | 5.1 |
| Real consumption | 0.2 | 1.3 | 2.5 | 3.8 | 5.0 | 6.6 | 7.8 | 8.6 |
| Accelerator model | | | | | | | | |
| Real GDP | −0.7 | −0.1 | 0.3 | 0.7 | 0.9 | 2.0 | 2.8 | 3.3 |
| Real consumption | 0.1 | 1.2 | 2.1 | 3.2 | 4.2 | 5.1 | 5.9 | 6.4 |
| Investment model | | | | | | | | |
| Real GDP | −0.4 | −0.3 | −0.2 | 0.0 | 0.3 | 1.3 | 2.1 | 2.5 |
| Real consumption | 0.1 | 0.7 | 1.2 | 1.9 | 2.6 | 3.4 | 3.9 | 4.5 |
| US only | | | | | | | | |
| Real GDP | 1.0 | 2.1 | 2.3 | 2.3 | 2.1 | 1.9 | 1.6 | 1.4 |
| Real consumption | 0.7 | 1.9 | 2.6 | 3.3 | 3.7 | 3.9 | 4.0 | 3.9 |

Table A2 (cont.)

| | 1993 | 1994 | 1995 | 1996 | 1997 | 1998 | 1999 | 2000 |
|---|---|---|---|---|---|---|---|---|
| **Canada** | | | | | | | | |
| Military spending | −0.5 | −0.9 | −1.5 | −2.1 | −2.6 | −2.7 | −2.8 | −2.9 |
| Main case | | | | | | | | |
|   Real GDP | −0.1 | 0.5 | 0.6 | 0.5 | 0.5 | 1.3 | 1.7 | 2.0 |
|   Real consumption | 0.2 | 0.7 | 1.3 | 1.8 | 2.4 | 2.9 | 3.4 | 3.6 |
| Accelerator model | | | | | | | | |
|   Real GDP | −0.3 | 0.4 | 0.6 | 0.6 | 0.6 | 0.9 | 1.1 | 1.2 |
|   Real consumption | 0.2 | 0.8 | 1.3 | 1.7 | 2.2 | 2.6 | 2.7 | 3.0 |
| Investment model | | | | | | | | |
|   Real GDP | 0.0 | 0.4 | 0.4 | 0.4 | 0.3 | 0.5 | 0.6 | 0.7 |
|   Real consumption | 0.2 | 0.5 | 0.8 | 1.0 | 1.3 | 1.5 | 1.6 | 1.8 |
| US only | | | | | | | | |
|   Real GDP | 0.1 | 0.5 | 0.7 | 0.8 | 1.0 | 1.5 | 1.6 | 1.6 |
|   Real consumption | 0.1 | 0.6 | 1.1 | 1.6 | 2.1 | 2.6 | 2.9 | 3.1 |
| **Smaller industrial countries** | | | | | | | | |
| Military spending | −1.6 | −3.4 | −5.1 | −7.1 | −9.1 | −9.3 | −9.6 | −9.8 |
| Main case | | | | | | | | |
|   Real GDP | −0.9 | 0.1 | 0.9 | 1.0 | 0.7 | 3.1 | 5.0 | 6.3 |
|   Real consumption | 0.3 | 1.8 | 3.2 | 4.6 | 6.0 | 7.7 | 9.1 | 10.0 |
| Accelerator model | | | | | | | | |
|   Real GDP | −1.3 | −0.1 | 0.7 | 1.4 | 1.6 | 2.3 | 2.8 | 3.4 |
|   Real consumption | 0.4 | 1.8 | 3.1 | 4.4 | 5.5 | 6.5 | 7.3 | 7.9 |
| Investment model | | | | | | | | |
|   Real GDP | −0.3 | 0.4 | 0.6 | 0.8 | 0.9 | 1.7 | 2.0 | 2.3 |
|   Real consumption | 0.4 | 1.4 | 2.3 | 3.1 | 3.9 | 4.5 | 5.0 | 5.5 |
| US only | | | | | | | | |
|   Real GDP | 0.1 | 0.4 | 0.7 | 0.8 | 1.0 | 1.4 | 1.6 | 1.6 |
|   Real consumption | 0.1 | 0.6 | 1.1 | 1.5 | 2.0 | 2.5 | 2.8 | 3.0 |

Table A3 **Present value of costs and benefits and reducing military spending**

| | In US$ 1992 | | | % 1992 GDP | | |
|---|---|---|---|---|---|---|
| | 1993 to 2000 | Beyond 2000 | Total gain | 1993 to 2000 | Beyond 2000 | Total gain |
| Industrial countries | −750 | −6025 | −6775 | −4.3 | −34.2 | −38.5 |
| Military spending | | | | | | |
| Base case | | | | | | |
|     Real GDP | 120 | 2794 | 2913 | 0.7 | 15.9 | 16.6 |
|     Real consumption | 446 | 4933 | 5379 | 2.5 | 28.0 | 30.6 |
|     Investment | | 3090 | 3090 | | 17.6 | 17.6 |
| Accelerator model | | | | | | |
| Accelerator model | 58 | 1910 | 1968 | 0.3 | 10.9 | 11.2 |
|     Real GDP | 384 | 4116 | 4500 | 2.2 | 23.4 | 25.6 |
|     Real consumption | | 2387 | 2387 | | 13.6 | 13.6 |
|     Investment | | | | | | |
| Investment model | | | | | | |
|     Real GDP | 43 | 1494 | 1538 | 0.2 | 8.5 | 8.7 |
|     Real consumption | 299 | 3201 | 3499 | 1.7 | 18.2 | 19.9 |
|     Investment | | 1715 | 1715 | | 9.7 | 9.7 |
| US only | | | | | | |
|     Real GDP | 107 | 1357 | 1464 | 0.6 | 7.7 | 8.3 |
|     Real consumption | 319 | 3139 | 3457 | 1.8 | 17.8 | 19.7 |
|     Investment | | 1702 | 1702 | | 9.7 | 9.7 |
| Net debtor developing countries | | | | | | |
| Military spending | −230 | −1879 | −2109 | −4.6 | −37.3 | −41.8 |
| Base case | | | | | | |
|     Real GDP | 60 | 2776 | 2836 | 1.2 | 55.1 | 56.3 |
|     Real consumption | 57 | 1667 | 1724 | 1.1 | 33.1 | 34.2 |
|     Investment | | 2246 | 2246 | | 44.6 | 44.6 |
| Accelerator model | | | | | | |
|     Real GDP | 28 | 2436 | 2464 | 0.6 | 48.3 | 48.9 |
|     Real consumption | 15 | 1075 | 1090 | 0.3 | 21.3 | 21.6 |
|     Investment | | 3094 | 3094 | | 61.4 | 61.4 |
| Investment model | | | | | | |
|     Real GDP | 10 | 2051 | 2061 | 0.2 | 40.7 | 40.9 |
|     Real consumption | 17 | 938 | 955 | 0.3 | 18.6 | 18.9 |
|     Investment | | 2838 | 2838 | | 56.3 | 56.3 |
| US only | | | | | | |
|     Real GDP | 7 | 159 | 166 | 0.1 | 3.2 | 3.3 |
|     Real consumption | 11 | 164 | 175 | 0.2 | 3.2 | 3.5 |
|     Investment | | 18 | 18 | | 0.4 | 0.4 |
| United States | | | | | | |
| Military spending | −415 | −3329 | −3744 | −7.0 | −55.8 | −62.8 |
| Base case | | | | | | |
|     Real GDP | 39 | 946 | 985 | 0.7 | 15.9 | 16.5 |
|     Real consumption | 211 | 2255 | 2465 | 3.5 | 37.8 | 41.4 |

215

Table A3    (*cont.*)

| | In US$ 1992 | | | % 1992 GDP | | |
|---|---|---|---|---|---|---|
| | 1993 to 2000 | Beyond 2000 | Total gain | 1993 to 2000 | Beyond 2000 | Total gain |
| Investment | | 1012 | 1012 | | 17.0 | 17.0 |
| Accelerator model | | | | | | |
| Real GDP | 13 | 672 | 685 | 0.2 | 11.3 | 11.5 |
| Real consumption | 188 | 1972 | 2159 | 3.1 | 33.1 | 36.2 |
| Investment | | 836 | 836 | | 14.0 | 14.0 |
| Investment model | | | | | | |
| Real GDP | 15 | 561 | 577 | 0.3 | 9.4 | 9.7 |
| Real consumption | 161 | 1662 | 1823 | 2.7 | 27.9 | 30.6 |
| Investment | | 637 | 637 | | 10.7 | 10.7 |
| US only | | | | | | |
| Real GDP | 15 | 676 | 691 | 0.3 | 11.3 | 11.6 |
| Real consumption | 170 | 1830 | 2000 | 2.8 | 30.7 | 33.5 |
| Investment | | 765 | 765 | | 12.8 | 12.8 |
| Japan | | | | | | |
| Military spending | −46 | −367 | −413 | −1.2 | −9.3 | −10.4 |
| Base case | | | | | | |
| Real GDP | 40 | 458 | 499 | 1.0 | 11.6 | 12.6 |
| Real consumption | 65 | 642 | 707 | 1.6 | 16.2 | 17.9 |
| Investment | | 550 | 550 | | 13.9 | 13.9 |
| Accelerator model | | | | | | |
| Real GDP | 31 | 367 | 398 | 0.8 | 9.3 | 10.1 |
| Real consumption | 54 | 520 | 574 | 1.4 | 13.1 | 14.5 |
| Investment | | 458 | 458 | | 11.6 | 11.6 |
| Investment model | | | | | | |
| Real GDP | 21 | 245 | 266 | 0.5 | 6.2 | 6.7 |
| Real consumption | 38 | 367 | 404 | 0.9 | 9.3 | 10.2 |
| Investment | | 306 | 306 | | 7.7 | 7.7 |
| US only | | | | | | |
| Real GDP | 28 | 275 | 303 | 0.7 | 7.0 | 7.6 |
| Real consumption | 36 | 336 | 372 | 0.9 | 8.5 | 9.4 |
| Investment | | 306 | 306 | | 7.7 | 7.7 |
| Germany | | | | | | |
| Military spending | −54 | −433 | −486 | −3.4 | −27.5 | −30.9 |
| Base case | | | | | | |
| Real GDP | 12 | 224 | 236 | 0.8 | 14.2 | 15.0 |
| Real consumption | 29 | 322 | 351 | 1.8 | 20.5 | 22.3 |
| Investment | | 305 | 305 | | 19.4 | 19.4 |
| Accelerator model | | | | | | |
| Real GDP | 6 | 147 | 154 | 0.4 | 9.4 | 9.8 |
| Real consumption | 24 | 261 | 285 | 1.5 | 16.6 | 18.1 |
| Investment | | 226 | 226 | | 14.4 | 14.4 |

Table A3   *(cont.)*

| | In US$ 1992 | | | % 1992 GDP | | |
|---|---|---|---|---|---|---|
| | 1993 to 2000 | Beyond 2000 | Total gain | 1993 to 2000 | Beyond 2000 | Total gain |
| **Investment model** | | | | | | |
| Real GDP | 4 | 113 | 117 | 0.3 | 7.2 | 7.5 |
| Real consumption | 18 | 197 | 215 | 1.1 | 12.5 | 13.6 |
| Investment | | 132 | 132 | | 8.4 | 8.4 |
| **US only** | | | | | | |
| Real GDP | 12 | 111 | 123 | 0.8 | 7.0 | 7.8 |
| Real consumption | 16 | 165 | 181 | 1.0 | 10.5 | 11.5 |
| Investment | | 122 | 122 | | 7.7 | 7.7 |
| **France** | | | | | | |
| Military spending | −37 | −297 | −334 | −3.0 | −24.1 | −27.1 |
| **Base case** | | | | | | |
| Real GDP | 3 | 190 | 193 | 0.3 | 15.4 | 15.7 |
| Real consumption | 18 | 241 | 259 | 1.5 | 19.5 | 21.0 |
| Investment | | 166 | 166 | | 13.5 | 13.5 |
| **Accelerator model** | | | | | | |
| Real GDP | 0 | 138 | 138 | 0.0 | 11.2 | 11.2 |
| Real consumption | 16 | 199 | 214 | 1.3 | 16.1 | 17.4 |
| Investment | | 127 | 127 | | 10.3 | 10.3 |
| **Investment model** | | | | | | |
| Real GDP | 0 | 114 | 114 | 0.0 | 9.2 | 9.2 |
| Real consumption | 12 | 153 | 165 | 1.0 | 12.4 | 13.4 |
| Investment | | 153 | 153 | | 12.4 | 12.4 |
| **US only** | | | | | | |
| Real GDP | 6 | 33 | 39 | 0.5 | 2.7 | 3.2 |
| Real consumption | 10 | 82 | 91 | 0.8 | 6.6 | 7.4 |
| Investment | | 55 | 55 | | 4.5 | 4.5 |
| **United Kingdom** | | | | | | |
| Military spending | −43 | −348 | −391 | −4.6 | −36.8 | −41.3 |
| **Base case** | | | | | | |
| Real GDP | 8 | 181 | 189 | 0.8 | 19.1 | 19.9 |
| Real consumption | 16 | 232 | 247 | 1.6 | 24.5 | 26.1 |
| Investment | | 174 | 174 | | 18.4 | 18.4 |
| **Accelerator model** | | | | | | |
| Real GDP | −5 | 130 | 125 | −0.6 | 13.8 | 13.2 |
| Real consumption | 13 | 188 | 201 | 1.4 | 19.9 | 21.3 |
| Investment | | 138 | 138 | | 14.5 | 14.5 |
| **Investment model** | | | | | | |
| Real GDP | −5 | 101 | 96 | −0.5 | 10.7 | 10.2 |
| Real consumption | 9 | 138 | 147 | 0.9 | 14.5 | 15.5 |
| Investment | | 101 | 101 | | 10.7 | 10.7 |

Table A3   (*cont.*)

|  | In US$ 1992 | | | % 1992 GDP | | |
|---|---|---|---|---|---|---|
|  | 1993 to 2000 | Beyond 2000 | Total gain | 1993 to 2000 | Beyond 2000 | Total gain |
| **US only** | | | | | | |
| Real GDP | 8 | 29 | 37 | 0.9 | 3.1 | 3.9 |
| Real consumption | 15 | 109 | 123 | 1.5 | 11.5 | 13.0 |
| Investment |  | 27 | 27 |  | 2.8 | 2.8 |
| **Italy** | | | | | | |
| Military spending | −26 | −211 | −238 | −2.6 | −20.5 | −23.1 |
| Base case | | | | | | |
| Real GDP | 11 | 188 | 199 | 1.1 | 18.2 | 19.3 |
| Real consumption | 29 | 314 | 342 | 2.8 | 30.4 | 33.2 |
| Investment |  | 181 | 181 |  | 17.5 | 17.5 |
| Accelerator model | | | | | | |
| Real GDP | 7 | 119 | 126 | 0.7 | 11.6 | 12.2 |
| Real consumption | 23 | 235 | 258 | 2.2 | 22.8 | 25.0 |
| Investment |  | 133 | 133 |  | 12.9 | 12.9 |
| Investment model | | | | | | |
| Real GDP | 4 | 92 | 96 | 0.4 | 8.9 | 9.3 |
| Real consumption | 14 | 164 | 178 | 1.4 | 15.9 | 17.3 |
| Investment |  | 96 | 96 |  | 9.3 | 9.3 |
| US only | | | | | | |
| Real GDP | 12 | 51 | 64 | 1.2 | 5.0 | 6.2 |
| Real consumption | 20 | 143 | 163 | 1.9 | 13.9 | 15.8 |
| Investment |  | 47 | 47 |  | 4.6 | 4.6 |
| **Canada** | | | | | | |
| Military spending | −13 | −107 | −120 | −2.4 | −19.5 | −21.9 |
| Base case | | | | | | |
| Real GDP | 6 | 73 | 79 | 1.0 | 13.4 | 14.4 |
| Real consumption | 13 | 133 | 146 | 2.4 | 24.4 | 26.8 |
| Investment |  | 81 | 81 |  | 14.8 | 14.8 |
| Accelerator model | | | | | | |
| Real GDP | 4 | 43 | 47 | 0.8 | 7.9 | 8.7 |
| Real consumption | 12 | 110 | 122 | 2.1 | 20.1 | 22.2 |
| Investment |  | 59 | 59 |  | 10.8 | 10.8 |
| Investment model | | | | | | |
| Real GDP | 3 | 27 | 29 | 0.5 | 4.9 | 5.4 |
| Real consumption | 7 | 67 | 74 | 1.3 | 12.2 | 13.5 |
| Investment |  | 30 | 30 |  | 5.6 | 5.6 |
| US only | | | | | | |
| Real GDP | 6 | 60 | 66 | 1.1 | 11.0 | 12.1 |
| Real consumption | 11 | 113 | 125 | 2.0 | 20.7 | 22.8 |
| Investment |  | 66 | 66 |  | 12.1 | 12.1 |

Table A3   (*cont.*)

| | In US$ 1992 | | | % 1992 GDP | | |
|---|---|---|---|---|---|---|
| | 1993 to 2000 | Beyond 2000 | Total gain | 1993 to 2000 | Beyond 2000 | Total gain |
| Smaller industrial countries | | | | | | |
| Military spending | −45 | −359 | −404 | −1.9 | −15.3 | −17.2 |
| Base case | | | | | | |
| Real GDP | 12 | 230 | 242 | 0.5 | 9.8 | 10.3 |
| Real consumption | 34 | 366 | 400 | 1.4 | 15.6 | 17.1 |
| Investment | | 304 | 304 | | 13.0 | 13.0 |
| Accelerator model | | | | | | |
| Real GDP | 8 | 123 | 131 | 0.4 | 5.2 | 5.6 |
| Real consumption | 29 | 288 | 317 | 1.3 | 12.3 | 13.6 |
| Investment | | 214 | 214 | | 9.1 | 9.1 |
| Investment model | | | | | | |
| Real GDP | 7 | 84 | 91 | 0.3 | 3.6 | 3.9 |
| Real consumption | 21 | 201 | 222 | 0.9 | 8.6 | 9.5 |
| Investment | | 139 | 139 | | 5.9 | 5.9 |
| US only | | | | | | |
| Real GDP | 6 | 58 | 64 | 0.3 | 2.5 | 2.7 |
| Real consumption | 11 | 110 | 121 | 0.5 | 4.7 | 5.2 |
| Investment | | 155 | 155 | | 6.6 | 6.6 |

Source:  Tables A1 and A2.

# Comments on chapter 8

## 1. Kimio Uno

How well do we understand the things we did not before the simulation? That is, how much is imbedded in the explicit and implicit assumptions of the model? Simulation results are only as good as the assumptions that went into the model and we start by examining the basic nature of the model.

Some of the crucial assumptions of the model employed for the experiment, the IMF MULTIMOD, are as follows.

1. It is a rational expectations model, i.e. economic agents are forward looking and future economic situations feed back into the behaviour in the current period.
2. The monetary authorities follow a target path for the money supply.
3. The level of productive investment in the economy is unaffected by the cut in military spending, i.e. military expenditures have no positive spillover on to productive capacity.
4. It is a single sector model.
5. We are in the world of a well-functioning market economy. Thus, the main portion of the model looks like this:

| | |
|---|---|
| Money supply: | MS = MS (i.e., targeted) |
| Money demand: | MD = f (Y) |
| Interest rate: | i = f (MS(t + 1), …, MD(t + 1), …) |
| Investment: | I = f (i, YD(t + 1), YD(t + 2), …) |
| Consumption: | C = f (YD(t + 1), YD(t + 2), …) |
| GDP: | Y = C + I + G (i.e., military spending is reduced) |
| Disposable income: | YD = (Y − TA) |
| Taxes: | TA = G |

Under these assumptions, the authors were able to predict that, although both private consumption and investment could fall in the short run, "by the sixth year of the simulation after all decreases in military expenditures have stopped, the economic performance of industrial countries is considerably improved."

This is a very welcome consequence but is contrary to the popular belief that reduction in military spending will have a negative economic impact. Let us start by reducing military expenditures by 20 per cent for five years. Aggregate demand is that much reduced. However, lower government spending will induce lower interest rates while allowing tax cuts (or reduction of fiscal deficit). Remember that money supply is following a target path, despite a short-term downturn of the economy. This then induces higher investment, giving rise to higher future growth. Forward-looking consumers also increase consumption anticipating higher disposable income, despite falling income today.

Compare this with conventional thinking where economic agents are *not* forward looking but react to the current situation and monetary authorities do *not* follow a predetermined path but react to the real side of the economy. We now have a system where some of the equations in the system above are replaced by the following.

| | |
|---|---|
| Money supply: | MS = f (Y) |
| Investment: | I = f (i, YD(t), YD(t − 1), …) |
| Consumption: | C = f (YD(t), YD(t − 1), …) |

Even when the rest of the model remains exactly the same, we will have a totally different result. Arms reduction now dampens GDP in the current period. Both businesses and households react to this fact, and not to future prospects. Reduced spending by government, business, and the consumer will also have a negative multiplier effect,

221

further reducing the aggregate demand. Money supply now follows the ever-shrinking real side, giving no room for lower interest rates even in the face of declining demand for money.

What if we had such a thing as a defence industry? (see the authors' assumption 3, which already seems to violate their single sector assumption.) In essence, we are now saying that production function in a particular economic sector (i) is distinct from the others.

$$Vi = f (Ki, Li; Ai)$$

We are now relaxing the single sector assumption above and saying that production facilities (K), workers (L), and technology (A) in the defence industry are somehow distinct from the rest of the economy. We are now confronted with a conversion problem. How difficult this can be is anybody's guess, but there was considerable discussion highlighting this issue during the Conference.

The defence industry (say, sector m), faced with declining demand for its products, would have to shift to civilian products (change in product mix Vm) by retooling its factories (Km and Am). Workers (Lm) would also have to be retrained. Otherwise they would have to be absorbed by other sectors or go unemployed. If the rest of the economy is prosperous, this can be done fairly easily; when it is not, conversion may prove difficult.

An easy way out for the defence industry is to turn to exports of military hardware. Should this happen, the regional balance of power around importing countries could be upset, triggering a regional arms race. Thus we see that successful conversion is the key in realizing the peace dividend on a global scale.

Can we leave the conversion process to the working of the market mechanism? Or do we need a policy package aimed at smoothing out the process? As the authors have shown, very much depends on the behaviour of the economic agents. If in reality business and the consumer are not forward looking, it seems essential to provide an overall scenario for the conversion process to which everyone (including the monetary and fiscal authorities) can agree. If this can be done, individual economic agents in segmented markets may start moving towards a well-functioning, single market. It seems also essential to create favourable macroeconomic conditions in the future, so that redundant workers in one sector can be absorbed by others.

## 2. Sanjay Pradhan

This paper deals with a very important subject – the potential impact of gains from simultaneous global reductions in military expenditures. The results are what one would expect and indeed wish – specifically, despite the initial fall in GDP, private consumption and private investment rise, and the net present value of welfare is positive and significant. Hence, the desirability of global reductions in military expenditure. The paper constitutes a well written and important contribution to this crucial subject. I would like to raise some issues and comments that, if addressed more frontally, could enhance the empirical robustness of the paper and make it more persuasive for policy makers.

Specifically, the outcomes of this exercise, as in any other simulation, are driven by some crucial assumptions. However, some of these crucial assumptions are quite contentious, their validity uncertain, and sensitivity analysis is not robust enough to give sufficient confidence about the results. Equally significant, the assumptions run the risk of overlooking some of the most particular and contentious economic and political features of military expenditures.

The first crucial assumption made in the bulk of the paper is that all military expenditures are unproductive, i.e., military expenditures do not include any investment. Cuts in these unproductive expenditures are assumed to translate into tax cuts, which result in an increase in private consumption (which is derived as the measure of welfare), and in private investment, which results in future growth in consumption. Consequently, the results flow tautologically from this simple assumption about the lack of an investment component in military expenditure. The paper and the results could, therefore, be about any government transfer programme, or wasteful expenditure, and not military expenditure *per se*. The main case, therefore, ducks the basic question of whether military expenditures consist of any investment; if so, how much, and what will be the impact of that investment component. Yet, these are precisely the controversies that have been raging in the academic literature since Benoit, and in policy debates. The paper *does* try a policy option towards the end: the investment model, which assumes that one-third of military expenditure is investment. In this scenario, the benefits are significantly reduced but still important. It would be important to reflect and investigate here several empirical issues: what is the investment content of military expenditures; is the one-third share an upper hand; is there a break-even share where the results would be reversed?

The second crucial assumption concerns the security implications of the key policy change modelled – 20 per cent reduction in military expenditures for every country. The paper contends that "no conclusions are offered or implied as to the security implications of this policy." This contention, however, does not appear to be accurate. Since the paper does not incorporate any impact on private investment on account of possibly decreased security stemming from reductions in military expenditures, it is *in effect* assuming that proportionate decreases in military expenditures across countries are security neutral. First, it would be important to make this assumption explicit because even more so than in the previous issue about investment content of military expenditure, it fails to take account of the peculiar dimension of military expenditure – its security impact. Secondly, there is no reason to believe that a 20 per cent reduction in every country's military expenditures is security neutral across countries. Whether it is so would depend on initial conditions or initial size of the expenditure, of the country, the extent of external threat, and whether security is a *linear function* of military expenditures, which it need not be: for instance, if a country needs a critical mass of security expenditures as a deterrent against a particularly large or aggressive neighbour that is spending excessively on the military to begin with. And, if these 20 per cent reductions are not security neutral, then they will have an impact on private investment and growth differentially and significantly affecting the results. More importantly, this issue points to the real challenge in this area: specifically, if the kind of policy change being modelled in the paper is to be translated into actual reality, the real challenge will be to figure out what reductions in military expenditures for different countries or different blocks of countries will be security neutral, and what the impact or gain from these reductions will be.

In addition to reflecting further on these assumptions, this paper or future related research could usefully investigate the impact of a richer disaggregation of developing countries. At present, there is only one disaggregation of net creditor and debtor countries. Perhaps a more meaningful and interesting classification could be in terms of arms producing or arms exporting/importing countries. In addition, it would further be useful to examine the employment impact of these changes on countries. Even though private consumption and investment rise as military expenditure falls, what will be the impact here?

This would shed light on the likely political cost, given, in addition, that benefits occur primarily in the long run while output falls in the short run.

These suggestions for further clarification and robustness notwithstanding, it is important not to detract from or lose sight of the essential, significant, useful message of the paper – i.e., global reductions in military expenditures will lead to a net increase in welfare. The real challenge and indeed the real opportunity under present global conditions is to forge and implement a consensus in the international community for a coordinated reduction in military expenditures. Economic analysis, if sufficiently bolstered and persuasive, can provide the technical ammunition to accomplish this. The real challenge, however, is political, and I personally think that a *deeper* approach than a preoccupation with military expenditures *per se* is called for. Military expenditures, after all, are a *manifestation* of the problem of underlying tensions and conflicts. The real challenge is to resolve underlying conflicts within regions and across regions through the United Nations and regional security institutions, in the new international world order through some kind of global security guarantee mechanism that will permit a coordinated global reduction in military expenditures and the realization of welfare gains across countries.

# Reference

Benoit, E. (1978). "Growth and defence in developing countries." *Economic Development and Cultural Change* 26(2), pp. 271–280.

# 9

# Some macroeconomic aspects of reductions in military expenditure

Simon Cunningham and Kenneth G. Ruffing

## Introduction

The potential gains from a reduction of military expenditures have been the subject of extensive debate for some time.[1] In 1991, the transformation of the Soviet Union into the Commonwealth of Independent States gave considerable impetus to the debate on the "peace dividend" in the developed market economies. As long as the former existed, there was a case for its potential opponents to remain vigilant and not to revise drastically their military spending plans.

The "new thinking" in Soviet foreign policy introduced by General-Secretary and, later, President Mikhail S. Gorbachev had, as one of its aims, the reduction in the size of the Soviet military budget and the conversion of military industries to civilian production. However, conversion efforts in the Soviet Union did not meet with the success that had been hoped for, in that civilian production did not increase sharply as military production fell.[2] This was surprising to some observers, as it was claimed that one of the advantages of the centrally planned economic system was that it enabled resources to be redirected quickly to those areas where they were needed.[3] Recent discussions on conversion have confirmed that the nature of the economic system is itself a very important factor to consider in any analysis of this issue.

In the short run, cuts in military expenditure will have an effect on domestic demand. At a time of economic difficulty, when there might be a need for a boost to demand, this macroeconomic effect could complicate matters. Yet a reduction in military expenditure can free resources for alternative uses and so lead to greater long-term growth of the economy. It is aspects of the medium- to long-term transition to a peace economy that will be analysed in this paper.

## Military expenditure in the world

Table 1 gives some of the main aggregates of military expenditure in 1989, according to the United States Disarmament Agency. The figures show military expenditure, the size of the armed services, arms imports and arms exports, with the percentage contribution of each country or group of countries to the aggregate for the world. The developing countries accounted for only 15 per cent of military expenditure and 9 per cent of arms exports, but for 62 per cent of the world's military forces and nearly 70 per cent of arms imports. The developed market economies, on the other hand, accounted for 50 per cent of military spending, and 43 per cent of arms exports, but only 20 per cent of the world's armed forces and 23 per cent of world arms imports.

In 1989, the economies in transition still accounted for 35 per cent of the world's military spending, 18 per cent of the world's military forces, and 47 per cent of world arms transfers. The figures for the military expenditure of the economies in transition were, in the past, shrouded in secrecy and many experts thought that those published by the United States were too high. However, developments since 1989 have certainly reduced the share of the economies in transition in both global military expenditure and in total military forces. Moreover, apart from the lack of reliable statistics, the very transition process from a centrally planned economy to a market economy will necessarily make any macroeconomic assessment of the possible effects of reductions in military spending extremely difficult. We are justified, then, in concentrating our attention on the developed market economies, not only because of their importance in the global military sector and the relative sophistication of quantitative economic models for these countries, but also because the future direc-

Table 1  The distribution of major items of global military expenditures

| Country | Military spending | | Military forces | | Arms imports | | Arms exports | |
|---|---|---|---|---|---|---|---|---|
| World | 1,035,100 | (100.00) | 28,290 | (100.00) | 45,320 | (100.00) | 45,430 | (100.00) |
| United States | 304,100 | (29.38) | 2,241 | (7.92) | 1,600 | (3.53) | 11,200 | (24.65) |
| Other developed market economies | 214,357 | (20.71) | 3,477 | (12.29) | 8,915 | (19.67) | 8,620 | (18.97) |
| Total developed market economies | 518,457 | (50.09) | 5,718 | (20.21) | 10,515 | (23.20) | 19,820 | (43.63) |
| Economies in transition | 365,700 | (35.33) | 4,952 | (17.50) | 3,150 | (6.95) | 21,480 | (47.28) |
| Former USSR | 311,000 | (30,05) | 3,700 | (13.08) | 900 | (1.99) | 19,600 | (43.14) |
| Other | 54,700 | (5.28) | 1,252 | (4.43) | 2,250 | (4.96) | 1,880 | (4.14) |
| Total of above | 884,157 | (85.42) | 10,670 | (37.72) | 13,665 | (30.15) | 41,300 | (90.91) |
| Developing countries | 150,943 | (14.58) | 17,620 | (62.28) | 31,655 | (69.85) | 4,130 | (9.09) |
| China | 22,330 | (2.16) | 3,903 | (13.80) | 110 | (0.24) | 2,000 | (4.40) |

Source: United States Arms Control and Disarmament Agency (1990). *World Military Expenditures and Arms Transfers.*
Note: Numbers in parentheses are percentages.

tion of military expenditure can be predicted with some confidence – downwards. The same confidence cannot be expressed in respect of future trends in developing countries, but the potential for reallocating public expenditures from the military sector in developed market economies to growth enhancing investment in developing countries is explored in the scenario analysis discussed later. With the present concern in developed countries over military spending in developing countries, it can be reasonably assumed that such investment would go to developing countries that were reducing their military expenditures.

The Cold War certainly played a role in fuelling arms races in developing countries and in prolonging conflicts there. Since such conflicts were often seen by the major alliances as being primarily a reflection of their ideological differences, and also largely caused by military assistance from the ideological rival to one party in a dispute, there was an incentive for all parties to look for a military solution. The resort to the military option was reflected in military assistance being extended to developing countries for strategic reasons. The consequences of the military assistance will long survive the end of the Cold War, as in the case of Somalia, into which both sides poured weaponry.

With the end of ideological confrontation, there is now a far greater possibility for the United Nations and other regional bodies to be effective in finding solutions to many conflicts. The results for developing countries of the end of the Cold War could, then, be low military expenditures and faster development as resources absorbed in military expenditure, including arms imports, are redirected to civilian purposes and as the death and destruction caused by conflicts give way to reconciliation and a national consensus on peaceful development within democratic norms. On the other hand, the recent tragic events in Somalia and Yugoslavia show that such an optimistic outlook for all developing countries cannot be automatically assumed.

## Military manpower

Table 2 shows the size of the armed services of some of the principal developed market economies between 1960 and 1991. In France and the United Kingdom, the end of their colonial empires was reflected in a sharp fall in the total size of their armed forces between 1960 and 1970. At the same time, Germany was assuming a more active role in NATO and its armed forces expanded rapidly. Japan's armed forces

Table 2   **Armed forces in selected countries (thousands)**

|      | United States | Japan | Germany | France | United Kingdom | Total |
|------|---------------|-------|---------|--------|----------------|-------|
| 1960 | 2,514 | 206 | 270 | 781 | 520 | 4,291 |
| 1965 | 2,723 | 225 | 441 | 510 | 500 | 4,399 |
| 1968 | 3,547 | 235 | 440 | 505 | 405 | 5,132 |
| 1970 | 3,066 | 259 | 466 | 506 | 373 | 4,670 |
| 1975 | 2,130 | 236 | 495 | 503 | 345 | 3,709 |
| 1980 | 2,050 | 242 | 495 | 495 | 329 | 3,611 |
| 1985 | 2,152 | 243 | 478 | 464 | 327 | 3,664 |
| 1990 | 2,118 | 249 | 469 | 461 | 306 | 3,603 |
| 1991 | 2,030 | 246 | 476 | 453 | 300 | 3,505 |

Source: International Institute for Strategic Studies, *The Military Balance*, various years.

expanded broadly in step with population, although they remain comparatively small: in 1988, they were equivalent to 0.2 per cent of the population, as compared to 0.9 per cent for NATO as a whole.[4] The size of the armed forces of the United States reached a peak in 1968, at over 3.5 millions, at the height of that country's commitment to the Viet Nam War. By 1980, when the United States had turned to an all-volunteer force, the size of its armed services had fallen to just over 2 million.

The military build-up of the 1980s resulted in very large increases in military expenditure – in the case of the United States by 38 per cent in real terms between 1981 and 1986. However, the size of the armed services increased less – in the United States, by 5 per cent between 1980 and 1985. In many other countries, the size of the armed services fell. The combined armed forces of the European members of NATO were larger than the total of the armed forces of the United States, but there was relatively little change over the 10-year period. NATO includes Turkey whose armed forces were greater than those of any other member except the United States.

The expansion of military expenditure after 1980 could largely be accounted for by expansion of the procurement item of military budgets as countries improved the quality of equipment deployed. Figure 1 shows how between 1981 and 1987, NATO's procurement of major weapon systems in real terms increased by 54 per cent. With the relaxation of tensions after the advent to power in the Soviet Union of General-Secretary Mikhail S. Gorbachev, NATO procurement fell between 1987 and 1990 by 16 per cent.

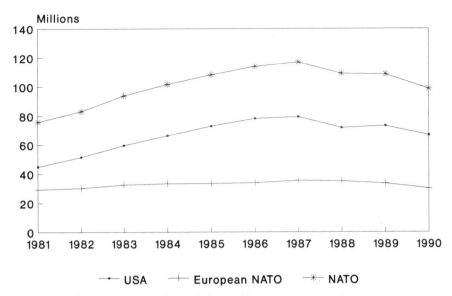

Fig. 1 **NATO procurement, 1981–1990 (constant 1988 US$) (Source: *SIPRI Yearbook 1991*. Oxford University Press, New York and Oxford)**

The earlier build-up was very heavily concentrated in the United States: procurement there rose by 77 per cent between 1981 and 1987. Whereas in 1981 United States procurement of major weapons systems accounted for 59 per cent of NATO's total, by 1987, it accounted for 68 per cent.[5] This reflects the high level of sophistication of the weaponry employed and, also, United States possession and development of nuclear forces. In Japan, the industrial country with the largest military expenditure outside NATO, expenditure on procurement also rose rapidly in the 1980s.

The emphasis on procurement reflected the fact that the industrial countries were drawing on their comparative advantage in high technology as against manpower and attempting to build up military forces that would be able to stop a mass conventional attack, especially by tank forces, in Europe. Another reason for the concentration on procurement was the direction of population trends which constrained the pool of labour available for the armed services. Table 3 shows the rate of increase in population of the industrialized countries. In all regions, this slowed down markedly between 1950 and 1955, and 1985 and 1990, whereas for the world as a whole, there was relatively little change.

The result of this slow-down was that the numbers of those aged

231

Table 3  **Population growth rates in the developed market economies, 1950–2005 (%)**

| Country group | 1950–1955 | 1985–1990 | 2000–2005 |
|---|---|---|---|
| Northern Europe | 0.37 | 0.25 | 0.14 |
| Southern Europe | 0.84 | 0.24 | 0.16 |
| Western Europe | 0.83 | 0.24 | 0.03 |
| Australia–New Zealand | 2.33 | 1.28 | 0.89 |
| Japan | 1.43 | 0.43 | 0.31 |
| Northern America | 1.80 | 0.82 | 0.55 |
| Eastern Europe | 1.02 | 0.27 | 0.30 |
| Soviet Union | 1.71 | 0.78 | 0.61 |
| World | 1.79 | 1.74 | 1.47 |

Source: *World Population Prospects, 1990*, United Nations publication, Sales No. E.91.XIII.4.

between 17 and 30, the potential pool for military manpower, fell. In the case of NATO, this pool reached a peak in the mid-1980s.[6] One implication drawn at that time was that "most countries may be forced to recruit women to fill a greater proportion of their military forces support echelons."[7]

Women did assume a greater importance in the armed forces of several countries although this may have been more a reflection of general social change. Between 1979 and 1991, the percentage of women in the total active armed services of Canada, the United Kingdom, and the United States increased from 5.6, 4.7, and 6.6 per cent respectively, to 10.9, 6.0, and 11.0 per cent respectively.

In spite of recruitment efforts, population trends could have been expected to put pressure on the military wage bill, especially if the supply elasticity of military personnel with respect to military wages was low, as appears to be the case, at least from the experience of the United Kingdom.[8] Increasing levels of conscription was not a favoured option. In many industrial countries, conscription had been abandoned by 1980, and both the number of conscripts and their length of service were generally smaller by the end of the decade.

## The composition of military spending

The effect of these influences on military expenditure was reflected in its composition. Table 4 shows the composition of the military budgets of a group of developed market economies as reported in the United Nations standardized reporting instrument. At its inception

Table 4  Comparison of major categories of defence spending 1978–1990 (%)

| | | Personnel | O&M | Total | Procurement | Construction | Total | R&D | Total |
|---|---|---|---|---|---|---|---|---|---|
| 1979 | Australia | 50.4 | 26.2 | 76.6 | 16.7 | 3.6 | 20.3 | 3.1 | 100.0 |
| 1989/90 | Australia | 40.9 | 27.6 | 68.5 | 21.6 | 7.6 | 29.1 | 2.4 | 100.0 |
| 1979 | Austria | 47.9 | 20.2 | 68.1 | 23.6 | 8.3 | 31.8 | 0.1 | 100.0 |
| 1990 | Austria | 56.3 | 17.8 | 74.0 | 20.1 | 5.9 | 26.0 | 0.0 | 100.0 |
| 1978 | Belgium | 55.4 | 19.5 | 74.9 | 18.7 | 6.4 | 25.1 | 0.0 | 100.0 |
| 1987 | Belgium | 55.3 | 23.6 | 78.9 | 17.9 | 3.2 | 21.0 | 0.0 | 100.0 |
| 1978/79 | Canada | 55.1 | 28.7 | 83.8 | 12.9 | 2.5 | 15.4 | 0.8 | 100.0 |
| 1989/90 | Canada | 46.9 | 29.8 | 76.7 | 19.0 | 2.9 | 21.9 | 1.4 | 100.0 |
| 1980 | France | 36.8 | 27.1 | 63.9 | 18.8 | 4.3 | 23.1 | 13.0 | 100.0 |
| 1990 | France | 32.5 | 20.8 | 53.2 | 25.8 | 4.8 | 30.5 | 16.2 | 100.0 |
| 1978 | Germany | 41.4 | 28.2 | 69.6 | 19.0 | 7.0 | 26.0 | 4.4 | 100.0 |
| 1989 | Germany | 44.7 | 24.5 | 69.3 | 20.2 | 5.1 | 25.3 | 5.4 | 100.0 |
| 1980 | Italy | 49.0 | 23.9 | 72.9 | 24.0 | 1.8 | 25.8 | 1.3 | 100.0 |
| 1990 | Italy | 47.9 | 25.8 | 73.7 | 20.7 | 3.1 | 23.8 | 2.6 | 100.0 |
| 1978 | Netherlands | 56.7 | 19.4 | 76.1 | 19.6 | 3.4 | 23.0 | 0.9 | 100.0 |
| 1989 | Netherlands | 48.7 | 26.5 | 75.2 | 20.6 | 4.0 | 24.6 | 0.2 | 100.0 |
| 1978/79 | New Zealand | 59.4 | 29.3 | 88.7 | 7.4 | 3.1 | 10.5 | 0.8 | 100.0 |
| 1989/90 | New Zealand | 38.3 | 29.2 | 67.4 | 17.1 | 15.5 | 32.6 | 0.0 | 100.0 |
| 1978 | Norway | 45.7 | 27.4 | 73.1 | 21.0 | 5.1 | 26.1 | 0.8 | 100.0 |
| 1990 | Norway | 36.4 | 28.5 | 65.0 | 24.4 | 10.6 | 35.0 | 0.0 | 100.0 |
| 1978/79 | Sweden | 40.4 | 19.2 | 59.6 | 29.3 | 5.6 | 34.8 | 5.6 | 100.0 |
| 1989/90 | Sweden | 34.9 | 24.3 | 59.2 | 26.0 | 3.0 | 29.1 | 11.8 | 100.0 |
| 1977/78 | United States | 49.0 | 20.5 | 69.5 | 20.3 | 1.8 | 22.1 | 8.4 | 100.0 |
| 1988/89 | United States | 35.3 | 21.7 | 56.9 | 29.6 | 1.8 | 31.4 | 11.6 | 100.0 |

Source: Department of Economic and Social Development of the United Nations Secretariat, based on *Reduction of Military Budgets: Military Expenditures* in standardized form reported by states, various years (United Nations publication).

233

relatively few countries replied to the Secretary-General's request to use this instrument, and so a comparison is possible between only a limited number of countries. The table gives figures for the industrial countries that replied when the reporting instrument was instituted.

In almost all of these countries, the percentage of military expenditure accounted for by procurement increased from 20 to nearly 30 per cent in the course of the decade. The exceptions were Austria and Sweden, the two neutral countries in the group, and Belgium and Italy. The share of United States expenditure accounted for by procurement rose by 50 per cent in the course of the decade. As could be expected, with the volume and quality of equipment increasing over time, the share of the budget going to operations and maintenance also rose in many countries.

Military research and development is a small percentage of military expenditure in all except the major weapons producers shown in the table: France, Germany, and the United States. The large share of research and development in the total for France reflects the independent development of its nuclear capability. Similarly, Sweden's military research and development absorbs a relatively large percentage of its expenditure because its policy of armed neutrality has entailed the development of its own military production.

The large category of military expenditure whose importance tended to decline as emphasis was placed on military procurement was expenditure on personnel. In the case of the United States, in particular, this fell from nearly 50 per cent of total military expenditure to 35 per cent in the course of the decade. However, in all countries expenditure on personnel remained the largest single item in the military budget.

## Effects of reductions in military expenditure on its components

An immediate effect of diminished tensions has been the scaling-down of the desired size of armed forces. With members of the Commonwealth of Independent States ceasing to be perceived as a potential military threat to the NATO countries, the need for NATO to have such large numbers of armed forces in Europe has diminished. Plans have already been made to reduce the size of armed forces. A reduction in the United States from 2 million in 1991 to 1.6 million persons is foreseen by 1995. In July 1990, the United Kingdom announced plans to cut its armed forces from 312,000 to 255,000, with the forces in Germany being halved from 55,000 to 20,000–

25,000.[9] The German armed forces are to be reduced to 370,000 as against a combined total of the forces of the Federal Republic and the former German Democratic Republic of 607,000 in 1990. As the number of the armed services falls, the number of civilian employees of the armed forces will also fall. A reduction in the desired number of active service personnel will put a downward pressure on the service wage bill, as there will be less reason to raise service remuneration to attract recruits.

The decline in procurement can be expected to continue through the 1990s. With smaller armed forces, much military equipment will be added to inventory or scrapped. These cuts can be expected to exceed those that would be dictated by the Conventional Forces in Europe agreement once it enters into force.[10] Furthermore, with the Cold War over, weapon systems that were being planned to meet the Soviet threat are coming under increasing scrutiny and orders are being scaled back or cancelled. This applies not just to nuclear missiles and strategic bombers, but also to conventional weapons.

The growing sophistication of new equipment, even if purchased in smaller quantities than before, exerts an upward pressure on the operations and maintenance item in military budgets. Training and equipment purchases will also be directed towards responding to a greater variety of challenges than in the past when the military threat posed by the Soviet Union dominated military thinking and planning. In this connection it may be noted that, apart from the United States, only two developed countries, France and the United Kingdom, deployed land, air, and sea forces in the Gulf. The United States deployed 2,000 tanks, the United Kingdom 177 tanks and France 40 tanks.[11] This disparity is partly accounted for by the much larger size of the United States' armed forces, but it also revealed the difficulty that other countries had in sending armed forces for action outside Europe.

Military research and development in the United States, which accounts for the bulk of such spending, expanded more rapidly in the course of the 1980s than overall military spending. After 1987, it stabilized in real terms.[12] Military research expenditure can be expected to fall in the future. However, the United States can also be expected to maintain a defence industrial base and to remain in the forefront of military technology. It has been suggested that the focus of the Pentagon be shifted from building weapons to an approach revolving around laboratory research and only limited production, with full-scale production starting when the need arose.[13]

## The public debate over defence expenditure

Decisions on levels of military spending and force levels are matters of public debate. The present public debate about the military is probably more searching than that which took place at previous times when military spending was winding down, as after the Korean and Vietnamese Wars in the case of the United States, or after the decisions by former colonial powers to accede to demands for independence. Even after these events, the principal military threat that they perceived remained – the vast conventional forces, supported by nuclear forces, of the Soviet Union.

At the present time, this military posture has to be rethought, bearing in mind the commitment of forces to United Nations operations and the formation of regional intervention forces. NATO has decided to form a Rapid Reaction Corps made up of four divisions and available for deployment to any part of NATO.[14] However, a common European defence policy raises many issues, especially concerning the relationship with NATO, that could take some time to resolve.[15] The difficulty of forming a united European policy to help resolve the situation in ex-Yugoslavia has highlighted the problems involved in any form of military cooperation that goes beyond repelling a direct attack on a friend of ally. Such cooperation requires a political mandate which cannot be assured in the case of struggles in third countries where the potential participants might not even be able to agree among themselves on the purpose and nature of any intervention.

The outcome of defence reassessments in countries that are not directly involved in NATO or the European theatre is more difficult to assess. This applies with particular force to Japan whose military spending is comparatively small – 1 per cent of GNP. Japan has in recent years modernized its forces by increasing its procurement expenditure.

Governments have made estimates of the future size of their military establishments and of their anticipated military spending. However, it is probable that these plans will be revised in the next few years. The likelihood is that such revisions will be downwards rather than upwards. In the case of the United States, estimates of future defence spending have been revised downwards in recent years. Even the proposed revisions have been seen as inadequate by some, including the nominee for Defense Secretary in the new Administration.[16]

## The military sector in different countries

Table 5 shows the relative orders of magnitude of military expenditure in the developed market economies in 1989, as given by the US government. Countries have been ranked according to their military expenditure. The percentage figures show the military burden within each country rather than the importance of each country in the overall global military economy, as in table 1.

In 1989, the United States devoted 5.8 per cent of its GNP to military expenditure – a larger percentage than any other industrialized country except Greece. Of the seven major economies, only two, France and the United Kingdom, devoted more than 3 per cent of their GNP to defence. For almost all other countries, less than 3 per cent of GNP was devoted to defence. Germany and Japan devoted 2.8 per cent and 1 per cent, respectively, of their GNP to defence.

The military expenditure of the United States was about 50 per cent greater than that of all the other industrialized countries combined, but the size of its armed forces was only about two-thirds of those of the other countries. The armed forces of several other countries account for a larger percentage of the population than in the case of the United States, but in these countries reliance was placed upon conscripts. Countries without conscription, such as Canada, Japan, and the United Kingdom, had smaller armed forces in relation to the population.

The United States exported more arms than all the other developed market economies put together, and its exports of arms were a larger percentage of total exports than in the case of any other country. Imports of arms constituted a small percentage of imports in all the developed market economies with the exception of Greece.[17] In general, the figures for imports and exports of arms changed much more year by year than did those for military expenditure or the size of the armed services. Furthermore, different sources give different relative orders of magnitude for arms transfers.[18] These statistics show that in the military sector the United States is more dominant than in other sectors such as total world trade. Therefore, changes in military spending in the United States dwarf the effects of such possible changes elsewhere. A reduction in military expenditure to 3 per cent of United States GNP by 1997, which is envisaged by some scenarios,[19] means a reduction by two percentage points of United States GNP over five years which would be significant if the slow annual growth in output experienced recently were not to pick up.

Table 5  **The military burden in the developed market economies, 1989**

| Country | Military expenditure (US$mn) | Military expenditure as percentage of GNP | Military forces (thousands) | Military forces per thousand of population | Arms imports (US$m) | Arms exports (US$m) | Arms as percentage of total imports | Arms as percentage of total exports |
|---|---|---|---|---|---|---|---|---|
| United States | 304,100 | 5.8 | 2,241 | 9.0 | 1,600 | 11,200 | 0.3 | 3.1 |
| France | 35,260 | 3.7 | 554 | 9.9 | 210 | 2,700 | 0.1 | 1.5 |
| United Kingdom | 34,630 | 4.2 | 318 | 5.6 | 650 | 3,000 | 0.3 | 2.0 |
| Germany | 33,600 | 2.8 | 503 | 8.1 | 875 | 1,200 | 0.3 | 0.4 |
| Japan | 28,410 | 1.0 | 247 | 2.0 | 1,400 | 110 | 0.7 | 0.0 |
| Italy | 20,720 | 2.4 | 533 | 9.3 | 300 | 60 | 0.2 | 0.0 |
| Canada | 10,840 | 2.0 | 88 | 3.4 | 190 | 410 | 0.2 | 0.3 |
| Spain | 7,775 | 2.1 | 277 | 7.1 | 750 | 130 | 1.0 | 0.3 |
| Netherlands | 6,399 | 2.9 | 106 | 7.1 | 480 | 140 | 0.5 | 0.1 |
| Australia | 6,153 | 2.3 | 70 | 4.2 | 675 | 80 | 1.5 | 0.2 |
| Sweden | 4,872 | 2.6 | 62 | 7.4 | 70 | 575 | 0.1 | 1.1 |
| Belgium | 3,881 | 2.5 | 110 | 11.1 | 220 | 20 | 0.2 | 0.0 |
| Switzerland | 3,806 | 2.1 | 17 | 2.5 | 300 | 60 | 0.5 | 0.1 |
| South Africa | 3,786 | 4.4 | 100 | 2.6 | 100 | 0 | 0.5 | 0.0 |
| Greece | 3,097 | 5.9 | 201 | 20.1 | 2,000 | 0 | 12.4 | 0.0 |
| Norway | 2,925 | 3.3 | 43 | 10.2 | 340 | 30 | 1.4 | 0.1 |
| Denmark | 2,184 | 2.2 | 31 | 6.0 | 110 | 20 | 0.4 | 0.1 |
| Finland | 1,788 | 1.6 | 39 | 7.9 | 20 | 0 | 0.1 | 0.0 |
| Portugal | 1,457 | 3.3 | 104 | 10.1 | 60 | 40 | 0.3 | 0.3 |
| Austria | 1,402 | 1.1 | 48 | 6.3 | 100 | 40 | 0.3 | 0.1 |
| New Zealand | 847 | 2.2 | 12 | 3.8 | 50 | 0 | 0.6 | 0.0 |
| Ireland | 449 | 1.6 | 13 | 3.7 | 5 | 0 | 0.0 | 0.0 |
| Luxembourg | 76 | 0.9 | 1 | 2.6 | 10 | 5 | .. | .. |
| Non-United States | 214,357 | | 3,477 | | 8,915 | 8,620 | | |
| USSR | 311,000 | 11.7 | 3,700 | 12.8 | 900 | 19,600 | 0.8 | 17.9 |

Source: United States Arms Control and Disarmament Agency (1991). *World Military Expenditures and Arms Transfers, 1990.* Washington, D.C.

238

## Historical experience of disarmament

In some situations in the past, it has been claimed that military spending has had a favourable impact on economic conditions and stimulated economic growth, notably when alternative ways of creating employment seemed beyond reach. Recent empirical work testing the connection between economic growth and defence spending has also often produced conflicting results.[20]

However, there are few exact historical parallels to the nature of the decrease in military expenditure that is now anticipated, notably in the United States. At the end of World War II, military expenditure decreased rapidly in the United States from over 40 per cent of GNP in 1944 to 7 per cent in 1947. However, the rapid build-up of military expenditure during the war years was considered at the time to be a temporary phenomenon. Civilian employees were often put to work making military products, but using their existing skills, as in the welding together of Liberty ships by civilian welders. With the end of the war, there was no question but that civilian workers would resume their civilian occupations. Similarly, the United States had mobilized a large conscript army which was rapidly demobilized at the end of the war. The pent-up demand for goods and services, which resulted not just from the war years but also from the Depression years of the 1930s, helped keep employment high in the transition to a peace economy and provided demand that enabled firms to reconvert back to their original lines of production quickly.[21] Furthermore, many women who had entered the labour force to help the war effort left to become housewives and mothers when the war was over.

At the end of the war, there was little or no support for the maintenance of high military expenditures or sizeable armed services. However, it was soon discovered that the pre-war world could not be reconstituted. The European colonial powers had to adjust to withdrawal from their empires. The United States defence strategy was also profoundly affected by the development of new weapons – the long-range bomber, the jet fighter, the V-1 flying bomb, the V-2 rocket, and the atomic bomb. It could no longer rely on its continental isolation for immunity from attack. It had also assumed a role of international leadership.

After the Soviet Union developed the atomic bomb in 1949, the United States felt that it could not depend on its possession of atomic weapons to deter any possible aggression, but considered it necessary to foster the creation of a defence industrial base which would produce weapons superior to those possessed by the Soviet Union. The defence industry remained in private hands and expanded with the progress of the Cold War.

The magnitude and nature of the perceived threat of the Cold War to national survival thus brought about the creation of a powerful "military industrial complex" in the United States in a way that World War II had not.[22] Much of the discussion in the United States concerns what kind of defence industrial base the country needs now that the Soviet threat has been removed. It is widely accepted that the country should retain a defence industrial base that would enable it to produce the most technologically advanced weaponry.[23]

## The defence industry in the industrialized countries

In 1989, of the 100 largest arms-producing companies in the industrialized countries in terms of sales, 47 were domiciled in the United States, and their total sales were $106.2 billion (in US dollars).[24] A total of 42 companies were domiciled in Western Europe and had sales of $52.5 billion. Of these, the United Kingdom accounted for 14 companies with sales of $17.2 billion, France for nine companies with sales of $16.3 billion and Germany for seven companies with sales of $7.6 billion. Japan had six of the 100 largest arms-producing companies and their total sales were $6.2 billion. The developing countries had five companies with total sales of $3.7 billion.

Arms sales do not account for all of the output of the arms-producing companies. Table 6 gives figures for the 10 largest arms-producing companies, ranked by their sales in 1989. There was a considerable difference in their reliance on arms sales. Northrop, the California-based aircraft producer, derived about half of its revenue from the B-2 bomber programme. As early as 1989, it foresaw cutbacks in the B-2 programme and began to institute layoffs.[25] In January 1992, the Administration announced that it would shut down production of this bomber after 20 had been produced. Northrop was the only one of the 10 largest companies to post a loss in 1989. On the other hand, the largest of the 10 in terms of total sales and employment, the automobile giant, General Motors, derived only 4 per cent of its sales from arms. What an individual company supplies is sometimes as much a determinant of its vulnerability to defence cuts as the percentage of sales accounted for by arms. General Dynamics, for instance, is a diversified weapons producer, making missiles and

Table 6 **The largest arms-producing companies among the market economies**

| Rank | Name | Country | Arms sales in 1989 | Total sales in 1989 | Arms as percentage of total sales | Profit (US$m) | Employment in 1989 |
|------|------|---------|--------------------|---------------------|-----------------------------------|---------------|--------------------|
| 1 | McDonnell Douglas | United States | 8,500 | 14,581 | 58.3 | 219 | 128,000 |
| 2 | General Dynamics | United States | 8,400 | 10,053 | 83.6 | 293 | 103,000 |
| 3 | Lockheed | United States | 7,350 | 9,932 | 74.0 | 2 | 82,500 |
| 4 | British Aerospace | United Kingdom | 6,300 | 14,898 | 42.3 | 546 | 125,000 |
| 5 | General Electric | United States | 6,250 | 54,574 | 11.5 | 3,939 | 292,000 |
| 6 | General Motors | United States | 5,500 | 126,932 | 4.3 | 4,224 | 775,000 |
| 7 | Raytheon | United States | 5,330 | 8,796 | 60.6 | 529 | 77,600 |
| 8 | Boeing | United States | 4,800 | 20,276 | 23.7 | 973 | 164,500 |
| 9 | Northrop | United States | 4,700 | 5,248 | 89.6 | −81 | 41,000 |
| 10 | Rockwell International | United States | 4,500 | 12,633 | 35.6 | 735 | 109,000 |

Source: *SIPRI Yearbook 1991* (1991). Oxford University Press, New York and Oxford, p. 311.

electronics, for which the market held up better in 1989 than for military aircraft; it showed a profit in 1989. Lockheed, on the other hand, barely made a profit on a similar volume of sales.

## The effects on labour markets of the transition to lower military spending

Large-scale inter-sectoral reallocation of labour can be expected to have both positive and negative effects. If capital productivity is higher in non-defence sectors, the reallocation of production can be expected to increase the average productivity of the economy. To the extent that labour is absorbed in other industries, such as services, without significant increases in investment, real wages would have a tendency to fall. And, of course, transitory unemployment would increase. Whether the net effects would be positive for the economy as a whole is an empirical question as is the incidence of the positive and negative effects on particular industries and localities.

With cancellations in arms purchases, the major companies are resorting to layoffs. Estimates of those who will eventually be affected vary. A study group found that federal cuts in military spending could result in the loss of between 210,000 to 420,000 jobs in Los Angeles County by 1995 as military spending there falls from $8.88 billion in 1990 to between $3.5 and $4.9 billion.[26] This county received more federal military dollars than any other in the United States and in December 1991 had 225,600 workers directly employed in the aerospace industry, accounting for 5.3 per cent of non-farm employment and 28.3 per cent of manufacturing jobs. Besides the prime contractors, the subcontractors and suppliers would also be affected.

To assess the net effects on employment of changes in military spending, two factors have to be taken into consideration – the rate at which new jobs are being created in a region, and the transferability of displaced workers to non-defence activities. A disaggregated analysis for the United States attempted to calculate the effects of cumulative reductions in military expenditure between 1990 and 1995.[27] Some of the results are given in table 7. In 1988, there were 1,337,900 active duty service personnel in the United States and 936,900 civilians working for the Department of Defense. These are known magnitudes. An estimate for the number of employees in defence-related industries was 3.4 million, equivalent to 3 per cent of total employment. A 3 per cent annual cut in military spending would result in the annual loss of 102,000 jobs in the private sector and a 6 per cent an-

Table 7  **Estimates of potential defence-related employment losses in the United States under different scenarios**

| | |
|---|---:|
| Active duty personnel in 1988 | 1,338,000 |
| Civilian Department of Defense in 1988 | 937,000 |
| Private sector in 1988 | 3,400,000 |
| Total defence-related employment in 1988 | 5,675,000 |
| Total employment in 1988 | 115,049,000 |
| Private sector defence employment as a percentage of total employment | 3.0 |
| Private sector workers potentially displaced by a 3% cut in defence spending | 102,000 |
| Private sector employees potentially displaced by a 6% cut in defence spending | 204,000 |
| Gains in annual total employment in 1988–1989 | 2,325,000 |
| Ratio between gain in total employment and losses in defence related employment: | |
|     for a 3% defence cut | 22.8:1 |
|     for a 6% defence cut | 11.4:1 |

Source: David D. Whitehead (1991). "FYI: the impact of private-sector defense cuts on regions in the United States." *Federal Reserve Bank of Atlanta Economic Review*, March/April.

nual cut in an annual loss of 204,000 jobs.[28] However, between 1988 and 1989 total annual employment in the United States economy grew by 2.3 million, meaning that 11 and 22 times as many jobs were generated as would have been lost by a 6 per cent and 3 per cent annual cut in defence spending, respectively.

In the North-East of the United States, potential absorption rates[29] tended to be lower as employment growth was small and the number of potentially displaced defence employees high. California, on the other hand, saw the greatest absolute loss in defence-related employment, but had the largest absolute change in employment and so its absorption rate was near the national average. A study for the United Kingdom and for the OECD countries came to a similar conclusion: the share of military expenditure is not a significant influence on the unemployment rate, except in the case of major wars when aggregate demand and employment rise rapidly.[30]

Such calculations can show that if the economy is performing well, as in the OECD countries in the late 1980s, the absorption of defence-sector workers should proceed in a reasonable manner. Between 1980 and 1989, the number of employees on non-farm payrolls in the United States expanded from 90.4 to 108.4 million – by about 2 million persons a year. An annual loss of just over 200,000 jobs from a 6 per cent cut in military expenditure is small in comparison. However, with the recession, total employment has fallen by about a million between the end of 1990 and the end of 1991.[31] To exacerbate matters, about half of the 3.14 million workers in private sector defence-related employment in 1988, or 1.55 million people, were in the manufacturing sector.[32] This sector is small and was already shrinking before the recession: it fell from 20.3 million employees in 1980 to 19.4 million in 1989. With the recession, the sector shrunk even more rapidly – to 18.4 million employees at the end of 1991. In these circumstances, the loss of jobs from, say, a 6 per cent cut in defence expenditure begins to appear large.

Job losses in the defence industry can be particularly severe for a particular community, as the figures for Los Angeles County indicate. At a time of recession they are doubly severe. One estimate was that defence cut-backs in the United States were responsible for about 25 per cent of lost jobs and industrial production between July 1990 and February 1992.[33] Salaries in the defence industry tended to be higher than those in other industries, not only for scientists, engineers, and other professionals but also for production workers.[34] Even if defence workers are able to find new employment, they might have to accept a cut in salary.

As illustrated by the decline in jobs in the manufacturing sector in the United States in the 1980s, at a time when total employment increased, the economy is constantly changing, with some jobs being lost to be replaced by others. The potential job availabilities for discharged defence-related workers will also depend on government action in the wake of defence cuts. Government could decide to do nothing when defence expenditure declines, or it could offset the decreases in various ways: by increasing its own purchases of civilian goods and services, by cutting personal taxes by the amounts of the reductions, by increasing transfer payments or grants to states and local government. These different policies would lead to different results for key macroeconomic variables such as interest rates, the budget deficit, the inflation rate, real disposable income, and productivity. They would also lead to different demands for labour: for instance, if taxes were cut and consumer demand rose, employment would be likely to increase for the manufacture of consumer goods. On the other hand, if grants were given to states and local authorities, they would tend to employ more teachers, court officials, and highway maintenance workers.[35]

## Other effects on defence-related industries

Besides laying off workers and shutting down production facilities, another strategy that defence companies are adopting to cut costs and become more competitive is to merge with other national producers or to cooperate with companies in other countries. Companies in the United States have tended to merge with other US companies, while in Europe, where the arms sales of individual companies tend to be smaller, joint companies are being formed by the main producers of engines, military electronics, missiles, and helicopters.[36]

Military revenue helped some companies compete in international markets. Furthermore, lessons learned from military production have been applied to similar civilian products, particularly in the aircraft industry.[37] With the prospective decline in military orders, manufacturers will have to ensure that their civilian production is profitable. This is doubly important if the market for commercial aircraft is depressed – in 1991, orders for new commercial jets were $32 billion, as compared to a peak of $90 billion in 1989.[38]

In military applications, many of the large companies that are arms producers purchase their supplies from other countries, in particular Japan, which is pre-eminent in many technologies required for military applications. Japan supplies about 50 per cent of the world's semiconductors and it alone can supply the semiconductors used in some weapon systems.[39]

The use of Japanese technology in US weapon systems has highlighted that military technology is no longer setting the pace for civilian technology, as was frequently the case earlier. Rather, the reverse appears to be true, with the military trying to adapt for their purposes technologies that had been developed for civilian uses. Military specifications for some products in electronics tend to be less demanding now than for civilian products, a reverse of early experience.

These developments suggest that a switch of resources from military to civilian research would not depress the long-run technological advance of a society and thereby harm its competitiveness and potential economic growth. However, there is not a limited pool of scientific talent which is either employed in defence or civilian research: changes in military and civilian research and development can often move in the same direction.[40] At the present time, after reaching a peak in 1989, it appears that both private and government research and development spending in the United States are falling as a result of the recession and the military cut-backs.[41] Moreover, the pool of scientific talent itself grows as a result of government policies: defence needs can lead to increases in universities' output of scientists. Migration and the greater entry of women into the scientific field also contribute to the supply of research scientists.

It is sometimes argued that military production was not sufficiently competitive to prepare companies for civilian production. Cost considerations were secondary to performance considerations, and the defence ministries were not as demanding customers as private consumers. Within the military establishment, it was generally accepted that military personnel would be trained at great cost to operate technologically advanced equipment, whereas the emphasis in civilian markets is on making equipment "user friendly." An element of competition was introduced by having companies compete for defence contracts and by the existence of competitors in export markets, but this was not thought to be as intense as competition in civilian markets.

Some companies have made the transition from military to civilian production successfully with overall sales expanding and civilian sales taking up a greater percentage of total sales. Others have failed to diversify into a new line of business.[42] The case for using public money to assist in conversion attempts has been resisted because of general scepticism about government intervention in industry.[43] Decisions on conversion will, then, ultimately be taken by private businesses who will have the responsibility for the success or failure.[44]

The strategy of the previous US Administration was that matters should be left in the hands of the companies themselves. The basic philosophy was that the government should not intervene to steer companies toward new areas of production or to subsidize the transition: it should, in fact, treat defence companies just like other companies which are facing a loss in demand. Some special steps have, though, been taken.[45]

Criticisms have been that legislation has not gone far enough, and in particular that support was not given to small businesses used as subcontractors by the main arms-producing companies, and that unemployment compensation was not extended for a longer period.[46] A more radical criticism has been that there is no plan for conversion to a civilian economy, and that legislation should mandate company-based advance planning for conversion.[47] The general view of the Bush Administration was that the proposed defence budget changes "do not seem to call for new and extraordinary economic adjustment or conversion programmes. Public adjustment supports already available are broadly adequate for the portended changes."[48]

In the matter of putting to alternative uses military bases that are to be closed down, local governments have been largely successful in generating new employment opportunities. Most former military bases have been turned into industrial and office parks. Others were used for educational establishments. From the records of 100 communities over a 25-year period to the mid-1980s, it was estimated that the loss of employment due to the base closings was 93,000, but that the new employment generated was 138,000.[49]

## The environmental costs of transition to a smaller military establishment

During the 40 years of the Cold War, and particularly during the early years, there was a relatively small appreciation of the hazards of nuclear power and of the environmental damage that was being caused. Now attention can be directed from producing nuclear weapons to cleaning up the environment. The environment was not polluted only by nuclear programmes and the leaking of radioactive wastes into the soil. Chemical by-products were also disposed of in an unsafe fashion and unexploded shells were left on firing ranges.

The scale of the clean-up is likely to be very large, particularly in the United States which had the largest military establishment, and a large nuclear programme. The Pentagon had by autumn 1991 investigated 17,500 sites on 1,855 installations in the United States and found that 11,000 were likely to warrant future restoration work.[50] These estimates exclude environmental damage in installations outside the United States. In fiscal year 1993, $3.7 billion was earmarked in the defence budget for the clean-up of pollution on military bases. A further $5.5 billion was requested for cleaning up the pollution from the Department of Energy's nuclear weapon programmes. As the clean-up progresses, new technologies could be developed that would reduce costs; further evidence of pollution could also be produced. In these circumstances, estimates of the time-scale and eventual total cost of the clean-up are necessarily subject to wide margins of error. One estimate for the total cost over 30 years of removing contamination from military bases and Energy Department sites was $400 billion.[51] This clean-up work could provide alternative sources of revenue for military contractors, although doubts have been expressed on whether such work could compensate for the cancellation of military production.[52]

## The costs of weapon destruction

With the enhanced emphasis on environmental protection, weapon destruction is likely to be more costly than before. In the 1960s, for instance, the primary method of disposing of the US chemical weapons and munitions was dumping at sea. In 1969, the National Academy of Science called for an environmentally sound method. In 1984, the United States formally adopted direct incineration as the preferred method to destroy its chemical stocks.[53] Its first full-scale destruction facility is the Johnston Atoll Chemical Disposal System (JACADS) in the Pacific. Eventually, the United States hopes to have a destruction facility at each of its nine chemical stockpile sites. As safety is the overriding concern in destruction, delays and rising costs can be expected. Between 1985 and 1988, the estimated cost of the United States' chemical destruction programme doubled.[54] One recent estimate of the cost of destroying the United States chemical weapons, including verification costs, was over $6 billion.[55]

Similar considerations apply to the destruction of nuclear weapons, where environmental concerns and safety should be the first priorities. The size of the reduction depends on the final outcome of negotiations and unilateral steps. In 1991, before the START treaty was signed, it was estimated that the strategic forces of the Soviet Union and the United States had a total of 10,877 and 11,602 warheads, respectively. If implemented, it was calculated that the START treaty would have cut these to 6,940 and 8,592 warheads, respectively, by the late 1990s.[56] However, in June 1992, Presidents Bush and Yeltsin reached an agreement to go even further and reduce their arsenals of strategic missiles to between 3,000 and 3,500 each by the year 2003.

A very considerable expense will have to be incurred by the developed market economies in destroying not only their own but also in assisting the destruction of the nuclear weapons of the Commonwealth of Independent States. In 1991, the US Congress voted to set aside $400 million to help the Commonwealth destroy its weapons of mass destruction. It is impossible to estimate the final cost of the destruction of nuclear weapons because of the lack of experience in this field.[57]

The platforms on which weapon systems are mounted, such as tanks, ships, and aircraft, cannot easily be converted to civilian use: for instance, it is probably cheaper to buy a tractor or a fire engine than to convert the chassis of a tank to one, and cheaper to build a freighter than to use a decommissioned destroyer for cargo.[58] However, the environmental and safety factors in the destruction of conventional weapons are not so complicated as with chemical or nuclear weapons. The technology of cutting up equipment and melting down the scraps to recover the original metal is well known. The cost of labour seems the determining factor in the cost of destruction: it takes between 300 and 500 man-hours to cut up a tank whose scrap value would be about $4,000.[59]

The destruction of conventional equipment could not, then, be expected to place insuperable costs on the countries undertaking it. However, destruction is made necessary not just by the terms of arms reduction agreements,[60] but also to prevent the weapons being recommissioned or sold.

## The cost of verification

The technology to verify arms-reduction agreements is continually developing. As with the destruction of nuclear weapons, it is therefore difficult to begin to estimate the costs of verification. However, verification technologies could have important civilian applications. For instance, French experiments with Thomson-CSF airborne radar used to detect submarine periscopes indicated that this system had the potential for locating tuna shoals more accurately.[61] In turn, this could render obsolete the practice of drift-net fishing for tuna which has led to the netting and killing of dolphins. It is also possible to envisage the sharing and mutual development by different countries of verification technologies which would lead to a reduction in costs.

## An overall assessment of the economic costs of moving to a lower military establishment

In the short term, the various costs associated with the implementation of disarmament measures, whether or not undertaken as a result of agreements, are substantial and could absorb a significant portion of the peace dividend. However, it is important to look at longer-term aspects of the different costs. Environmental clean-up costs are being incurred because of a perceived necessity. The end of the Cold War allowed attention to be directed to the environmental consequences of much military activity, but environmental clean-up could not have been indefinitely delayed, and further delays would only have added to total eventual costs. Similarly, with arm-reduction agreements, costs of verification and of weapons destruction have to be incurred.

Many of the tasks frequently have or could have a direct civilian application. This is the case with environmental clean-ups and verification techniques. The experience that enterprises obtain in these military-related activities could help prepare them for subsequent civilian operations: the short-term costs involved could lead to longer-term civilian benefits.

Recent research indicates that enterprises moving from military to civilian production often find that it is more economic to shut down existing production facilities and build new facilities for civilian production than to attempt to convert the former to civilian production. The view that conversion would be a matter of mechanical re-engineering of facilities from military to civilian production was cast into doubt by the experience of the Soviet Union; the experience of the market economies confirms that such a short-term change-over is seldom realistic. If the longer-term structural adjustment of economies towards a position where the military sector and military production are considerably smaller is successful, the benefits should certainly outweigh the costs of the transition.

## Modelling the medium-term effects of arms reductions

The above discussion shows some of the likely benefits and costs of reductions in military expenditure. The global models that we have presently available could not be expected to capture all these effects but they can shed light on the principal macroeconomic effects.

In general, as will be seen below, the global model analysis supports the conclusions reached above. The deflationary macroeconomic effects in developed market economies are sufficiently small as to pose no major problem of adjustment using conventional tools of fiscal and monetary policy. Although relatively small in relation to GDP in developed market economies, government budgetary savings – if used to finance investment in reforming developing countries and the economies in transition of Central and Eastern Europe – could significantly underpin growth in these countries.

250

## Macroeconomic policy simulations using the world econometric model of Project LINK

In the scenarios shown in table 8, it was assumed that the four major developed market economies where the ratio of military expenditure to GDP was estimated to be above 2 per cent in 1992 would reduce them over a period of four years or less. In the case of the United States, where the ratio was estimated to be 5.3 per cent in 1992, it was reduced to 3 per cent by 1996, almost one percentage point less than in the baseline forecast.[62] In the cases of the United Kingdom, France, and Germany (West), the ratio was reduced from current levels of 3.7, 3.3, and 2.4 per cent, respectively, to 2 per cent. It should be emphasized that in the baseline LINK forecast of the world economy, a reduction in the ratio of military expenditures in the United States from 5.3 per cent in 1992 to 3.8 per cent by 1996 had already been assumed based on the Bush Administration's proposals. Specific assumption about reduction in military budgets had not, however, been made in the case of the other three countries.

Since the reductions in military spending are small, the effects on aggregate output are also small, but by no means negligible. For the developed market economies as a group there would be a cumulative reduction in output of nearly 1 per cent by 1997, taking into account the international demand multiplier of the LINK system. The negative impact in percentage terms would be greatest for the United Kingdom and least for the countries making no expenditure cuts, but losing from the reduction in world demand for their exports.

The losses to GNP are small enough to be compensated by some combination of increased expenditures on other programmes or by interest rate reductions or some combination of the two. Coordinated interest rate reductions of 25 basis points were assumed in 1994 and 1995 and reductions of 50 basis points (from baseline) in 1996 and 1997. The effect of the interest rate reductions alone would be to restore almost half of the loss in demand caused by the military expenditure reductions (scenario B in table 8).

In scenario C (table 8) it was assumed that part of the budgetary savings would be used to finance transfers to developing countries implementing structural adjustment programmes, and to the Central and Eastern European economies in transition, including the constituent republics of the former Soviet Union. Increasing transfers by $19 billion in 1993 and progressively to about $60 billion by 1997

Table 8  **The LINK model scenario analyses**[a]

| Scenarios / Impact | GDP in world | GDP in developed market economies | GDP in developing countries Total: Recipient | | GDP in former USSR | GDP in 5 countries of Central Europe | World trade volume | Inflation in developed market economies | Unemployment in developed market economies |
|---|---|---|---|---|---|---|---|---|---|
| After 1, 3, 5 yrs | | | | | | | | | |
| A. Reduce military spending in 4 industrial countries | -0.1 | -0.2 | -0.0: | -0.0 | -0.0 | -0.0 | -0.1 | 0.0 | -0.0 |
| | -0.4 | -0.5 | -0.1: | -0.0 | -0.1 | -0.1 | -0.7 | -0.1 | -0.0 |
| | -0.7 | -0.8 | -0.1: | -0.1 | -0.1 | -0.1 | -1.2 | -0.2 | -0.0 |
| B. Partially offset reductions by reducing interest rates in G7 | -0.1 | -0.2 | -0.1: | -0.0 | -0.0 | -0.0 | -0.1 | -0.1 | -0.0 |
| | -0.3 | -0.4 | -0.1: | -0.0 | -0.1 | -0.1 | -0.6 | -0.1 | -0.0 |
| | -0.4 | -0.5 | -0.1: | -0.1 | -0.1 | -0.1 | -0.9 | -0.1 | -0.0 |
| C. Increase net transfers to developing countries and economies in transition combined with A and B | 0.1 | -0.0 | 0.4: | 1.3 | 0.4 | 0.5 | 0.5 | 0.0 | 0.0 |
| | 0.2 | 0.1 | 0.9: | 2.9 | 0.7 | 1.5 | 1.1 | 0.0 | 0.0 |
| | 0.4 | 0.2 | 1.0: | 3.2 | 1.0 | 2.2 | 1.3 | 0.0 | 0.0 |
| D. Reallocate military spending to investment in export sector in developing countries | -0.0 | -0.1 | 0.1: | 0.4 | 0.0 | 0.0 | 0.0 | 0.0 | 0.0 |
| | -0.2 | -0.3 | 0.4: | 1.4 | 0.0 | 0.0 | -0.2 | -0.1 | 0.0 |
| | -0.3 | -0.6 | 0.7: | 2.4 | -0.1 | 0.0 | -0.5 | -0.1 | 0.0 |
| E. Composite of C and D | 0.0 | -0.1 | 0.4: | 1.4 | 0.4 | 0.6 | 0.5 | 0.0 | 0.0 |
| | 0.0 | -0.3 | 1.1: | 3.6 | 0.6 | 1.5 | 0.8 | 0.0 | 0.0 |
| | 0.0 | -0.4 | 1.4: | 4.6 | 0.7 | 2.2 | 0.7 | -0.1 | 0.0 |

Notes:

Scenario A:  Military spending in 4 large industrial countries reduced by $19 billion in 1993 increasing to $118 billion in 1997. Dollars are US dollars.

Scenario B:  Deflationary effect of scenario A partially offset by reductions in interest rates in G7 countries by 25 basis points in 1994 and 1995 and by 50 basis points in 1996 and 1997.

Scenario C:  Scenario B combined with additional net transfers to Central Europe and former Soviet Union of $7 billion in 1993 increasing to $25 billion in 1997; additional net transfers to selected developing countries of $12 billion in 1993 increasing to $34 billion in 1997.

Scenario D:  Reallocation of military spending to investment in the export sector in developing countries equivalent to 3% of GDP per year.

Scenario E:  Scenarios C and D combined.

a.  Impact expressed in percentage deviation from baseline.

would constitute a substantial contribution to accelerating growth in these struggling countries, but beginning in 1994 military expenditure reductions would also leave scope for central government budget deficit reductions of somewhat more than $25 billion per year in 1994 and 1995, and nearly $60 billion per year in 1996 and 1997, facilitating the interest rate reductions mentioned above.

The injection of further demand stimulus in the form of increased exports to the countries receiving the government transfers would, together with the interest rate reductions, completely offset the initial deflationary impact of the military spending cuts resulting in virtually no change to unemployment levels and inflation rates in the developed market economies.

The effects on the countries receiving the transfer would be proportionately much greater. Recipient developing countries would experience a one percentage point increase in their GDP growth rates for three years, after which GDP would remain three percentage points higher than in the baseline scenario, as the growth rate would return to its baseline value by 1997. Since the capital transfers to the five Central European countries would be proportionately somewhat larger, their economies would expand cumulatively by about two percentage points as compared with the baseline. Because of its greater size the economy of the former Soviet Union would expand by only about 1 per cent as a result of the transfers. The effects of this composite scenario on world trade would be to increase its volume by about 1.3 per cent over a five-year period.

Military spending not only absorbs an unnecessarily large fraction of output in developed market economies, but it absorbs even greater proportions in many developing countries and has until recently in the economies in transition of Central and Eastern Europe and the former USSR. Regarding the latter countries, however, the baseline projection itself embodies the assumption that significant reductions in military spending will occur and that a large portion of the industrial capacity used to supply the military sector will be converted to production of civilian goods. Hence, no further adjustments were made to these countries in the LINK simulation.

As regards the developing countries, however, the following assumptions were made. Starting from current levels those recipient developing countries with military expenditures above 2 per cent of GDP were assumed to reduce them to this level over a period of years (varying depending on the size of the reductions). It was further assumed that the resources thus released would be used to increase investment in the external sector, leading to increases in exports. Since on average the increases in investment/GDP ratios amounted to about three percentage points and since the average implicit efficiency of capital as measured by the incremental capital output ratio (ICOR) in the LINK models of developing countries is about 3, GDP growth rates could be permanently raised by about 1 per cent as compared with the baseline projection (scenario D).

When scenarios C and D are combined (scenario D) the results are additive and are quite striking, especially for the transfer-recipient countries whose GDP is increased cumulatively by nearly six percentage points over a five-year period. For the developed market economies and for the world as a whole, the effects on GDP inflation and unemployment are approximately neutral.

## The future for the peace dividend

These simulations indicate that, even in the short to medium term, there is indeed a peace dividend, and that the policies governments pursue will determine its eventual impact. However, the main lesson from the discussions about the peace dividend may be that the greatest peace dividend coming from the end of the Cold War is peace itself and that international action and cooperation are required to achieve it.

A critical issue concerning military spending and industrial re-organization in the developed market economies is what will happen in the United States, the pre-eminent military power. Now that the strategic situation has changed radically, the United States is looking at its military structure and reviewing the options. Some suggestions might be controversial[63] and the Executive and Legislature and the media can be expected to review very carefully the contingencies that the armed forces are supposed to meet, and their implications for force levels. Alternatives, often involving an enhanced role for international cooperation, particularly through the United Nations, are often invoked. The dispatch in December 1992 of US troops to Somalia to stabilize the country and avert famine by ensuring food deliveries is an example of the novel use of military power.

The force of arguments for a careful scrutiny of the defence posture comes from the growing appreciation that a country's security and its international standing do not just depend upon its military strength, but also upon the robustness of its economy, which reflects its domestic spending priorities, and upon its ability to participate in international cooperation. Security can never be measured solely in terms of an individual country's military strength, but also depends upon the confidence it can place in its neighbours and other countries, their mutually beneficial economic cooperation, the stability of its import supplies, and the ensured access to markets for its exports, as long as they remain competitive.

The result of the Clinton Administration's assessment of the kind of role the United States expects to play in the world, and, by implication, the kind of military it will have, is of profound importance not just for the country itself, but for the overall global community.

With the end of the Cold War, the participation of United States forces in peace-keeping operations can be envisaged. The recent Somali operation showed how US participation is often vital for the success of any large-scale operation. The concept of peace-keeping is itself being refined with experience and, unfortunately, new conflicts. In this connection, it has been suggested by a former United Nations official that countries which find it difficult to pay their assessments for peace-keeping should shift this cost to the defence budget rather than the diplomatic or foreign aid budgets which tend to be much smaller.[64]

The econometric results described above show that there is certainly no justification for slowing down the reduction in military expenditures in order to benefit a sagging civilian economy in the short run. In the longer term, then, the question of a peace dividend can be seen not so much as one of how to spend a given volume of resources, or to compensate for the short-term demand-reducing effects of cuts in military expenditure, but of how the military structure and the resources that it presently absorbs should be redesigned to support a new system of global relations. The large volume of resources presently absorbed by the military are potentially available for helping resolve some of the most important problems on the global agenda and making possible sustained socio-economic advance in a peaceful international environment.

## Notes

1. Much of this paper relies on chapter VI of the *World Economic Survey 1992*, United Nations publication, Sales No. E.92.II.C.1.
2. For an analysis of conversion in the former Soviet Union, see Stanislav Menshikov (1992). "Experiences of Soviet Conversion," paper prepared for the ECAAR-AEA Joint Panel on Utilizing Military Funds for Economic Development, New Orleans, 3 January (mimeographed); and Michael Checinski (1991), "The conversion of the Soviet arms industry." *Osteuropa Wirtschaft* 36(1).
3. See Julian Cooper (1991), "The Soviet Defence Industry and Conversion: The Regional

Dimension." In Liba Paukert and Peter Richards, *Defence Expenditure, Industrial Conversion and Local Employment*. International Labour Office, Geneva, p. 158.

4. United States Arms Control and Disarmament Agency (1989), *World Military Expenditure and Arms Transfers 1989*. Washington, D.C., pp. 35 and 52.

5. Figures from Stockholm International Peace Research Institute (1991), *SIPRI Yearbook 1991*. Oxford University Press, New York and Oxford, p. 132.

6. See International Institute for Strategic Studies (1983), *The Military Balance 1983–1984*. Brassey's, London, pp. 145–146.

7. ibid., p. 145.

8. See Ridge, Michael, and Ron Smith (1991), "UK military manpower and substitutability." *Defence Economics* 2(4), p. 285.

9. *The Economist*, 28 July 1990, p. 47.

10. The Conventional Forces in Europe Treaty was signed (but not ratified) in November 1990, by which time it was clear that "NATO forces would be reduced to levels far below the maximum allowed by the Treaty." International Institute for Strategic Studies (1991). *The Military Balance 1991–1992*. Brassey's, London, p. 229.

11. International Institute for Strategic Studies, *The Military Balance 1991–1992*, op. cit., pp. 238–239.

12. *SIPRI Yearbook 1991*, op. cit., p. 125.

13. *The New York Times*, 24 January 1992 and 22 February 1992. Some military contractors have argued that without actually producing the weapons that were designed, they would lose the ability to do so, and that it would be almost impossible to start production from scratch.

14. International Institute for Strategic Studies, *The Military Balance 1991–1992*, op. cit., p. 231.

15. See *The Economist*, 2 November 1991, for a description of some of the various suggestions.

16. For instance, whereas the Administration has proposed that the military budget in 1997 should be $291 billion, entailing a savings of $43 billion between 1993 and 1997, the Chairman of the House Armed Services Committee, Representative Les Aspin, proposed four different options designed to face different configurations of threats. The outcomes for 1997 were expenditures of $231, $246, $270 and $295 billions. The Chairman argued in favour of spelling out the options since the taxpayers were buying defence "for dealing with certain potential contingencies or threats, and they don't want to spend more than is necessary." (*The New York Times*, 23 February 1992).

17. However, in 1989, Greece's imports of arms were considerably larger than in other years.

18. The other principal source of information for arms transfers is SIPRI, which gives figures for exports of "major weapons" in constant prices.

19. See *Business Week*, 24 February 1992.

20. For instance, in a recent issue of *Defence Economics* 2(1) (1990), three articles analysed the relationship between defence spending and economic growth. H. Somnetz Atsesoglu and Michael J. Mueller in "Defence spending and economic growth" concluded that "a larger defence spending leads to a higher economic growth, and vice versa" (p. 26). They calculated that the loss of output coming from a 10 per cent annual reduction in defence spending from 1990 to 1995 would constitute 2.8 per cent of real output in 1995 (p. 25).

Chi Huang and Alex Mintz in "Ridge regression analysis of the defence-growth tradeoff in the United States" found that "the results showed no significant, direct tradeoff between defence spending and economic growth" (p. 36).

Finally, W. Robert J. Alexander in "The impact of defence spending on economic growth: A multi-sectoral approach to defence spending and economic growth with evidence from developed countries" concluded that "we are unable to reject the hypothesis that defence spending has no significant impact on economic growth for a group of developed countries. We are able, though, to point out the relatively low productivity of the defence sector. Even if we are unable to discount the possibility of a positive spin-off from spending on defence, resources are more productively employed in another sector from which the spin-off may be just as high or higher."

21. For an analysis of how the post-war change-over in American industry was a "reconversion" rather than a "conversion" see Kenneth L. Adelman and Norman R. Augustine (1992), "Defense conversion." *Foreign Affairs* 71(2).

22. Two countries that had built up a military-industrial complex before the war were Germany and Japan, but their large defence industries were dismantled and destroyed after the war. See Lutz Köllner "The National Experience of the Federal Republic of Germany." In *Conversion: Economic Adjustments in an Era of Arms Reduction (Volume II): Disarmament Topical Papers No. 5*. United Nations publication, Sales No. E.91.IX.7; and Isamu Miyazaki, "Conversion from military to civilian industry." *Challenges to Multilateral Disarmament in the Post-Cold-War and Post-Gulf-War Period: Disarmament Topical Papers No. 6*. United Nations publication, Sales No. E. 91.IX.18. The example of Germany, which surely also applies to Japan, was that "the Germans surrendered neither their know-how nor their propensity to work hard and succeeded in compensating for the military defeat in the great economic upswing that was to follow" (Köllner, op. cit., p. 151).

23. For a discussion of the concept of the defence industrial base, see Jonathan Ratner and Celia Thomas (1990), "The defence industrial base and foreign supply of defence goods." *Defence Economics* 2 (1), pp. 57–58. The authors pointed out how the National Defense Authorization Act, Fiscal Year 1989 directed the Secretary of Defense to formulate plans to strengthen the United States defence industrial base.

24. All figures in this paragraph are from *SIPRI Yearbook 1991*, op. cit., p. 286.

25. Betty G. Lall and John Tepper Marlin (1991), *Building a Peace Economy*. Westview Press, Boulder, Colo., p. 14.

26. Estimate by the Los Angeles Aerospace Task Force reported in *The New York Times*, 18 March 1992.

27. David D. Whitehead (1991), "FYI: The impact of private-sector defense cuts on regions in the United States." *Federal Reserve of Atlanta Economic Review*, March/April, pp. 30–41.

28. Another estimate for the United States as a whole was that over the next six years, 1.3 million people would lose jobs in the defence industry and the military services (Professor Seymour Melman, Chairman of the National Commission for Economic Conversion and Disarmament, writing in *The New York Times*, 27 February 1992).

29. The absorption rate can be defined as the ratio between the new jobs being created elsewhere in the economy and the losses of jobs in the defence industry.

30. Paul Dunne and Ron Smith (1990), "Military expenditure and unemployment in the OECD." *Defence Economics* 1(1), pp. 70–71.

31. Figures from United States Department of Labor, Bureau of Labor Statistics, *Employment and Earnings*. Washington, D.C., various issues.

32. Norman C. Saunders (1990), "Defence spending in the 1990's – the effect of deeper cuts." *Monthly Labor Review*. United States Department of Labor, Bureau of Labor Statistics, Washington D.C., October, p. 4. The conclusion of this study was that "although the effects (of reductions in defence spending) tend to be relatively minor at the aggregate level, they may be significant in certain industries and occupations most closely tied to the Department of Defense. While other industries and occupations may suffer from significant defense cutbacks, other industries and occupations may improve as a result of offsetting economic factors", p. 15.

33. *Business Week*, 24 February 1992.

34. Liba Paukert and Peter Richards, "Employment impact of industrial conversion: A comparative analysis." In Paukert and Richards, op. cit., p. 212.

35. Saunders, op. cit., p. 12.

36. *SIPRI Yearbook 1991*, op. cit., pp. 287–291.

37. For instance, the Boeing 707 jetliner was derived in part from the KC-135 tanker produced for the United States Air Force (*The New York Times*, 15 March 1992).

38. *The Economist*, 7 March 1992.

39. See Professor Hajime Karatsu (1991), "Weapons running on Japanese technology keep increasing in an era when technology for the public has priority." *Shukan Toyo Keizai*, Tokyo, 3 March, translated in United States Government Foreign Broadcast Information Service *Daily Report. Supplement: East Asia – Japan – Defense Related Issues*, 13 May 1991.

40. See Murray Weidenbaum (1990), "Defence spending and the American economy: how much change in the offing." *Defence Economics* 1(3), pp. 236–237.

41. *The New York Times*, 21 February 1992.

42. Adelman and Augustine, op. cit., concluded that "The reason for this solid record of failure (in conversion) is simple: defense work has little in common with civilian work." They argued that detailed research had not identified a successful product in the United States economy that was developed through a military to civilian conversion (p. 27). On the other hand, Jurgen Brauer and John Tepper Marlin believe that the conversion history of the late 1960s and early 1970s deserves "a second, more careful look." See (1992) "Converting resources from military to non-military uses." *Journal of Economic Perspectives* 6 (4), p. 150.

43. cf. Murray Weidenbaum, op. cit., p. 241.

44. Experience suggests that the elements for successful diversification include: "(1) planning for change before cuts; (2) thorough market research; (3) an understanding of cost minimization; (4) using the existing workforce; (5) technology transfer; (6) persistence in the face of a long-term payoff; and (7) committed leadership." From (1985) *Economic Adjustment and Conversion*, a report prepared by the Economic Adjustment Committee and the Office of Economic Adjustment, Department of Defense, Washington, D.C., cited in Lall and Marlin, op. cit., p. 21.

45. The Defense Economic Adjustment Diversification, Conversion and Stabilization Act 1990 provided $200 million in funding for community and worker-centred adjustment assistance. Of this amount, $150 million is to be provided by the Department of Defense to the Job Training Partnership Act programmes of the Department of Labor and $50 million to the Department of Commerce's Economic Development Administration for disbursements as planning grants to communities adversely affected by defence cuts.

   The National Defense Authorization Act for Fiscal Year 1992 (Public Law 102-90) included provisions to fund technology programmes, such as high definition display, through the Defense Advanced Research Projects Agency, and also increased funding for research and development of manufacturing technologies. The American Technology Preeminence Act of 1991 (Public Law 102-245) authorized funding for the Department of Commerce's programmes relating to technology and established two commissions, the "National Commission on Reducing Capital Costs for Emerging Technology" and the "Commission on Technology and Procurement" to investigate and report on methods of promoting technology development in the United States and on the role of federal procurement policies in fostering and maintaining a technology base, respectively.

   The National Defense Authorization Act for Fiscal Year 1992 also contained provisions for voluntary separation incentive and special separation benefits programmes for military personnel who leave the services early.

46. See Lall and Marlin, op. cit., p. 81.

47. See Melmann, op. cit., and Lall and Marlin, op. cit., p. 78. The "Defense Economic Adjustment Act," has been introduced by Representative Ted Weiss for many years without becoming law. Its key provision was that at every defence facility employing at least 100 persons an Alternative Use Committee composed of not less than eight members with equal representation of the facility's management and labour should be established.

48. Robert M. Rauner, "The national experience of the United States." In *Disarmament Topical Papers 5: Conversion: Economic Adjustments in an Era of Arms Reduction (Volume II)*. United Nations publication, Sales No. E.91.IX.7, p. 100. Mr. Rauner is the Director of the Office of Economic Adjustment of the Department of Defense.

49. See Lall and Marlin, op. cit., pp. 30–31.

50. *The New York Times*, 5 August 1991.
51. ibid.
52. *The Economist*, 25 January 1992.
53. Stephen J. Ledogar, "Issues relating to the destruction of weapons, including environmental impact." In *Disarmament Topical Papers 8: Challenges to Multilateral Disarmament in the Post-Cold-War and Post-Gulf-War Period*. United Nations publication, Sales No. E.91.IX.18, pp. 276–277.
54. *SIPRI Yearbook 1991*, op. cit., p. 94.
55. Hendtik Wagenmakers. "Future of monitoring and verification." In *Disarmament Topical Papers 8*, op. cit., p. 222.
56. Figures given in *The New York Times*, 30 January 1992. Different figures are given in the International Institute for Strategic Studies, *The Military Balance 1991–1992*, op. cit., pp. 219–220. However, whereas the treaty limited each side to 6,000 START-countable warheads, this limit could be breached legally because "the counting rules set artificial figures for warheads attributed to each delivery weapon which can in some cases be exceeded" (p. 216).
57. Ledogar, op. cit., p. 286.
58. Alan Shaw, "Problems arising from putting disarmament measures into effect." In ibid., p. 266.
59. Ledogar, op. cit., p. 282.
60. Article VIII of the Treaty on Conventional Armed Forces in Europe mandates how reduction in armaments is achieved, in ways that do not permit export: in the case of artillery, for instance, by "destruction or placement on static display, or, in the case of self-propelled artillery, by use as ground targets" (*SIPRI Yearbook 1991*, op. cit., p. 468).
61. Keith Hayward and Trevor Taylor, "Military hardware." *Disarmament Topical Papers 5: Conversion: Economic Adjustments in an Era of Arms Reduction (Volume II)*. United Nations publication, Sales No. E.91.IX.7, p. 263.
62. When extended to 1997, this would imply a level of defence expenditures of about $225 billion, similar to the lowest figure among the options proposed recently by the Secretary of Defense designate (see n. 16 above).
63. A recent document that caused considerable debate was the Pentagon's 18 February 1992 draft of the Defense Planning Guidance for the fiscal years 1994–1999. Although this document was classified, excerpts of it have appeared in the United States press. (*The New York Times*, 8 March 1992).
64. Sir Brian Urquhart reported in *The New York Review of Books*, 9 April 1992, p. 42. The media and some legislators in the United States have taken up the suggestion that peace-keeping be funded from the defence budget.

# Comments on chapter 9

**Akira Onishi**

In order to realize the peaceful perspective for which humankind is thirsting, we need to achieve economic growth that does not depend on military expansion. And to achieve sustainable economic development compatible with the changing global environment while reducing North-South economic differences, we need to carry forward global arms reduction through international cooperation with an enhanced role for United Nations organizations. This may indeed be seen as nothing less than a prerequisite for the global human society as we approach the twenty-first century.

Based on comparative simulation analyses using the Project LINK world economic model, Simon Cunningham and Kenneth Ruffing demonstrated quantitatively either positive or negative impacts which arms reduction of the major developed market economies would bring about, not only on their own economies, but on the rest of the global economy. It is worth noting that global arms reduction seems likely to give a positive impetus in the long-term perspective to the developed market economies, developing economies, and planned market economies in transition, according to scenario C where an increased ODA originating from arms reduction is incorporated. However, in scenario E where increased exports of developing countries to the developed market economies are incorporated, it is also shown that the developed market economies might be suffering from negative shocks. In order to offset a part of the negative impact derived from global arms reduction, we need some additional policy scenario such as an increased civilian R&D for exporting high technology products from the developed market economies to the developing economies. Then we can reasonably expect the positive impacts of arms reduction on the developed market economies and the global economy as well as in terms of real GDP and trade expansion. To advance the building of a peaceful world economic perspective as we approach the next century, I would like to advocate their policy stances and simulation results.

In order to confirm simulation results made by the Project LINK model, I have used the FUGI global modal to analyse the same sorts of impacts on the world economy that would arise in the event that a freeze of all countries' military budgets was carried out on a global basis starting from 1992.

In the scenario for global arms reduction which I would like to discuss here, it is first of all hypothesized that military expenditures are restricted, starting from 1992, not only in the United States and former USSR but throughout the world. More specifically, in this scenario military expenditures are frozen at 1991 levels, with no further increments in budgeted military expenditures allowed during the period 1991–2000.

Secondly, in the developed market economies, one-half the amount of financial resources in annual budget increases that would otherwise have been allotted to military expenditures under the baseline conditions is directed to domestic expenditures with non-military objectives such as public investment, R&D for future technology to reconcile economic development with global environment, energy savings, and anti-pollution investment, etc., while the remaining one-half goes into official development assistance to developing countries.

Thirdly, this global arms reduction scenario proposes that in the case of developing economies and the planned market economies in transition, the total amount of financial resources that would otherwise go into military increases be directed to domestic capital formation for building infrastructures for export-oriented growth and environment protection, etc. From the above, it is seen that for the developing economies there is much wisdom in the aim of slowing down or stopping the purchase of weapons and redirecting funds to investment in domestic non-military plant and equipment.

The most important consideration, however, is that in the global military freeze scenario we could expect large-scale increases in official development assistance from the developed to the developing countries, and planned market economies in transition. As a result, the economic growth rates of the aid-receiving countries would tend to accelerate. More precisely, averaged over the period 1991–1995, the real growth rates in the developing economies would be 0.53 percentage points above the baseline and 1.04 percentage points greater when averaged over the period 1991–2000, giving a real GDP in 2000 that is much greater than in the baseline scenario.

Looking at the comparative simulation results for economic growth, the baseline 4.4 per cent estimate for average annual real growth in the developing economies during the period 1991–2000 rises to 5.4 per cent in the global disarmament scenario. It is thus seen that in this military freeze scenario the degree of acceleration in the economic growth rates of the developing countries may be expected to become greater the longer the length of time over which the limitations on military expenditures have been in effect.

Under such circumstances, we may expect that the United States will greatly lessen its trade and current balance of payments' deficit as a result of the world trade expansion during the period 1993–2000. When we consider that examples of what are called "economic conflicts" between Japan and the United States are principally caused by the fact that at present Japan's trade *vis-à-vis* the United States shows a very large surplus, limitations on military expenditures may be expected to ameliorate these economic conflicts.

The current situation is one in which relatively larger US military expenditures (about 5.3 per cent of its GDP) are eating up funds that could otherwise be channelled into public and private non-military investment. In Japan, on the other hand, the burden of military expenditures is relatively small (about 1 per cent of its GDP), while expenditures on non-military research and development are growing, thus pushing up productivity in the manufacturing industries in a way that is creating significant imbalances with respect to the United States. This gives rise to a situation in which Japan tends to manufacture moderately priced and high-quality consumer products while in many cases similar US manufactures are at a disadvantage with respect to price and/or quality, as a result of which economic conflicts between Japan and the United States may possibly increase.

By the same token, if we were able to expect that the United States would make greater efforts in practical, non-military research and development with the financial and human resources made available through holding down military expenditures, with the result that the United States can produce higher-quality goods with accompanying improvements in productivity, we could certainly see such a situation as working in a positive way to diminish conflicts between the United States and Japan.

All things considered, however, the point that should continue to be given uppermost consideration in our "military freeze" scenario is

Table 1 **Arms reductions scenario simulations using the Fugi model: Annual growth rates of real GDP for the period 1991–2000 (%)**

| | Baseline 1991–2000 | Deviations from the baseline arms-reduction scenarios | | |
| --- | --- | --- | --- | --- |
| | | 1991–1995 | 1996–2000 | 1991–2000 |
| World | 2.6 | 0.075 | 1.231 | 0.651 |
| Developed market economies | 2.3 | −0.135 | 0.677 | 0.269 |
| OECD | 2.3 | −0.137 | 0.687 | 0.274 |
| The Major Seven | 2.3 | −0.176 | 0.775 | 0.298 |
| Japan | 3.7 | 0.369 | 1.529 | 0.948 |
| USA | 2.1 | −0.597 | 0.684 | 0.041 |
| EC | 2.3 | 0.140 | 0.367 | 0.254 |
| Developing market econo- mies | 4.4 | 0.532 | 1.552 | 1.041 |
| Asia Pacific | 6.7 | 0.613 | 1.662 | 1.137 |
| East Asia | 8.0 | 0.149 | 1.327 | 0.739 |
| China | 8.7 | −0.019 | 2.322 | 1.149 |
| ASEAN | 6.0 | 0.780 | 2.065 | 1.423 |
| Other Asia and Pacific | 4.9 | 0.770 | 1.561 | 1.165 |
| Middle East | 2.7 | 0.264 | 1.360 | 0.811 |
| Africa | 1.9 | 0.153 | 0.453 | 0.303 |
| Latin America and Caribbean | 2.3 | 0.685 | 1.851 | 1.265 |
| Planned market economies in transition | | | | |
| Former USSR and East Europe | −2.1 | 0.668 | 2.820 | 1.739 |
| Former USSR | −2.5 | 0.642 | 2.216 | 1.426 |

Source: Projections and simulations using the Fugi global model.

the effect of such a military freeze on "North-South issues." A major objective of the United Nations International Development Strategy for the decade 1991–2000 is to reduce the gap in "North-South" per capita incomes. Although this objective has been invested with great expectations, the present prospect seems to lack signs that the gap is being narrowed overall.

If one is to accord credibility to the simulations made using the global models, there should be ways to prepare for governmental policy changes that can achieve a positive breakthrough toward overcoming the economic and military dilemmas which we currently face. In other words, by starting now to prepare global plans for a lessening of military expenditures, the possibility arises for improving the welfare of human beings everywhere, through a process of elevating each country's true national strengths, not in terms of "military powers" but in terms of each country' s constructive, non-military economic strengths. Based on such strengthened economic powers derived from global arms reduction, we will be able to cope with complex global issues brought about by the destruction of the environment, failures in economic development, lack of peace and security, as well as violation of human rights, and advance the building of a peaceful world as we approach the twenty-first century.

Part 4
Political economy of sustainable
reductions in military spending

# 10

# A new international order and its implications for arms reductions

Robert S. McNamara

## Introduction

This paper will put forward the proposition that if the nations of the world – developed and developing alike – take advantage of the end of the Cold War to move toward a system of collective security, a system in which the Security Council and other multinational organizations play major roles, the risk of war will be substantially reduced and, as a consequence, military expenditures can be cut dramatically.

Although there has been clear evidence for several years that the Cold War was ending, nations across the globe have been slow to revise their foreign and defence policies, and slow to strengthen regional and international security organizations to reflect that fact.

In the United States, for example, in 1991 defence expenditures totalled $300 billion. In constant dollars that was 40 per cent more than a decade ago, and only 7 per cent less than at the height of the Viet Nam War. Moreover, the President's five-year defence programme, presented to Congress in January 1992, projects that expenditures will decline only very gradually from the 1991 levels. Defence outlays in 1997, in constant dollars, are estimated to be approximately 15 per cent higher than some 21 years earlier, under

President Nixon, in the midst of the Cold War. Such a defence programme is not consistent with my view of the post-Cold War world.

Before nations can respond in an optimum manner to the end of the Cold War, they need a vision of a world which would not be dominated by East-West rivalry, a rivalry which for more than 40 years has shaped foreign and defence programmes across the globe.

## Post-Cold War world: A world of conflict

As the Iraqi invasion and the Yugoslavian civil war demonstrate, the world of the future will not be a world without conflict, conflict between disparate groups within nations, and conflict extending across national borders. Racial and ethnic differences will remain. Political revolutions will erupt as societies advance. Historical disputes over political boundaries will continue. Economic differentials among nations, as the technological revolution of the twenty-first century spreads unevenly across the globe, will increase.

In the past 45 years, 125 wars, leading to 40 million deaths, have taken place in the third world. Third world military expenditures now approximate $200 billion per year. They quintupled in constant dollars between 1960 and the mid-1980s, and are approximately 5 per cent of GDP, only slightly less than the total amount the developing countries spend on health and education.

It is often suggested that the third world was turned into an ideological battleground by the Cold War and the rivalries of the great powers. That rivalry was a contributing factor, but the underlying causes for third world conflict existed before the origin of the Cold War and will almost certainly continue even though it has ended.

In those respects, therefore, the world of the future will not be different from the world of the past – conflicts within and between nations will not disappear.

But it is also clear that in the twenty-first century relations among nations will differ dramatically from those of the post-war decades. In the post-war years the United States had the power – and to a considerable degree it exercised that power – to shape the world as it chose. In the next century, that will not be possible. While remaining the world's strongest nation, the United States will live in a multipolar world and its foreign policy and defence programmes must be adjusted to that reality.

Japan is destined to play a larger and larger role on the world scene, exercising greater political power and, hopefully, assuming greater political and economic responsibility. The same can be said of Western Europe, which will have taken a giant step toward economic integration by the end of this year. From that is bound to follow greater political unity – despite the opposition to the Maastricht Treaty – which will strengthen Europe's power in world politics.

And by the middle of the next century several of the countries, of what we now think of as the third world – in particular, China – will have so increased in size and economic power as to be major participants in decisions affecting relations among nations. India is likely to have a population of 1.6 billion, Nigeria 400 million, and Brazil 300 million. If China achieves its economic goals for the year 2000, and if it then moves forward during the next 50 years at satisfactory but not spectacular growth rates, the income per capita of its approximately 1.6 billion people in 2050 may be roughly equal to that of the British in 1965. China's total GNP would approximate that of the United States, Western Europe, or Japan, and very likely would substantially exceed that of Russia. These figures, are, of course, highly speculative. I point to them simply to emphasize the magnitude of the changes which lie ahead and the need to begin now to adjust our goals, our policies, and our institutions to take account of them.

In such a multipolar world there is, clearly, need for developing new relationships both among the great powers and between the great powers and third world nations.

## Vision of a new world order

I believe that, at a minimum, the new order should accomplish five objectives. It should:
1. Provide to all states guarantees against external aggression.
2. Codify, and provide means of protecting, the rights of minorities within states.
3. Establish a mechanism for resolution of regional conflicts without unilateral action by the great powers.
4. Commit the great powers to termination of military support of conflicts between third world nations and conflicts between opposition political parties within those nations.
5. Increase the flow of both technical and financial assistance to the developing countries to help them accelerate their rates of social and economic advance.

In sum, we should strive to move toward a world in which relations among nations would be based on the rule of law, a world in which national security would be supported by a system of collective security, with conflict resolution and peace-keeping functions performed by multilateral institutions – a reorganized and strengthened United Nations and new and expanded regional organizations.

That is my vision of the post-Cold War world.

## An alternative vision of the post-Cold War world

In contrast to my vision, many political theorists predict a return to the power politics of the nineteenth century. They claim that as ideological competition between East and West is reduced, there will be a reversion to more traditional relationships. They say that major powers will be guided by basic territorial and economic imperatives: that the United States, Russia, China, India, Japan, and Western Europe will seek to assert themselves in their own regions while competing for dominance in other areas of the world where conditions are fluid.

This view has been expressed, for example, by Michael J. Sandel, a political theorist at Harvard, who said: "The end of the Cold War does not mean an end of global competition between the Superpowers. Once the ideological dimension fades, what you are left with is not peace and harmony, but old-fashioned global politics based on dominant powers competing for influence and pursuing their internal interests."[1]

Professor Sandel's conception of relations among nations in the post-Cold War world is historically well founded, but I would argue it is not consistent with the increasingly interdependent world – interdependent economically, environmentally, and in terms of security – into which we are now moving. In that interdependent world, I do not believe any nation will be able to stand alone. The UN Charter offers a far more appropriate framework for relations among nations in such a world than does the doctrine of power politics.

In contrast to Professor Sandel, Carl Kaysen, former director of the Institute of Advanced Studies at Princeton, wrote in *International Security* that:

The international system that relies on the national use of military force as the ultimate guarantor of security, and the threat of its use as the basis of order, is not the only possible one. To seek a different system ... is no longer the pursuit of an illusion, but a necessary effort toward a necessary goal.[2]

This is exactly what I propose we undertake.

## A system of collective security

To repeat, such a new world order would require:
– Renunciation by the great powers of the use of force in disputes among themselves.
– Renunciation by the great powers of unilateral action in dealing with regional conflicts.
– Agreement by the Security Council that regional conflicts endangering territorial integrity will be dealt with through the application of economic sanctions and, if necessary, military action, imposed by collective decisions and utilizing multinational forces.
Such a world will need leaders.

The leadership role may shift among nations depending on the issue at hand. Often it will be fulfilled by the United States. However, in such a system of collective security, whenever the United States plays a leadership role it must accept collective decision-making. Correspondingly, other nations – including Japan, for example – should accept a sharing of the risks and the costs: the political risks, the financial costs, and the risk of casualties and bloodshed.

Had the United States, and the other major powers made clear their conception of, and support for, such a system of collective security, and had they stated they would not only pursue their own political interests through diplomacy without the use of military force, but would seek to protect third world nations against attack by other nations, the Iraqi action might well have been deterred.

## Arms reductions: Nuclear forces

While steps are being taken to establish a world-wide system of collective security, the arms control negotiations which have been underway should be expanded rapidly in scope and accelerated in time.

Particular attention should be given to establishing long-term goals for nuclear forces. There are today approximately 40,000 nuclear warheads in the world, with a destructive power over one million times that of the Hiroshima bomb. Even assuming that the reductions called for by the SALT and START treaties and the "Joint Understanding" signed by Bush and Yeltsin are implemented, the stock of nuclear warheads of the existing nuclear powers is not likely to be reduced below 10,000 by the year 2003. The danger of nuclear war – the risk of destruction of societies across the globe – will have been lowered but not eliminated. Can we go further? Surely the answer must be yes.

More and more political and military leaders are accepting that basic changes in the world's approach to nuclear weapons are required. Some are going so far as to state that the long-term objective should be to return, in so far as is practical, to a non-nuclear world.

That is a very controversial proposition. Leading Western security experts – both military and civilian – continue to believe that the threat of the use of nuclear weapons prevents war. Zbigniew Brzezinski, President Carter's National Security Advisor, has said with reference to a proposal for eliminating nuclear weapons: "It is a plan for making the world safe for conventional warfare. I am therefore not enthusiastic about it." A recent report of an Advisory Committee, appointed by the US Secretary of Defense, Richard Cheney, makes essentially the same point. However, even if one accepts their argument, it must be recognized that their deterrent to conventional force aggression carries a very high long-term cost: the risk of a nuclear exchange.

Gerard Smith, President Nixon's arms negotiator, has pointed out that recently disclosed, formerly highly classified, documents of the Eisenhower Administration indicate that Secretary of State John Foster Dulles had recognized this problem nearly 50 years ago. In 1954, writing in a top secret assessment of internal strategy, Dulles said, "The increased destructiveness of nuclear weapons and the approach of effective atomic parity are creating a situation in which general war would threaten the destruction of Western civilization and of the Soviet regime and in which national objectives could not be obtained through a general war even if a military victory were won." Dulles went so far as to state "Atomic power was too vast a power to be left for the military use of any one country." Its use, he thought, should be "internationalized for security purposes." He proposed, therefore, to "universalize the capacity of atomic thermo-nuclear weapons to deter aggression" by transferring control of nuclear forces to a veto-less United Nations Security Council.[3]

Should we not begin immediately to debate the merits of alternative long-term objectives for nuclear forces of existing nuclear powers, choosing for example, from among:

- A continuation of the present strategy of "extended deterrence" –
  as recommended in the Advisory Committee's report which I referred to above – but with each side limited to approximately 3,500
  warheads, or
- a minimum deterrent force – as recommended a few months ago by
  a committee of the U.S. National Academy of Sciences – with each
  major nuclear power retaining 1,000 to 2,000 warheads, or
- as I myself would prefer, a return, in so far as practicable, to a non-
  nuclear world.

## Controlling proliferation of weapons of mass destruction

And should not the world debate as well how best to deal with the
proliferation of weapons of mass destruction and with the export of
arms to the third world?

Over the last three decades, efforts have been made to limit the
spread of nuclear, biological, and chemical weapons. The Treaty on
the Non-Proliferation of Nuclear Weapons of 1968 and the Biological
Weapons Convention of 1972 have done much to slow the spread of
these categories of weapons. Yet, in 1991, at least three countries, in
addition to the five declared nuclear powers, are believed to possess
nuclear weapons, and three are said to have a biological weapons
capability. Other nations are carrying out research that could place
them in these categories.

Although substantial efforts have gone into negotiating a chemical
weapons treaty since 1968, and an agreement has been transmitted to
the United Nations which will consider the pact later this year, several countries, including China, Indonesia, Pakistan, and Russia have
indicated they have not decided whether they will sign it. Moreover,
for years, informal international guidelines on the transfer of chemical precursors have been poorly implemented and enforced. Fifteen
countries are now believed either to possess or to be in the process of
acquiring chemical weapons. As many as 11 other countries may also
possess or be on the way to possessing a chemical weapons capability.
Global stocks are huge and it is not clear when, or with what assurance, they will be destroyed. And developing a monitoring system
to give high confidence that civilian chemical production facilities
are not being diverted, secretly, to production of weapons will be
extremely difficult.

Of equally great concern, some 25 countries have longer-range
ballistic missiles in their inventories, capable of delivering weapons of

mass destruction on the territory of their adversaries. About three-quarters of these countries have or are in the process of acquiring production capability. The Missile Technology Control Regime is limited in scope and in membership. Only the transfer of production facilities is explicitly banned, and several important suppliers, notably Russia and China, are not members. It has been reported recently that China is expanding its sales of ballistic missiles to third world countries.

Twenty countries possess or have the capability of producing at least two of these categories of weapons: the five permanent members of the United Nations Security Council plus Israel, North Korea, South Africa, Iraq, Syria, India, Pakistan, Egypt, Taiwan, Iran, Libya, South Korea, Argentina, Brazil, and Cuba. Most of these have or are believed to be developing a capability in three or four of the categories.

It is clear, therefore, that the international community needs to redouble its efforts to limit the spread and prevent the use of nuclear, chemical, and biological weapons and ballistic missiles. Inspection and export-control regimes already in place should be strengthened. The treaty banning chemical weapons should be ratified and restrictions on the production, possession, and use of ballistic missiles and related systems must be negotiated.

Returning to a non-nuclear world, in so far as it may be achievable, would greatly strengthen the hand of those who seek to control or even eliminate chemical, biological, and ballistic missile arsenals throughout the world. One of the main complaints of the non-nuclear developing countries has been that the non-proliferation treaty is a discriminatory agreement that prevents such countries from acquiring nuclear weapons without requiring those already possessing them to dismantle their arsenals. From this point of view, the Biological Weapons Convention and the Chemical Weapons Treaty, which do not distinguish between "haves" and "have nots," are preferable models.

In order to truly stop the proliferation of weapons of mass destruction and the means of delivering them, I see no alternative to some form of collective, coercive action by the Security Council. To begin with, the Council should agree to prohibit the development, production, or purchase of nuclear, chemical, and biological weapons and ballistic missiles by nations not now possessing them. Countries in violation of relevant Security Council resolutions would be subject to strict economic sanctions on the part of the international community. If sanctions failed to alter the behaviour of the government in question, a United Nations military force would be given a mandate to eliminate the production capability and any stocks that had been produced or otherwise acquired. Countries now in possession of such weapons of mass destruction would be subject, as well, to international inspection and control and would be asked to approve a treaty prohibiting "First Use."

## The potential for reductions in military expenditures

As we move toward a system providing for collective action against military aggression wherever it may occur, military budgets throughout the world – in both developed and developing countries – can be reduced substantially. They now total nearly $1 trillion (US dollars) per year. I believe that during this decade the amount could be cut in half. The huge savings of $500 billion per year could be used to address the pressing human and physical infrastructure needs across the globe.

In the case of the United States, it should be possible, within six to eight years, to cut military expenditures from the 1989 level of 6 per cent of GNP to below 3 per cent. And military expenditures of the third world, which, as I have said now total some $200 billion per year, over 4 per cent of GNP, should be reduced, by the end of the century, to 2 per cent.

## Arms transfers to the third world

Between 1978 and 1988, the third world imported $371 billion of arms (nearly $450 billion at 1988 prices), or more than three-quarters of the arms traded internationally. While these figures reflect the relative lack of domestic production capability in the third world and a legitimate concern to protect national sovereignty, there clearly is great scope for reducing third world military expenditures by reducing arms imports.

Two major factors have driven the arms trade: supply and demand. Both must be addressed. The United States and the former Soviet Union tended to use arms transfers as a means of maintaining political support in strategically located third world nations. For many of the Western Europeans, and some of the emerging third world suppliers (in particular China and Brazil), economic considerations have been paramount. Over the last decade or so, economic considerations have become increasingly important for the former Soviet Union.

But the demand for weapons is strong, too, and many third world governments have actively sought to purchase arms. One of the most important demand factors is involvement in an ongoing conflict – internal or external. Of the top 15 third world arms importers, who together account for about three-quarters of the arms imported by the third world, 13 have been party to conflicts of many years' duration. Iran and Iraq were at war from 1980 to 1988. Egypt, Syria, and Israel have all been involved in the Middle East conflict. Saudi Arabia has believed itself threatened by other regional powers, notably Iran and Iraq. Algeria has been involved in disputes with neighbouring Morocco and Libya. Ethiopia, Afghanistan, and Angola have conducted civil wars while Viet Nam, Libya, Pakistan, and India are parties to long-standing regional disputes.

An extremely important factor affecting how many weapons a government will import is the availability of financing. Seven of the top 15 third world importers have had access to petrodollars (Iraq, Egypt, Saudi Arabia, Syria, Libya, Iran, and Algeria). The availability of security assistance – in the form of outright grants of subsidized credits – from both the United States and the former Soviet Union was instrumental in allowing a number of third world governments to build up sizeable arsenals. Over the last decade, five of the top 15 third world arms importers have received many of their arms free of charge from their superpower patron or at highly subsidized rates (India, Cuba, Israel, Viet Nam, and Egypt).

The United States is the only country for which reliable, detailed security assistance figures are available. The three main components of US security assistance are the Military Assistance Program (MAP), which provides grant aid; Economic Support Fund (ESF), which provides balance of payments support and finances commodity import programmes, increasingly on a grant basis; and the Foreign Military Sales (FMS) programme, which enables countries to purchase military hardware and services on credit.

In fiscal 1989, seven countries received 80 per cent of the $468 million MAP funds appropriated (El Salvador, Honduras, the Philippines, Thailand, Turkey, Greece, and Kenya). Nine shared in the $4.3 billion appropriated under FMS (Israel, Egypt, Pakistan, Greece, Turkey, Portugal, Morocco, Jordan, and Tunisia). Two of these, Israel and Egypt, received nearly 75 per cent of the FMS credits, and all of these credits were forgiven, that is, converted into grants. Nearly 80 per cent of the $3.6 billion appropriated for fiscal year 1989 under ESF went to five countries (Israel, Egypt, Pakistan, El Salvador, and the Philippines). Israel and Egypt alone received nearly 60 per cent of the ESF appropriation. In fact, Israel and Egypt received nearly two-thirds of the $8.4 billion in FMS, ESF, and MAP funds allocated in fiscal year 1989.

While very little is known about the scale and terms of the former Soviet security assistance, it is clear that the new republics will not be able to support any kind of massive aid beyond their borders. Military assistance to Cuba has already been cut and India, for example, will probably be required to pay in hard currency for whatever weapons and arms-production technology it imports from Russia.

Another source of military assistance for at least some third world countries has been oil-surplus countries of the Middle East. Saudi Arabia, Algeria, Kuwait, and the United Arab Emirates have provided varying amounts of grants and credits, primarily to other Muslim countries such as Pakistan, Sudan, Iraq, Syria, and Egypt.

Not all of the weapons procured by developing countries must be imported. While upwards of 54 third world countries have some domestic arms production capacity, nine countries (excluding China) produce nearly all of the major weapons manufactured in the third world. The investments needed to create this capacity have been significant, particularly in terms of foreign exchange.

There is an additional factor, important but hard to assess, in the financing of military outlays: fungibility. Common sense – and some evidence – suggests that the availability of general-purpose external balance of payments or budget financing enables governments to spend more on the military, if they are so minded, than would otherwise be possible. In my view, it is bad economics and bad policy for the donor nations and the international financial institutions to continue to behave as if the funding of stabilization adjustment and development programmes can be separated from the financing of military expenditures.

The combination of wars and arms procurement (both domestic and from abroad) has caused a number of third world countries to bear a very high military expenditure burden. To the extent that security assistance takes the form of loans, involves barter trade, or causes additional security-related outlays, it adds to that burden. The two regions with the highest levels of military expenditures over the last decade are the Middle East and East Asia. It is in these two regions that many of the unresolved conflicts of the post-war period have been located and that many of the major third world arms importers and arms producers are found. At the same time, it is important to recall that relatively low regional shares can hide rather large individual outlays in the security sector. Countries such as Libya, Mozambique, Ethiopia, Morocco, Zambia, Zimbabwe, Afghanistan, Pakistan, Argentina, and Nicaragua devote a significant proportion of both their GNP and their central government expenditures to the military. And all have been involved in major conflicts over the last decade or more; several are among the top 15 third world arms importers.

The introduction of the system of collective security, with its guarantee by the Security Council and by regional organizations of the territorial integrity of member states, would reduce the demand for arms in the third world. The international organizations should agree, as well, to actively assist countries in finding negotiated solutions to conflicts.

An important element in the global collective security system would be the strengthening of existing regional organizations such as the Organization of American States and the Organization of African Unity, as well as the creation of such groups in Asia and the Middle East. These bodies would, ideally, come to function as regional arms of the Security Council.

There is, of course, the danger that the shrinking military forces of East and West, and the effectiveness of high-tech weapons in the Gulf War, will cause industrialized-country arms producers and their governments to seek new markets in the third world – as the United States and Russia did recently with the sale of high-technology aircraft to Saudi Arabia, Taiwan, and China. Such actions point to the importance of negotiating agreements among arms-producing countries to limit exports.

As has been said, external security considerations play an important role in determining the level of expenditure on the arms forces for a number of third world countries. Yet some developing nations that have not engaged in conflict for many years and are under no obvious external threat still allocate considerable portions of their budgets and gross product to the security sector. Preserving a strong internal power posture is an important objective of many armed forces in the third world today. In fact, in some countries, it is the primary objective.

Where governments have armed themselves against their own

people in an attempt to maintain themselves in power and their members in positions of privilege, the general public often has limited access to the policy-making process and the formal economic system. Under these conditions, conflicts among élites as they vie for power and between the government and groups suffering discrimination or repression are inevitable. International and regional conflict resolution must therefore be matched by internal conflict resolution strategies.

## The social costs of third world military expenditures

Pakistan, with defence expenditures approximating 6.5 per cent of GNP, is an example of a country where military outlays severely penalize development.

Islamabad has been involved in a long-standing conflict with India, which has flared into war three times since the end of World War II. Negotiated settlements of the outstanding territorial disputes between India and Pakistan, coupled with a Security Council guarantee of territorial integrity, are essential if military expenditures – and the pressure for nuclear arms – are to be reduced.

At the same time, while an end to regional conflicts should enable both India and Pakistan to reduce their procurement of weapons and their overall level of military expenditure substantially, it must be recognized that the armed forces, particularly in Pakistan, have for many years played domestic roles. The political and social conditions that have given rise to military involvement in Pakistan's domestic affairs must be addressed for the benefits of increased regional stability to be felt fully. Both countries have significant unmet political and economic developmental needs, at least some of which could be overcome if additional funding were available.

In 1987, for example, only 52 per cent of Pakistani school-age children of both sexes were enrolled in primary education facilities, and only 19 per cent were receiving secondary school education. For girls, the figures were 35 and 11 per cent respectively. Even in the lower and lower-middle income Asian countries such as Sri Lanka, China, and the Philippines, primary school enrolment for children of both sexes in 1987 ranged between 95 and 100 per cent; total secondary school enrolment ranged between 43 and 68 per cent. Almost all school-age girls in these countries were enrolled in primary school and between 37 and 69 per cent in secondary school.

Health care statistics offer a similar picture. In countries such as

Chile, Argentina, Mexico, Costa Rica, and Panama, the population per nursing person ranged from 370 : 1 to 880 : 1 in the mid-1980s, and infant mortality in 1988 ranged from 20 to 46 per thousand live births. In contrast, there were some 4,900 Pakistanis per nursing person and infant mortality for Pakistan stood at 107.

While it is extremely difficult to draw hard and fast conclusions about the relationship between poverty and military expenditures from statistics such as these, it is clear that a country such as Costa Rica, which has only an 8,000-man Civil and Rural Guard force and devoted about 0.7 per cent of its GNP to military-related expenditures during the 1980s, has more resources at its disposal for social and economic programmes than countries that spend nearly an order of magnitude more on the military.

One of the most important effects of military expenditures, which has serious implications for political advance and for economic growth and development in the third world, is the degree to which it strengthens the political influence of the armed forces at the expense of civilian groups within society. In many parts of the third world, economic systems function primarily to benefit a relatively limited number of people, and political systems are frequently manipulated to guarantee continued élite dominance. If development that meets the needs of all social groups is to occur, however, there must be, among other things, a relatively equitable distribution of resources. This, in turn, relies on the existence of a political system that both allows all groups to articulate their demands and is capable of producing workable compromises between competing interests. The greater the political power of the security forces, the less likely it is that the requirements for democratic governance will be met.

## "Conditionality" in relation to military expenditures

The role of the military is, of course, the prerogative of each government. The international community none the less needs to identify ways in which it can reward those countries that reduce their security-related expenditures in favour of development. Therefore, I strongly urge the linking of financial assistance, both from OECD nations and from multilateral financial institutions, through conditionality, to movement toward "optimal levels" of military expenditures. The optimal levels should take account, of course, of the external threat. The conditionality could take the form of the proposal contained in *Facing One World*, the report of the "Independent Group on

Financial Flows to Developing Countries," chaired by former German Chancellor Helmut Schmidt. The Group, which included ex-Presidents or ex-Prime Ministers of Nigeria, Peru, Canada, and Korea, urged that, when decisions concerning allocations of foreign aid are made, special consideration be given to countries spending less than 2 per cent of their GNP in the security sector. I am conscious that application of such conditionality will be difficult and contentious. Nevertheless, it is, I believe, an essential part of the solution to the waste represented by excessive military spending in poor countries.

## Conclusion

In sum, with the end of the Cold War, I do believe we can create a New International Order.

If together we are bold – if East and West and North and South dare break out of the mind sets that have guided our actions for the past four decades – we can reshape international institutions, as well as relations among nations, and we can reduce the military expenditures, which have been a derivative of such relations – in ways that will lead to a far more peaceful world and a far more prosperous world for all of the peoples of our interdependent globe.

It is the first time in my adult life we have had such an opportunity. Should we not seize it?

## Notes

1. *New York Times*, 31 December 1989.
2. Kaysen, Carl (1990). "Is War Obsolete?" *International Security* 14(4), p. 63.
3. In (1990). "John Foster Dulles and the Diplomacy of the Cold War." Princeton, Princeton University Press.

# 11

# Enhancing peace and development: Foreign aid and military expenditure in developing countries

Nicole Ball

### Bringing the military into the development dialogue

For the developing world, the "Cold War" was characterized by high levels of conflict (resulting in some 40 million deaths), arms proliferation, and the diversion of valuable human and financial resources from development to the military sector. Even in countries with no obvious internal or external security threats, high military budgets resulting from the military's central role in the political system drained available financing from the productive sectors. As a result, at the end of the 1980s, military spending in nearly a fifth of the developing countries exceeded combined expenditures on health and education – sometimes by a wide margin.[1] Many years of insufficient financing had caused civil-sector infrastructure, such as transportation and communications networks, to deteriorate severely, further crippling weak economies.

There are now growing concerns that the demand for capital may soon exceed supply. Many of the OECD countries have important unmet domestic needs of their own, and the recession of the early 1990s is causing some of them to reduce aid budgets. The transition to market economies in Eastern Europe and the successor states to the Soviet Union is generating enormous demands on capital. Following the "lost decade of development opportunities" during which social welfare, productive capacity, and infrastructure declined in large parts of the developing world, the requirements for investment in the third world are also substantial.[2] This confluence of events makes it vital that all available capital resources be used as efficiently as possible.

There is thus a clear and urgent need to bring military issues into the development dialogue. The serious imbalances that exist between military spending and development financing in many countries underscore the fact that military budgets can no longer be immune from review as they have been so often in the past.

During the Cold War era, the international official lending community virtually ignored the possibility that non-military external funding might be diverted to the military sector.[3] Lenders now privately admit that financing provided for non-military purposes, particularly balance-of-payments funding and budget support, enables governments to spend more on the military if they are so inclined.[4] As a result, many lenders have begun to question all aspects of resource allocation in borrower countries. They are stressing the economic benefits that could flow from transferring resources from unproductive uses – including military expenditures – to more productive undertakings.

The arms-reduction process currently under way in the industrial countries has given greater authority to these calls for military reform in the developing world. The European Community, for example, has taken the position that:

... in a period in which donor countries are engaged in a process leading to levels of armament not exceeding sufficiency levels, development co-operation with governments which maintain much larger military structures than needed will become difficult to justify.[5]

Several bilateral lenders have enunciated policies linking their disbursements of aid to changes in the military sphere of recipient countries. The World Bank and the International Monetary Fund have begun to collect information on resources allocated to the security sector. The World Bank and the bilateral lenders are also supporting moves toward demilitarization on the part of member states, for example, by helping to reintegrate demobilized soldiers into civilian life. The growing willingness of the bilateral aid agencies and the multilateral development institutions to confront these issues is an important first step in enlarging the development debate to confront this once-taboo subject.

This paper begins by briefly reviewing the twin goals of military reform proposed for the developing world – enhanced security and enhanced development. It then describes several categories of potential reformers in the developing world and considers the different kinds of economic leverage available to lenders. Drawing on the experience of the international lending community over the last two or three years, a number of external strategies for promoting military reform are outlined. The paper concludes by proposing a series of actions that lenders can take to help developing countries implement a reform process.[6]

## Enhancing security and development

Development and security are closely intertwined. Stable political environments are a necessary component of sustained development. Successful development, the fruits of which are reasonably equitably shared, can be a source of domestic land regional stability. High levels of military spending, the inability to resolve conflicts peacefully, and the use of security forces to prevent the emergence of representative domestic political systems can reduce opportunities for development and further erode security.

Most of the military reform objectives that have been discussed by the international community reflect the twin objectives of enhancing both security and development. They include: smaller, less costly military forces; the elimination of wasteful expenditure; the promotion of transparency and accountability in the military budgeting process; reductions in defence-industrial sectors; conventional arms transfer control; commitment to non-proliferation, non-intervention, and non-aggression; depoliticization of the armed forces; conflict resolution; and the creation of collective security mechanisms.

Both regional security and development could be enhanced, for example, if governments were assisted in strengthening their capacity to manage public expenditure in the military sector at the same time as multilateral mechanisms were established to provide a forum for discussing security issues of concern to regional parties. In a situation characterized by trust, greater transparency and accountability in the military budget process enhances security. Transparency and accountability in the military budgeting process is also vital for efficient resource management, a cornerstone of successful economic development. To the extent that they strengthen civilian control over the military, transparency and accountability in the military sector can support political development, reduce the likelihood of internal conflict, and create a stable environment in which development can take place.

## The reformers

Clearly, an important consideration in devising strategies for linking external financing to changes in the military sector is the attitude of the borrowers. Only on rare occasions can governments be compelled to modify policies – on any issue – if they are seriously opposed to reform. What is more, forcing a reluctant government to adopt a new policy can be counter-productive if the reform does not produce positive results within a reasonable period of time. Such a government may open itself to serious domestic criticism for having adopted a politically unpopular course of action without obtaining any benefits.

There is a wide spectrum of opinion on the need for military reform among developing countries, ranging from governments already undertaking reform to those with no interest in it at all. Countries that are opposed to military reform include those with authoritarian governments led by the armed forces or governments dependent on the military for essential support, such as the one installed in Haiti following the *coup d'état* against President Jean-Bertrand Aristide in September 1991.

At the other end of the spectrum are governments seeking assistance for reforms they have already decided to implement. Some countries – for example Angola, Cambodia, El Salvador, and Uganda – have recently settled disputes and need external financial support for demobilization of troops and economic reconstruction. Also in this category are newly democratizing countries such as Argentina and Chile, whose civilian governments may request external support, both financial and political, to restrict the power of the armed forces and their call on national resources.

Between these extremes lie countries whose governments are divided on the desirability of reform, either in general or with regard to specific reform strategies. The armed forces often play an important role in the political, and perhaps economic, life of these countries, and external support can be instrumental in helping civilians in

285

government confront pressure from military establishments. Barber Conable, Jr., former President of the World Bank, has commented that: "Weak or uncertain civilian governments may publicly protest, as invasion of their sovereignty, admonitions that arms expenditures be reduced. I speak from experience when I say that such pressure may be privately welcomed by the new democracies."[7]

Officials responsible for financial management and economic development are frequently among the first to welcome military reform designed to limit the armed forces' access to resources. Government leaders seeking to reduce the domestic political power of the armed forces or to improve a country's security situation by resolving outstanding conflicts may also encourage reform. Official aid institutions urging lower military expenditure on the government of Uganda – where the military has absorbed one-third or more of the national budget in recent years – received a sympathetic hearing in 1990/91 from some senior government officials. In June 1992, the Army Council announced a plan for deep cuts in the Ugandan military.[8]

Receptivity to reform proposals can be increased by demonstrating that there are gains as well as costs associated with the suggested changes. The armed forces may initially find it difficult to identify gains in the reform process. Their share of national resources may decline; the force may be reduced in size; weapons procurement may shrink; and certain categories of weapons may be prohibited entirely. The vast majority of the political and financial gains accrue elsewhere.

Some governments may therefore be willing to make concessions to the armed forces in exchange for agreement on the central elements in the reform package. A smaller, defence-oriented force, less capable of meddling in domestic politics or of entangling the country in foreign conflicts may, for example, be exchanged for the military's right to procure certain weapons or higher salaries for the officers and men who remain under arms. Such trade-offs are currently being discussed in Argentina, Chile, and Uganda.

The nature of a country's security environment is crucial in determining its willingness to restructure the armed forces and reduce the military budget. Some countries have militaries that are demonstrably larger than warranted by security needs, either because the military's role has been largely an internal, political one or because external or internal conflicts have been resolved – for example, Argentina, Chile, most West African states, Uganda, and the members of ASEAN. Other governments, however, must address a broad range of security issues before they can make significant changes in budgets, force levels, and armaments – notably the states in the Middle East, India and Pakistan, Myanmar, North and South Korea, Sudan, Somalia, and Sri Lanka.

The official lenders find it easiest to work with governments that have already decided to implement some kind of military reform, arguing that the decision on how much to spend on the military and how to allocate government resources most efficiently are properly the domain of national governments. It is much harder for them to force the issue on governments with little or no interest in military reform or, most important but most difficult of all, on countries where underlying security imbalances must be corrected before the armed forces and the military budget can be significantly reduced in size. In this latter group of countries, where the security environment is not conducive to large-scale reductions in military budgets, political pressure from the major powers, from regional governments, and from multilateral political institutions will be an important ingredient in the process of creating the conditions for military reform.

## Types of leverage

Once having decided to press for military reform, the international community has several economic tools at its disposal. The most commonly discussed options are development assistance and other official financing, trade, investment, and technology transfer.

### Aid and other official financing

To date, the debate on using economic tools to influence change in the military sector of developing countries has focused almost exclusively on aid and other types of official financial flows. This should come as no surprise, since that debate has thus far occurred primarily within the international lending community.

The dependence of individual countries on aid varies considerably. The countries that rely most heavily on concessional aid – official development assistance (ODA) – tend to be the poorest ones, with the least diversified economies. As a group, the sub-Saharan African countries are most aid-dependent. Official development assistance in 1989–1990 provided nearly 14 per cent of the GNP in Kenya, 42 per cent in Somalia, and possibly as much as 83 per cent of Mozambique's national wealth.[9]

287

While there are good reasons to believe that the military is absorbing too many resources in a number of the most aid-dependent countries, the same problem exists in other countries that receive very little or no ODA. There is a very real possibility that lenders may find themselves pressing for military reform in the economically weakest countries, while some of the major military powers in the developing world may escape control. The military in aid-dependent countries such as Mozambique and Uganda admittedly absorbs a sizeable portion of national resources. The same is true, however, in India, Pakistan, and Israel – where ODA accounts for less than 5 per cent of GNP – and in South Korea, Chile, and Saudi Arabia – which receive no aid at all. These non-aid-dependent countries, many of which have domestic arms industries and are capable of producing weapons of mass destruction, pose potentially greater threats to regional peace and stability than do the impoverished aid-dependent states.[10]

Concessional aid is of course not the only form that official financial flows from the industrial countries to the developing world can take. Some countries in which only a small portion of national product derives from ODA none the less require lender assistance to carry out specific projects of importance. These countries may also need IMF credits to stabilize their economies and IMF approval of their economic policies to open the door for non-concessional public and private lending.

Thus, there may be some leverage even in negotiations with countries such as India and Pakistan, which receive only modest ODA, and even countries such as Argentina and Chile, which receive none at all.[11] At the same time, it is clear that official financial flows cannot bear the entire burden of promoting military reform. Bilateral lenders need to consider ways of using other economic tools, such as trade, investment, and technology transfer, to influence government policies.

## Supplier groups

A number of defence technology supplier groups in the security sphere are designed to limit access to the know-how and material required to produce weapons of mass destruction and ballistic missiles. These are the London Club (nuclear), the Australia Group (chemical and biological warfare agents), and the Missile Technology Control Regime (longer-range ballistic missiles).[12]

That these groups have been less than totally effective is evident in the capabilities that countries such as Iraq and Pakistan have been able to acquire by purchasing restricted technology from their members. Indeed, the failure of industrial-country governments to police adequately their own corporations – which has resulted in the diffusion of highly sophisticated weapons technology – is one reason why these same governments are now so interested in military reform.

The experience of the Gulf War and the subsequent revelations of Iraq's capabilities in the nuclear and chemical spheres have prompted the supplier countries to strengthen these groups. At the suggestion of the United States, for example, the number of chemicals used to produce chemical warfare agents controlled by the Australia Group was increased in May 1991 to 50.[13]

Governments have also begun to enforce legislation and guidelines more stringently. For instance, in March 1992, the German government announced plans to open a new federal export office, to hire additional customs officials, and to make violations of German export regulations and of UN embargoes punishable by up to 15 years in prison. In October 1991, Japan Aviation Electronics Industry was banned from exporting for 18 months after having sold Iran missile guidance and aircraft navigation components in violation of Japan's Foreign Exchange and Foreign Trade Control Law.[14]

Enforcement is crucial if clandestine efforts to acquire these weapons are to be successfully combated. While the elimination of programmes to develop weapons of mass destruction may not by itself result in a significant decrease in a country's military budget, it should have a positive effect on inter-state relations and ultimately contribute to a regional security environment that is sufficiently stable to allow governments to engage in mutual spending reductions.

## Sanctions

Trade and investment sanctions are one of the most extreme forms of pressure and frequently are not successful in forcing governments to change policy.[15] But when governments are not at all dependent on external financing and routinely seek to circumvent restrictions imposed by supplier groups, the only way to influence their policy may be by restricting other forms of economic activity.

The US Congress has for several years been seeking to suspend China's most-favoured-nation (MFN) trading status unless, among other things, Beijing acceded to the Nuclear Non-Proliferation Treaty (which it has now done) and adhered to guidelines established under the Missile Technology Control Regime (MTCR). In February 1992, the US Senate joined the House of Representatives in agreeing to continue to extend MFN to China only if conditions relating to human rights, trade practices, and nuclear and missile proliferation are met. President George Bush vetoed this legislation, and Congress was unable to override the veto. In the fall of 1992, MFN opponents again brought the issue before Congress.[16]

The Bush Administration has not, however, entirely eschewed restricting trade to promote its non-proliferation objectives. As a result of significant pressure from the United States, including sanctions imposed on the sale of high-performance computers in June 1991, the Chinese government agreed to abide by the provisions of the MTCR and provided a somewhat vaguely worded statement to this effect in mid-February 1992. Although questions have been raised about the trustworthiness of China's government on this issue, US intelligence sources stated at the time that they had not observed any recent violations of the Non-Proliferation Treaty or the MTCR by China. Washington therefore agreed to lift the computer sale sanctions in February 1992, promising, however, that they would be reinstituted if further violations occurred.[17]

Following reports in late March 1992 that China was negotiating with Iran for the sale of guidance systems that could be used in ballistic missiles, the US Department of State essentially conceded that China had not yet ended all sales of missile technology prohibited under the MTCR. Testifying before the US Congress in early April, Assistant Secretary of State Richard Solomon characterized US policy toward China's missile sales as "a process of trying to turn the spigot off." Rather than immediately reinstitute sanctions, the US government planned to hold technical meetings with the Chinese to discuss what adherence to the MTCR implies.[18]

Sanctions are most effective when they are supported by all of a country's trade partners and are strictly adhered to by all parties. The more countries that must join in sanctions to make them work, and the longer they must remain in force to effect change, the harder it is to obtain strict adherence. The sanctions imposed on Iraq by the United Nations in August 1990 have never been airtight. Although they continue in force, they do not yet appear to have significantly influenced Saddam Hussein's policies. The various sanctions imposed on South Africa by the United Nations prohibiting the transfer of weapons and weapon production technology have also been only partially effective. Although the cost to South Africa of procuring weapons surely increased as a result of the 1963 and 1977 UN embargoes, South Africa has none the less been able to procure a substantial amount of weaponry from abroad as well as from domestic industry.[19] The UN sanctions on Libya designed to force Moammar Gaddhafi to extradite two Libyans implicated in the December 1988 bombing of Pan American's Flight 103 are viewed by most analysts as quite weak.

The strengthening of international and regional bodies such as the United Nations and the Organization of American States might lead to the increased use of economic sanctions, but it is unlikely that the world community will impose comprehensive economic sanctions with any degree of frequency. For one thing, the widespread moral outrage at Iraq's invasion of Kuwait and South Africa's repression of the majority of its population will probably be duplicated only rarely. For another, it is difficult to justify cutting off all or most economic contact with very poor countries. The OAS-imposed embargo on Haiti following the military overthrow of that country's elected president has been widely criticized in view of the hardships it has imposed on Haiti's poorest citizens.

Efforts specifically targeted to prevent countries from acquiring certain military capabilities might be more broadly acceptable than comprehensive economic sanctions against entire populations. Defence technology suppliers could penalize governments and firms acquiring material directly involved in the manufacture of nuclear, chemical, and biological weapons and ballistic missiles – for example, by cutting off access to highly desirable but non-essential goods (such as sophisticated computers), or by limiting but not halting trade (such as revoking MFN status).[20]

Although control regimes and sanctions can play an important role in limiting the number and kinds of weapons that countries procure and the types of policies their governments pursue, the current debate on influencing the allocation of resources between military security and development has focused primarily on official financial flows. The following two sections will therefore examine the ways in which lenders can use official financing to encourage military reform and suggest some next steps for the international community in this area.

## External strategies for reform

Efforts by the international lending community to promote reform in the military or any other sector can be divided into three broad categories: persuasion, support, and pressure. There are some important differences in the strategies that bilateral lenders can adopt and those open to the multilateral lenders such as the World Bank and the IMF.

The bilateral institutions are able to address overtly political issues. They are best suited to take the initiative in using economic tools to alter government policies in areas such as weapons procurement and conflict resolution. They may also have the capability (although not in their aid agencies) to evaluate the security needs of other governments. The Bank and the Fund have taken the position that military expenditure is an economic as well as a political–strategic issue. However, their mandate is to strengthen the economies of member governments, and the objective of enhancing security will be secondary, at the very best. Thus Japan can insist that North Korea dismantle the Yongbyon plutonium facility as one criterion for normalizing political and economic relations and threaten to cut aid to China if Beijing proceeds with plans to purchase an aircraft carrier from Ukraine.[21] The World Bank, however, is likely to rely more on persuasion, support for reform-minded governments, and pressure in economic and social sectors designed to squeeze the military budget.

The following is a survey of lender strategies that either have been applied or currently are under consideration. While they are described here as discrete entities, these strategies are in practice complementary. Circumstances in the borrower country will play an important role in determining which strategies are used and the combination and sequence in which they are applied.

## Persuasion

Persuasion has played a central role in recent efforts to bring military budgets and policies into the development dialogue. In 1989, IMF Managing Director Michel Camdessus and then World Bank President Barber Conable began speaking out about the conflict between military spending and development financing. This signalled the beginning of a campaign aimed at the institutions' employees as well as at recipients of Bank and Fund financing.

In addition to public statements by top management, a number of in-house seminars, meetings, and training sessions examining military expenditure issues have taken place. The April 1991 World Bank Annual Conference on Development Economics, for example, took military spending as one of its main topics and gave the issue a high profile by having former World Bank President Robert McNamara address the possibility of limiting military budgets in the developing world.

The Bank/Fund campaign has influenced bilateral donors. Policy makers in several donor countries have stated privately that these public statements on military reform by the international financial institutions legitimized the issue within their own governments. In turn, the growing acceptance on the part of bilateral donors of the view that official financing can be used to reduce competition between military spending and development has provided important support for Bank and Fund officials who find it difficult consistently or repeatedly to take positions that are significantly at variance with those of their major shareholders.

The public statements by the Bank/Fund leadership have served notice to the recipients of international financing that the rules of the game are changing. Henceforth, military spending will be viewed as an economic as well as a strategic/political issue. In September 1989, then World Bank President Barber Conable noted: "It is important to place military spending decisions on the same footing as other fiscal decisions, to examine possible trade-offs more systematically, and to explore ways to bring military spending into better balance with development priorities."[22]

At the 1991 joint Bank/Fund Annual Meetings, IMF Managing Director Michel Camdessus noted that:

to help countries to identify areas of unproductive or wasteful spending ... is, of course, just an extension and intensification of our traditional work to help countries improve their macroeconomic policies. As regards military spending, [a]n immediate priority must be to collect full and accurate information, and analyze the economic implications ... [T]he Fund does not intend to interfere with [member governments'] sovereign decisions when dealing with their national security. But the importance of these expenditures is such that their economic implications are a proper subject for our attention.[23]

The same message is being delivered to individual countries privately, as part of the policy dialogue between lenders and borrowers. In countries where the details of military budgets are shared among a relatively few individuals and security-related policies are formulated by an equally small group, merely discussing the importance of treating the military budget in the same fashion as other portions of the budget is a significant event. Reviewing military spending, even if available only in aggregate terms, will not only provide lenders with

293

data but will also constitute a first step toward making military-related data available to civilian members of the government and, ultimately, to the public.

Putting governments "on notice" that lenders are concerned about existing patterns of resource allocation should be a precondition for pressure. Several pieces of legislation were introduced into the US Congress during 1992 which seek to promote military reform by preventing US executive directors at the World Bank and the IMF from voting in favour of lending to countries where military expenditure exceeds certain measures, for example its share in gross national product (GNP) or its size compared with health and education expenditure.[24] Such an approach is not likely to achieve the desired ends.

Governments that are opposed to military reform predictably will respond negatively to blanket cut-offs. Disrupting bilateral relations in this way will only complicate the process of identifying potential allies within the government or educating government officials about the desirability of better budgeting practices and the benefits of greater transparency and lower expenditures in the military sector. Some governments may be very aware that their military spending is excessive and want to change their priorities. They may not, however, control the military budgeting process and therefore need assistance in raising the issue with their armed forces. External support, beginning with policy dialogue, can be very fruitful in such cases.

Furthermore, it may be desirable to reward countries that make steady progress in reducing military budgets from very high levels, even if expenditure remains relatively high for a period of years. Pakistan's military budget absorbed approximately 7 per cent of GNP at the beginning of the 1990s. To take one example, even if military expenditure could be reduced by 10 per cent a year, it would be six years before the US executive director at the Bank and the Fund could vote in favour of loans to Pakistan if a 3.6 per cent of GNP ceiling on borrowers' military budgets were approved by the Congress as called for in the legislation sponsored by Senator Cranston.

Policy dialogue is important for another reason. The degree to which borrowers feel ownership of reform programmes crucially affects the success or failure of these programmes. It is important that lenders avoid imposing a particular course of action on borrowers. Even governments that are contemplating inaugurating their own reform process and would welcome external support are sensitive in this regard.

It is thus important to identify multilateral forums in which military expenditure and other related issues can be raised in a non-confrontational fashion. The Global Coalition for Africa – whose members include African governments, bilateral donors, and multilateral organizations – is addressing the possibility of reducing military expenditure as one element of improved governance.[25] In Central America, consultations between regional governments and the European Community and its members under the San José accords or under the Partnership for Democracy and Development (which involves all OECD governments) could be broadened to include the opportunities for lowering military spending.

The UN Development Programme (UNDP) began in 1991 to address security and development in its annual *Human Development Report*, stating that:

If a government chooses to spend more on its army than on its people, it cannot be regarded as committed to human development, and this bias should certainly count against it in aid negotiations. High military expenditure should be a legitimate area of policy dialogue in all forums of development cooperation.[26]

Forums within the United Nations system include the UNDP Governing Council and UNDP-chaired Round Tables.

## Support

External support – which can take various forms, depending on the nature of the reforms pursued and the borrower's own resources – can facilitate efforts by borrower governments to implement change in the military sector.

Financial support can help governments absorb extra costs associated with reform, such as compensating soldiers released from the armed forces or workers laid off as a result of the rationalization of the defence-industrial sector. In 1991, Argentina and the World Bank began negotiating a loan that would support the privatization of firms in the defence industry that produce goods primarily for the civilian market.[27] Several of Nicaragua and Uganda's major lenders are working with those governments to underwrite programmes designed to integrate demobilized soldiers into the civilian economy.

Technical support can provide skilled manpower or equipment to carry out tasks, such as the destruction of weapons, the integration of former soldiers into the civilian economy, or the privatization/conversion of military industries. The Organization of American States provided demobilized Nicaragua Resistance soldiers with construction materials and farm implements to assist their transition to civilian life while bilateral donors have provided training to enhance their skills.[28]

Diplomatic support may be important in bringing adversaries to the negotiating table, preventing negotiations from breaking down or making concessions that facilitate the resolution of regional disputes. To remove obstacles to an agreement between North and South Korea on nuclear matters, the United States withdrew all of its own nuclear weapons stationed in South Korea and overrode its standard practice of neither confirming nor denying the presence of US nuclear weapons abroad by allowing the South Korean government to announce that South Korea was nuclear-free. It also cancelled major US–South Korean military manoeuvres and agreed to meet bilaterally with North Korea.

In the 1990s, the international lending community increasingly will be called upon to provide assistance to countries emerging from long periods of conflict. Although signing a formal agreement is clearly a significant event, actual implementation of the agreement is crucial to ending the conflict. Lenders could use their assistance both to encourage settlement of these disputes and to ensure that settlement agreements are implemented. External financing could be linked to carrying out verifiable measures such as agreeing to a cease-fire, signing a peace accord, officially ending hostilities, opening certain facilities for mutual or international inspection, and reducing troop levels.

The treaty that ended the civil war in El Salvador contains over 100 dates by which specific actions must occur in the economic, social, military, and political spheres.[29] Lending institutions will not themselves be involved in restructuring the armed forces or in setting the appropriate level of military expenditure. They will, however, be well placed to ensure that social and economic development are given priority from the start.[30]

Initial estimates suggest that El Salvador will require some $1.8 billion (US dollars) over five years to repair war damage and meet development needs neglected during the war. Linking the delivery of assistance to meeting key dates specified in the treaty could promote both development and stability. At the beginning of January 1992, the World Bank announced that it would convene a conference to coordinate external assistance to El Salvador, once the ceasefire had gone into effect. The meeting, held in Washington, D.C. on 10 March 1992, resulted in pledges to provide $800 million worth of assistance.[31]

## Pressure without conditions

The World Bank and the IMF have stated very clearly that they will not apply military-related conditions to their lending.[32] If policy dialogue is to be a credible tool for these two institutions, however, they must have some means of motivating borrowers to re-examine the resources allocated to the security sector.

The World Bank has pioneered a form of pressure implicitly rather than explicitly aimed at the military sector. The Bank's objective is to encourage countries to provide adequate funding to meet their economic and social goals. As part of its structural adjustment lending programmes (SALs), performance targets are set in development sectors that require the reallocation of domestic resources.[33] The intention is to force governments to shift funds from unproductive sectors, including the military, to productive ones. By focusing on strengthening the economy and guaranteeing that development sectors are fully funded rather than on reducing military spending *per se*, the Bank hopes to deflect criticism that it is meddling in the internal politics of member governments.

A similar strategy is available to the IMF when it sets targets for cutting fiscal deficits. Some governments may need to identify such substantial budgetary savings to meet IMF deficit reduction targets that it will be hard to avoid cutting spending in the military sector. While it remains to be seen how successful strategies of this nature can be in actually reducing military budgets, recent experience with Pakistan (discussed in the following section) and Uganda suggests that a coalition of bilateral and multilateral lenders can pressure even very reluctant governments into making some concessions.

## Specific conditionality

Although there is a wide variety of methods by which military reform can be promoted, a good deal of attention, particularly in the public debate, has focused upon the single tool known as conditionality. Under this strategy, an economic benefit (such as external financing, debt relief, trade, or technology transfer) is provided only if the recipient of that benefit agrees to undertake or abstain from a specific action.

Many borrowing countries have expressed displeasure at the possibility that such linkages may be extended to the military sphere. They argue that demanding reductions in military spending without reference to security needs is a dangerous exercise. In their view, only the country concerned has the capacity to define these needs and to decide how resources should be allocated to meet them.

Control over security policy, the armed forces, and the military budget have traditionally been among the most closely guarded prerogatives of states. None the less, during the Cold War, the major powers routinely influenced the security sector in many developing countries. While some developing-country governments were critical of this external involvement, others welcomed it as a means of strengthening their position *vis-à-vis* that of their opponents, both domestic and foreign.

Virtually every country in the developing world has received some portion of the billions of dollars of military hardware, training, technology, and aid that the United States, the Soviet Union, their allies in Eastern and Western Europe, and a few oil-rich developing countries provided on concessional terms during the Cold War.[34]

Security assistance has enabled some countries, for example South Korea in the 1950s and Israel since the mid-1970s, to maintain military establishments significantly larger than any they could have supported solely with domestic resources. More important, security assistance has allowed many states (Viet Nam, Afghanistan, El Salvador, and Ethiopia, among others) to conduct wars – often against domestic opponents. Still other countries (for example Israel and its Arab neighbours, India, and Pakistan) have been able to avoid the difficult political compromises that must be made if long-standing conflicts that drive arms races and from time to time erupt into open warfare are to be resolved. Some of these wars have not only relied on the financial and material backing of external states but have also involved direct intervention by one or more of the major powers.

The collapse of Soviet power, the subsequent disintegration of the Soviet Union, and the revelations about Iraq's nuclear arms-production capabilities following the Gulf War altered to some degree both the nature and content of external involvement in developing-country security sectors. The major powers are now calling for conflict resolution, non-proliferation, and lower military expenditure. Although the arms trade continues apace, subsidies are no longer as widely available as in the past. As a result, governments that were content to make use of external support to build up their military establishments and pursue local and regional disputes now object to efforts to limit the size and armaments of their armed forces, arguing that this constitutes an infringement of their sovereignty.

The lack of consultation associated with conditionality raises concerns in the developing world. It is widely agreed by lenders and borrowers that far greater efforts must be made to jointly assess evidence that reform is in the self-interest of particular governments. At the same time, however, it is important that lenders not allow their desire to persuade rather than force borrowers to change policy to serve as a rationale for maintaining the status quo in the military sector. The losses in terms of human, financial, and material resources that conflicts, excessive arms procurement, and high military budgets have incurred in the developing world over the last four decades render the sovereignty argument increasingly invalid. It may at times be necessary to place conditions on economic cooperation to force a government to reconsider a policy that is internationally viewed as unacceptable.

Conditionality can take several forms and be applied with varying degrees of stringency. Most lenders are reluctant to identify specific military expenditure targets that borrowers *must* meet to obtain financing. Aid suspension and other forms of sanctions have, however, been applied, particularly by the United States, in response to specific activities such as military *coups d'état*, efforts by non-nuclear powers to obtain nuclear weapons, and failure to negotiate in good faith. Thus, Washington sought to encourage the Israeli government to enter into significant negotiations with the Palestinians and several of its Arab neighbours by placing conditions on the $10 billion in housing loan guarantees requested by Israel in 1991.

Bilateral donors may increasingly link specific conditions to particular *actions* by individual countries to promote non-proliferation, conflict resolution, and regional arms control in the developing world. In contrast, specific conditions related to the level of a country's military *expenditure* will probably be used only rarely by the bilateral lenders. A consensus may be evolving that lower military budgets are preferable, but there is no agreement on what constitutes an appropriate level of expenditure in this sector. The size and composition of the military force (and hence the military budget) necessary to guarantee security varies from country to country. Lenders are therefore disinclined to insist that borrowers reduce military spending by a specific amount. Instead, they tend to speak of measurable, sustained progress toward lower levels of expenditure.

A possible exception might be the establishment of a military expenditure threshold. In October 1991, World Bank President Lewis Preston noted that governments have the sovereign right to determine the level of military spending but added that: "If we found a situation where defense expenditure was 35 to 40 per cent of the [government] budget, we might wonder if it was an appropriate use for [World Bank] funds." A few months later, his predecessor, Barber Conable, suggested that it might not be sensible to lend money to countries whose military spending exceeded 5 per cent of GNP.[35]

Although it is the policy of both the World Bank and the IMF not to apply specific military conditions to their lending, there is some evidence to suggest that they may, in fact, have attempted to link their financing to reductions in military spending in South Asia. The disbursement of the last tranche of a four-year structural adjustment facility (SAF) to Pakistan valued at $250 million reportedly was held up at least in part because Islamabad was unwilling to discuss reductions in its military budget as part of an effort to cut the total budget deficit. Press reports indicated that the IMF had demanded a 9 per cent drop in military spending.[36] An additional $250 million from the World Bank was said to have been withheld for the same reason.

Germany and Japan have also expressed dissatisfaction with the level of Pakistan's military spending. Although Islamabad has yet to announce reductions in military spending, it has talked of freezing the military budget in real terms and has plans to increase budgetary allocations for health, housing, education, and rural development.[37]

India has reportedly also been subject to pressure from the Bank and the Fund to lower its military spending, although the exact nature of the pressure is unclear. Press reports have claimed that reduced military spending was "an IMF requirement" for obtaining new loans from the Fund. Fund staff members have said privately that no outright demands were made. However the discussions between the Fund and the Indian government proceeded, India's military spending is being reduced, and in mid-September 1991 the IMF approved nearly $3 billion in loans to India.[38]

It can be argued that India has made some progress in several problem areas. The standby credit agreed upon in 1991 requires the fiscal deficit to be reduced to 5 per cent in 1992 (compared with 6.5 per cent in 1991 and 8 to 9 per cent in 1990). Military spending has also reportedly declined in real terms. Just how accurately official Indian budget figures reflect military spending is, however, open to question. India continues to engage in barter trade with Russia for military equipment and technology despite the Soviet Union's (and Russia's) intention to end barter trade at the beginning of 1991.

## "Carrots" instead of "sticks"

Lenders may choose not to impose specific conditions on their aid but to give preference to governments whose performance is favourable (allocative conditionality). While lenders are required to take many factors into account when distributing their funding, by spring 1992 Germany was already applying this strategy in the military sector, and Canada and Japan were developing policies in this area.[39] The Japanese government is particularly interested in rewarding good behaviour, reserving denial of aid for rare occasions when governments fail to pursue certain policies. In a statement at an informal meeting of the OECD's Development Assistance Committee in April 1992, the Japanese representative noted:

> ... two types of policy approaches should be employed ... One ... is the so-called "positive linkage," which means extending assistance to those countries that are making positive efforts to restructure their economy by reducing their military expenditures and arms trade....
>
> The other approach is the so-called "negative linkage," which means cutting or reducing assistance in light of negative development. In principle, it is more desirable to make use of the former approach. However, cases may arise where donors should make use of the latter approach after they have exhausted other means of communication, such as policy dialogue. Even in such cases, donors need to remember that their objective is to promote development, rather than to punish countries.[40]

A reward-based strategy is grounded upon the premise that changes in behaviour are more likely to result from positive reinforcement than from punishment. While such an assessment may be valid for governments with a fairly firm commitment to reform, it is unclear how much leverage this sort of strategy provides over less committed countries.

Furthermore, desirable as it may be to offer the carrot rather than the stick, allocative conditionality virtually always requires official lenders to *shift* resources from one country to another. Japan, whose aid budget has been expanding more rapidly than most other DAC members, may find it easier to reallocate resources. In contrast, the United States, where a substantial portion of aid resources are earmarked by Congress for specific countries, and countries such as Sweden where aid budgets are shrinking, face greater limits on their capacity to reallocate assistance.

One reason why allocative conditionality is particularly attractive to the bilateral lenders is that it enables them to register their displeasure with a borrower's policies but does not immediately jeopardize existing projects. It may take several years for a shift to be felt as old projects are completed. This gives borrowers the opportunity to adjust their policies to obtain new funding. Another method of allocating resources to indicate dissatisfaction with the borrower government without actually cutting assistance is to channel funding through non-governmental organizations. This is a tactic that is apparently increasingly favoured by some donors, notably Canada, the Netherlands, and the Nordic countries.

## Proposals to enhance development and security

The international official lending community has made substantial progress since the days when military issues were virtually never raised in the context of development policy or financing. It is no longer possible to ignore the impact that the armed forces have on a country's prospects for sustained development. According to the OECD's Development Assistance Committee, military expenditure "will be ... of continuing concern and attention in the years ahead, and can be expected to feature prominently in aid allocation decisions by donors, both bilaterally and collectively in such fora as Consultative Groups, etc."[41]

Of the numerous tools available to promote military reform among borrowing countries, lenders have thus far focused on policy dialogue, structural adjustment, deficit-reduction targets designed to squeeze military budgets, and financial and technical support for those few governments that have requested assistance to privatize military industries or integrate demobilized soldiers into the civilian economy. Specific conditionality, focused mainly on specific activities such as proliferation or the military's domestic political role in particular countries, has also been employed, primarily by the United States.

The formulation and implementation of policies to encourage change are none the less still at an early stage, and there is considerable uncertainty among lenders about how far and how rapidly they can and should proceed. The following proposals suggest the direction in which the international lending community might take the next steps to enhance both development and security in borrower countries.

1. *All members of the international lending community should actively seek to create an enabling environment for military reform in the developing world.* Now that the potential competition between military spending and development has been acknowledged, all lenders should adopt policies that will actively promote reform in the military sector, rather than simply punishing bad behaviour, passively rewarding good behaviour, or limiting their involvement to reform-minded governments.

It may at times prove necessary to attach specific conditions to economic interactions with borrower countries. The core of lenders' policies should, however, be policy dialogue and financial, technical, and diplomatic support designed to assist governments in changing their behaviour and policies in the military sector, in placing the military sector on the same footing as other portions of the government, and in altering the balance between expenditures on the armed forces and those on development. The objectives of these policies should include establishing greater transparency and accountability in the military sector; encouraging civilian control over the armed forces, paramilitary groups, and the police; supporting reductions in the size of military forces; and promoting the creation of new security arrangements that will enable governments to provide enhanced security at lower levels of expenditure.

One of the most important contributions that lenders can make in this regard is to integrate the military sector into normal development practice. Strengthening the capacity of governments to manage the public sector, improving the efficiency of public-sector expenditures, and supporting market-oriented reforms each have military components. All too often, these components have been ignored.

The substantial economic and social costs incurred since 1945 as a result of conflicts, arms proliferation, and excessively large military sectors have made it increasingly difficult to carry out fiscal and institutional reforms without considering how the military sector contributes to the problems these reforms are designed to overcome. To take just one example, the armed forces own and operate non-military businesses in many borrower countries. When these are inefficiently operated, they can become dependent on budget subsidies, siphoning off resources from development sectors. Such enterprises should be included in privatization programmes designed to reduce the burden of the public sector on the economy.[42] What is more, the economic viability of arms-production facilities should also be discussed, although governments will frequently continue to subsidize their domestic arms industry for foreign policy reasons that lending institutions cannot affect.

Each lender must determine where its own comparative advantage lies, what specific reforms it can promote, and which of the available policy tools are most appropriate for it to employ. Whatever instruments lenders find most suitable to their purposes and whichever reform objectives they are able to promote, lenders must be as consistent as possible in the application of their policy to demonstrate the high priority they accord military reform.

2. *The international political and development communities should coordinate their efforts to promote reduced emphasis on the military sector in developing countries.* Two types of coordination are necessary: within the international lending community and between lenders and political institutions.

With regard to the former, the definition of military reform will vary among lenders, who will adopt diverse strategies to encourage borrowers to revise their military priorities. But to the extent that the official lenders can agree on the *objectives* of their military reform policies, they will be more successful in promoting change among borrowing governments.

If the official lenders could also agree on the countries whose military spending gives cause for concern, they could act through consultative groups, aid consortia, and UNDP Round Tables to press for reform. A number of lending institutions are already targeting India, Pakistan, and Uganda because of, among other things, the clear competition between military spending and resources available for development in these countries.

OECD members began in the spring of 1992 to explore the possibility of using the Development Assistance Committee (DAC) as a forum for systematically exchanging views on topics such as reducing military spending and promoting democratization and good governance. It may be some time before formal coordination evolves. In the interim, OECD members should make use of their contact in the DAC and elsewhere to review jointly their policies towards specific countries on an informal basis.

Lenders can assist in the demilitarization and reconstruction of economies in the wake of conflict. The World Bank and some bilateral donors have already been approached by several governments for this purpose. Reconstruction financing needs are considerable in countries such as Angola, Cambodia, El Salvador, Nicaragua, and Uganda. As more and more conflicts are resolved in the coming years, the demands for funding will grow. Strong support from the multilateral financial institutions – which are the source of a significant share of the available capital – will be crucial in helping to consolidate the peace.

For such efforts on the part of lenders to succeed, however, it is important that they not be undercut by other policies in the political realm. It is clearly counter-productive for lenders to fund reintegration schemes for demobilized soldiers in a particular country to reduce the economic burden of the defence sector while they or their DAC partners are promoting and subsidizing arms transfers to the same government. Coordination between lenders and the political community is vital.

In countries where political settlements are required, or where non-proliferation and arms transfer control demand urgent attention, external financing and other *economic* tools will help promote reform only when they are linked to broader diplomatic efforts to guarantee the security of the state, its government, and its citizenry. Through their foreign affairs and defence ministries, the bilateral lenders can participate in negotiations designed to terminate conflicts, provide security guarantees, assist in disarming soldiers and guerrilla forces as part of the demobilization process, and provide training for those who continue to serve in the military and police forces. The United Nations and regional organizations such as the Organization of African Unity can play a similar role. The lenders can then use their economic leverage to support these efforts.

For example, lenders could support conflict resolution by funding activities such as destroying weapons, verifying troop withdrawals, or monitoring cease-fires. They could also provide financial "carrots" to the parties to the conflict once negotiations reach an advanced stage. Outside mediators could determine which concessions are sufficiently significant to warrant some form of assistance from lenders.

Although the bilateral donors and multilateral organizations such as the United Nations are best suited to begin this process, it would be worth exploring whether the multilateral development banks (the World Bank and the African, Asian, and Inter-American regional development banks) could join in by temporarily withholding assistance to convince governments to begin serious negotiations. The World Bank, for example, participated in the January 1992 decision of the Consultative Group for Kenya to withhold new loans for six months in response to Nairobi's lack of progress in moving towards multi-party democracy. If in particular cases bilateral lenders agreed that a high level of military spending or an ongoing conflict constitutes a serious obstacle to development, and that only negotiations to resolve underlying security imbalances can lead to lower military spending, multilateral development bank action might be justifiable on economic grounds.

3. *Bilateral donors and UN agencies should agree upon common security-related characteristics that any country receiving their financial support will possess.* These characteristics should reflect universally agreed upon norms. As a start, DAC members might agree that borrowers will:

- Have signed, ratified, and implemented international arms-control treaties such as the Nuclear Non-Proliferation Treaty, the Biological Weapons Convention, and the soon-to-be completed chemical weapons treaty, or be party to internationally recognized alternative arrangements such as the full-scope nuclear safeguards agreement concluded between Argentina and Brazil with the International Atomic Energy Agency;
- Not contravene such treaties and regimes by covertly developing the capability to produce weapons of mass destruction and ballistic missiles or by assisting other countries to develop such weapons;
- Respect the territorial integrity of other countries by supporting non-aggression and non-intervention;
- Participate in dialogues designed to increase regional security and stability;
- Negotiate in good faith as necessary to end long-standing conflicts, both internal and external;
- Participate in the United Nations standardized military expenditure reporting exercise and the UN arms transfer register; and,
- Subject the military sector to the same scrutiny and discipline as other public-sector expenditure.

4. *The official lenders should promote the understanding that transparency and accountability in the military budgeting process do not undermine security.* Transparency has both domestic and international dimensions. While confidentiality is necessary in some areas to protect external security, basic information on the size, structure, and financing of the military, as well as on the budgeting process itself, tends to be publicly available in the OECD countries. Their se-

curity has in no way been compromised by this level of transparency, even at the height of the Cold War. Indeed, one of the premises of the Conference on Security and Cooperation in Europe process is that greater transparency can produce greater security among countries.[43]

Transparency and accountability in the military sector are part of the efficient and prudent management of public resources that characterizes good governance. Withholding *basic* information about the military sector has no purpose other than to protect the defence budget from public scrutiny. Secrecy frequently leads to the misallocation of domestic resources, undermining a country's economic stability. Sound economic practice requires that budgets for all public-sector activities be treated in the same manner and be open to the same degree of public scrutiny.

To underline the commitment of the international lending community to greater transparency, the International Monetary Fund should move rapidly to implement the mandate it received from its Board of Directors in September 1991 to measure and analyse the military spending of member governments as part of Article IV consultations. Similarly, the World Bank should include the military sector in all public-expenditure reviews it conducts of borrower countries. The bilateral donors should orient their aid policies toward supporting enhanced transparency in the military sector.

It is important that the military budgeting process be controlled by professional civilian financial managers and that all military expenditures be clearly identified and placed on-budget. The armed forces must justify programmes in terms of a realistic threat and provide complete cost analyses of all proposed programmes. Trade-offs between the military and other sectors must be made explicit, and actual outlays need to be carefully monitored. Lenders should work with borrower governments to see that such practices are institutionalized. By encouraging governments to introduce a wide range of standard budgeting practices in the military sector, lenders can make a significant contribution to enhanced civilian control over the military, which is crucial to reducing military budgets.

Realistic appraisals of each country's security environment are an important part of this process. The official lenders should encourage borrowers to base their military budgeting on detailed assessments of their country's security requirements and alternative (diplomatic as well as military) means of addressing these needs. Some governments may not have the technical capacity to conduct threat assessments entirely on their own. In these cases, lenders could fund technical assistance by civilian analysts.

Although some developing countries already publish information on their military sectors and budgets, this practice is not widespread. Lenders should encourage borrowers to present detailed military budgets to their executive branches and legislatures in a timely fashion so that a full review and debate of their contents can occur prior to the beginning of each fiscal year.

The international official lending community, particularly members of the DAC, may also wish to promote transparency by giving preference in aid allocations to governments that participate in the unified military expenditure reporting system of the United Nations and the forthcoming UN arms transfer register. Only a handful of developing countries have ever participated in the expenditure reporting system since its inception in the early 1980s. The security of those which have done so – including regional rivals Argentina, Brazil, and Chile – has not been impaired as a result.

Yet another method of increasing transparency would be for regional groups to follow the lead of the Conference on Security and Cooperation in Europe and create regional reporting mechanisms to cover a variety of military indicators. Lenders and borrowers participating in organizations such as the Global Coalition for Africa might explore the opportunities for such regional initiatives. Finally, borrowers and lenders could agree that the international official lending community should include aggregate information collected in the course of regular economic reviews in appropriate publications, such as the IMF's *Government Finance Yearbook* – a practice that could significantly upgrade the quality of data available to the public.

5. *Bilateral donors should acknowledge that military reform is a two-way street by matching their policies in the security sector with those expected of developing countries, wherever possible.* To build credibility and avoid charges of discrimination and unwarranted interference in borrowers' affairs, lenders and developed nations in general should be willing to accept the same norms for themselves that they are applying to developing countries. There is considerable scope for military expenditure reductions throughout the world, as military spending in most of the developed world remains substantially higher than justified, given the end of East-West rivalry. To the extent possible, future international arms control agreements and supplier groups should be universal in membership and non-discrim-

inatory in scope, treating all states alike. When military intervention in the developing world is necessary, it should be multilateral, not unilateral, in nature, and given legitimacy in some broadly accepted way, for example by occurring under the aegis of the United Nations or a regional organization.

One of the areas of greatest disparity between the objectives the industrial countries are pursuing in the developing world and their own behaviour is the arms trade. With the exception of Iceland, all OECD members export weapons.[44] Several of them either export only a very small amount of arms or sell only to other industrial countries. However, some of the largest OECD members, notably the United States, France, and the United Kingdom, export a substantial amount of arms to the developing world and are currently seeking to expand their share of the market in the face of declining domestic orders. A portion of these transfers – for example the nearly $4.7 billion in arms transferred by the United States in FY1991 under the Foreign Military Financing programme – are government subsidized.

While all governments have the right to equip armed forces to defend their sovereignty, and many countries have no domestic arms production capacity, countries that aggressively promote arms sales seriously undermine their ability to promote military reform. IMF Managing Director Camdessus has urged arms-exporting countries to eliminate subsidies associated with arms transfers. Such a move – which could have an impact on the long-term viability of some arms producers in the industrial world – would offer concrete proof that the industrial countries do not expect all concessions to be made by the borrowing countries.

As a first step, the OECD Understanding on Export Credit ("the Consensus"), which limits the amount of conditionality for most civilian merchandise, could be extended to armaments and other military equipment. As a second step, OECD countries could agree among themselves to eliminate the small subsidy allowed by the Consensus, and to not sell arms on unrealistic credit terms to uncreditworthy countries, thus compounding these countries' debt problems. This would require concerted action between the DAC and the Export Finance Group of the OECD Trade Committee.

6. *Bilateral donor governments should instruct their representatives on the governing boards of the international financial institutions to support efforts by these organizations to promote changes in the military sectors that will strengthen the capacity of all of their members for sustained economic growth and development.* Because the degree to

which the multilateral institutions can promote military reform depends heavily on the support they receive from their major shareholders, the bilateral donors should support data collection and data transparency, inclusion of the military sector in economic analyses, and efforts to use financial assistance to demilitarize economies, including, if necessary, the reduction or suspension of funding.

## Conclusion

The end of the Cold War has produced significant changes in relations between and within states. Democratization, conflict resolution, non-aggression, collective security, multilateralism, and compromise are beginning to replace authoritarianism, war, military alliances, unilateral action, and confrontation as internationally accepted modes of behaviour.

Yet many of the problems of the Cold War era are still very much with us. The proliferation of chemical, biological, and nuclear weapons and ballistic missiles remains a danger. Strong industrial pressures persist to maintain and, if possible, expand exports of conventional weaponry. Low rates of economic growth and social progress and numerous unresolved conflicts, including serious ethnic, religious, and national disputes, threaten long-term stability in many parts of the developing world, Eastern Europe, and the former Soviet Union.

From the perspective of the industrial world, the defining relationship of the 1945–1990 period was the hostility between the United States and the Soviet Union. The Cold War admittedly left its mark on many inter- and intra-state relations in Africa, Asia, Latin America, and the Middle East, but its influence in these parts of the world was frequently exaggerated. Local and regional conflicts derived from local and regional disagreements, many of which pre-dated the Cold War and many of which have survived it.[45]

It would be unrealistic to assume that conflict can be eradicated. It can, however, be channelled into non-military avenues, and the norms defining acceptable behaviour on the part of governments, both towards their neighbours and towards their own citizens, can be changed. The challenge of the 1990s and succeeding decades is to ensure that the emergent trend towards international cooperation and domestic participation is maintained and strengthened.

The international official lending community clearly has a role to play in this process by using its resources to enhance both development and security. The international lending institutions can help to change norms relating to secrecy in the military sector, the domestic role of the military, the spread of weapons and weapon-production technology, and the appropriate means of settling disputes within and among states. Where the objective is primarily developmental, for example transparency and accountability in the budgetary process, lenders can act on their own initiative. Where the objective is primarily to alter the security environment, for example non-proliferation of weapons of mass destruction, the official lending community will need to work in tandem with international and national political institutions.

The use of economic tools to affect policy always runs the risk of producing charges of unwarranted interference in the affairs of those states that are the object of reform efforts. There are two ways in which the official lending institutions can overcome at least some of this resistance. The first is by engaging in discussions with groups of borrowers. In these discussions, the accent should be on how these lenders can help developing countries implement mutually agreed-upon policies. Such dialogues might take place within the framework of existing regional or international institutions or among ad hoc groups of countries assembled for the purpose of resolving specific local or regional problems.[46] In either case, conflict resolution, security guarantees, confidence-building measures, and economic incentives all would be vital components of the process.

The second means by which lenders can gain the confidence of borrowers is to accept *themselves* the new norms in the security sphere. Arms-control agreements should be universal and non-discriminatory in scope. Military budgets should be reduced in all countries allocating more than a modest share, say 10 per cent, of their central government expenditure to the security sector. When military intervention is necessary, it should be multilateral, not unilateral, in nature. Encouraging military reform in the South gains legitimacy when combined with military reform in the North.

In the final analysis, however, military reform in developing countries will occur only if governments in those countries accept the need for change. They must take a hard look at their priorities and devise policies that will promote reduced tensions and increase development. This will require compromises to be struck, both domestically and among states. The industrial countries can underline their commitment to the emerging norms by making them the cornerstone of their own policies. They can also help to instil new modes of behaviour by conditioning relations with other countries on adherence to these norms. But it is ultimately the people and the governments of developing countries who must seize the opportunities presented by recent changes in the international system to create a more equitable and prosperous future for themselves.

## Notes

1. Available data suggest that there is a particularly large discrepancy between military spending and outlays in social sectors in Angola, Bolivia, Brunei, Chad, China, Egypt, Ethiopia, Iran, Iraq, Israel, Jordan, Oman, Pakistan, Peru, Sudan, Syria, Uganda, and the United Arab Emirates. See Robert McNamara, "The Post-Cold War World: Implications for Military Expenditures in the Developing Countries." Proceedings of the World Bank Annual Conference on Development Economics, 1991; Supplement to the World Bank *Economic Review* and the World Bank *Research Observer*, Lawrence H. Summers and Shekhar Shah, eds., Washington, D.C., World Bank, March 1992, pp. 122–124; and World Bank, *The Challenge of Development: World Development Report 1991*. New York, Oxford University Press, 1991, p. 142. Also on this point see United Nations Development Programme, *Human Development Report 1991*, New York, Oxford University Press, 1991, pp. 80–83; and *Human Development Report 1992*, New York, Oxford University Press, 1992, pp. 84–86.

2. As the demand from Eastern Europe and the former Soviet Union has grown and the implementation of the capital increase agreed upon in 1990 has been delayed, the IMF's cash resources are rapidly approaching a worryingly low level. See George Graham, "IMF Cash Resources 'Facing Strain'." *Financial Times*, 11 September 1992, p. 6.

   The chaos that struck the European currency markets in September 1992 has reportedly led several important bilateral lenders – such as Sweden – to reduce aid allocations as part of austerity measures. See, Stuart Auerbach, "Europe Crisis Likely to Hurt 3rd World Aid." *The Washington Post*, 25 September 1992, pp. F1, F2.

   In the developing world, certain regions (sub-Saharan Africa and Latin America) and social groups (women and girls) have been affected more severely by the adverse conditions of the 1980s than others. The World Bank, *Poverty: World Development Report 1990*. New York, Oxford University Press, 1990, pp. 1–2.

3. Throughout this paper, the terms "international official lending community," "official lenders," and "lenders" are used interchangeably for both multilateral lending institutions such as the World Bank and bilateral aid agencies such as the U.S. Agency for International Development. The terms "bilateral donors," "bilateral lenders," or simply "donors" denote – according to context – either the governments that extend aid or their bilateral aid agencies.

4. A well-documented example of fungibility occurred when Iraq used export credits and loan guarantees approved by the Reagan and Bush administrations in the late 1980s to free up resources for arms procurement. See Murray Waas and Douglas Frantz, "Bush Had Long Supported Aid for Iraq." *Los Angeles Times*, 24 February 1992; Douglas Frantz and Murray Waas, "Secret Effort by Bush in '89 Helped Hussein Build Iraq's War Machine." *Los Angeles Times*, 24 February 1992; Paul Houston, "House Banking Committee to Probe Reports on Aid to Iraq." *Los Angeles Times*, 25 February 1992; and Douglas Frantz and Murray Waas, "U.S. Loans Indirectly Financed Iraq Military." *Los Angeles Times*, 25 February 1992.

5. Council of the European Communities, General Secretariat, Press Release, 1538th Session of the Council on Cooperation and Development, Brussels, 9555/91 (Press 217), Preliminary Version, 28 November 1991, p. 16.

6. The issues raised here are of course relevant to the debate on official lending to the new

republics of the former Soviet Union. None the less, this paper does not specifically attempt to apply them to the successor states of the Soviet Union.

7. Barber B. Conable, Jr., "Growth – Not Guns," *The Washington Post*, 24 December 1991.

8. "Army Council Issues Criteria for Reducing Army," Radio Uganda, 5 June 1992, reproduced by the Foreign Broadcast Information Service. FBIS-AFR-92-110, 8 June 1992, pp. 10–11. See also Keith Richburg, "Rule Brings Stability to Uganda; Aid Donors Look for Looser Rein." *The Washington Post*, 3 March 1992.

   The implications of this decision for the military budget are at present uncertain, since salaries in the military sector – as in other portions of the civil service – are unreasonably low and the military would like to upgrade its equipment.

9. Development Assistance Committee, *Development Co-Operation 1991 Report*. Paris, OECD, 1991, table 19, p. 189. DAC officials state that the very high figure for Mozambique results from the difficulty in accurately measuring that country's GNP but note that irrespective of the exact figure, Mozambique's aid dependence is substantial.

   Among sub-Saharan African countries, Ethiopia, Ghana, Kenya, Lesotho, Madagascar, Rwanda, the Sahel Group, Uganda, and Zambia relied on ODA to provide between 10 and 20 per cent of their GNP in 1989–1990. Others that derived more than 10 per cent of their national product from ODA in 1989–1990 include Bangladesh, Bolivia, Egypt, Indochina, Jordan, Nepal, and Papua New Guinea.

10. What is more, to the extent that development succeeds, the number of countries that derive a sizeable share of their GNP from aid will decline, and donor leverage will be eroded. For most of the aid-dependent states, however, this is not a near-term consideration.

11. The leverage donors can exert over recipients can at times far outweigh the amount of ODA provided, since at the margin even a modest amount of aid can be critical.

12. For a description of these supplier groups, see Zachary S. Davis, *Non-Proliferation Regimes: A Comparative Analysis of Policies to Control the Spread of Nuclear, Chemical and Biological Weapons and Missiles*. 91-334 ENR, Washington, D.C., Congressional Research Service, 1 April 1991.

13. For example, see, "Non-proliferation Efforts Bolstered." *US Department of State Dispatch*, 20 July 1992, pp. 569–571.

14. On Germany, see "Bonn to Block Export for Arms." *Financial Times*, 12 March 1992; on Japan, see Robert Thomson. "Japanese Company Under Export Ban in Iranian Missiles Row," *Financial Times*, 26–27 October 1991. Japan Aviation, a subsidiary of NEC, apparently began exporting military equipment to Iran in 1983.

15. Gary C. Hufbauer and Jeffrey J. Schott, assisted by Kimberly Ann Elliott, *Economic Sanctions in Support of Foreign Policy Goals*, Policy Analyses in International Economics No. 6, Washington, D.C., Institute for International Economics, October 1983, provides a useful survey of the successes and failures of efforts to impose sanctions since World War I.

16. Guy Gugliotta, "Senate Backs China Trade Conditions." *The Washington Post*, 26 February 1992; Jim Mann, "Bush Vetoes Limits on China Trade." *Los Angeles Times* [Washington edition], 3 March 1992; Jim Mann, "Senate Fails to Override Veto on China Policy." *Los Angeles Times* [Washington Edition], 19 March 1992, p. A3; Arnold Kanter, "US Policy Objectives and MFN Status for China." *US Department of State Dispatch*, 6 July 1992, pp. 551–554; and Don Oberdorfer, "U.S. Decries China's Sale of Reactor, But Clears the Way for Satellite Deal." *The Washington Post*, 12 September 1992.

   It is also interesting to observe that while the Bush administration has opposed withdrawing MFN status from China, it has threatened to increase tariffs on certain goods imported from China if Beijing fails to improve access for US goods to the Chinese market by, for example, adopting internationally approved product testing and certification standards and ending discriminatory import licensing practices. See Richard Lawrence, "U.S. Sets Mid-August Target for China Market-Access Pact." *Journal of Commerce*, 17 July 1992, and Yvonne Preston, "China Resists US Pressure to Cut Tariffs." *Financial Times*, 17 September 1992.

17. "Baker Defends Move to End US Sanctions Against China." *The Journal of Commerce*, 25 February 1992, and Elaine Sciolino, "C.I.A. Chief Says North Koreans Plan to Make Secret Atom Arms," *The New York Times*, 26 February 1992.

18. Jim Mann, "U.S. Fears China is Seeking Missile Deal with Iran." *Los Angeles Times* [Washington edition], 3 April 1992.

19. See, for example, Douglas McDaniel, *Economic Sanctions: Issues Raised by the Sanctions Against Iraq*, 92-370 F, Washington, D.C.: Congressional Research Service, 17 April 1992; and Signe Landgren, *Embargo Disimplemented: South Africa's Military Industry*, Oxford, Oxford University Press, for Stockholm International Peace Research Institute, 1989.

20. Current US legislation provides for sanctions against both foreign individuals and companies under the Missile Technology Control Regime (Title XVII of the National Defense Authorization Act of 1990), and against foreign individuals, companies, and countries under the Chemical and Biological Weapons Control and Warfare Elimination Act of 1991, Title V of Public Law 102-138, 28 October 1991.

21. Growing concern over North Korea's nuclear programme in the wake of the Gulf War prompted Tokyo to announce on 30 October 1991, that before it would recognize or trade with Pyongyang, North Korea would have to dismantle its plutonium processing plant at Yongbyon. Lawyers Alliance for World Security with the Washington Council on Non-Proliferation, *North Korea: Do They or Don't They Have the Bomb?*, Washington, D.C., 1992, p. 16.

    On the purchase of the carrier from Ukraine, see Sam Jameson, "Japanese Official Criticizes China's 'Fussing'," *Los Angeles Times* [Washington Edition], 8 September 1992.

22. Barber Conable, Joint Bank/Fund Annual Meetings, 25 September 1989.

23. Michel Camdessus, Board of Governors, 1991 Annual Meetings, Bangkok, Thailand, Press Release No. 64, 17 October 1991, p. 2.

24. Two of these pieces of legislation are s.2162, "Third World Development and Threat Reduction Act of 1992," sponsored by Senators Harkin, Adams, Bingaman, and Wirth (limiting lending to countries where military expenditure does not exceed combined health and education spending), and s.2157, "Developing Countries Demilitarization Act of 1992," sponsored by Senator Cranston (limiting lending to countries devoting less than 3.6 per cent of their GNP to the military). Neither of these bills would apply to Israel, which received 20 per cent of the international development, humanitarian, and security assistance provided by the United States during FY 1991. The restrictions in both bills would apply only to developing countries, defined as having per capita GNPs of less than \$4,000 (s.2162) or \$4,300 (s.2157). World Bank data indicate that Israel had a per capita GNP of nearly \$10,000 in 1989.

25. Global Coalition for Africa, *Reducing Military Expenditure in Africa*. Document GCA/AC.2/04/4/92, prepared for the Second Advisory Committee Meeting, Kampala, Uganda, 8–9 May 1992. For a report of the meeting at which this paper was presented, see, Ernest Harsch, "African Reforms Under the Spotlight." *Africa Recovery*, August 1992, pp. 10–11.

26. United Nations Development Programme, *Human Development Report 1991*. op. cit., p. 83. The UNDP has established a working group on operational criteria for identifying excessive military expenditure, which will report on its findings in 1993.

27. "Layoffs Planned for Military Industry Employees." *Buenos Aires Herald*, 23 September 1991, p. 7, reproduced in FBIS-LAT-91-186, 25 September 1991, pp. 26–27.

28. Santiago Murray, "Building Towards Reconciliation." *Americas*, 1992, vol. 44, no. 3, pp. 52–53.

29. Trevor Rowe, "Salvadorans Reach Final Accord." *The Washington Post*, 15 January 1992, and Edward Cody, "Salvadorans Sign Accord Ending 12-Year War." *The Washington Post*, 17 January 1992.

30. A number of DAC members and some multilateral organizations may play a dual role. Their aid agencies will focus on economic and social development while other parts of the

bureaucracy may be asked to become involved in political and security affairs such as providing professional training to reconstituted armed forces, supervising elections and so on. The European Community agreed in late February 1992 to fund an ECU 1.5 million programme to promote human rights in Central America that will, among other things, provide professional training for regional police and armed forces. See Patrick Blum, "El Salvador Clinches Aid from EC." *Financial Times*, 26 February 1992.

31. Stephen Fidler, "World Bank to Call El Salvador Aid Conference," *Financial Times*, 3 January 1992, and Bernard Aronson, "Consolidating Peace and Democracy in El Salvador." *US Department of State Dispatch*, 20 July 1992, p. 578.
32. Jonathan E. Sanford, *Multilateral Development Banks: Issues for Congress*. IB87218, Washington, D.C., Congressional Research Service, 13 March 1992, p. 13.
33. The Bank's third review of structural adjustment lending programmes concludes that the Bank needs to give greater attention to development outcomes, rather than merely specifying expenditure targets.
34. For a review of security assistance during most of the Cold War period, see Nicole Ball, *Security and Economy*. Princeton, N.J., Princeton University Press, 1988, pp. 237–294.
35. Paul Blustein, "World Bank, IMF to Press Defense Cuts: Institutions Hint at Withholding Loans." *The Washington Post*, 19 October 1991, p. B1, and Conable, "Growth – Not Guns." op. cit.
36. "IMF-IBRD Assistance Conditional on 9 p.c. Defence Cut." *Dawn*, 14 September 1991.
37. "Defense Spending Freeze May Appease Creditors." *The Muslim*, 1 April 1992, reprinted in FBIS-NES-92-064, and Farhan Bokhari, "Pakistan Raises Tax Base to Cut Budget Deficit." *Financial Times*, 15 May 1992.
38. K.K. Sharma, "Indian Companies Bear Brunt of Austere Budget." *Financial Times*, 25 July 1991.

    In late October, Michel Camdessus visited India and made the following comments: "It is gratifying that India has already taken meaningful steps to reduce expenditures on defense, which have fallen as a share of GDP from 3 1/2 per cent in the late 1980s to below 3 per cent in the current budget. In a few days, I shall be visiting Pakistan also. What a fine example it will be to the rest of the developing world, if these two great nations can transfer substantial human and financial resources to activities that will more directly contribute to growth and to the reduction of poverty." Michel Camdessus, "India Implements Courageous and Far-Reaching Economic Program." *IMF Survey*, 18 November 1991, p. 339.

39. Nicole Ball, *Pressing for Peace: Can Aid Induce Reform?*, Policy Essay no. 6, Washington, D.C., Overseas Development Council, 1992, pp. 46–48. Japan's Official Development Assistance Charter, approved 30 June 1992, calls for Japanese ODA to be provided "in accordance with the principles of the United Nations Charter (especially sovereign equality and non-intervention in domestic matters), as well as the following four principles. (1) Environmental conservation and development should be pursued in tandem. (2) Any use of ODA for military purposes or for aggravation of international conflicts should be avoided. (3) Full attention should be paid to trends in recipient countries' military expenditures, their development and production of mass destruction weapons and missiles, their export and import of arms, etc., so as to maintain and strengthen international peace and stability, and from the viewpoint that developing countries should place appropriate priorities in the allocation of their resources on their own economic and social development. (4) Full attention should be paid to efforts for promoting democratization and introduction of a market-oriented economy, and the situation regarding the securing of basic human rights and freedoms in the recipient country."

    On 5 November the Director-General of Japan's Economic Cooperation Bureau, Takao Kawakami, indicated that Japanese policy would emphasize transparency in the military sector, trends in military spending, policy dialogue to convince governments of the need for reform, and multilateral cooperation. "Japan's ODA Policies for a Peace Initiative." Address by Mr. Takao Kawakami, Director-General, Economic Cooperation Bureau, Ministry of Foreign Affairs, Tokyo Conference on Arms Reduction and Economic Development in the Post-Cold War Era, 5 November 1992, mimeo.

40. Statement by Mr. Nobuyuki Sugimoto, Director of Multilateral Cooperation Division, Economic Cooperation Bureau, Ministry of Foreign Affairs, at the Informal Meeting on Participatory Democracy and Good Governance, Paris, 9 April 1992, p. 3.

41. Development Assistance Committee, *Development Co-operation 1991 Report.* op. cit., p. 19.

42. This is occurring in Argentina and is planned for Bolivia. On the latter, see Chris Philipsborn, "Privatisation Plans Delayed in Bolivia." *Financial Times*, 24 September 1992.

43. "Vienna Document 1992." *US Department of State Dispatch Supplement*, July 1992, describes the information on military forces that CSCE members will be exchanging on an annual basis.

44. The 24 OECD countries in descending order as arms exporters based on data, in billions of 1989 US dollars, for 1979–1989 are: United States ($133.8), France ($47.7), United Kingdom ($33.0), Germany ($20.4), Italy ($11.9), Canada ($5.8), Switzerland ($5.4), Spain ($4.4), Netherlands ($3.9), Sweden ($3.1), Belgium ($2.8), Japan ($2.1), Austria ($1.8), Portugal ($1.2), Finland ($1.0), Australia ($0.8), Norway ($0.7), Turkey ($0.5), Greece ($0.45), Denmark ($0.4), Ireland ($0.01), New Zealand ($0.01), Luxembourg ($0.005), and Iceland ($0.0). U.S. Arms Control and Disarmament Agency, *World Military Expenditures*, op. cit., table II.

45. McNamara, "The Post-Cold War World." op. cit., pp. 97–98.

46. See, for example, Enrique ter Horst, "Mechanism for Reduction of Third World Military Expenditure: Disarmament for Development Conferences or Round Tables," New York, October 1990, mimeo, which suggests bringing together under the auspices of the United Nations neighbouring countries with outstanding security problems and a consortium of donors created for the purpose of reducing regional tensions and promoting development.

316

# Comments on chapter 11

## 1. Raimo Väyrynen

Nicole Ball rightly points out in her paper that there is a worldwide shortage of capital. This is due, in part, to the massive needs of reconstruction in the former Soviet Union and in Eastern Central Europe, and not only there. The development needs of China and Southern Africa as well as the rebuilding of the infrastructure of the US economy figure among the tasks demanding inputs from the international capital market. The imbalance between the demand and supply of capital tends to drive up the interest rates and to reinforce the instability of the international financial markets.

In these circumstances, there is a dire need to create new sources of funding for various development needs. It is only natural that attention be paid to military expenditures for which the world spent immense sums during the Cold War. Now that the Cold War is supposedly over, there are credible political arguments for cutting down military expenditures and converting military industries into civilian uses. These policies could be acceptable if military allocations were to strengthen national defence against threats by adversaries. With the direct threats melting away, there is no corresponding need to build up military capabilities to thwart them off. If such capabilities were, on the other hand, results of the activities by interest groups and their coalitions, such as the military–industrial complex, the new security environment in great power relations does not necessarily lead to disarmament. On the contrary, the military establishments try to develop arguments for the continuation of high levels of military preparedness.

The idea of tapping the pool of military resources for development purposes is by no means novel, although it might have now gained new policy relevance. Back in 1974 the Soviet Foreign Minister, Andrei Gromyko, suggested that all the permanent members of the UN Security Council reduce their military spending by 10 per cent, and a further 10 per cent out of the sum be transferred to developing countries. The idea refined in the 1980s in the UN debates on disarmament and development ("Disdev") resulted in various proposals to establish a Disarmament Fund for Development. Military budget cut-backs of major powers could be collected into this fund for distribution to the third world. The International Conference on the Relationship between Disarmament and Development, held in 1987 under UN auspices, failed, however, to support these proposals.

A flaw in these suggestions was their mechanical nature. It was assumed that money could be collected by administrative decrees and distributed to those in need. Such a redistributive mechanism is hardly feasible in the reality of international relations. The big military spenders have been traditionally reluctant to cut back their budgets, and even if they have done so, as happens today, they prefer to use the resources so released for domestic purposes. In addition, any redistributive strategies should take the existence of the markets into account and design approaches compatible with them.

Nicole Ball departs from the premise that there is a preference in the international community and, indeed, a need for national military reforms. Such reforms are often opposed by recalcitrant political and military leaders. In order to get reforms moving the international lenders and other relevant actors could use a variety of levers, especially aid and other official financial flows, to spark the change. Ball advocates active initiatives and coordination by the international lenders to promote military reforms by a variety of specific measures. The question is not of her personal advocacy only, but many an international institution may be ripe for a policy change in this regard.

In the future the aid flows will be more dependent on the compliance of the recipients with central arms-control and non-proliferation arrangements, such as the NPT and the MTCR, greater transparency in military allocations, and non-aggression in inter-state relations. Furthermore, such objectives are contemplated not only by the international lending institutions but some governments too have been visibly moving in this direction. Thus, the Japanese government states in its Development Assistance Charter of 30 June 1992 as follows: "full attention should be paid to the trends in recipient countries' military expenditures, their development and production of weapons and missiles of mass destruction, their export and import of arms, etc., so as to maintain and strengthen international peace and stability, and from the viewpoint that developing countries should place appropriate priorities in the allocation of their resources on their own economic and social development." The sentence may be long, but it contains novel elements in the governmental thinking on the preconditions and role of development assistance.

Placing conditions on the granting of aid has been criticized on several counts. It has been pointed out, for instance, that conditionality amounts to the interference in the internal affairs of the recipient country. In addition, it has been observed, relying often on research on the effects of negative economic sanctions, that conditionality may not be an effective policy instrument. Instead, rewards should be used to persuade the recipient to reorient its military and other policies. Dr. Ball deals in detail with these counterarguments and emphasizes the need of dialogue and different forms of cooperation between the lender and the recipient as a precondition for viable results in military reforms. She also prudently recognizes the limits of reward-based strategies.

As a matter of fact, Russia would provide interesting material for a case-study on the possibilities of steering military reforms by external economic aid. Admittedly, Russia is an extreme case because of its great-power status, but this also makes it fascinating. The Western powers aim at dismantling the striking power of Russian strategic weapons (and that of Belarus, and Ukraine as well), reducing its conventional weapons and manpower and converting its military doctrine into a non-offensive one. At the same time, Russia is dependent and is becoming increasingly so, on external economic assistance both from international lending institutions and individual governments. Will these two policies be coupled and aid flows used to promote military reforms in a major Euro-Asian power, and not only in the South?

It seems to me that Dr. Ball overlooks a couple of issues that are pertinent in the debates and policies concerning the relationship be-

319

tween peace and development. The military dominance in national politics is not only related to the allocation of resources between civilian and military purposes, development and production of destabilizing weapons and their exports. The military dominance may also be associated with the other aspect of peace, i.e., human rights, democracy, and repression. Military rulers are usually less inclined than civilian ones to honour various values and commitments intended to permit the self-realization of individuals.

The consideration of this positive aspect of peace leads to new problems in the thinking and action on conditionality. The limitation on military spending, the conversion of military industries, and the ban on weapons exports are all instrumental policies that the lending institutions and the recipient governments can discuss on rational grounds. It is much more difficult to address such value-based issues as human rights, democracy, and repression. To make aid conditional, for example, on compliance with human rights invites, as reality amply shows, complications and conflicts. Even though it is easier to deal with interest-oriented military issues, the question of value standards and norms cannot be omitted either. In effect, the external pressures to give up repression and to promote democracy may have much greater immediate significance for individual citizens in recipient countries than the reductions in military budgets. Weapons do not necessarily kill, but repression does. The Human Development Report 1992 by the United Nations Development Programme (UNDP) has done a major service for the international community by focusing on the human aspects of development.

Another aspect that should not be overlooked in the peace-development debate relates to the shrinking official development aid (ODA). It currently amounts to 0.35 per cent of the combined GNP of the OECD countries compared with the international target of 0.7 per cent. The share of ODA has been declining, in addition, over time, and there are several reasons, such as the long-term recession in most industrial countries and the end of the political competition associated with the Cold War, suggesting that the decline will continue into the 1990s. At the same time, there is an increasing need for development funds in the South. The UNDP report shows, among other things, that the 10 countries in which 72 per cent of the developing countries' poor people live, receive only 27 per cent of all ODA.

It appears that the aid and other development flows will be more discriminatory in the future. The major lending agencies and governments have a greater chance than before of imposing political and humanitarian conditions on the recipient countries. So far, at least some governments in the South have even been able to be lenders to each other and thus formulate the conditions for receiving and utilizing aid. There are now signs that industrial countries are becoming more prone to criticize the policies of recipient governments and dictate the conditions of their aid flows.

This trend seems to suggest that the preconditions for resorting to the politics of conditionality are becoming stronger; conditionality may be used more often and by more governments and new types may be created. In that sense, Nicole Ball touches upon, in her rich paper, an important and relevant topic. The issue is not easy, however. On the other hand, the use of the aid lever to transform the political systems of developing countries to a more democratic, humane, and demilitarized direction, must certainly be welcome.

The results of international pressures to enhance democracy and good governance in individual countries may have been limited, but yet they cannot be neglected. In a sense, the promotion of multi-party elections and their international supervision shows that the world is gradually moving towards common international standards pertaining to democracy and human rights. If these standards are grossly violated the international community can resort to economic sanctions, at it has done in the Serbian case, to punish deviant behaviour.

On the other hand, the growing imbalance between the supply of development funding and the need for it in developing countries can well encourage unilateral and imperial tendencies in the North. The major donors may use development assistance to impose their own political will on the recipients and direct aid to purposes that do not have a priority from economic and humanitarian points of view. In fact, a global covenant should be established on the allocation of development aid for genuine development needs instead of promoting unilateral political or economic interests. The promotion of military reforms by international lending policies is only one and perhaps a rather limited task in this totality.

## 2. Zhu Manli

I have been listening with great interest to the presentations made by Dr. Ball and other speakers over the past two days. I greatly appreciate their valuable efforts to explore ways to advance arms control and disarmament for the common good of mankind, and I have benefited from some of their insights.

I wish to congratulate Dr. Ball for the thought-provoking paper she has prepared and the balanced and non-confrontational approach she favours. I think I can share some of her views, such as the promotion of policy dialogues, etc., and I take no issue with the suggestion of exploring the idea of transparency. However, I find it difficult to embrace the idea of conditionality or the resort to the use of stick and carrot when listening to the discussions over the reduction of military expenditure in developing countries. I believe we should be very careful with the idea of imposing conditions or sanctions because the problem we are facing is not at all simple, rather it is a problem of many dimensions: historical, political, economic, scientific, and technological, etc. Here I would like to emphasize three points.

First, differentiations should be made while deliberating the issue of military outlays. According to the UN Charter, all nations have the right to obtain legitimate self-defence capabilities in order to strengthen their national defences. Therefore, distinctions should be made between legitimate defence needs and excessive arms build-up. While there are cases of unjustifiably high levels of military expenditures in the developing world, many developing countries still lack sufficient defence capabilities to protect their legitimate security interests. The reason why they should make some reasonable defence efforts is not difficult to understand. The post-Cold War world is not tranquil. Despite the fact that the East–West confrontation is over, that some regional issues have been resolved or are tending towards resolution, and that headway has been made in the realm of disarmament, factors of instability still exist today. The international situation is turbulent and volatile due to the serious imbalances of power, the intertwining of contradictions old and new, the existence of hegemony and power politics, and the aggravation of the North–South problem. It is therefore quite natural and beyond reproach that they should make reasonable defence efforts.

By saying so, I do not mean to suggest that developing countries should go beyond their legitimate defence needs and work for excessive arms build-up or high levels of military expenditure. In order to develop their national economies and raise the living standard of their people, all countries, developed or developing, should keep a tight rein on their military spending.

In passing, I would like to say a few words about China's military spending. It has been suggested on several occasions during the discussions that "China's military spending poses a sort of problem to the region and even to the world." But one would find the concern unjustified if the issue is looked at carefully. The Chinese people are working hard to develop their national economy. In order to secure a long-term peaceful international environment, China is pursuing an independent foreign policy of peace. At home it tries hard to concentrate its human, material, and financial resources on economic development. Therefore, since 1985 it has cut down the size of its military forces by one million. It has also kept its military spending at a low level over the past decade. In 1979 its defence spending accounted for 17.5 per cent of government expenditure, which was reduced to 10.5 per cent in 1985, and 8.7 per cent in 1991. Even in absolute terms the defence outlay is limited. In 1992 it is about US$6 billion, much less than that of many other countries. China is opposed to the arms race, and will never go in for excessively high levels of military spending. Some participants asked about a so-called purchase of an anti-aircraft carrier by China. The report that China is buying an anti-aircraft carrier from a certain country is unfounded. China does not have the need nor the intention to do so. Given the eased overall international situation, and relative stability in Asia and the Pacific in particular, China will continue to concentrate its efforts on economic development.

Secondly, while it is commendable to try to curtail excessive military spending, attention should be paid to both the North and the South. Although reductions have been made in some developed countries and are welcome by the people of the world, the lion's share of the world's total military expenditure is taken by the developed world. Countries with the biggest military outlays have special responsibilities in military spending reductions.

Thirdly, as an endless variety characterizes the situations of the nations of the world, arms control and disarmament are sure to undergo a long and arduous progress. All countries, big or small, strong or weak, should work together, on an equal footing, to advance arms control and disarmament through consultation. Therefore, an indiscriminate use of conditionality or resort to the use of stick and carrot will be inappropriate, often impractical, and sometimes turn out to be counter-productive. Such a practice may give rise to tensions in international relations and set up roadblocks to the economic development of developing countries. Caution is well advised in this regard.

# 12

# Economic incentives for demilitarization

Somnath Sen

## I. Introduction

Recent changes in the international political climate, often termed
the end of the Cold War, has brought a rapid transformation in the
realm of arms control. Structural and systemic changes, induced by
political transition and economic difficulties, have led to fast declines
in military expenditure and arms acquisition. Traditional methods of
arms control, such as verifiable treaties, have had lesser impact on
arms reduction compared to fundamental politico/economic changes.
It is clear that such political and economic changes have acted as
inducements or incentives towards arms reductions and possible
demilitarization. Nowhere is this more evident than in the Central
and Eastern European countries where political transformation has
impelled active participation in arms-control treaties and economic
collapse has forced landslide conversion – both contributing to arms
reduction and demilitarization.

Among developing countries the trend is more mixed. On the one
hand, economic and budgetary constraints in the 1980s have been
acute enough to cause rapid falls in defence spending and arms importation even in regions, such as the Middle East, where they have
been excessively high during the last two to three decades. On the

other hand, political changes, although substantial, have been far less significant so that many conflicts (explicit and implicit) still remain. Arms-control treaties, or regional collective security organizations such as the Conference on Security and Cooperation in Europe, are still conspicuous by their absence in the third world. Again, conflict resolution has made impressive gains over the last few years (Ethiopia, Afghanistan, Nicaragua, Cambodia) but incipient conflicts still remain a potential problem for the future (Angola, Afghanistan). Thus, the intrinsic fear remains that demilitarization currently observed among developing nations could be only a temporary phenomenon, at least for some regions and countries. Economic difficulty has been the single most contributory cause and catalyst for reductions in defence spending and arms purchases. Thus the question arises that when economic fortunes improve will arms acquisition rise again? It may not be fortuitous that during the late 1980s the maximum decline in military spending took place in Africa and Latin America – regions suffering the most from economic difficulties. At the same time, the highest regional growth in defence spending occurred in South-East Asia which coincidentally also witnessed the highest growth in per capita income. This phenomenon also calls into question the usual causality that security is relatively independent and exogenous to growth. It could be possible that high growth actually causes defence spending rises (defence is a "luxury" public good with a positive income effect after a threshold), except when there are very specific security and external threats to a country.

If economic factors are indeed crucial in motivating much of military expenditures and defence procurement, then clearly it is important to analyse economic incentives and sanctions that could in principle produce lower militarization. It is of course problematic to define militarization (see Deger, 1986 for a detailed discussion). For the purpose of this paper militarization will be related to a number of "input" measures such as defence spending (or various ratios thereof), arms acquisition through production or importation, and the size of the armed forces. The central issue of this paper is to analyse whether economic incentives can produce demilitarization and what are the problems inherent in such an approach, which tends to interrelate two very distinct concerns. These concerns are those of security and development, which have generally been kept separate in the past in terms of policy formulation – even though conceptually they were both considered important and vaguely interrelated. It is also assumed in the discussion that follows that the incentives and sanctions would come from the major powers (both politically and economically) while the demilitarization and arms reduction will have to be conducted by the developing countries. Thus there is an asymmetric relationship, which incidentally also extends to asymmetric information about possible intentions of various types of countries.

There is a practical problem of classification so that in some of the case-studies below we discuss the former Soviet Union (FSU), which could be a recipient of incentives to speed up demilitarization and therefore in this context is not a major power. However, the general concept of the distinction should be clear. But the framework also raises a much broader question as to whether such an asymmetricity is equitable and indeed efficient. Is it optimal for developing countries to proceed rapidly with demilitarization when military expenditure decline is slow in the OECD countries and the proportion of these countries in the world total arms trade is rising. However, a proper evaluation of this issue is beyond the scope of this paper and will only be briefly touched upon in the very last concluding section.

The framework we need to construct, therefore, has two types of "agents" – the major powers and the developing countries. In the narrow confines of foreign aid these could be called the donors and recipients. The former are concerned, in these analyses, with international development (hence the interest in transfers such as aid or trade concessions) as well as international security (which is believed to be best achieved through lower levels of militarization in developing countries now that superpower and alliance rivalry is over). The latter are concerned with national development (hence the demand for transfers) as well as national security. However, for individual developing countries or even among regional groups (such as ASEAN) it is not the case that lower levels of militarization would necessarily enhance security. Particularly for large and (relatively) rich developing countries the attempt to reduce military spending or arms acquisition could lower perceived security and hence national welfare. There would need to be a compensating increase in foreign aid to counteract this perceived loss of security. For smaller and poorer countries, often threatened by belligerent neighbours, clearly a general regional demilitarization would be welfare enhancing.

A central dilemma, in the search for economic incentives for demilitarization, arises therefore from the fact that a military expenditure increase is often considered to be an input measure of greater security by many developing countries. However, it is also clear that military spending in an adversarial world, either between opposing countries or alliances, exhibits the classic properties of a "prisoner's dilemma game." Concerned only with its own security, each country tends to overspend, compared to the optimum commensurate with the joint security needs of the conflictual parties, as well as their budgetary and economic constraints, simply because the relations with other countries are adversarial. Like most such games, the cooperative solution is preferable in increasing the welfare of both participants. Under viable and verifiable arms-control measures when military spending is reduced by both countries (or in the region), total welfare can increase. This is because the search for common security is enhanced since both countries reduce their threats to each other by cutting defence spending together. At the same time, the resources released from the military towards socio-economic needs increase growth and enhance development. Unfortunately such arms-reduction measures were rare in the past for the major powers and are still uncommon in the developing world except perhaps in Latin America over the last few years. The pursuit of national security alone, through more armaments and forces, reduced the security of the perceived enemy who in turn pursued a similar go-it-alone militarized security policy. This relentless pursuit of military security, whenever economically feasible, sometimes produced deterrence and sometimes threatened peace through an unstable arms race. But it always reduced regional or collective security and also seriously and adversely affected other aspects of security (political, economic). The reasons for not cooperating are familiar both from theoretical game theory as well as experience: mutual distrust, difficulties of communication, lack of an institutional framework, high degree of uncertainty in an area involving national security, major risks in the event of failures, and asymmetric information sets as between the participants.

The central question is how external agencies (such as aid donors, multilateral organizations, the great powers) can provide sufficient *economic* incentives and sanctions that can produce a virtuous cycle of demilitarization, which will also imply a greater level of regional security. For example, there is now quite a widespread discussion among policy makers as to whether foreign aid could and should be utilized as an incentive mechanism to force countries to reduce military spending. It has been suggested (see Schmidt, 1989; McNamara, 1992) that countries with defence spending below 2 per cent of GNP should be given favourable treatment in foreign aid allocation; it is also clear that the obverse side of the issue would be to penalize countries that spend more than 2 per cent, unless pressing security needs can be used to justify their defence burden. The formal and analytical linkages between "defence conditionality" and economic aid are explored in Deger and Sen (1992).

These forms of analyses take a rather narrow view of economic incentives and (de)militarization. On the one hand they focus on economic aid, which is but one, albeit the most important, of a number of instruments available to external governments and agencies. On the other hand, they concentrate on military expenditure alone without looking at related variables such as procurement spending (which could be the most destabilizing), arms imports, or the size of the armed forces. What we should be looking at is really a whole range of incentives and we should also try to construct broader measures of demilitarization. Even if the ultimate policy focus is confined to aid and defence burden, there is no reason why the conceptual discussion should be focused to this narrow point of view. Rather, it may be dangerous to draw broad conclusions from the narrow focus, and the impact of policy could be adverse. This paper therefore attempts to look at the more general problem first and then tries to glean some specific conclusions.

The paper is organized as follows. Section 2 sets out a theoretical framework that has two objectives. First, to look at behaviourial patterns of adversarial developing countries determining their military expenditures in terms of non-cooperative games. Secondly to see how demilitarized outcomes are achievable through either security guarantees or economic incentives. Section 3 analyses the nature and impact of such incentives in terms of five criteria: are they optimal; are they equitable; are they efficient; are they additional; are they affordable. The final section concludes stressing the obligation of the major political and economic powers towards their own demilitarization – otherwise the process could be unsustainable.

## II. An analytical framework

There are two aspects of the analytical framework that need to concern us here. The first relates to the action-reaction mechanism that causes military expenditure expansion in developing countries arms races and are thought to be necessary for the preservation of security. Unless we can understand the reasons why countries spend on the military even though they face major resource constraints it will not be possible to devise incentive-compatible methods of arms control.

Secondly, when countries are locked in adversarial arms races what external agencies can do to alleviate the problem. Both these phenomena can be understood by some simple game theoretic concepts.

The core model has been developed to understand environmental cooperation (see Sandler 1992a, b) but can be easily adapted towards the discussion at hand. Indeed, there are quite a few issues in environmental economics that have close parallels to arms control and can be usefully studied by economists. Consider two countries that believe that military expenditure provides security and hence enhances their social welfare. The aggregate welfare of society depends on economic development and security, both having positive marginal utilities, and is represented by a social welfare function measured in some units. The two countries have the option of reducing defence spending or keeping it at the same initial level. Call these countries, somewhat unimaginatively but without causing offence, countries A and B.

If one country unilaterally reduces military spending both countries can gain (for various reasons) in terms of social welfare, but the demilitarizing country also suffers some losses. So for example, if country A cuts spending on the military by $x$ per cent then it loses 60 units of social welfare in terms of reducing its security and increasing the threat from the other (belligerent) country. Henceforth, all gains or losses or pay-offs will be denoted by numbers signifying units of social welfare. Country A, however, gains 50 from resources reallocated to development. At the same time, this unilateral act of disarmament or demilitarization by A reduces the threat for country B and enhances the latter's security leading to a gain of 50 for B.

The essential point of this simple game theoretic model, which mimics the behaviour of many developing regions' arms races, is that even unilateral military reductions lead to a gain for both participants (for different reasons) and therefore seem a reasonable strategy to employ. However, as the pay-off matrix of table 1 shows, the final outcome is similar to a prisoner's dilemma game. In each of the four boxes of table 1 (labelled I, II, III, IV) are the net gains made by A and B consequent to reducing or maintaining defence spending. In box I, since both countries reduce, their potential net gains or pay-offs are 40: a loss of 60 due to insecurity from own reduction; a gain of 50 from reallocation of resources from own reduction; a gain of 50 due to better security from the reduction of the opposing country. In box II, country A reduces but B does not. Hence, A suffers a net loss of 10 denoted with a minus sign; B gains 50 due to the unilateral

Table 1 **Hypothetical two country game of (de)militarization: Prisoner's dilemma**

|  |  | Country B | |
|---|---|---|---|
|  |  | Reduce defence spending | Maintain defence spending |
| Country A | Reduce defence spending | [I]<br>40, 40 | [II]<br>−10, 50 |
|  | Maintain defence spending | [III]<br>50, −10 | [IV]<br>0, 0 |

measure taken by A. Box III is similar to II with country labels changed. Box IV denotes no change either way.

Now it is clear why the Nash equilibrium will be given by box IV. Consider country A, which is considering each option separately, to either reduce or maintain defence spending, and calculating its net gain or loss given what B can possibly do. If B decides to reduce defence expenditure A should maintain its level (with pay-off 50 in box III) rather than reduce (with pay-off 40 in box I) since the former gives it higher utility. If B decides to maintain its original defence spending then A compares its pay-offs (in box II and IV) and observes that reducing its military expenditures gives it a pay-off of −10 while maintaining the original level for A gives it a pay-off of 0. Hence, in either case A should optimally choose to maintain its military spending and not reduce. Similarly, B chooses in like fashion and does not reduce defence spending. Both countries do the best they can and make optimal choices from their own point of view. Both end up with pay-offs in box IV, no change, while the optimum from a global or supra-national or external coordinator's point of view is clearly box I with pay-offs of 40 each.

It is obvious that this model is simple and the reason for non-cooperation is that neither communicates with each other and accepts policy coordination. I could add uncertainty and probabilistic choices but would be able to get similar conclusions. However, *the model is elemental but not elementary*. There are many instances of stable arms races (see Deger and Sen, 1984) where it is difficult to achieve even modest disarmament simply because of lack of coordination and co-operation. The causes of such an action-reaction mechanism are beyond the scope of this paper but its existence is empirically validated.

Table 2  **Hypothetical two country game of (de)militarization: Impact of incentives**

|  |  | Country B | |
|---|---|---|---|
|  |  | Reduce defence spending [I] | Maintain defence spending [II] |
| Country A | Reduce defence spending | 60, 60 | 10, 50 |
|  | Maintain defence spending | [III] 50, 10 | [IV] 0, 0 |

The central issue here is whether external agencies do have a role to play in transforming this outcome into a more globally optima outcome.

I consider two alternative scenarios where an external agency intervenes. I choose my numbers such that table 2 represents the outcome of the game for both scenarios. In the first case, each country is given a security guarantee by an outside power that by unilaterally reducing its defence spending, its security loss will be less than that depicted in table 1. This time therefore, a country reducing unilaterally its military expenditures will suffer a welfare loss of 40 (rather than 60 as in table 1). The gains remain the same, i.e. reduction by any one country gives a gain of 50 to both countries. Thus in box I of table 2, both A and B potentially reduce and their pay-offs are as depicted (40 loss due to own reduction, 50 gain from own reduction, 50 gain from other's reduction). Now it is clear that the preferred choice for both countries would be given by box I of table 2. When A is deciding on its choice (reduce or maintain), it sees what B could be possibly doing. If B reduces then A should also reduce since its higher pay-off is 60 (box I). If B maintains, then again A should reduce because out of the two alternatives the pay-off for reduction at 10 is higher (box II). Either way, A should reduce and, inverting the names of the countries, B should do likewise. Known, trusted, and verifiable security guarantees that reduced losses in welfare arising from unilateral reductions can overturn the prisoner's dilemma result of table I.

Consider the second scenario, where there is an economic incentive (more foreign aid or trade concessions) for the country willing to reduce its defence spending. If a country unilaterally reduces its military expenditures it loses 60 (due to security and threat) while both countries gain 50. The case until now is similar to table 1. But now if foreign transfers are given as a reward and there is an additional gain of 20 for the reducing country then we get the globally optimum situation depicted in table 2. In box I both countries reduce and their pay-offs are: 50 gain from own reduction; 50 gain from other country reduction; 20 gain from foreign aid or transfer; 60 loss due to greater insecurity; net pay-off is 60. In box II of table 2, country A loses 60 and gains $50 + 20 = 70$ from own reductions alone. Country B makes a net gain of 50 by not changing. And so on for box III and IV. It is easily verified that box I is preferred by both acting individually and non-cooperatively but attaining the global optimum.

The moral is clear. Even if countries refuse to cooperate, or mistrust each other, or act from their own narrow national self-interest, it is possible for incentives to work. These could be either political or economic. The nature of political security guarantees are set out in McNamara (1992) and these are practical policy prescriptions underpinning the foregoing theoretical construct. The nature of economic incentives are issues like foreign aid and defence conditionality that the Development Assistance Committee (DAC) and OECD donors are currently discussing. We analyse the practical problems of economic incentives in the next section.

### III. Economic incentives and demilitarization

As mentioned earlier, there are five criteria by which we could possibly judge the use of economic incentives to foster demilitarization and arms control. Although I analyse economic incentives overall, and do not restrict myself to foreign aid alone even though this is probably the most direct incentive, I shall use the terms "donors" and "recipients" to mean respectively the agents who provide the incentives and those who are expected to demilitarize. These five criteria relate to whether such measures and relationships between donors and recipients are: optimal; efficient; equitable; additional; and finally, affordable. There are obvious overlaps between these concepts but it helps to keep them analytically separate.

It must also be stressed initially that although we often analyse relations between governments, ultimately the central issues in economic and military relationships are about the development and security of people. If the interests of the population in general are hurt due to the misdemeanours of governments then clearly the whole objective of any incentive scheme is destroyed. In particular, if link-ing foreign aid with military spending reductions means that the poor in developing countries are to be denied assistance because their gov-ernment is overtly pursuing a militaristic policy then we have to be extra careful of such policies. This is a classic example of the "micro-macro dilemma" in foreign aid. At the macroeconomic or govern-mental level certain apparently desirable policies are pursued but which could have adverse consequences at the micro-economic or in-dividual level. In all the discussion that follows, this distinction should be kept in mind even though it may not be explicitly mentioned.

Optimality requires that the measures are joint-welfare maximiz-ing, i.e., the interests of both sets of countries are taken into account in policy formulation. The incentive programme may be non-optimal if there is a high risk that the outcome will turn out to be different from what the original intentions were. This could be the case if a single policy instrument of the donor is focused on a single targeted objective that the recipients are expected to attain. Even leaving out the immense practical problem of setting out the precise level of the single target (such as that military expenditure as share of GDP should not rise above 2 per cent) there are analytical difficulties with the narrow focus. At the same time, if donors are only interested in juggling with one economic instrument, say foreign aid, then it is easy to make mistakes.

Consider the case of linking foreign economic assistance with re-ductions in military expenditure shares in GDP – a one target, one instrument example. If there are definitional or measurement errors, which are in any case formidable, then even the definition of defence burden becomes problematic (see appendix 1 of Deger and Sen, 1991). Should domestic military spending include foreign military aid? Should arms imports be added when it is known that procure-ment budgets do not include foreign arms? How should government purchases be priced when the Ministry of Defence could be buying arms from state-owned military enterprises? Should costs of demobi-lization be included in military or civilian budgets? If this ratio is high does this mean that military spending is relatively high or that na-tional income is low? If military spending is relatively stable over time (Deger, 1986) and income could fluctuate due to crop failures or commodity price collapse then how stable is this ratio? Should one take into consideration long-run trends or moving averages? These are all difficult issues and Sen (1990) has a longer discussion. My purpose here is simply to point out that concentrating on one possibly ill-defined target – reduction of the military burden – may not be optimal.

Another problem of course is that countries could accept foreign aid and promise to reduce defence spending and then renege on their promises. This could happen either because perceived security threats are sought to be magnified, or if the need for receiving foreign aid is reduced. This problem, of dynamic inconsistency, arises often in economic transactions when there is asymmetric information between principal (donor) and agent (recipient) and it is difficult to monitor and check on information, perception, and action. The usual method to avoid dynamic inconsistency is through binding pre-commitment, but this is difficult to enforce. In the case of foreign aid this pre-commitment could be the threat of withdrawal. However, it is not easy to withdraw aid. Much of foreign aid could be in sunk costs or irreversible projects which just cannot be easily withdrawn if the recipient reneges. In any case, given the micro-macro dilemma, mentioned above, it is not clear that donors should withdraw midway through projects.

My suggestion is that donors should expand the range of targets or indicators of militarization so that excessive reliance on one or the other does not make the costs of wrong policies excessively high. One way of doing this is to look at a number of indicators simultaneously, such as military expenditure share of GDP, defence expenditure share of total government expenditure or in relation to key socio-economic expenditures such as on health and education, arms trade as a proportion of total international or third world weapons importation and (to capture the public good nature of security) defence spending per capita.

One important step would be to construct a demilitarization index which would be a composite index, aggregating over the various measures just mentioned, so that countries could be compared with each other or across time to see the progress they are making in reducing militarization. Similar to the UNDP Human Development Index, a relative demilitarization index (DMI) can be constructed which aggregates over a number of targets that donors wish to monitor.

The DMI would be defined by the following equation for any country labelled $j$:

$$\text{DMI}_j = 1 - \left\{ \frac{1}{n} \sum_{i=1}^{n} I_{ij} \right\}$$

where $I_{ij}$ is a relative measure of militarization defined for country $j$ and militarization indicator $i$. Therefore:

$$I_{ij} = \left\{ \frac{X_{ij} - X_i^{opt}}{X_i^{max} - X_i^{opt}} \right\}$$

where $X_{ij}$ is some militarization indicator $i$ for country $j$, $X_i^{opt}$ is the optimum value of that indicator, as defined by the donors, and $X_i^{max}$ is the maximum value within the sample set. The relative measure $I_{ij}$ should be positive and vary between 0 and 1. Therefore, if any country has its $X_{ij}$ *less* than the optimum then the corresponding $I_{ij}$ is set equal to zero. Defined in this fashion, the DMI can take a maximum value of 1 (all $I_{ij}$ equals zero) or a minimum value of zero (all $I_{ij}$ equals unity).

Consider the 2 per cent rule suggested by Schmidt (1989). Here the militarization indicator is the defence expenditure share in GDP. The optimum value is 2 per cent. Let the maximum value of the military burden among the set of countries being considered for economic aid and incentives be 10 per cent. Suppose a specific country has a military burden of 4 per cent. Then the corresponding militarization indicator, $I_{ij}$ is 0.25. If the country under consideration spent 2 per cent or less the indicator equals zero and therefore the contribution to the DMI is the highest. If that country spent 10 per cent, i.e., the maximum, then the value of the $I_{ij}$ would be 1 and the contribution to the DMI would be the lowest. In similar fashion one could consider $X_{ij}$ to be the share of defence in central government expenditure (or as a proportion of health and education expenditures); the share of arms imports in total third world arms imports; log of per capita military spending. Clearly, for tractability the number of indicators of militarization (the variable $n$ in the DMI) should not be too large but certainly should be greater than 1 or 2. Defining the value of $X_{ij}^{opt}$ for each indicator is a matter of further research, as are also refinements to the index necessary in the presence of measurement errors.

The general argument is that targets should be widened and their numbers increased if optimal policy rules are to succeed. Parallel to this is the corresponding widening of the menu of incentives. Simply focusing on foreign aid, as has been the case with recent policy discussions, is again non-optimal. The range of policy options available to the so-called donors are large and there could be substitution among them. This could also alleviate the contentious issue of burden sharing. If one country can contribute more in one area of incentives and less in another then clearly there would be less criticism of who is not paying fair shares.

Therefore, economic incentives should encompass the following types of measures. Direct payments, independent of all other considerations, for countries going through the phase of demilitarization such as after a systemic change in regime (as in Central and Eastern Europe) or after a war (as in Southern Africa) or after conflict resolution (as in Central or Latin America). These payments could be for industrial conversion of military industries (as in the European Bank for Reconstruction and Development plans to aid Soviet conversion) or for the elimination of weapons of mass destruction. These payments could be money paid to former soldiers who are being demobilized at the cessation of hostilities but require special attention due to the potential for future civil conflict. The Swedish International Development Agency has indeed initiated some schemes but far more needs to be done. In particular, the expertise and skills required for such programmes need to be built up. It must be stressed that such direct transfers for demilitarization go far beyond the standard issues of economic assistance and therefore require special attention and a different framework.

A particularly special case deserves some attention. This refers to the US foreign assistance from its defence budget to the FSU for the elimination of weapons of mass destruction as well as the control of proliferation by giving employment to nuclear scientists to stay in their own countries rather than migrate with their deadly skills. This is quite a dramatic example of the incentive–demilitarization nexus from the point of view of the US government. In fiscal year (FY) 1992, $500 million (dollars are US dollars) were allocated from the US defence budget for weapons destruction and humanitarian aid (Deger, 1993) for the FSU. Most of the aid will go for eliminating weapons of mass destruction (such as nuclear weapons) as also to provide employment for unemployed scientists who could migrate to unstable countries and increase the dangers of proliferation. The incentive here is clearly working in favour of demilitarization. However, the amount is so little compared to both the demand for such economic incentives as well as in relation to total US foreign aid that its impact is not significant from the point of view of arms reduction.

The second measure could be trade concessions, within the multilateral framework set up by GATT regulations. Already Most Favoured Nation (MFN) status is being linked to non-economic criteria such as human rights. These could be extended to countries facing special problems due to attempted demilitarization. In the same way, regional economic cooperation could be utilized as an incentive for countries wishing to shed their military past. Clearly, economic considerations would be the most important criterion for entry into say ASEAN or NAFTA, but it is time, in the changing world order, to include political factors more directly into the entry negotiations. One special area, where far more attention will be focused in the coming years, is in the protection of the environment. Here the process of militarization is intricately linked to environmental conflicts. A very flexible set of measures would be needed for environmental conflict resolution and the prevention of environmental tensions erupting into open hostilities.

Clearly the most important incentive is foreign aid (Tinbergen, 1990) and we do not wish to minimize its major role. The basic issues regarding optimum aid policy in the presence of "defence conditionality" are discussed in detail in Deger and Sen (1991, 1992b). Practical policy measures, as to how one can design optimum policies, are also presented in those papers. Here I simply wish to stress that fungibility of aid remains a major issue. If economic aid is increased, under the promise of demilitarization, then it is possible that some leakages could occur since countries feel that their security and national welfare has decreased. Thus there is an incentive for recipients to avoid stringent conditions and the control of fungible resources is difficult to monitor for the donors.

Another point to note is that substantial military aid is still provided to developing countries, overwhelmingly by the United States, and this sustains the trade in arms, which is a major cause of third world militarization. For the United States, in FY 1993, development and humanitarian assistance requested by the President's budget authority was $8.4 billion while security assistance (which also includes some economic aid) was about $7.4 billion. Around one-third of US aid is for predominantly military purposes and this is a major stimulus to the trade in arms. Although there has been considerable change in intentions, not much has changed in terms of actual policy in the US foreign aid programmes in terms of the interrelationships between economic and security relations with allies. The Congressional Budget Office puts this succinctly:

As the world has changed during the last three years, so have the stated goals of the US foreign aid program. Instead of strengthening security relationships, they now emphasize strengthening democracy and promoting

337

market economies. In meeting these new goals, however, the Administration relies on existing programs. Funding levels of the proposed budget for most programs differ only marginally from current levels. The request remains oriented towards the Middle East and southern Europe. (CBO, 1992)

The central issue is that arms sales can make profits to beleaguered defence industries and replace declining domestic procurement with additional foreign demand. So, from the individual firm's point of view there are few negative externalities. Rather, if defence technology exhibits increasing returns then an increase in output (sales) will bring down the unit price, making it more attractive to more potential buyers. It is the government which has to deal with the adverse security implications of arms sold abroad. When the government's security interests are identified with militarization and rearmament then clearly there is little chance of active arms transfer control to succeed. Essentially, *economic incentives could be used for militarization* rather than the stated objective of this topic, i.e. economic incentives for demilitarization.

On the other hand, there are also recent examples where the US administration has used the leverage of economic incentives to foster arms control. In FY 1993 both Pakistan and the Philippines are to receive less security assistance compared to previous years, reflecting for the former country the Administration's displeasure at the nuclear weapons programme while for the latter country the fact that Clark and Subic Bay US military bases are to be closed. For Pakistan this could lead to a re-evaluation of the utility of being a nuclear threshold state and thus reducing defence spending on possible nuclear arms; while for the Philippines it will imply lower long-term domestic expenditures required to maintain the infrastructural facilities in the neighbourhood of the bases.

The second criterion for judging economic incentives for demilitarization is that of efficiency. Clearly, the choice of efficient policy is related to the previous discussion on optimality. There are two reasons for wanting developing countries to spend less on the military and arms imports. The first relates to the enhancement of regional security and the second relates to the release of resources for developmental purposes. In a first best situation it is efficient to target security policy towards demilitarization and economic policy towards resource increase. However, in a constrained second best situation such clear-cut targeting may not be possible due to the interaction between targets and policy instruments. Thus the use of economic incentives could be efficient. However, the role of security guarantees are also important and developing countries, who feel genuinely threatened by foreign military forces or internal insurrections, should be provided with some form of security protection. Only then will the economic incentives and sanctions work efficiently.

In terms of equity, the distinction made earlier between peoples and governments, a specific example of the micro-macro dilemma, needs to be remembered. If a government is highly militarized and it is punished through the reduction of foreign transfers then it is the people who might ultimately suffer. At the macroeconomic level the leverage of foreign transfer or incentive may produce some benefits if successful; however, at the micro-economic level the costs of failure of such a leverage might mean misery for the people who were the final beneficiaries of the transfer. The probabilities of success and failure in implementing such policies must be estimated as well as the gains and losses that could accrue to different sets of agents (the government and the people). Policy makers therefore need to calculate the expected (or probability weighted) pay-off of the policy.

In addition, the reduction of foreign transfers due to sanctions could exacerbate government budget constraints. It is not clear what category of government expenditure exhibits resilience. But there is some evidence that when aggregate spending by governments is reduced then economic or developmental expenditures and their share are reduced the most, while the share of defence in the budget remains stable. Thus the threat of sanctions might produce a reduction in developmental finance that could be counter-productive for long-run development. Certainly, such measures will be inequitable from the point of view of the population concerned even if it does harm the recipient government.

The next criterion, particularly important for the recipients, is whether all these new initiatives would lead to additional resources. The issue of additionality is particularly important in the case of economic assistance. In a sense the proposed set of extra conditionality will increase the "price" or "cost" of foreign aid and could well lead to a change in the supply and demand functions of economic assistance from abroad. If for example the "price" of foreign aid for each level of supply is raised through additional conditionality the supply function will shift upwards and the final equilibrium will lead to a loss of "consumer's surplus." Unless additional resources are provided to compensate for such a loss the recipients in aggregate would be worse off. It is also possible to think of an impasse, where

339

governments of major recipients refuse such terms because aid levels are too low in any case to compensate for security losses and major donors are concerned about the adverse impact on the recipient economy in general if sanctions are imposed. It is therefore imperative that additional resources are provided and foreign aid volumes are substantially increased to provide true incentives. It is certainly possible in the current political climate to reduce military spending in the major donor countries – which are also the largest military spenders in the world – and to use at least some proportion of freed resources to expand foreign economic aid programmes, albeit with stricter controls.

There is a great need for much higher levels of foreign transfers through aid to mitigate the impact of additional tying of aid towards the security criterion. At the same time, the future will see new demands for aid not only from newly independent countries (such as in the FSU), but also from new concerns such as environmental protection and preserving minimum levels of environmental security. The final question is whether these levels are affordable from the donor's point of view. At a time of international budgetary constraints it is indeed difficult to talk about affordability since the initial reaction would be negative. Indeed, there is a general pessimism about increasing government-to-government transfers arising out of military expenditure cuts among the major powers; the UN World Economic Survey 1992 claims that the peace dividend has vanished. However, the various costing of the disarmament or peace dividend shows that the potential for freeing resources does indeed exist. Even realistic assessments (see Deger and Sen, 1990a; Sen, 1991; Deger, 1992) imply that foreign aid allocations can rise somewhat from international demilitarization although not on the grandiose scale projected by, for example, the Human Development Report 1991.

Instead of doing another round of costing on the peace dividend, I will go the other way and show by comparison the cost of war. The purpose is to demonstrate that the international economy spent a considerable amount of financial and physical resources during the short-lived Gulf War because the political will existed. If then the world is serious about using economic incentives to further the cause of peace then a similar political will is required. Spending for war is always easier than spending for peace but asymmetricity should not be so large.

Just as the long-term peace dividend is slow in coming, the cost of modern wars is becoming increasingly prohibitive. The total cost of the Gulf War has been extremely high even though estimates are still imprecise. In addition to the usual military and war related expenditures there are also the economic opportunity costs. Alternative estimates have been made in 1991 about the possible economic implications of the Gulf crisis on developing countries. A report (ODI, 1991) by the London-based Overseas Development Institute claimed:

at least 40 low and middle income countries suffered an impact of more than 1% of GNP; 16 of them over 2%, including countries as distinct from the Gulf as Jamaica and Paraguay. The Indian states of Kerala and Gujarat, with a population over 70 million, would join them, if they were separate countries. The total direct cost for low income countries is at least 3.2 billion dollars, when lower middle income countries are included, it is at least 12 billion dollars.

The International Monetary Fund (IMF, 1991), in its analysis of the costs of the crisis and the impact of post-war reconstruction claims: "Thus, for the world as a whole the combined effect of the war in the Middle East and reconstruction will be a substantial net budgetary cost, thereby reducing the supply of saving that otherwise would have been available to finance investment in new capital goods." According to IMF estimates, the Gulf crisis caused a fall in GDP of all net debtor countries of the world taken together, amounting to 1.1 per cent of their GNP. The maximum losses suffered were in the debtor countries of the Middle East (including Iraq, Jordan, Egypt, and Yemen) whose GNP in total fell from baseline projections by about 23.1 per cent. According to my own estimates the fall in GDP, for the world as a whole, would be about $30 to $35 billion in 1991 alone. In addition, the cost of the war, for the Allied forces, itself would be around $50 to $60 billion, most of which was spent for Operation Desert Storm. Table 3 gives some data of allied contributions to the war and an indication of the costs of the US war effort. These are conservative estimates; press reports claim that the cost of financing the war was in the region of $80 to $100 billion. Even without costing the reconstruction of Kuwait and Iraq as well as the military spending and value of weapons losses for Iraq, which are not known, the total costs (economic and military) comes to *at least $80 billion and possibly $95 billion*. If these unidentified elements are included, given the vast destruction of this conflict, the total monetary cost could easily exceed $100 billion.

It is instructive to note how far these vast sums of money would go towards the promotion of sustainable development. At the United

341

Table 3  **Cost of Operation Desert Shield/Desert Storm Gulf War (figures are in US$bn)**

| Country contribution | Cost |
|---|---|
| Saudi Arabia | 16.8 |
| Kuwait | 16.1 |
| UAE | 4.1 |
| Japan | 10.0 |
| Germany | 6.5 |
| Korea | 0.4 |
| USA | 7.1 |
| Total | 61.1 |

Source: Annual Report to the President and the Congress by the US Secretary of Defense, February 1992 (USGPO 1992).

Nations Conference on Environment and Development (UNCED) at Rio in June 1992 the major constraint seemed to be financial transfers from the North to the South for environmental protection. The maximum that the OECD countries could promise was an additional $10 billion in foreign aid for environmental protection; this is about one-sixth of the sum that the major powers alone spent in the Gulf War of 1991. The World Bank (1992) estimates that environmental protection for the South would require by the year 2000 a sum of resources equivalent to 1.4 per cent of combined developing countries' GDP. Using the same estimated ratio for the early 1990s a sum of around $50 billion may be required for global protection. The Gulf War costs could have financed two years of such resource use for the whole third world. In addition, physical resource transfers, for example from military to civilian R&D (Deger and Sen, 1990b) could considerably help the needs of environment protection.

## IV. Concluding remarks

This paper has proposed a basic framework within which economic incentives as a tool for demilitarization can be studied. It has argued that the range of policy instruments needs to be widened. More care is necessary to define indices of (de)militarization in developing countries. The policy set has to be equitable and efficient and should try to take into account the interests of both developing and developed countries. If foreign aid is to be used for such non-economic purposes, thus raising its cost to recipients, the total volume of economic assistance needs to be raised substantially as a compensating variation. Finally, the macro-micro dilemma has to be addressed, i.e. in an attempt to punish or reward governments the population of the country should not suffer in the process.

The paper's principal focus has been the donor–recipient relationship. However, much of international militarization – in terms of the indicators just discussed – are concentrated in the advanced industrial nations of the world. There have to be symmetric adjustments in both North and South. Otherwise, the divisions in political perceptions will widen and will match the divisions in economic performance. In addition, the growing commercialization of political relations means that contradictory policies could be pursued. For example, at the same time as developing countries of the South are asked to demilitarize there is greater emphasis by arms suppliers of the North to buy subsidized weapons due to the domestic crisis of the defence industries. Even within the South the fastest growing or richer developing countries will suffer the least if sanctions are imposed. Unless the rewards are particularly high the gainers will not have received sufficient benefits. In a global context, such hardening of the terms of transfers without a corresponding rise in the volume of transfers, could be counter-productive in the long run. Hence the paper ends with a plea: if economic incentives are to be used effectively for world peace and security, and there is great scope for doing so, the content and volume of incentives must be expanded.

# References

Congressional Budget Office (CBO) (1992). *An Analysis of the President's Budgetary Proposals for Fiscal Year 1993*. CBO, Washington, D.C.

Deger, S. (1986). *Military Expenditure in Third World Countries: The Economic Effects*. Routledge & Kegan Paul, London.

—— (1992). "The disarmament dividend: Problems and prospects." Paper prepared for UNICEF.

—— (1993). "World military expenditure." In *SIPRI Yearbook 1993: World Armaments and Disarmament*. Oxford University Press, Oxford.

Deger, S., and Sen, S. (1984). "Optimal control and differential game models of military expenditure in less developed countries." *Journal of Economic Dynamics and Control* 7.

—— (1990a). *Military Expenditure: The Political Economy of International Security*. Oxford University Press, Oxford.

—— (1990b). "The re-orientation of military R&D for civilian purpose." In J. Rotblat and F. Blackaby, eds., *Towards a Secure World in the 21st Century Annals of Pugwash 1990*. Taylor and Francis, London.

—— (1991). "Military expenditure, foreign aid and economic development." Paper prepared for the *World Bank Annual Conference on Development Economics*, Washington, D.C., April.

—— (1992a). "World military expenditure." In *SIPRI Yearbook 1992: World Armaments and Disarmament*. Oxford University Press, Oxford.

—— (1992b). "Military expenditure, aid and economic development." *Proceedings of the World Bank Annual Conference on Development Economics 1991*. The World Bank, Washington, D.C.

Hewitt, D.P. (1991). "Military expenditure: International comparison of trends." *International Monetary Fund WP/91/54*, IMF, Washington, D.C.

*Human Development Report 1991* (1991). United Nations Development Programme, New York 1991.

International Monetary Fund (IMF) (1991). *World Economic Outlook*, IMF, Washington, D.C.

McNamara, R.S. (1992). "The post-Cold War world: Implications for military expenditure reductions in the developing countries." *Proceedings of the World Bank Annual Conference on Development Economics 1991*. The World Bank, Washington, D.C.

ODI (1991). *The Economic Impact of the Gulf Crisis on Third World Countries*. Report of the Overseas Development Institute. The World Development Movement, Oxford.

Sandler, T. (1992a). *Collective Action: Theory and Applications*. Harvester Wheatsheaf, UK.

—— (1992b). "After the cold war, secure the global commons." *Challenge* 35, July/August.

Schmidt, H. (1989). *Facing One World: Report of the Independent Group on Financial Flows to Developing Countries*. United Nations University Tokyo.

Sen S. (1990). "Military expenditure data: methods and measurement." *World Bank Research Symposium on Military Expenditure*. Washington, D.C., December.

—— (1991). "Debt and international security." In *SIPRI Yearbook 1991: World Armaments and Disarmament*. Oxford University Press, Oxford.

—— (1992). "The economics of conversion: Transforming swords to ploughshares." In G. Bird, ed., *Economic Reform in Eastern Europe*. Edward Elgar, Aldershot, UK.

Tinbergen, J. (1990). *World Security and Equity*. Edward Elgar, Aldershot, UK.

*United Nations World Economic Survey 1992*. United Nations, New York.

World Bank (1992). *World Development Report 1992: Development and Environment*. World Bank, Washington, D.C.

# Comments on chapter 12

**Mihály Simai**

The paper has been an important and interesting contribution to the discussion. The main theoretical and practical issues of the paper are and will be for some time in the centre of international debate. Could economic incentives be resulting in major international moves toward demilitarization, what exactly are those incentives, and how strong are they in different countries? In searching for the answers, Somnath Sen develops a model in which two types of countries exist: two agents, the major powers and the developing countries. He concentrates on the problems of the developing world.

In my comments I am going to look at the issues from a different perspective. In my view, in order to understand the role of economic incentives for demilitarization, it is necessary to understand to what extent economic factors comprised incentives for militarization in general, and especially in the developing countries. In order to find the appropriate answers one must of course clarify or define the concept of militarization. In *Webster's Dictionary*, militarization is defined in two ways: to equip with armies or prepare for war psychologically and militarily. Even from the brief definitions given by *Webster's* it is evident that militarization is a multidimensional process with political, ideological, techno-economic, and institutional components.

In its political and ideological dimensions, militarization has often been considered as a cult of the military, an advocate of violence, and a manipulator of society in the interests of the military establishment. In human history different ideologies "incorporated" militarization and militarism and in certain regimes they have been practised from cradle to grave.

In economic terms of militarization one should differentiate first of all between the macroeconomics and micro-economics of militarization. In macroeconomic perspectives militarization has meant the redistribution of incomes through the budget in favour of the defence sectors, including the army and its related institutions and the military–industrial complexes. In micro-economic perspectives militarization has meant a production and consumption system, which has functioned outside the framework of the normal market relations and developed its own logic and motivation.

In its institutional dimension, militarization has meant the subordination of different non-military institutions (education, research, propaganda, parliaments, local governments etc.) to the interests and needs of the military. This process in many cases is accompanied by an atmosphere of suspicion and secrecy practised in hierarchical, dictatorial regimes.

Among the macroeconomic incentives of militarization in the developed industrial countries, the role of defence expenditures as "automatic" or built-in stabilizers has been emphasized (especially in the United States) eliminating the spectre of secular stagnation. The high profits, the high level of employment, the large number of sub-contractors have been mentioned among the most important micro-economic incentives. (In the United States in the mid-1980s there were 37,000 prime contractor firms, over 100,000 subcontractors, three million people employed in defence industries and allied laboratories, one million direct civilian employees of the Department of Defense, and two million in the uniformed armed forces.

The economy (and the society) of the highly militarized nations has been paying of course a very high price. It has been evident that the high burden of defence expenditures played a major role in ruining the economy of the Soviet Union and in its dismemberment. The other country which has been paying a high socio-economic price for militarization is the United States. The large and unmanageable budgetary deficit, the international indebtedness of that country, the erosion of her international competitive position, the distortion of the R&D sector have been some of the adverse macroeconomic consequences. Seymour Melman, one of the American experts and critics of militarization, wrote in the preface of his book *The Permanent War Economy* in 1974:

Traditional economic competence of every sort is being eroded by the state capitalist directorate that elevates inefficiency to a national purpose, that disables the market system, that destroys the value of the currency, and that diminishes decision power of all institutions other than its own. Industrial productivity, the foundation of every nation's economic growth, is being eroded by the relentlessly predatory effects of military economy. (Melman, 1985)

The non-economic dimension and incentives for militarization in the developing countries have been even stronger than in the industrial world. First of all the two opposing military blocks and the global nature of their confrontation extended their military interests and strategies to their client states in the developing world. The disappearance of this factor from global politics in the post-Cold War era may become a disincentive for militarization in the future.

The share of the developing countries in the total global military expenditures has been about 20 per cent on average in the past 20 years. Extreme forms of militarization in the developing world took place in the military dictatorial regimes, where the army had practically unlimited power over society. The post-World War II era produced some of the worst military dictatorial regimes in human history (in certain cases one or another external power provided active support for them).

The answer to the question, what are the economic incentives for militarization in the developing countries, would require a convincing answer to another question: how large armies and defence expenditures could be justified by "legitimate security interests" and "not excessive" in those countries? In the present world however, where there are not yet strong and credible intentional multilateral security guarantees, it is almost impossible to give a concrete answer. But what is the tolerable level? Any country which increases its spending on the military has to decide on the incidence of the increases on other items, like social expenditures, productive investments, or in the increase of budgetary revenues through higher taxes. The macroeconomic implications of increasing military expenditures in the developing countries are even more detrimental from the point of view of socio-economic development than in the industrial world.

The fact that in most of the developing countries, the proportion of defence expenditures declined in the total budget during recent years was however not the consequence of the general recognition of this reality. There was a rather unconventional incentive: the increase of interest payments. Beyond the external and internal political needs, there are also rather important micro-economic interests, pressures, and incentives for the increase of military expenditures in the developing countries.

1. The armies of developing countries constitute a built-in force and a source of constant pressure for the increase of defence expenditures, even without an apparent enemy, or external conflict. As they are still the only central, organized, and most efficient institutions in many countries, they are able to achieve the increases. The importance of the armies in the stabilization of power for the local élite is also a key factor which strengthens the role of the military. The armies of the developing countries are increasingly costly. They are no longer barefoot guerilla armies. The example of high-tech armies of the developed world has increasingly influenced their arsenal.

2. According to NATO data, about half of the defence expenditures is spent on salaries. The data about the structure of defence expenditure in the developing countries has been sporadic and uncertain. There is however enough evidence that the army as a source of income for its members and for the local enterpreneurs who supply goods and render services could be a relatively important micro-economic incentive for sustaining high defence expenditures.

3. The arms trade has created a strong interconnected lobby, which includes local and foreign military, politicians, local enterpreneurs and international arms merchants and producers. The end of the Cold War did not terminate the arms trade or the era of client states. There are dangers that in the world of close to 200 states where the length of the frontiers is on the increase and there are many new sources of "small conflicts," the spread of military production capacities may increase the number of arms suppliers and their client states. New dependent regimes may emerge in the arms market, restructuring, in fact regionalizing, the arms business.

I agree of course with Somnath Sen that strong economic incentives must be created through different channels but I do not consider the economic incentives only as sufficiently strong and efficient instruments for demilitarization. He correctly states: "spending for war is always easier than spending for peace," and the asymmetry between the two should not be so large. I stress however, that the incentives for demilitarization should not be confined to economic sticks and carrots only. The causes and the symptoms of militarization must be attacked simultaneously.

In the world of the late twentieth century it is also necessary that a global framework of collective security should support the economic incentives. These include:

1. an agreement of the main military powers of the world on a comprehensive programme of demilitarization;
2. a network of global agreements which would promote progress towards a more equitable and democratic system of international cooperation;
3. firm and credible guarantees for the security of all nations against the new large, medium, and small power games. Those guarantees must be supported by sufficiently strong global and regional institutions which combine moral pressure, "forceful persuasion," and if needed rapidly deployable military forces.

A reformed UN system may develop all those instruments.

# Reference

Melman, Seymour (1974 rev. edn. 1989). *The Permanent War Economy*. Simon and Schuster, New York.

# 13

# Arms reduction in the Middle East: Between credibility and illusion

Amin Hewedy

## I. Introduction

The end of the Cold War altered the basic principles of the old international order based on the balance of power and mutual nuclear deterrence between the United States and the USSR. Strangely, it ended in a lukewarm peace in contrast with the cold peace that usually follows a hot war. There was no act of capitulation as in Compiègne in 1918 or in Rheims in 1945.[1] Because the Cold War ended peacefully, both the victors and the vanquished hoped for a new world order based on coordination and mutual dependence more than contradiction and enmity. This new trend was examined in the Gulf crisis caused by the Iraqi invasion of Kuwait on 2 August 1990. The pre-war preparations to build the coalition under Operation Desert Shield showed a new unprecedented international trend for cooperation under a common purpose.

On 16 January 1991, Operation Desert Shield took effect, and in his speech announcing the hostilities President George Bush spoke about a "New World Order where the rule of law governs the conduct of nations and in which a credible United Nations can use its peace-keeping role to fulfil the promise and the vision of the UN's founders."

The speech brought hopes all over the world despite the ambiguity of the "New World Order" the President spoke about. It was vague and undefined. Yet there was a feeling that the world order depending on the balance of power will be replaced by a world order of community of power – the combination of all against the wrongdoer. All nations are expected to respond to challenges to international order from a common perspective and by united opposition.

But as time passed, hopes began to fade and nations, particularly in the Middle East, started to compare slogans and declarations on one hand and actions and policies on the other. The world is still living in turbulence and distinctions among its various districts, if we look at it as a big unified city. The Middle East is one of the most unstable districts in the world, with wars among states, violence inside states, encroachment on vital interests, and different regional hegemonies. In spite of that the different states consider legitimacy as an important base of world order, yet each state measures this in the manner in which it serves its vital interests, thus overlooking the interests of others. Some look at legitimacy through history, others through geography and geopolitics. Some consider force as a means, others consider justice, moderation, and mutual understanding as tools.[2] The region exists in strange and insecure situations where right is always enforced to be confronted by a might that imports its tools from the central states by arms and technology transfer.

## II. The real contemporary international order

Calling the contemporary international order a new order is not accurate or factual because we have to raise two questions: new in what? and new for whom? In the bipolar order the world used to live under *détente* on the basis of mutual nuclear deterrence which excluded direct confrontations between the big powers, as this meant the end of the world. But at the same time it permitted direct confrontations by using force in regional conflicts which are wars by proxy, in reality because of the arms and technology transfer from the centre to the periphery. But after the drastic changes that happened after the fall of the Soviet Union as a state, and communism as a doctrine, the world has to live under *entente*. *Détente* is an agreement between powers with different interests while *entente* is an agreement between powers with common interests. This does not mean the end of regional confrontations by using force, nor the end of conflicts on international or regional levels which President Richard Nixon calls

351

"Perfect Peace,"[3] because this is merely an illusion. The globe will live in "real peace" which means living with conflicts and crises and trying to solve them by using every means available at regional level; at the same time excluding the use of force on the international level.

The main cause of the Middle East turbulence was crisis management, or enforcing the status quo through the imbalance of forces using three dangerous means: arms transfer to build suitable polarization to serve the big powers' interests, technological transfer to control the direction of events, and capital transfer for completely vanquishing the region. Enforcing stability or even peace on the basis of the imbalance of forces is merely an illusion because the result is always either bad agreements or continuous encroachments. Bad agreements are temporary because the balance of forces between the signatories can be changed on one side and because they do not remove the main causes of the conflict on the other side. Real peace cannot be achieved except under wise agreements based on the balance of interests as well as the balance of forces. In such agreements, the individual state sacrifices some of its interests in favour of the collective interests and security of all the regional players.[4] The situation in the Middle East is still disturbed and gloomy in spite of the trials done after the Madrid Conference in 1991. In spite of the goodwill of all players, arms and technological transfers for achieving peace will not prevent the selective enforcement of the Security Council's resolutions. What is permissible for one state is prohibitory on others. Regional stability cannot be fulfilled under a nuclear umbrella, weapons of mass destruction, "conventional-plus"[5] superiority, conventional arsenals, or an imbalance of forces. The Palestinians, for example, are fighting their "Intifada" with stones against the formidable weaponry of "Zahal." Stability can be achieved only through incomplete satisfaction of the regional states on the basis of mutual security, controlling diffusion of power, and abolishing – not encircling – the real causes of conflicts. Central stability – even after the dissolution of the Soviet Union – will be merely an illusion as long as regional instability lasts. It will be possible to build a new international order if accurate answers can be given to the following questions:

1. What does security mean? It is complete security for one regional state? Or mutual security for all regional states? Is it by annexing territories or by normalizing relations with one's neighbours on the basis of justice?

2. Justice. Is it to the mighty? Or to the right?
3. Balance of forces? Or balance of interests?
4. Legitimacy? Is it enforced regionally on the basis of parity or enforced selectively?
5. Self-determination to the people without a territory? Or to the people on their land?
6. Arms reduction or arms control to all regional states? To certain states in the region?

Unless the contemporary international order is changed from a regional viewpoint, it will remain:

1. chaotic and anarchic where international law will be ebbing away;
2. merely an order of the giants against the pygmies and the rich against the poor;
3. believing in power and force, respecting the status quo, and undermining historical rights. Legitimacy is the product of might not of right.

A great and drastic strategic change occurred after the collapse of the USSR. Regional friends and antagonists are aligned side by side under the American umbrella. According to this new relationship, the role of the United States changed from an accelerator to that of a mediator, to a partner, and now to the main director of all regional crises.

## III. Arms and technology transfer in the bipolar order

In the bipolar international order which faded with the collapse of the Soviet Union, and under the nuclear balance which existed, it was impossible for the two big powers to change the equilibrium in the central regions, leaving only one course to fulfil this in the periphery. The Middle East was and still is one of the most important regions for any global strategy. This fact led to the fearful arms race, and polarization to change the regional balance to benefit the central powers, to build some regional clients into becoming regional big powers, in order to defend the big powers' interests by proxy and the management of crisis on the basis of the rivalry between the two big powers without underestimating the real causes of regional conflicts. According to this strategy, American foreign policy was based on three main pillars:

1. it was not permissible for Soviet arms to match US arms in regional conflicts;

2. to build Israel as a big regional power through sophisticated arms and technology transfer, and strategic agreements to deepen their mutual cooperation in security fields;
3. crisis management through the changes in the balance of power using the strategy of linkage with other conflicts in different parts of the world.

Accordingly arms sales became the chief means of diplomacy as arms transfer had a greater impact on changing policies than assisting in building dams or giving economic aid, and was certainly more lucrative. The US arms delivery to some Arab States[6] ensured the technological gap with Israel because the US deliveries to Tel-Aviv were more sophisticated and on easier terms. The American arms deliveries to the Arabs were for cash and were in fact used to reduce the unit cost of defence items for the United States by recycling petrodollars and extending production runs, as well as spreading development outlays. Every one billion dollars' worth of exported weapons saves the Pentagon $70 million in unit costs. That means the Pentagon gains $700 million out of the $1 billion worth of arms the Saudis import annually.

So the US arms-transfer policy was a key strategy aimed at controlling the region and preventing the Soviets from making a breakthrough by weakening the Arabs and at the same time strengthening Israel. Hereunder is an excerpt from the US Presidential Directives which consolidate these ideas. Arms transfer can:[7]

a. demonstrate that the US has enduring interest in the security of its friends and partners and that it will not allow them to be at a military disadvantage.
b. foster regional and internal stability, thus encouraging peaceful resolution of disputes noting whether the transfer is consistent with US interests in maintaining stability within the regions where friends of America have different objectives.
c. First-line-systems may not suit the needs of many countries and this leads to the concentration on adaptations of military equipment for sale abroad.[8]

*Under this directive many regional wars and invasions took place, and the regions lived with instability and encroachments.*

The Presidential statement on 16 July 1981 spoke of the Administration's policy on non-proliferation, as *further* proliferation would pose severe threat to international peace, regional and global stability, and the security interests of the United States and other countries. The US responsibility is urgent because of the ominous events in the Middle East and the United States must put all its capabilities to the task to improve regional and global stability and reduce motivations that will drive countries towards the build-up of nuclear arsenals. The statement specially emphasized the following:[9]

1. The United States will seek to prevent the spread of nuclear arms to *additional* countries.
2. The United States will strive to reduce the motivation for acquiring nuclear arms by working to improve regional and global security;
3. She will continue to support adherence to the Treaty on Non-Proliferation of Nuclear Weapons and the Treaty for the Prohibition of Nuclear Weapons in Latin America (Treaty of Tlatelolco);
4. She will strongly support the International Atomic Energy Agency (IAEA) to provide for an improved international safeguard;
5. She will continue to inhibit the transfer of sensitive nuclear material, equipment or technology, particularly where there is danger of proliferation.

At the time of the statement, nuclear proliferation in the region was active and accelerating. The UN Secretary-General submitted a report to the General Assembly at its fortieth session regarding the dangerous path Israel's nuclear armament and developments were leading to. The General Assembly in its report took note of the Secretary-General's report and expressed its deep alarm over the fact that Israel had developed a technical capability of manufacturing nuclear weapons and possessed the means of delivering such weapons; then called on all states and other parties and institutions to terminate forthwith all nuclear collaboration with Israel, and also requested the Secretary-General to "give maximum publicity to its report, to follow Israeli military activity closely and report thereon as appropriate ..."[10] On the matter of following Israeli military activities, the Secretary-General prepared a study on the subject with the assistance of qualified experts which was then submitted to the General Assembly and discussed in the yearly sessions without any result despite the fact that the report stated "There is no doubt that Israel has the technical capability to manufacture nuclear weapons and possesses the means of delivery of such weapons, to targets in the area."

The same thing happened with the Missile Technology Control Regime (MTCR), Geneva 1987. It has been adapted selectively. Consequently, different kinds of rockets – especially the intermediate and long range ground-to-ground missiles – which can attack both counter-value and counter-force targets are found in many regional states.

That policy was disastrous to the regional states, including Israel. The situation forced the US Comptroller General to write in his report of 24 June 1983 to the Chairman of the Senate Committee on Foreign Relations and the Chairman of the House of Representatives of the same corresponding committee the following:

The major objectives of U.S. assistance to Israel include demonstrating U.S. political support for an ally and providing for the defense of Israel. Israel receives more U.S. security assistance and also more liberal terms and concessions than other countries. However, it continues to seek additional help because it perceives potential threats from other M.E. nations which in some cases also obtain advanced U.S. weaponry. Congress has approved increases in the Israeli programme and included more grants and forgiven loans. Even so, Israel is faced with the need to finance new military loans as well as make payments on mature outstanding loans. GAO believes the trends toward increasing assistance requirements, greater relaxation of restrictions on the use of security assistance funds, and the provision of assistance under terms others may ask for will continue unless Israel can reach a peaceful settlement with her Arab neighbors. Without this, the U.S. is faced with questions concerning the spiralling Middle East arms race, the impact of providing concessions with assistance, and the Israeli military debt situation.[11]

During the Cold War era the Middle East suffered not only from regional conflicts but also from the rivalry between the two big powers. The bipolar international order was a curse to the Middle East states because under the rules of the game the big powers played with regional crises and avoided solving them.

## IV. Arms-technology transfer in the contemporary unipolar order

President Bush proposed an initiative to halt the spread of conventional and unconventional weapons in the Middle East during his visit on 29 May 1991 to the American Air Force Academy in Colorado shortly after the end of Operation Desert Storm. In broad terms he spoke about his initiative which featured supplier guidelines on conventional arms exports, barriers to exports that contribute to weapons of mass destruction, a freeze now and a ban later on surface-to-surface missiles in the region, as well as a ban on the production of nuclear weapons material. "Halting the proliferation of conventional and unconventional weapons in the Middle East *while supporting the legitimate need of every state to defend itself* will require the cooperation of many states in the region and around the world. It won't be easy, but the path to peace never is."[12] (See appendix A.)

On 8 and 9 June 1991 the first important step for implementation was taken at the Paris conference attended by representatives of the five major suppliers of arms – the United States, the USSR, France, the United Kingdom, and China. Fundamental elements were discussed at the meeting: guidelines on conventional arms transfers and preventing the transfer of weapons of mass destruction and ground-to-ground missiles, and a set of specific control proposals for the region to implement. The most important point of the meeting was the declaration that the conferees "supported the objective of establishing a weapons of mass destruction free zone."

The G7 leaders of the Economic Summit held in London on 16 July 1991 underscored their commitment to combat the dangers to world security created by the proliferation of nuclear, biological, and chemical weapons and associated missile delivery systems (appendix B). On 18 October 1991 five permanent members of the United Nations Security Council – the United States, China, France, the United Kingdom, and the USSR – met in London to discuss guidelines aimed at creating a serious, responsible, and prudent attitude of restraint regarding arms transfers to the Middle East. They agreed to inform each other about transfers, to consider them only if they meet legitimate self-defence, avoiding transfers which might prolong or aggravate an existing armed conflict, and to initiate a UN register of arms transfers (appendix C).

All these good wishes and successive initiatives and meetings did not prevent weapons of all sorts proliferating in the region publicly or covertly. Some sources indicated that the United States was the chief supplier.[13] And thus, while the diplomats talk of peace to the international public, they simultaneously allow arms and technology transfers to the region. America, for example, agreed to ship $13 billions' worth of weapons to the unstable region since the end of the Gulf War. Military arsenals, specially in the Gulf, are being rebuilt from the supply of conventional and unconventional arms. While the allies destroyed the Iraqi arsenals under cover of UN legitimacy, Israel in the West and Iran in the East are receiving weapons from everywhere. Thus, regional hegemonies are enhanced and regional balance is shaky. Israel, on one side, refuses to come to peace with the Arabs, and Iran, on the other hand, cooperated with the Arab

357

Islands in the Gulf and constructed a Silkworm missile base in Abu-Mousa island which had recently capitulated. Israel, living in a nightmare caused by the firing of Scud missiles during the Gulf War on some of its cities, is actively developing its Arrow Anti-missile System to intercept the so-called Arab missiles by using military aid and is exchanging Patriot technology with Chinese weaponry.

This regional disorder caused by arms proliferation has its political and economic dogmas which end with a strange and dangerous outcome: the illusion of regional arms control. Some believe that any moratorium on arms sales to the Middle East or sellers' cartel to manage the flow of arms into the region, proposed restrictions on conventional-plus weaponry, or enforcing a zone free from weapons of mass destruction – are workable ideas. President Richard Nixon, in his last book, *Seize the Moment: America's Challenge in a One-Superpower World*, gives four reasons why conventional arms-control proposals are inadvisable and unfeasible.[14]

1. A moratorium would impede the ability of regional states to equip themselves with defence requirements.
2. The differences among Middle East states and their potential threats make it difficult to enforce stability, or enable a cartel to determine appropriate arms levels for each state.
3. The economic incentives for arms exporters would soon lead to invasions or violations of agreed-upon limits.
4. Enforced conventional arms control would have the perverse effect of prompting countries to develop weapons of mass destruction as force equalizers.

The former President of the United States ends his views with a very discouraging proposal. "Maintaining the balance of military power remains the best formula for Middle East security, and selling arms represents an indispensable instrument in preserving that balance." The view is similar to the US official policy for conventional arms transfer in the region. On testifying before Congress on 27 June 1991 both Mr. Frederick Smith, director of the Office of Near Eastern and South Asian Affairs of the Department of Defense, and Mr. Richard Clarke, Assistant Secretary of State for Political-Military Affairs, said,

The administration will only seek to transfer arms that strengthen a country's ability to deter and if necessary defend itself. This is totally consistent with the President's arms control initiative. Five major weapons sales to the region since the war have already occurred and in their travels to the region they were tripping all over suppliers offering to sell more weapons. Arms transfers are not inherently good or evil. They are an instrument in achieving the goal of regional stability. The United States is the only nation that informs the public and the rest of the world about arms sales before they became final. Other countries do not and this is destabilizing because it does not bring the transparency necessary to confidence and stability.[15]

Who will consider the regional states' need for arms sales? Who will consider the quantity and quality of the transfers? Who is responsible for limiting the regional potentialities and capabilities even by using force? Up till now the answer is ambiguous. What about tomorrow? Nobody can tell.

Adding to this turmoil is the complete change of rules in the arms and technology transfers from the centre to the periphery. The sales are simply made now on a commercial basis to get hard currency and keep military industry lines afloat. The Russian and East European countries have even unveiled their secrets of sophisticated weaponry. Reports from Farnborough Fair near London in September 1992 speak about British and American companies marketing Russian weaponry in spite of the competition with Western arms. During the fair President Bush declared two important deals: one with Taiwan (160 F-16 Falcons) and the other with Saudi Arabia (72 F-15 Eagles) which were met with enthusiasm and delight by MacDonald Douglas. Furious competition is taking place in the Gulf between the American General Dynamics Company (the Abrahams M-1A2 tank) and the British Vickers Company (the Challenger 2 tank). The volume of the deal is 1,000 tanks: 200–250 tanks for Kuwait, 500 tanks for the Saudis and 390 tanks for the United Arab Emirates. The new rules do not only permit the proliferation of technology and arms but also experts, with their know-how of all kinds in the military industry.

Under such conditions, arms reduction in the Middle East is an illusion and this will last for years to come. The incentives for proliferation are not limited as hoped, but enhance destabilization in an international and regional environment.

## V. Reflections

Regional conflicts force the Middle East states to enlarge their military arsenals despite their lack of economic basis. In such an environment the military capabilities of the states increase while their overall national capabilities decrease, which then threaten the national security of the nations. The allocation of national resources is the crucial element in restoring the general balance of the states. This sensitive allocation is called "The 3-dimensional allocation – the decision makers' trilemma."[16] The three allocations which cause the trilemma are defence-oriented allocations, system-oriented allocations, and export-oriented allocations. Should the export-oriented be overlooked a dangerous development follows. The deficit in the current balance of payments would increase, the position of the national economy and its constituents on the international capital markets would deteriorate, foreign indebtedness would reach a point which would prevent further borrowing, and the state will be in danger of bankruptcy. Similar results will happen if the other dimensions are neglected. Any attempt to give preference to one of the three dimensions to the neglect or exclusion of the other two would end in the failure to provide for survival (table 1).

The enhancements of the domestic burdens of armaments due to the enormous defence expenditures divert resources and efforts, thus hindering chances to solve social problems. The more one strives for security against external threats by an intensive build-up of arms, the more vulnerable one becomes to internal challenges caused by economic incompetence and social disruptions. The equilibrium between steps taken for security and procedures directed to build for peace is essential. Development cannot be achieved except by attaining security, and security cannot be restored except on the firm base of development. This difficult equation cannot be resolved

Table 1  **Central government expenditure (% of total expenditure)**

| Country | Defence 1972–1989 | Education 1972–1989 | Health 1972–1989 | Average annual growth rate 1965–1989 |
|---|---|---|---|---|
| Egypt | 14.4 | 11.9 | 6.6 | 4.2 |
| Iran | 11.7 | 19.3 | 7.1 | .05 |
| Jordan | 25.9 | 15.3 | 4.1 | – |
| Israel | 26.1 | 10.1 | 3.9 | 2.7 |
| Kuwait | 19.9 | 14 | 7.4 | – |
| UAE | 43.9 | 15 | 6.9 | – |
| Syria | 40.4 | 10.4 | 1.5 | 3.1 |
| Oman | 41.9 | 10.3 | 5.1 | 6.4 |
| Somalia | 23.3 | 5.5 | 7.2 | .03 |

Source: *World Development Report 1991–The Challenge of Development.* The World Bank, Oxford University Press.

under regional instability caused by contradictions and conflicts between the Middle East states, and at the same time these conflicts cannot be resolved by regional efforts only but also by international efforts which must concentrate on the elimination of the causes of conflicts and not escalate them by fanning the flames through arms sales.

Solving regional problems must be based on balancing interests and power not selectively but equally. Discriminatory arms control that seeks to restrict arms flows only to some selected regional states is not good policy because it leads to an arms race, particularly since weapons markets are becoming more numerous and available. It is not of real importance that international resolutions by the Security Council are despatched or issued. It is more important that these should be respected and executed by *all* members of the United Nations.

The emphasis is on the cut-off of supply of weapons at the source, because this is something that big suppliers can do now. A moratorium on military sales for a short period – one year for example – is essential. This will pave the way to solve some urgent problems and spare time for more comprehensive international agreements on arms control or reduction between the permanent five, the 12 members of the European Community, and the members of the Conference on Security and Cooperation in Europe. Arms sales should be banned in the following circumstances:

1. A state of war.
2. A high risk that a state will commit an aggression.
3. Gross violations of human rights and torture of citizens.
4. High defence expenditures.
5. Non-compliance with UN resolutions.
6. Refusal to join in arms-control negotiations.
7. Annexation of neighbouring territories through the use of force.

Punitive measures can be added such as a ban on both economic or military aid, prohibition of membership in international organizations for certain periods, cutting down the number of diplomatic representatives, economic sanctions, limitation in Olympic sports and other sports events, etc.

The initiatives of the big powers are merely an illusion under the contemporary rules. In a fearful and unchecked arms race, these initiatives threaten international and regional order and lead to the opening of a Pandora's box which could unleash all kinds of evils.

361

# Notes

1. Brzezinski, Dr. Zbigniew. *The Consequences of the End of the Cold War for International Security*. IISS, Adelphi Press, pt. 1, p. 265, Winter 1991/1992.
2. Hewedy, Amin (1982). *The New International Order*. UNU International Seminar, Yokohama, Japan, 29 November–3 December.
3. Nixon, Richard (1988). *Victory without War*. Sedgwick & Jackson, London, p. 56.
4. Hewedy, Amin (1989). *Militarization and Security in the Middle East and its Impact on Development and Democracy*. Pinter Publishers, London; St. Martin's Press, New York, p. 3.
5. The author means by conventional-plus: weapons of biological warfare, chemical warfare, rockets, scud missiles, etc.
6. Saudi Arabia, Kuwait, United Arab Emirates, etc.
7. *Survival*. IISS, Sept/Oct 1981.
8. Presidential Statement on Nuclear Non-Proliferation, 16 July 1981.
9. Ibid.
10. UN Resolution A/RES/39/147 of 1 January 1985, Geneva.
11. GAO/ID-83-51 24 June 1983. Library of the International Institute for Strategic Studies, 23 Tavistock Street, London.
12. Official text. USIS, Embassy of the United States of America, Cairo, 30 May 1991. This proposal was consolidated by a White House fact sheet 5/29/91/860 the same day explaining the initiative in several points such as supplier restraint, missiles, nuclear weapons, chemical weapons, and biological weapons.
13. Waller, Douglas. *Newsweek*, 22 June 1992.
14. Nixon, Richard (1992). *Seize the Moment: America's Challenge in a One-Superpower World*. Simon & Schuster, New York, p. 212.
15. The wireless file, US Information Agency, U.S. embassies in Cairo, NEA, "U.S. Says Responsible Arms Transfers Foster Stability." (Clarke and Smith testifying on ME arms sales).
16. Sedan, E. (1984). National Security and National Economy, *Symposium on Israeli Security Planning*. The Jaffa Center for Strategic Studies, Tel Aviv University, Praeger Publishers.

# Appendix A. Middle East arms control initiative

The following fact sheet on President Bush's Middle East arms-control initiative was issued by the White House on 29 May. (White House fact sheet 5/29/91 [860]).

Fulfilling the pledge he made in his March 6 address to a joint session of Congress, the president announced today a series of proposals intended to curb the spread of nuclear, chemical and biological weapons in the Middle East, as well as the missiles that can deliver them. The proposals also seek to restrain destabilizing conventional arms build-ups in the region.

The proposals would apply to the entire Middle East, including Iraq, Iran, Libya, Syria, Egypt, Lebanon, Israel, Jordan, Saudi Arabia, and the other states of the Maghreb and the Gulf Cooperation Council. They reflect our consultations with allies, governments in the region, and key suppliers of arms and technology.

The support of both arms exporters and importers will be essential to the success of the initiative. Since proliferation is a global problem, it must find a global solution. At the same time, the current situation in the Middle East poses unique dangers and opportunities. Thus, the president's proposal will concentrate on the Middle East as its starting point, while complementing other initiatives such as those taken by Prime Ministers John Major and Brian Mulroney. It includes the following elements.

362

## Supplier restraint

The initiative calls on the five major suppliers of conventional arms to meet at senior levels in the near future to discuss the establishment of guidelines for restraints on destabilizing transfers of conventional arms, as well as weapons of mass destruction and associated technology. France has agreed to host the initial meeting. (The United Kingdom, France, the Soviet Union, China, and the United States have supplied the vast majority of the conventional arms exported to the Middle East in the last decade.) At the same time, these guidelines will permit states in the region to acquire the conventional capabilities they legitimately need to deter and defend against military aggression.

- These discussions will be expanded to include other suppliers in order to obtain the broadest possible cooperation. The London Summit of the G7, to be hosted by the British in July, will provide an early opportunity to begin to engage other governments.
- To implement this regime the suppliers would commit
  1. to observe a general code of responsible arms transfers;
  2. to avoid destabilizing transfers; and
  3. to establish effective domestic export controls on the end-use of arms or other items to be transferred.
- The guidelines will include a mechanism for consultations among suppliers, who would
  1. notify one another in advance of certain arms sales;
  2. meet regularly to consult on arms transfers;
  3. consult on an ad hoc basis if a supplier believed guidelines were not being observed; and
  4. provide one another with an annual report on transfers.

## Missiles

The initiative proposes a freeze on the acquisition, production, and testing of surface-to-surface missiles by states in the region with a view to the ultimate elimination of such missiles from their arsenals.

- Suppliers would also step up efforts to coordinate export licensing for equipment, technology and services that could be used to manufacture surface-to-surface missiles. Export licenses would be provided only for peaceful end uses.

## Nuclear weapons

The initiative builds on existing institutions and focuses on activities directly related to nuclear weapons capability. The initiative would

- Call on regional states to implement a verifiable ban on the production and acquisition of weapons-usable nuclear material (enriched uranium or separated plutonium);
- Reiterate our call on all states in the region that have not already done so to accede to the Non-Proliferation Treaty;

– Reiterate our call to place all nuclear facilities in the region under International Atomic Energy Agency safeguards; and
– Continue to support the eventual creation of a regional nuclear weapon-free zone.

## Chemical weapons

The proposal will build on the president's recent initiate to achieve early completion of the global chemical weapons convention.
– The initiate calls for all states in the region to commit to becoming original parties to the convention.
– Given the history of possession and use of chemical weapons in the region the initiative also calls for regional states to institute confidence-building measures now by engaging in presignature implementation of appropriate Chemical Weapons Convention provisions.

## Biological weapons

As with the approach to chemical weapon controls, the proposals build on an existing global approach. The initiative would
– Call for strengthening the 1972 Biological Weapons Convention (BWC) through full implementation of existing BWC provisions and an improved mechanism for information exchange. These measures will be pursued at the five-year review conference of the BWC this September.
– Urge regional states to adopt biological weapons confidence-building measures.

This initiative complements our continuing support for the continuation of the U.N. Security Council embargo against arms transfers to Iraq, as well as the efforts of the U.N. Special Commission to eliminate Iraq's remaining capabilities to use or produce nuclear, chemical, and biological weapons and the missiles to deliver them.

## Appendix B. Summit leaders vow to expand non-proliferation regimes

London – The Economic Summit leaders July 16 underscored their commitment to combat the dangers to world security created by the proliferation of nuclear, biological and chemical weapons, and by associated missile delivery systems. (Summit Declaration on Arms 7/16/91 [1840]).

"We are determined to combat this menace by strengthening and expanding the non-proliferation regimes," the leaders said in a declaration on conventional arms transfers and nuclear, biological and chemical non-proliferation.

In the declaration on arms issues, the leaders also:
– said they would work for the early adoption of the proposed universal register of arms transfers under the auspices of the United Nations;
– advocated measures to prevent the building up of disproportionate arsenals and asked all countries to refrain from arms transfers which would be destabilizing or would exacerbate existing tensions;

- called "moderation in the level of military expenditure" a "key aspect" of sound economic policy and good government;
- pledged to provide every assistance to the U.S. Special Commission and the International Atomic Energy Agency (IAEA) so they can "fully carry out their tasks" associated with monitoring the destruction, removal or rendering harmless of Iraq's nuclear, biological and chemical warfare and missile capabilities;
- reaffirmed the importance of the nuclear Non-Proliferation Treaty (NPT) and urged all non-signatory states to subscribe to the agreement;
- encouraged all non-nuclear weapon states to submit all their nuclear activities to IAEA safeguards: and
- vowed to work for "a total and effective" ban on chemical and biological weapons.

Following is the text of the Declaration on Conventional Arms Transfers and Nuclear, Biological and Chemical Non-proliferation:

1. At our meeting in Houston last year, we, the heads of state and government and the representatives of the European Community, underlined the threats to international security posed by the proliferation of nuclear, biological and chemical weapons and of associated missile delivery systems. The Gulf crisis has highlighted the dangers posed by the unchecked spread of these weapons and by excessive holdings of conventional weapons. The responsibility to prevent the re-emergence of such dangers is to be shared by both arms suppliers and recipient countries as well as the international community as a whole. As is clear from the various initiatives which several of us have proposed jointly and individually, we are each determined to tackle, in appropriate fora, these dangers both in the Middle East and elsewhere.

## Conventional arms transfers

2. We accept that many states depend on arms imports to assure a reasonable level of security and the inherent right of self-defense is recognized in the U.N. Charter. Tensions will persist in international relations so long as underlying conflicts of interest are not resolved. But the Gulf conflict showed the way in which peace and stability can be undermined when a country is able to acquire a massive arsenal that goes far beyond the needs of self defense and threatens its neighbors. We are determined to ensure such abuse should not happen again. We believe that progress can be made if all states apply the three principles of transparency, consultation and action.

3. The principle of transparency should be extended to international transfers of conventional weapons and associated military technology. As a step in this direction we support the proposal for a universal register of arms transfers under the auspices of the United Nations, and will work for its early adoption. Such a register would alert the international community to an attempt by a state to build up holdings of conventional weapons beyond a reasonable level. Information should be provided by all states on a regular basis after transfers have taken place. We also urge greater openness about overall holdings of conventional weapons. We believe the provision of such data, and a procedure for seeking clarification, would be a valuable confidence and security building measure.

4. The principle of consultation should now be strengthened through the rapid

implementation of recent initiatives for discussions among leading arms exporters with the aim of agreeing a common approach to the guidelines which are applied in the transfer of conventional weapons. We welcome the recent opening of discussions on this subject. These include the encouraging talks in Paris among the Permanent Members of the U.N. Security Council on 8/9 July; as well as ongoing discussions within the framework of the European Community and its member states. Each of us will continue to play a constructive part in this important process, in these and other appropriate fora.

5. The principle of action requires all of us to take steps to prevent the building up of disproportionate arsenals. To that end all countries should refrain from arms transfers which would be destabilizing or would exacerbate existing tensions. Special restraint should be exercised in the transfer of advanced technology weapons and in sales to countries and areas of particular concern. A special effort should be made to define sensitive items and production capacity for advanced weapons, to the transfer of which similar restraints could be applied. All states should take steps to ensure that these criteria are strictly enforced. We intend to give these issues our continuing close attention.

6. Iraqi aggression and the ensuing Gulf war illustrate the huge costs to the international community of military conflict. We believe that moderation in the level of military expenditure is a key aspect of sound economic policy and good government. While all countries are struggling with competing claims on scarce resources, excessive spending on arms of all kinds divert resources from the overriding need to tackle economic development. It can also build up large debts without creating the means by which these may be serviced. We note with favour the recent report issued by the United Nations Development Programme (UNDP) and the recent decisions by several donor countries to take account of military expenditure where it is disproportionate when setting up aid programmes and encourage all other donor countries to take similar action. We welcome the attention which the managing director of the International Monetary Fund (IMF) and the president of the World Bank have recently given to excessive military spending, in the context of reducing unproductive public expenditure.

## Non-proliferation

7. We are deeply concerned about the proliferation of nuclear, biological and chemical weapons and missile delivery systems. We are determined to combat this menace by strengthening and expanding the nonproliferation regimes.

8. Iraq must fully abide by Security Council Resolution 687, which sets out requirements for the destruction, removal or rendering harmless under international supervision of its nuclear, biological, and chemical warfare and missile capabilities; as well as for verification and long-term monitoring to ensure that Iraq's capability for such weapon systems is not developed in the future. Consistent with the relevant U.N. resolutions, we will provide every assistance to the United Nations Special Commission and the International Atomic Energy Agency (IAEA) so that they can fully carry out their tasks.

9. In the nuclear field, we:
– Reaffirm our will to work to establish the widest possible consensus in favour of an

equitable and stable non-proliferation regime based on a balance between nuclear non-proliferation and the development of peaceful uses of nuclear energy;
- Reaffirm the importance of the nuclear Non-Proliferation Treaty (NPT) and call on all other non-signatory states to subscribe to this agreement;
- Call on all non-nuclear weapon states to submit all their nuclear activities to IAEA safeguards, which are the cornerstone of the international non-proliferation regime;
- Urge all supplier states to adopt and implement the Nuclear Suppliers Group guidelines.

We welcome the decision of Brazil and Argentina to conclude a full-scope safeguard agreement with the IAEA and to take steps to bring the Treaty of Tlatelolco into force, as well as the accession of South Africa to the NPT.

10. Each of us will work to achieve:
- Our common purpose of maintaining and reinforcing NPT regimes beyond 1995;
- A strengthened and improved IAEA safeguards system;
- New measures in the Nuclear Suppliers Group to ensure adequate export controls on dual-use items.

11. We anticipate that the Biological Weapons Review Conference in September will succeed in strengthening implementation of the convention's existing provisions by reinforcing and extending its confidence-building measures and exploring the scope for effective verification measures. Each of us will encourage accession to the convention by other states and urge all parties strictly to fulfill their obligations under the convention. We each believe that a successful Review Conference leading to strengthened implementation of the BWC, would make an important contribution to preventing the proliferation of biological weapons.

12. The successful negotiation of a strong, comprehensive, and effectively verifiable convention banning chemical weapons to which all states subscribe, is the best way to prevent the spread of chemical weapons. We welcome recent announcements by the United States which we believe will contribute to the swift conclusion of such a convention. We hope that the negotiation will be successfully concluded as soon as possible. We reaffirm our intention to become original parties to the convention. We urge others to become parties at the earliest opportunity so that it can enter into force as soon as possible.

13. We must also strengthen controls on exports which could contribute to the proliferation of biological and chemical weapons. We welcome the measures taken by members of the Australia Group and by other states on the control of exports of chemical weapons precursors and related equipment. We seek to achieve increasingly close convergence of practice between all exporting states. We urge all states to support these efforts.

14. Our aim is a total and effective ban on chemical and biological weapons. Use of such weapons is an outrage against humanity. In the event that a state uses such weapons each of us agrees to give immediate consideration to imposing severe measures against it both in the U.N. Security Council and elsewhere.

15. The spread of missile delivery systems has added a new dimension of instability to international security in many regions of the world. As the founders of the Missile Technology Control Regime (MTCR), we welcome its extension to many other states in the last two years. We endorse the joint appeal issued at the Tokyo MTCR meeting in March 1991 for all countries to adopt these guidelines. These are

367

intended to inhibit cooperation in the use of space for peaceful and scientific purposes.

16. We can make an important contribution to reducing the dangers of proliferation and conventional arms transfers. Our efforts and consultations on these issues, including other supplier countries, will be continued in all appropriate fora so as to establish a new climate of global restraint. We will only succeed if others, including recipient countries, support us and if the international community unites in a new effort to remove these threats which can imperil the safety of all our peoples.

## Appendix C. Major powers agree on Middle East arms transfer guidelines

London – The five permanent members of the United Nations Security Council concluded two days of talks in London October 18 by issuing a set of guidelines aimed at creating "a serious, responsible and prudent attitude of restraint regarding arms transfers" to the Middle East. (London communiqué by perm five [1070]).

The United States, China, France, the United Kingdom and the Soviet Union agreed to inform each other about transfers and to consider them only if they meet legitimate self-defence needs, are "an appropriate and proportionate" response to threats against the recipient, and would enhance that country's ability to participate in regional or other collective security arrangements.

They also agreed to avoid transfers which might prolong or aggravate an existing armed conflict, increase regional tension or contribute to regional instability, encourage international terrorism, or seriously undermine the recipient's economy.

Representatives of the five nations agreed to meet in the United States in the new year to continue their discussions on arms transfer restraints.

Following is the text of the final communiqué and annex of the London meeting:

1. In accordance with their agreement in Paris on 8 and 9 July 1991, representatives of the United States of America, the People's Republic of China, France, the United Kingdom of Great Britain and Northern Ireland, and the Union of Soviet Socialist Republics met in London on 17 and 18 October to take forward their discussions on issues related to conventional arms transfers and to the non-proliferation of weapons of mass destruction.
2. Recalling the statement which was issued in Paris on 9 July, they:
   - agreed on common guidelines for the export of conventional weapons (annexed). They expressed the hope that other arms exporting countries will adopt similar guidelines of restraint;
   - agreed to inform each other about transfers to the region of the Middle East, as a matter of priority, of tanks, armored combat vehicles, artillery, military aircraft and helicopters, naval vessels, and certain missile systems, without prejudice to existing commitments to other governments;
   - agreed to make arrangements to exchange information for the purpose of meaningful consultation, bearing in mind their shared concern to ensure the proper application of the agreed guidelines, and to continue discussions on how best to develop these arrangements on a global and regional basis in order to achieve this objective;

- welcomed work at the U.N. General Assembly on the early establishment of a U.N. register of conventional arms transfers, and supported the current consultations on this issue between a wide range of U.N. members in which they are actively participating. They called for universal support for this work;
- noted the threats to peace and stability posed by the proliferation of nuclear weapons, chemical and biological weapons, missiles, etc., and undertook to seek effective measures of non-proliferation and arms control in a fair, reasonable, comprehensive and balanced manner on a global as well as on a regional basis. They affirmed the importance of maintaining stringent and, so far as possible, harmonized guidelines for exports in this area. They embarked on a comparison of their national export controls on equipment related to weapons of mass destruction and agreed to examine the scope for further harmonization of those controls. They agreed to pursue discussions at their next meeting on these subjects;
- agreed to continue discussing the possibilities for lowering tension and arms levels, including the development of further measures of restraint concerning arms transfers and ways of encouraging regional and global efforts towards arms control and disarmament;
- agreed to continue to give these efforts high priority and meet again in the new year in the United States to take forward their discussions, and to meet regularly thereafter at least once a year.

## Guidelines for conventional arms transfers

The People's Republic of China, the French Republic, the Union of Soviet Socialist Republics, the United Kingdom of Great Britain and Northern Ireland, and the United States of America,
- recalling and affirming the principles which they stated as a result of their meeting in Paris on 8 and 9 July 1991,
- mindful of the dangers to peace and stability posed by the transfer of conventional weapons beyond levels needed for defensive purposes, reaffirming the inherent right to individual or collective self-defense recognized in Article 51 of the Charter of the United Nations, which implies that states have the right to acquire means of legitimate defense,
- recalling that in accordance with the Charter of the United Nations, U.N. Member States have undertaken to promote the establishment and maintenance of international peace and security with the least diversion for armaments of the world's human and economic resources,
- seeking to ensure that arms transferred are not used in violation of the purposes and principles of the U.N. Charter,
- mindful of their special responsibilities for the maintenance of international peace and security,
- reaffirming their commitment to seek effective measures to promote peace, security, stability and arms control on a global and regional basis in a fair reasonable, comprehensive and balanced manner,
- noting the importance of encouraging international commerce for peaceful purposes,

– determined to adopt a serious, responsible and prudent attitude of restraint regarding arms transfers, declare that, when considering under their national control procedures conventional arms transfers, they intend to observe rules of restraint, and to act in accordance with the following guidelines:

1. They will consider carefully whether proposed transfers will:
   a) promote the capabilities of the recipient to meet needs for legitimate self-defense;
   b) serve as an appropriate and proportionate response to the security and military threats confronting the recipient country;
   c) enhance the capability of the recipient to participate in regional or other collective arrangements or other measures consistent with the Charter of the United Nations or requested by the United Nations.

2. They will avoid transfers which would be would be likely to:
   a) prolong or aggravate an existing armed conflict;
   b) increase tension in a region or contribute to regional instability;
   c) introduce destabilizing military capabilities in the region;
   d) contravene embargoes or other relevant internationally agreed restraints to which they are parties;
   e) be used other than for the legitimate defense and security needs of the recipient state;
   f) support or encourage international terrorism;
   g) be used to interfere with the internal affairs of sovereign states;
   h) seriously undermine the recipient state's economy.

# Comments on chapter 13

**Susumu Ishida**

The Middle East has been an arena where major military confrontations have repeatedly occurred. We can remember four wars between Arab countries and Israel, the civil war between royalists and republicans in North Yemen, the Iran–Iraq War, the Gulf War and ongoing civil wars in both Lebanon and Sudan.

In the past the major military dynamics, having provoked confrontations behind the arena, have always been the bipolar order between the two superpowers. Fortunately, this bipolar order has ended with the collapse of the USSR. In all events, the Iran–Iraq War and the Gulf War have ceased (according to Dr. Amin Hewedy the Gulf War has not yet ceased), and the negotiations around the table between Israel and the Arabs have started. In a sense, the Middle Eastern countries and the people living there are now standing at the entrance to a new order with the sincere hope of achieving something different from what has militarily prevailed in the Middle East, including arms reduction.

We are very happy to have a chance to listen to a speech on arms reduction delivered by a most respectable speaker from the Middle East. Though Dr. Amin Hewedy's speech may have sounded pessimistic and discouraging enough, I am more sorry to read in his paper that under such conditions, arms reduction in the Middle East is an illusion and this will last for years to come. Dr. Hewedy is an ex-Minister of Defense and ex-Head of General Intelligence of Egypt and should know very well both what has happened and what is to happen. Therefore, the predictions in his speech are too implicative to be easily ignored.

But I would like to refer to a point which hopefully, someone else has already discussed in this conference or elsewhere; that is, the so-called principle of the legitimate need of every state to defend itself which is recognized in the UN Charter. The five permanent members of the UN Security Council who are at the same time the five major sellers of arms are willing to approve and agree on a principle that offers them many excuses to export and sell, that offers some of the Middle Eastern countries other excuses to import arms, and that can thus easily lead to an endless vicious cycle of the arms race.

The prerequisite of the legitimate need of every state to defend itself against outside military aggressions was possible mainly under the old bipolar order, but can be eliminated under the new unipolar order. The principle of the legitimate need of every state to defend itself must be changed to, for instance, "the legitimate need of every state to maintain its own security." In this new principle, the five major arms sellers and the Middle Eastern arms importers cannot find any excuse to export or import even major conventional or conventional-plus weapons, and thus actual arms reduction will go on.

One more point to which I would like to refer is that there are many things for the people and governments of the Middle East to do so as not to again be locked in a vicious circle of arms accumulation. Dr. Hewedy is proposing a ban on arms sales under circumstances consisting of seven items. His proposal must be supported universally. But, above all, it is necessary for the League of Arab States and the Organisation of Islamic Countries, etc. to endorse and promote it.

Admittedly, the Middle East has been at the mercy of big arms suppliers and some of the Middle Eastern countries have been encouraged to get involved in wars by proxy. In order for them to avoid being involved in the same pattern that has been repeated in the Middle East, they have to help themselves. The Middle Eastern initiatives are most needed to achieve arms reduction there.

As regards the so-called punitive measures, what those countries, including Japan, which provide ODA, but do not sell arms can do directly in respect of arms reduction, is limited. But, in the post-Cold War era, punitive measures such as imposing a ban or cutting financial assistance can be applied to those countries which export or import weapons against the arms-reduction policy. In order to make these punitive measures effective, they must be applied jointly by most of the donor countries depending, for instance, on resolutions of the United Nations.

Now we have learned enough lessons to teach us that military confrontations between Arab countries and Israel, between Arab and Arab, or between Arabs and Persians left nothing but misery, disaster, poverty, and minimal development among the people of the Middle East. There was no winner, but all parties involved in such military confrontations were losers in terms of economic development.

I am a researcher who has been studying the modern economic history of the Middle East, focusing on the case of Egypt since Muhammad Ali. I have found that the Middle East has suffered from two obstacles to its success in economic development in its modern history: that is, colonization by Western powers in the nineteenth century and the repeated wars in the Cold War era after World War II. I strongly hope that the Middle East can achieve arms reduction and enjoy a successful economic development in the post-Cold War era without any more wars in that region.

# 14

# Japan's ODA policies for a peace initiative

Takao Kawakami

It gives me great pleasure today to address this distinguished assembly on the subject of Japan's ODA policies for a peace initiative. As Parliamentary Vice-Minister Kakizawa said in his opening remarks, with the end of East–West confrontation, we are now at a crucial moment in the attainment of lasting world peace. Japan, as the world's largest ODA donor, is conscious of its immense responsibility in helping to establish a new order that will assure peace and prosperity for both developed and developing countries.

As a first step to making such a new order a reality, with OECD development assistance, member countries are now seeking ways to reallocate development resources of both donors and recipients.

The military spending of the developing countries is one of the most important issues to be discussed at present, not only in the context of arms reduction, but also in terms of ensuring sustainable economic development. We are keenly interested in this issue in Japan since Japan has achieved an economic growth, rapid and remarkable by any standards, since the end of World War II, owing at least in part to a relatively small military expenditure.

In my statement, I will focus on Japan's two ODA principles on military expenditure and on Japan's approach to the application of these principles. In so doing, I must say I will make my statement based on my personal views as well as on the government's official position.

To start with, allow me to say that Japan's ODA principles on military expenditures are included in our new Official Development Assistance Charter, announced after the Cabinet decision on 30 June of this year. Let me quote the relevant principles under today's subject-matter from that ODA Charter:

The first principle states:

Any use of ODA for military purpose or for aggravation of international conflicts should be avoided.

The second principle states:

Full attention should be paid to trends in recipient countries' military expenditure, their development and production of mass destruction weapons and missiles, their exports and imports of arms, etc., so as to maintain and strengthen international peace and stability, and from the viewpoint that developing countries should place appropriate priorities in the allocation of their resources for their own economic and social development.

Now let me explain a little about the background to the announcement of this charter, as one of the officials who closely participated in the drafting process.

The charter is intended mainly for both of the two major players in ODA: the Japanese taxpayers and recipients of Japan's ODA.

The two principles were laid down in view of the current international situation, and Japan's response as a donor to that situation.

After the collapse of the Cold War structure, ethnic as well as regional conflicts have broken out in various parts of the world, seriously impeding the development of many countries in the South.

It only suffices to look at the TV scenes of what is happening in Somalia, where civil war, compounded by severe drought, has resulted in immense and tragic human suffering, to understand the crucial importance of avoiding such conflicts as a precondition of a sound development. In other words, it is evident that development cannot take place without stability. Donors are confronted with such deep-rooted obstacles to development in many developing countries, and most donors realize it is absolutely necessary to pay due attention to military and other political aspects of the recipients when extending assistance.

At the same time, there also exists an economic reason to pay attention to military spending.

There have recently emerged substantial new claimants to concessional and non-concessional financial resources, including the need to assist Central and Eastern Europe and the former Soviet Union, as well as to cope with other growing global problems, such as environmental degradation, refugee outflow, drug abuse, and the spread of AIDS. Given that the Development Assistance Committee (DAC) members' ODA is not expected to increase substantially over the coming years because of financial constraints in major DAC members, scarcity of financial resources obliges us to seek other possible ways of expanding development resources. In this context, from this viewpoint of macroeconomic gap between supply and demand, I believe it is only natural that we turn our eyes to the military expenditure in developing countries, which amounted to approximately $160 billion in 1991 according to SIPRI.

Under such circumstances, Japan has reconfirmed its conviction derived from its own development experience. That is, simply stated, putting maximum resources into sound economic development, instead of military spending, certainly helps economic growth. That is one of the reasons why Japan, in its diplomacy, has put much emphasis on arms reduction, and, as stated in its ODA Charter, Japan intends to promote it through its foreign aid policy as well, which is an important tool of our diplomatic efforts.

Inasmuch as it is essential for any donor government to receive adequate public support for ODA, it has become increasingly difficult these days to start up or continue aid if the aid money is to be directly or indirectly diverted to military uses, or is not used most efficiently or effectively. In other words, it has clearly become difficult for any donor government to justify to its taxpayers extending aid to those developing countries engaged in large military spending. Japan is no exception to it.

Developing countries at present are thus asked more than ever to seek sound economic growth based on "good governance," which includes, among other conditions, efficient resource allocation, the promotion of political and economic reforms, and respect for human rights.

Furthermore, balanced reduction of military spending generally tends to contribute to regional stability, thus preparing propitious conditions for development. Civilian control may also be strengthened through the reduction of military spending, which in turn should lead to democratization and good governance in developing countries.

Now let me come back to the issues related to the implementation of those two principles that I mentioned earlier, namely, no use of ODA for military purpose, and linkage between ODA and military expenditure, and so forth.

As for the first principle, it means that goods and resources provided by aid should never be used for military purposes, which is nothing new with Japan's aid policy of the past, nor with the globally recognized definition of ODA, which is those flows "to be administered with the promotion of the economic development and welfare of the developing countries as its main objective." None the less, we have decided to reaffirm this point as a clear-stated principle, because of its political significance, especially in Japan. In implementing this principle, the government of Japan requires a recipient country, under the terms of the related Exchange of Notes, which constitutes an international agreement, to make proper use of the funds provided by Japan. In addition, review and certification of contracts as well as a dialogue on the use of aid by recipient countries are constantly carried out.

The second principle is simply a rephrasing of the guidelines announced by then Prime Minister Kaifu on 10 April 1991. In formulating the guidelines, we certainly drew painful lessons from the result of the military build-up of Iraq, which led to the Gulf crisis. The public in Japan strongly felt that there should be no more cases like this in the future. Thus the conviction that ODA policy should contribute to preventing any such escalation of regional tension was deepened and confirmed through that crisis.

In order to put this second principle into practice, I believe the following *five key points* need to be borne in mind.

The first key point is that *we need to pay full attention to "trends" in recipient countries' military expenditure, etc.* Military expenditures are closely related to the national security affairs of recipient countries, and it may often be difficult to expect drastic improvement of the situation in a short period of time.

The reason why "trends" are mentioned in the charter as the focus of attention is that we believe it is neither appropriate nor easy to set an absolute level or GNP ratio for military expenditure and arms trade as criteria for automatic application at a given time, without considering properly the national security concerns of the recipient. As we see it, it is more effective to look at the trends over a certain period of time as signals or indicators of the situation. Thus, I believe we will be in a position to be able to realize, for instance, the case of an abrupt increase of military spending which could well be judged to be excessive. Or a country that is making continuous reform efforts to reduce military expenditure could be singled out for reward.

Secondly, *improved transparency of military spending and transactions needs to be achieved.*

Before judging the "excessiveness" of military spending, related transparency needs to be secured. It is no easy task to obtain relevant military-related data and to accurately grasp the military spending and other transactions in developing countries. Not surprisingly, many developing countries tend to be reluctant to disclose such data. Available information published by such organizations as SIPRI, ACDA, and IISS may not match each other and additional information is often required to make a fair judgement. Therefore, it seems to me indispensable to take measures to improve data transparency. On this I will come back later.

Once transparency is adequately secured, we can then discuss what "excessive military expenditure" is. My personal and preliminary thoughts are that the following factors may be considered in determining what is *"excessive military expenditure"* for a specific developing country.

Quantitative factors could include:

*Trends* in the size of military expenditure and ratio of military expenditure to GNP.

*Trends* in the allocation of resources between military and development spending, such as the budget for education, health, welfare etc., especially their ratio to GNP and as a percentage of government spending.

Qualitative factors could include:

National security environment such as the threat posed by neighbouring countries; geographical situation of the country; existence of an alliance or cooperative security arrangements, or the absence thereof.

As indicated above, quantitative factors alone may not be sufficient to determine the "excessiveness" of military expenditure, and the situation of the developing country as a whole needs to be carefully assessed in order to judge whether the military expenditure in question is excessive or not. On the question of criteria, we cannot forget the following. Objective criteria are needed to reduce the element of subjective judgement. However, universally acceptable criteria are hard to come by, since, in attempting to construct objective criteria, they become more complex, and it becomes harder to make them operational. The discussion on this topic has just begun at DAC, and since Japan has taken the initiative in this regard, we would like to actively contribute to the course of this discussion, in spite of the possible difficulties as I mentioned above.

Thirdly, *policy dialogue is the central part of the implementation.* Policy dialogue is an essential way of encouraging reduction of excessive military expenditure, or discouraging increase in unnecessary military spending.

Policy dialogue is a vital process for achieving common recognition of the significance of reducing excessive military spending. Recipients are expected to understand that more efficient allocation of resources is crucial for their own sustainable development. Thus, avoiding such excessive military spending is something that developing countries themselves need to carry out. The objective here is naturally not to force developing countries to reduce military spending against their will and at the expense of their security, but to make common efforts between donors and recipients for the objective of promoting development.

On the other hand, in case the efforts through policy dialogue should not bear fruit, as the argument often goes, the possibility of applying some form of negative linkage, which may include aid reduction and aid withdrawal, might need to be considered. However, at present, the actual implementation of the negative linkage is by no means a simple process, and we are all, in a way, in the process of trial and error. In linking aid and military expenditure, unilateral action clumsily taken by donors could cause serious disruption in relations between donors and recipients or could simply be counterproductive from the viewpoint of promoting the objective of development. Therefore, caution and patience are quite in order. Drastic negative linkage such as suspension of aid could obviously be taken only as the last resort, after having exhausted other means like persuasion through policy dialogue, as I discussed above. Needless to say, our strong feeling is that we would rather not experience such an unfortunate situation.

Just a word about the so-called positive linkage. It is clear that desirable tendencies in a given developing country can generally be encouraged. More specifically, for example, the extension of donors' assistance to demobilization of recipients' armed forces or civilian conversion of their military industries may be a case in point.

The fourth point I would like to mention is *the need for international cooperation.* Japan's efforts alone cannot achieve the goal

379

discussed above, and we all need to cooperate both bilaterally and multilaterally in promoting a reduction in military spending. Multilateral institutions can play complementary roles along with bilateral donors. This is the reason why Japan has proposed or strongly supported including this issue of military expenditure and aid in various communiqués of the international meetings, such as the Economic Summits of industrialized democracies both in London and Munich, the 1991 and 1992 OECD Ministerial Conferences, and the 1991 DAC High Level Meeting. Based on my preliminary thoughts, I would like to suggest the following roles for multilateral institutions for your consideration today.

First, the IMF and the World Bank can play a role in monitoring and reviewing trends in military expenditure through their public expenditure reviews. Such efforts can substantially complement the efforts by bilateral donors to improve military expenditure data transparency. Since analysis by these institutions is considered to be politically neutral and objective, it goes without saying that the relevant data and analysis of public expenditure, including military expenditure, compiled by these multilateral institutions with a view to promoting the greatest possible allocation of resources to development, can be persuasive.

It is to be hoped that the IMF and the World Bank will provide bilateral donors with information about military expenditure through such forums as the OECD/DAC, the Consultative Group Meetings organized by the World Bank and the UNDP Roundtable, which are important occasions for multilateral policy dialogue with recipients.

Regional development banks, such as the EBRD and the ADB, can also play a similarly important role, always with due attention to the regional situation.

Secondly, the UN is another institution that can serve as a vehicle to improve the transparency of military-related data. The recently established UN Register of Conventional Arms Transfer, which was proposed jointly by Japan and the EC, is designed to increase the transparency of international arms transfers, and also of military stocks and procurement from domestic production in its member countries. Here again, for the sake of transparency, recipients are expected to provide relevant data and information for the UN Arms Register. Needless to say, donors should also report.

Thirdly, the Development Assistance Committee of OECD is an important forum in which both bilateral and multilateral donors can deepen their understanding of this matter, and exchange views on basic policy approaches. Japan has already proposed a possible role of DAC in this regard, and based on our proposal, DAC and the OECD Development Center will hold an experts' meeting early next year to examine the implication of military spending in developing countries for their development, and the donor's approach, to address this issue.

Based on the data provided by the multilateral institutions and bilateral donors, the DAC and the OECD Development Center could gather and analyse information on military spending in developing countries for the use of individual donors.

Lastly, *coherence of donors' policy is also indispensable.* As part of the donor efforts discussed above, it is important that bilateral donors reduce military aid, military exports, and military export credits to developing countries that are not justified under the changed international situation, and to make data related to such matters transparent. Otherwise, donors will not be able to maintain credibility in arguing for eliminating excessive military expenditure. Japan has been very conscious of this aspect, and we have consistently maintained the policy of non-arms exports and have not exported any weapons for over the last 20 years in spite of our potential capacity for doing so. In some of the other donor countries, such a policy shift may lead to significant repercussions, such as strong opposition on the part of arms producers, but it is essential to maintain consistency in policy.

Today, I attempted to put forward first steps of the ODA policies for a initiative, based on my preliminary thoughts. We do not live in a perfect world, and the elimination of excessive military expenditure will be a very complex and difficult process. None the less, we need to start somewhere. In a nutshell, I would propose that we focus on the issue of *transparency* in this initial stage. Distrust and hostility among nations, based on mutual fear and anxiety, need to be eliminated, if we are to reduce excessive military expenditure. If, at least, transparency is sufficiently attained, donors and recipients will be able to engage in serious, honest dialogue aimed at reducing military spending and promoting sustainable development in recipient countries. In order to move on to such a level of dialogue, cooperation and goodwill among bilateral donors, multilateral institutions, and developing countries are essential. In this regard, we need the public understanding of the importance of this issue in both donor and recipient countries. Japan, as one of the largest donors, is ready to continue to send strong messages on this score to both the recipients and to fellow donors.

I hope the ideas I have put forth here today will serve a useful purpose for triggering the discussions eventually leading to a desirable process of the *competition for arms reduction* at this moment after the end of the Cold War.

Before concluding, I would like to express my thanks for your kind attention. Let me also express my appreciation to all the participants at this conference and to the staff of the United Nations University for their outstanding work and for the high quality of the discussions.

Thank you.

# Contributors

Paul Armington, Director, International Economic Department, The World Bank, Washington, D.C.

Nicole Ball, Visiting Fellow, Overseas Development Council, Washington, D.C.

Tamim Bayoumi, Economist, Research Department, International Monetary Fund, Washington, D.C.

Jean-Claude Berthélemy, Administrator, OECD Development Centre, Paris.

Simon Cunningham, Senior Economic Affairs Officer, Department of Economic and Social Information and Policy Analysis, United Nations, New York.

Saadet Deger, Senior Researcher, Stockholm International Peace Research Institute, Stockholm.

Daniel Gallik, Senior Economist, U.S. Arms Control and Disarmament Agency, Washington, D.C.

Amin Hewedy, Former Minister of Defence, Government of Egypt, Cairo.

Daniel P. Hewitt, Senior Economist, European Department, International Monetary Fund, Washington, D.C.

Shinichi Ichimura, Vice President, Osaka International University, Osaka.

Takashi Inoguchi, Professor, Institute of Oriental Culture, University of Tokyo, Tokyo.

Susumu Ishida, Professor, Institute of Middle Eastern Studies, International University of Japan, Niigata.

Jalaleddin Jalali, Economist, International Economic Analysis and Prospects Division, The World Bank, Washington, D.C.

Takao Kawakami, Director-General, Economic Cooperation Bureau, Ministry of Foreign Affairs, Tokyo.

383

## Contributors

Lawrence R. Klein, Professor Emeritus, University of Pennsylvania, Philadelphia.

Warwick J. McKibbin, Senior Fellow, The Brookings Institution, Washington, D.C., and Professor of Economics, the Australian National University, Canberra.

Robert S. McNamara, Former President of the World Bank and former U.S. Secretary of Defense, Washington, D.C.

Akira Onishi, Vice President, Soka University, Tokyo.

Sanjay Pradhan, Senior Economist, The World Bank, Washington, D.C.

Kenneth G. Ruffing, Assistant Director, Economics, Finance and Information Services, Division for Sustainable Development, Department of Policy Coordination and Sustainable Development, United Nations, New York.

Jerald Schiff, Economist, Fiscal Affairs Department, International Monetary Fund, Washington, D.C.

Somnath Sen, Professor, University of Birmingham, Birmingham.

Mihály Simai, Director, World Institute for Development Economics Research, Helsinki.

Stephan S. Thurman, Principal Administrator, Economics Department, the OECD, Paris.

Kimio Uno, Professor, Keio University, Fujisawa.

Raimo Väyrynen, Professor, University of Helsinki, Helsinki.

Murray Weidenbaum, Director, Center for the Study of American Business, Washington University, St. Louis.

Zhu Manli, Secretary-General, Chinese People's Institute of Foreign Affairs, Beijing.